Helping Relationships

*Basic Concepts for the
Helping Professions*

ARTHUR W. COMBS
DONALD L. AVILA
WILLIAM W. PURKEY

University of Florida

ALLYN AND BACON, INC.   · BOSTON

Second printing . . . September, 1971

Library of Congress Catalog Card Number: 78–144036

Contents

Preface

This book was written for people entering or already engaged in some form of the helping professions. It attempts to answer these questions: "What ideas about human behavior have special value for understanding the helping relationship?" "What do these imply for effective practice in the helping professions?" This is not a psychology book in the usual sense of expounding concepts and showing how they are supported by logic and research. Instead, this book begins with principles of behavior already widely accepted among humanistically oriented psychologists and examines what such concepts mean for persons who work in the varied helping professions. In addition to the very old professions such as medicine, teaching, and the clergy, these include counselors, school psychologists, visiting teachers, social workers, nurses, play therapists, and, most recently a whole constellation of professions concerned with helping people in basic encounter, sensitivity training, and T-groups.

Each of the helping professions has emerged in response to practical human needs. Each has its own philosophy, techniques, and training procedures that are strongly defended by its adherents. Fundamentally, these professions are all alike in their basic aim—the optimum development of human beings. To achieve this goal, effective helpers need to be guided by the best we know of the dynamics of human behavior offered by the science of psychology.

Modern psychology, however, is a very broad field, and the concepts selected for inclusion in a book like this must necessarily represent a highly biased sample. This is inevitable, and the authors recognize that their choices have been deeply influenced by their peculiar goals and experiences. In all fairness to the reader therefore, it should be said at the outset that all three authors tend to look at human behavior from what has been called the humanistic orientation. Each began his professional training in orthodox, behavioristic psychology, but over the years they have increasingly learned to appreciate the special values of a humanistic frame of reference for the problems of the helping professions.

"Humanistic psychology" currently includes a wide variety of persons, practices, and beliefs. Among these, the authors have found that position described as "perceptual psychology" to be most pertinent for the helping professions. In their experience it speaks with special relevance to helpers and provides a framework for understanding students, clients, or patients immediately applicable to the practical problems helpers confront; so much so, in fact, that at times perceptual psychology has been called "the practitioner's psychology." Many of the concepts discussed in this volume are based upon perceptual approaches to understanding behavior, particularly the systematic outlines for perceptual psychology first proposed by Snygg and Combs in *Individual Behavior: A New Frame of Reference for Psychology,* New York: Harper & Bros., 1949, and revised by Combs in 1959.

The authors have spent their entire professional lives in the helping professions. Among those they have practiced are teaching, counseling, supervision, clinical psychology, administration, and school psychology. They have also been responsible for psychological phases in the training of nurses, teachers, social workers, administrators, and pastoral counselors. In the course of continuous dialogue with helpers in many fields, they have had opportunity to explore and refine psychological theory on one hand, and to test its applicability in the crucible of professional practice on the other.

For ease of reading. Professional helpers are called by a variety of names as are the persons they seek to aid. The latter can be called students, clients, patients, workers, or parishioners. Since there is no satisfactory generic name for helpees, there is a problem in nomenclature for persons writing about the helping professions. To avoid complications and contribute to easier reading therefore, the authors have limited the designation of helpees to *student, client,* and *patient.* However, readers should understand that these terms are interchangeable, and that the application of general principles is intended to apply to all helpees regardless of what they may be called by their respective helpers.

As a further contribution to ease of reading, the authors have adopted a form of documentation concentrated in a special Reference Index at the end of the volume. In place of footnoting and the inclusion of names and dates in parentheses in the pages of the text, interested readers will find pertinent references listed by page and line in the Reference Index.

An additional alphabetical listing of authors may be found in the Bibliography.

For deeper study. A book devoted to basic principles and their meaning for the professions cannot hope to deal with all topics in detail. Serious students will no doubt wish to become acquainted with original sources or pursue topics in greater depth. To meet these needs, Selected Readings, relevant to the topics in a particular chapter, have been listed at the end of each chapter. To make pertinent and original articles more readily available, many of the shorter Selected Readings have also been included in a companion volume, *The Helping Relationship Sourcebook.* Boston: Allyn and Bacon, 1971.

A WORD OF SPECIAL THANKS

To the many persons who have assisted in the production of this book the authors would like to express their deep appreciation. Special thanks are due the Foundations Department secretarial staff and to Mrs. Elsie Voss for much of the manuscript preparation.

To Mildred Combs, Howard Crouch, Sarah Hurst, Kay Ernst, Hannelore Wass, Mary Harriff, and James Bowers for their critical reviews of the manuscript in process.

To the authors and publishers who have so generously permitted quotation from their sources.

To the thousands of students, clients, and patients with whom the authors have worked and from whom they have learned so much. Out of the dialogue of those interactions, thinking was stimulated, hypotheses were formulated, subjected to critical examination and tested in the encounters of real life helping relationships.

The years spent in the helping professions have been a rare privilege for the authors. Few occupations are so greatly needed in current society or so deeply rewarding for its practitioners. That, in itself, is a highly fulfilling experience. If this book can serve, in turn, to assist new members of the helping professions toward a better understanding of themselves, their clients, and the processes of helping, the authors will rest content. What more could professional helpers ask than to write a helpful book?

AWC
DLA
WWP

1

What Is a
Professional Helper?

What is a professional helper and what can psychology offer to aid him in carrying out his professional tasks successfully? These are the problems this book is about. The formal study of human behavior is now nearly a hundred years old and the information psychologists have accumulated is nearly overwhelming. To select from this great mass those understandings most likely to be useful for helping persons, it is necessary, first, to ask two questions: What are the helping professions? What are effective helpers like?

THE "WHY" OF THE HELPING PROFESSIONS

Each new person born into our society must, in a comparatively few years, work his way through the public schools, marry, and find his way into one or more of the thousands of occupations required to keep our economy running. In one way or another, people must find solutions to the problem of fulfilling their own needs on the one hand and contributing to society's expectancies on the other. For a few people, life will be a marvelous experience, satisfying both for themselves and the society in which they live. Others will never achieve such high peaks of realization but, nevertheless, will manage to work out a tolerable balance between their own and society's needs. Many will succeed in meeting the demands of society well enough, but only at the cost of living in personal doubt and despair. Some deeply deprived people, more's the pity, will be unable to satisfy *either* the needs of society *or* their own. These people are not only disappointing to themselves; they are dangerous for the rest of us.

It is a great tragedy for everyone concerned when people are unable to realize the potentialities that lie within them. This unfortunate waste of talent poses one of the great social problems of our time. When societies were less complex and interdependent, the failure of individuals to achieve satisfactory growth and development could be overlooked. In today's world, human unhappiness has effects far beyond the individual himself. It reaches out to touch the lives of everyone. Frustrated people are likely to frustrate the rest of us. One angry driver on a freeway can endanger the lives of hundreds of innocent persons. A Lee Harvey Oswald armed with a rifle can turn our political world upside down.

Even if practical reasons for being concerned about fulfillment of human potential were not valid, we should still be concerned about helping people on purely humanitarian grounds. Frustration and unhappiness is not just a matter of economics. It is a human tragedy and that, in itself, would be reason enough to warrant concern. As a nation we have accepted the "pursuit of happiness" as an important value for our society. Even if we "never made a nickel" from achieving this goal, it would still be worth striving for, both for ourselves and for our fellow men, simply because life is better that way.

The basic idea of democracy is a belief in the dignity and integrity of man—not just a few men, but all men everywhere and of every kind and description. We believe that when men are free and informed, they can find their own best ways. Our forefathers dared to adopt this dream as a basic tenet of our way of life, and little by little, over the years, we have come closer and closer to making it a reality. The fulfillment of the democratic ideal, however, will depend upon how successful we are in producing people who can act with intelligence, independence, and responsibility. We must have people who are well-informed, who can make up their own minds, and who can be counted upon to behave in ways that contribute to the welfare of others as well as themselves. To aid in the achievement of these ends we have invented the "helping" professions. Some of these professions are rehabilitative in that they help the sick and discouraged, the casualties of the system. Some are preventive, seeking to forestall illness; most recently, some are concerned with helping people scale the highest levels of human possibilities. Some helping professions deal with problems of physical health, others with psychological well-being, and still others address themselves to social and political affairs. The people who work in these professions are called by many names. Among them are teachers, doctors, psychologists, social workers, nurses, supervisors, counselors, human relations experts, psychiatrists, visiting teachers, personnel workers, guidance counselors, child care specialists, encounter group leaders, group therapists, and many more. Each profession has its unique aspects, but all are concerned with the "people problem," helping people achieve more effective relationships between themselves and others or the world in which they live.

What is a profession? A profession is generally defined as a vocation requiring some special knowledge and skill. The special quality of a profession, however, which distinguishes it from more mechanical occupations is its dependence upon the professional worker as a thinking, creative being. The essence of his function is the application of human intelligence to the task at hand. Professional workers are problem-solvers. They begin their training from some field of intellectual content. Beyond this, the professions call for a high degree of worker self-discipline, skill in judgment, and adherence to an appropriate code of ethics. In addition, the helping professions, more specifically, are concerned with service to people. Their special responsibility is human welfare, a ministry to mankind.

WHAT MAKES AN EFFECTIVE HELPER?

KNOWLEDGE AND THE HELPING PROFESSIONS

It seems obvious that the effective professional helper must know his subject. However, almost everyone has had experience with people who knew their subject but were ineffective in putting it to work. We have seen intelligent doctors who failed in practice, gifted scholars who couldn't teach, brilliant ministers unable to hold a parish, and clever psychiatrists with obvious problems of their own. Clearly, knowledge alone is no guaranty of successful professional work.

The helping professions are applied professions and require *doing* something with knowledge. In all of the helping professions there exist the knowers and the doers, the scholars and the practitioners. In medicine, for example, there are specialists in anatomy or biochemistry and the physician who puts this information to work at the bedside of his patient. In education, there are scholars researching some aspect of knowledge and teachers helping students to know what it means. Psychology has its experimental psychologists investigating principles of human behavior and its counselors putting this information to work with clients. There are also sociologists examining the conflicting forces of the social scene and social workers helping clients to adjust to them.

While the knower and the practitioner may, of course, exist in the same skin, it does not follow that knowledge alone is enough to make an effective helper. This fact has been clearly demonstrated in many researches attempting to distinguish between good practitioners and poor ones in a number of the helping professions.

METHODS IN THE HELPING PROFESSIONS

It may come as a surprise to some of our readers to learn that what makes an effective helper is not a question of using right methods. Good and poor practitioners cannot be clearly discriminated on the basis of the methods they use. For example, a review of all the research available on good and poor teaching, sponsored by the National Education Association in 1961, was unable to discover any method of teaching which could be clearly shown to be associated with either good or poor teaching. This review covered hundreds of studies, and the conclusion seems unquestionably definitive. Apparently there is no such thing as a "good" or a "right" method of teaching. A review of research in the other helping professions seems to corroborate the point in those professions as well.

People seem to be helped by the darnedest things. We are frequently surprised by sudden waves of public enthusiasm over some weird new technique that is supposedly helpful to people in trouble. The strange thing about these methods is that often they really are helpful to their users. Doctors are well aware that nostrums with no demonstrable chemical value whatever frequently help a patient to get well if he believes they will help! It is probable that the reason why we cannot find specific methods associated with good helpers and poor ones is because it is the *meaning* of the method to the person on whom it is applied rather than the method itself which is the important factor.

The effects of stimuli on human behavior are not mechanical or chemical things like a prod with a pin or a doctor's prescription. A social worker of our acquaintance once discovered this the hard way. He was deeply concerned about the problems of the poor in the ghetto areas where he worked. In a well-meant effort to help these people, he pleaded with churches, clubs, and fraternal organizations in the wealthier sections of town to "adopt a block" in the slums. The idea was to provide the people in the ghetto areas with some of the things they desperately needed. Our friend was delighted when a number of organizations responded to his pleas and agreed to provide the funds for his project—only to have his good hopes dashed to the ground by the people who lived on the block he sought to help. They would have no part of his plan! In fact, they resented the condescension of the rich folks. They preferred to go it alone rather than suffer the humiliation of being patronized by outsiders. A few years later the same idea was advanced again, this time as a venture involving both rich and poor in a program of cooperative planning and work in which people put their hearts, minds, and muscles as well as their money. And this time it worked.

THE SELF AS INSTRUMENT CONCEPT

In examining the helping professions, it becomes apparent that the common characteristic of these activities is *instantaneous response*. That is to say, all of the helping professions seem to differ from more mechanical vocations in the immediacy of reaction required of the helper. For example, in teaching, when the child says something to his teacher, his teacher must respond instantaneously. The interchange between a teacher and her pupils will be different every moment, and the teacher must be prepared to react to each child in terms of the unique question, idea, problem, and concern that he is expressing at that particular instant. Similarly, the patient asking the nurse, "Am I going to get well?" must be answered. A delay in the nurse's answer while she stops to think of what she should say is already an answer. This immediate nature of helping relationships is characteristic, too, of the social worker and his client, the pastor and the parishioner, or the counselor and his client. All are dependent upon instant response.

Professional helpers must be thinking, problem-solving people; the primary tool with which they work is themselves. This understanding of the nature of the helping professions has been called the "self as instrument" concept. Effective operation in the helping professions is a question of the use of the helper's self, the peculiar way in which he is able to combine his knowledge and understanding with his own unique ways of putting it into operation to be helpful to others. We might state it formally as follows: *Effective helping relationships will be a function of the effective use of the helper's self in bringing about fulfillment of his own and society's purposes.*

The self as instrument concept helps to explain why the attempt to distinguish the helping professions on the basis of knowledge or method falters. If effective operation in the helping professions is a personal matter of the effective use of a self, then the search for a common knowledge or a common method is doomed before it begins. Since the self of each individual is unique, the search for a common uniqueness is, by definition, hopeless!

At this point we are confronted with a difficult problem. If effective helping calls for instantaneous response which fits the peculiar needs of the person to be helped, and if it depends upon the effective operation of the unique self of the helper, how can we hope to be sure the instantaneous use of the unique self will be good for the client? Helping, after all, must be a predictable process, one in which we can be sure the results will be positive. In answering this question, it is helpful to draw an analogy with a giant computer. The modern computer is a magnificent machine capable of taking in great quantities of data from outside and combining this information with that stored in its "memory bank" to give an almost instantaneous "best answer" for the complex of data it deals with. Like a human being, it provides appropriate responses to mountains of data. Now, the kind of answers the computer provides out of the data available to it is dependent upon the formula (the program) in the machine. Similarly, for human beings the peculiar responses occurring as a consequence of the circumstances in which people find themselves are also a product of the program in the person. But the formula in the human case is not a mathematical equation. It consists of the individual's perceptions, especially those we call values, beliefs, and purposes.

IMPORTANCE OF BELIEF

In an article on the nature of the helping relationship, Carl Rogers once observed that it didn't seem to make much difference how the helper behaved so long as his "intent" (purpose) was to be helpful. We are all familiar from personal experience how our own behavior is an expression of our beliefs. Indeed, this intimate effect of belief on behavior is so strong that it betrays us even when we consciously try to hide it. As the old Indian said, "What you do speaks so loudly I cannot hear what you say." Beliefs have a controlling, directing effect. This is especially true with respect to what we believe is important.

A beautiful young woman teaching first grade in one of our great cities had a magnificent head of blonde hair which she often wore in a "ponytail" down her back. For the first three days of the new school year, she wore her hair this way. Then, on Thursday morning of that first week she decided to wear it differently and put it up in a "bun" on top of her head. As often happens when a woman changes her hairdo, she looked quite different and one of the little boys in her class didn't recognize his teacher. Thinking he was in the wrong room, he turned away in confusion. Soon the bell rang for the start of the day and he found himself standing in the hall not knowing where to go or what to do. He was still there crying when a supervisor came along a bit later. Questioning the child, she could not discover what his teacher's name was. He didn't know. Nor did he know what room he belonged in. He'd looked in there and it was clearly not the right place! She said to him, "Come along. Let's go together and see if we can find your teacher." And they set out hand in hand, to see if they could find his classroom. They opened the doors of several rooms without any luck. Finally, they came to the right one. As the door to this one opened, the teacher, who was sitting at her desk, turned around, saw the little boy and said, "Why Joey! It's so good to see you! We wondered where you were and we're glad to have you back! We missed you so!" The little boy let go the supervisor's hand and threw himself into his teacher's arms. She gave him a hug, patted him softly, and he trotted off to his seat. This teacher believed that little boys are important.

Let's suppose she had not acted in this manner. She might very well have thought *other* things were important, in which case she would have behaved quite differently. For example, she might have thought that supervisors were important. In that case she probably would have said, "Why, good morning, Miss Jones. Do come in. We've been hoping you'd come to see us. Haven't we, boys and girls?" And the little boy would have been ignored. Or, she might have felt that the lesson was the important thing, in which case she would have seen the little boy's tardiness as an unwarranted interruption. For that matter, she might have "chewed him out." Or, she might have felt that discipline was important, in which case she could have punished him for being late. But, she didn't. She believed the little boy's feelings were important and so behaved in terms of these. So it is with each of us.

CONTROLLING FUNCTION OF BELIEFS

What we believe to be important inevitably determines the methods we use in dealing with other people. There are a vast number of methods one could conceivably use in establishing helping relationships. There are so many, in fact, that without some kind of philosophy or frame of reference for making choices, the helper is likely to remain forever ineffectual in human relationships rather than as a potent force for human welfare. A clear understanding of purposes and goals provides guidelines for the selection of appropriate methods of establishing helping relationships, and a frame of reference to determine choices from the great welter of possibilities. Without this the teacher or counselor may find himself behaving in such confused fashion that he, in turn, confuses the people he teaches or counsels.

There is a widespread belief that eclecticism—that is, the utilization of whatever seems best from whatever sources—is most likely to produce an effective teacher or counselor. Unfortunately, this seemingly logical and practical way of selecting one's methods of operation often misfires, producing what William Snyder once called "the Smorgasbord Approach in which a little of everything is tried." Some years ago at an American Psychological Association convention, a well-known psychologist was reporting upon a difficult counseling case which he and his staff had worked with. He described how, over the years, the staff had used a large number of methods with a patient. These methods, furthermore, were selected from a dozen different schools of thought. At the conclusion of this long description of the methods used and the results obtained, the psychologist concluded: "Well, now I've told you what we did with this client and what happened, but do not ask me why. The best I can say about this case is that the patient got better in the presence of the therapist!" There can surely be no doubt that eclecticism sometimes works. But then it is true that *almost anything* works with *some* people *sometimes* in *some* places. The competent professional worker cannot be content with so hit or miss an approach to his job. He needs a consistent philosophy of function which can guide him effectively in the selection of the particular methods he uses in establishing helping relationships.

What kind of behavior the professional worker is able to produce will be largely a question of the accuracy and appropriateness of the beliefs and understandings he has acquired in the course of his experience. Helpers must possess internal formulas that will produce behavior that we can be certain will be good for clients, students, patients, or employees. We are governed by perceptions in everything we do, from the simplest to the most complex of behaviors. We do not step out in the street unless we believe the cars will stop. Similarly, how we vote, what we seek from our institutions, even what we will fight for is determined by our beliefs about what form of government is most desirable.

It is often assumed that the proper approach to behavior is a coldly objective one. This approach has worked very well in our past experience in dealing with the material things of our world, and it is logical to assume that it will work for other events as well. Unfortunately, such logic only gets us into difficulties. People simply do not behave on the basis of cold and calculating reason, except with respect to problems that are unimportant to them. So it is that the psychologist can be objective about your children or mine, but not about his own. In the important events of life we are governed by our beliefs, our values, our understandings, and the things we think are important. To be sure that professional workers behave effectively then, it is necessary in the course of their training to provide them opportunities for discovering personal meanings which can be effective guides for the moment to moment behaviors they will be called upon to engage in during the course of their professional experience.

PRACTITIONER-SCHOLAR DILEMMA

This necessity of the professional training program to produce a change in the personal belief system of the student, as well as in what he knows, is at the basis of the misunderstandings which often occur between students and professors in colleges of arts and sciences on the one hand and students and teachers in professional schools on the other. One group is concerned primarily with knowledge, the other with behavior. So the scholar observes the nurse, the teacher, the counselor, or clinical psychologist and exclaims, "Mickey Mouse stuff! How unscientific can you get?" The professional workers on the other hand look at the work of the scholar and exclaim, "What good is that idea? So what! Imagine trying that with my patient!" (or student or client) Each observes the other through the glasses of his own values, beliefs, and decisions as to what is important and often finds the other wanting. This breakdown of understanding between scholars and practitioners sometimes becomes very bitter. It also creates confusion for the student who has decided to enter professional work. All of his past experience has usually been in educational settings deeply rooted in the scholarly tradition where the acquisition of knowledge and information was the primary goal. Coming into a professional program from this kind of background, he may then find it difficult to make the transition to a program which emphasizes beliefs, values, and personal meanings and which evaluates him in terms of what he *can do* rather than on what he *knows*.

Beginning students in the helping professions may even be heard complaining that they "aren't learning anything" because they are spending hours in observing, experimenting, and interminable talk. They believe they are not learning anything unless someone is telling them something new. They do not understand that beliefs, values, and purposes are not acquired from information alone but from the personal discovery of the *meaning* of information. One of the authors recalls, for example, sitting in a class with Carl Rogers twenty-five years ago and writing down in a notebook the principle: "It is essential that the counselor have an absolute respect for the dignity and integrity of his client." Now, twenty-five years later he is still discovering deeper and deeper meanings of that idea. So it is with beliefs. They, too, are the products of an individual's personal discovery of meaning, and they provide professional helpers the internal formulas for the determination of instantaneous behavior.

BELIEFS OF PROFESSIONAL WORKERS

A series of researches on the perceptual organization of workers in the helping professions carried on by Combs, his colleagues, and students at the University of Florida, sheds some light on the kinds of beliefs specifically related to effective professional work.[1] These studies examined the belief systems of teachers, counselors, professors, nurses, and Episcopal priests, and found a high degree of similarity in the perceptual organizations of the "good" workers in each of these fields. Good practitioners in these professions apparently have certain beliefs in common. Examining these beliefs more closely, the Florida investigators have sug-

---

1. Material on this and remaining pages in this chapter is largely drawn from Combs, A. W. et al. *Florida Studies in the Helping Professions,* University of Florida Social Science Monograph, Number 37, University of Florida Press, Gainesville, Fla., 1969. In this monograph the interested reader will find a much expanded discussion of the theory and development of this approach to the helping professions and a more detailed description of the research designed to test it.

gested five major categories into which the perceptions of effective helpers may be divided. The helper's beliefs concern the following:

1. his subject
2. what people are like
3. himself (that is, the helper's self-concept)
4. purposes—society's, his own, and those related to his peculiar helping task
5. approaches to his task

These categories are by no means definitive at this stage of our knowledge, but let us examine them briefly because they are suggestive guides to areas of human experience related to effective work in the helping professions.

1/ BELIEFS ABOUT HIS SUBJECT

We have already seen that a profession is a vocation requiring some specialized kind of knowledge. It goes without saying that an effective professional worker must be well-informed about his subject. We have also observed that mere knowledge is not enough to guarantee successful professional application. For effective professional work, knowledge about the subject must be so personally meaningful to the helper as to have the quality of belief. The practitioner, without commitment to his knowledge, cannot be counted upon to use what he knows when it is called for. Even an Einstein must *believe* in his theory to put it into practice. The teacher who *knows* that the children in her class differ widely from one another but does not *believe* this important fact cannot be expected to teach as though the information existed at all. It is precisely because the discovery of the meaning of information is so essential for the effective training of the professional worker that so much of his training is devoted to discussion, observation, experimentation, internship, and various forms of clinical experience. It is here he discovers the personal meaning of knowledge and converts it to belief.

2/ WHAT ARE PEOPLE LIKE?

Among the most important ideas in determining what we do as members of the helping professions are the ideas we hold about what people are like and why they behave as they do. If I believe a child is hungry, I will feed him. If I believe he is lonely, I will befriend him. If I think he needs to know, I will teach him. How we behave as helpers will depend upon the particular concepts we have about people and the ways in which they behave. Whether the ideas we hold about other people are accurate or false, if we believe them, they inescapably affect our behavior toward people. The goals we set for our professions, the methods we use, the rules we make, even the buildings we design will be dependent upon our understanding of the nature of persons. It is of vital importance, therefore, that professional helpers examine carefully what they believe to be true about the human beings with whom they work.

In the Florida studies mentioned above, good practitioners or "helpers" could be clearly distinguished from poor ones on the basis of some of the concepts they held about people. These differences between the good helpers and poor ones are listed below with an indication in each case of the profession for which each was found to be true. If the name of a profession is absent, it should not be supposed that this indicates the factor is not characteristic of that profession; it was not studied in these researches.

Able-unable.   Helpers perceive others as having the capacity to deal with their problems. They believe that people can find adequate solutions to events, as opposed to doubting the capacity of people to handle themselves and their lives (teachers, counselors, priests, and professors).

Friendly-unfriendly.   Helpers see others as being friendly and enhancing. They do not regard them as threatening to themselves, but see people as essentially well-intentioned rather than evil-intentioned (teachers and counselors).

Worthy-unworthy.   Helpers see other people as being of worth rather than unworthy. They see them as possessing a dignity and integrity which must be respected and maintained; they do not see people as unimportant beings whose integrity may be violated or treated as of little account (teachers, counselors, and professors).

Internally-externally motivated.   Helpers see people and their behavior as essentially developing from within rather than as a product of external events to be molded and directed; they see people as creative and dynamic rather than passive or inert (teachers and professors).

Dependable-undependable.   Helpers see people as essentially trustworthy and dependable in the sense of behaving in lawful ways. They regard the behavior of people as understandable rather than capricious, unpredictable, or negative (teachers, counselors, and professors).

Helpful-hindering. Helpers see people as being potentially fulfilling and enhancing to self rather than impeding or threatening. They regard people as important sources of satisfaction rather than as sources of frustration and suspicion (teachers).

From these results, it would appear that an important part of the training of the professional worker must be directed toward helping him arrive at clear, consistent, and accurate concepts of the nature of man and his behavior.

3/ WHAT AM I LIKE?

The helping professions demand the use of self as an instrument. Effective operation demands personal interaction. The helper must have the ability to share himself on the one hand and, at the same time, possess the capacity for extraordinary self-discipline. The giving of self called for in the helping professions is probably possible only in the degree to which the helper himself feels basically fulfilled. The deeply deprived self cannot afford to give itself away. A self must possess a satisfactory degree of adequacy before it can venture commitment and encounter. The task of professional workers is dependent upon entering into some kind of relationship with others. But, one cannot have a relationship with a nonentity. Effective helpers must be somebody. They must possess sufficient personal strength to make sharing possible. They need to feel personally adequate to deal effectively with life.

This same feeling of personal adequacy is also necessary for the other side of the coin—self-discipline. It is only when persons feel fundamentally adequate that self can be transcended and attention truly given to the needs of others. People who feel inadequate cannot afford the time and effort required to assist others as long as they feel deprived themselves. A number of psychologists, including the authors, have been deeply interested in the nature of self-fulfillment and personal adequacy. They have attempted in various ways to define the nature of the truly adequate, self-fulfilling, fully functioning personality, and to isolate some of the characteristics of these remarkable people. In the University of Florida studies on effective helpers, these characteristics also turned out to be associated with effective helping.

Identified-apart.   Helpers feel identified with rather than apart from others. The good helper tends to see himself as a part of all of mankind; he sees himself as identified with people rather than as withdrawn, removed, apart, or alienated from others (teachers, counselors, and priests).

Adequate-inadequate.   Helpers feel basically adequate rather than inadequate. The good helper generally sees himself as enough; as having what is needed to deal with his problems (teachers and counselors).

Trustworthy-untrustworthy.   Helpers feel trustworthy rather than untrustworthy. The good helper has trust in his own organization. He sees himself as essentially dependable or reliable and as having the potentiality for coping with events. This is opposed to seeing self in a tentative fashion with doubts about the potentiality and reliability of the organism (teachers).

Wanted-unwanted.   Helpers see themselves as wanted rather than unwanted. The good helper sees himself as essentially likeable, attractive (in a personal sense, not necessarily in physical appearance), wanted, and in general capable of bringing forth a warm response in those people important to him. This is opposed to feeling ignored, unwanted, or rejected by others (teachers).

Worthy-unworthy.   Helpers see themselves as worthy rather than unworthy. A good helper sees himself as a person of consequence, dignity, integrity, and worthy of respect, as opposed to being a person of little consequence who can be overlooked, discounted, and whose dignity and integrity do not matter (teachers).

Because beliefs about themselves are so very important, training programs for professional workers increasingly deal with the *person* of the helper. Thus, social workers and counselors are encouraged, even required sometimes, to enter into personal counseling relationships as a part of their professional training. Training programs for teachers, supervisors, school psychologists, and nurses are likewise more and more deeply interested in the personal qualities of people entering these professions.

4/ WHAT ARE MY PURPOSES?

Human behavior is always purposeful. How the professional helper operates will be dependent upon what he believes are the purposes of those with whom he must work, the purpose of the particular kind of helping profession in which he is involved, and his own personal and professional purposes at any moment. Each of us always behaves in terms of what seems to be important and appropriate. Some of the purposes of persons engaged in the helping professions are highly specific and related to the particular kind of helping function they are involved in. Others are much more general and seem to be held in common by a number of the helping professions.

In the studies of effective helpers carried out at the University of Florida, for example, good helpers could be distinguished from poor ones on the basis of the following purposes.

Freeing-controlling. Helpers perceive their purpose as one of freeing rather than of controlling people—that is to say, the helper sees the purpose of the helping task as one of assisting, releasing, and facilitating rather than as a matter of controlling, manipulating, coercing, blocking, or inhibiting behavior (teachers, counselors, and priests).

Larger issues-smaller ones. Helpers tend to be more concerned with larger rather than smaller issues. They tend to view events in a broad rather than a narrow perspective. They are concerned with the larger connotations of events and with more extensive implications rather than with the immediate and specific. They are not exclusively concerned with details, but can perceive beyond the immediate to the future (teachers and counselors).

Self-revealing—self-concealing. Helpers are more likely to be self-revealing than self-concealing. They are willing to disclose the self. They can treat their feelings and shortcomings as important and significant rather than hide or cover them up. They seem willing to be themselves (teachers and counselors).

Involved-alienated. Helpers tend to be personally involved with rather than alienated from the people they work with. The helper sees his appropriate role as one of commitment to the helping process and willingness to enter into interaction, as opposed to being inert or remaining aloof or remote from interaction (teachers and priests).

Process-oriented—goal-oriented. Helpers are concerned with furthering processes rather than achieving goals. They seem to see their appropriate role as one of encouraging and facilitating the process of search and discovery as opposed to promoting or working toward a personal goal or preconceived solution (teachers).

Altruistic-narcissistic.   Helpers have altruistic purposes rather than narcissistic ones. Their purposes are more oriented toward aiding and assisting other people rather than attending to their own personal or selfish goals (counselors).

5/ APPROACHES TO THE TASK

The helper's beliefs about suitable approaches to his task seem to have important determining effects on the success with which he carries out his helping role. These beliefs determine how he approaches his client, student, or patient, and the particular methods he chooses to accomplish his purposes. In the Florida studies, for example, good helpers could be distinguished from poor ones quite clearly in terms of their task orientations as follows:

People-things.   The basic approach of the helper is directed more toward people than things—that is to say, his orientation is human rather than with objects, events, rules, regulations, and the like (teachers, counselors, and priests).

Perceptual-objective.   Effective practitioners are more likely to approach their clients subjectively or phenomenologically. They are more concerned with the perceptual experience of their subjects than with the objective facts (counselors and teachers).

PURPOSE OF THIS BOOK

The making of a professional helper is a purely personal matter. Learning to use the self as an effective instrument cannot be learned from a book—it is a matter of personal discovery, a problem in *becoming*. The making of a helper is not so much a matter of learning *how* to teach, to nurse, to counsel, but of *becoming* a teacher, nurse, or counselor. Growth of personal meaning and the unique development of the helper's own system of beliefs are required. Some of the beliefs that enter into the making of a helper are so very personal that information from outside sources will be of little value to the helper. Others require interaction with the world of ideas, and it is here that a book can be of assistance.

Of the five areas of beliefs and understandings required for effective professional work mentioned above, this book is primarily concerned with the second—the problem of what people are like and why they behave as they do. This is a matter fundamental to all of the helping professions. It is also a field in which the understandings accumulated by the science of psychology can make an important contribution to the growth of the professional worker. The authors have asked themselves, "What are the most important and useful ideas about people and their behavior that psychology has to offer which may be helpful to persons in the helping professions?" These are described in the pages to follow. Some of the ideas developed in these covers may also be helpful to the reader in formulating his beliefs about himself, his purposes, and perhaps even about his methods and subject matter. For the most part, however, those understandings will have to be explored in other places, in other ways, and with other people.

SELECTED READINGS

Starred entries indicate appearance in whole or in part in Donald L. Avila, Arthur W. Combs, and William W. Purkey, *The Helping Relationship Sourcebook* (Boston: Allyn & Bacon, 1971).

* Arkoff, A. Some workers in improvement, *Adjustment and mental health.* New York: McGraw Hill, 1968, pp. 284–307.

Carkhuff, R. R. & Berenson, B. G. *Beyond counseling and therapy.* New York: Holt, Rinehart & Winston, 1967.

* Combs, A. W. et al. *Florida studies in the helping professions.* (University of Florida Social Science Monograph No. 37) University of Florida Press, Gainesville, Fla., 1969.

Combs, A. W. & Soper, D. W. Perceptual organization of effective counselors. *Journal of Counseling Psychology,* 1963, **10,** 222–226.

Fiedler, F. E. The concept of an ideal therapeutic relationship. *Journal of Consulting Psychology,* 1950, **14,** 239–245(b).

Frymier, J. R. Professionalism in context. *Ohio State Law Journal.* 1965, **26,** 53–65(a).

* Rogers, C. R. The characteristics of a helping relationship. *Personnel and Guidance Journal,* 1958, **37,** 6–16.

Rogers, C. R. *On becoming a person.* Boston: Houghton Mifflin, 1961.

2

Two Ways of
Looking at Behavior

Throughout man's history, the methods he has used to deal with people have been the inevitable outgrowth of his beliefs about the nature of human beings. People who believed themselves to be "the chosen ones" while other people were "of no account" often enslaved their neighbors and treated them as less than human. When it was believed that mental illness was a consequence of "being possessed of the devil," the methods devised to cure such conditions were unbelievably cruel, designed to "drive the devil out." Whatever beliefs people have had about the nature of man and his behavior have always determined the ways they sought to deal with others. We need but look about us to observe how differently people behave toward children depending upon whether they see them as "delightful," "friendly," "willing," "stubborn," "lazy," "sneaky," or "ignorant." It makes a great deal of difference what we think people are like.

The helping relationships we attempt to construct will also depend upon what we believe about the nature of those we have to deal with. Inaccurate understandings about what people are like will, almost certainly, lead to inefficiency and confusion in working with them. It may even result in failure. To create effective and efficient helping relationships, we need the very best and most accurate understandings about people that we can possibly acquire.

In earliest times our concepts about the nature of man and his behavior were derived from folklore and tradition. Later on they were

18

largely formulated from philosophical or theological sources. More recently, we have learned to apply the methods of sciences such as psychology, anthropology, and sociology, which are designed to explore the nature of man's behavior in all kinds of settings. As a result of these investigations, psychologists have learned to look at human behavior from two broad frames of reference.

The term "frame of reference" is used to describe the basic position from which observations are made in the development of scientific theory. Two of these are currently in wide use in the study of behavior. One has been called the "external approach" because it makes its observations of people from the point of view of an outsider, someone looking on at the process. It has also been called the "objective frame of reference." This is the approach which most of us use in our daily lives as we observe the behavior of people around us. It is also the frame of reference for observing behavior most used by psychologists since the 1890's when psychology first began to apply the methods of the physical sciences to the study of man's behavior.

In more recent years a second frame of reference has been increasingly employed by social scientists. This one is called the "internal approach" because it attempts understanding, not from the point of view of an outsider but from the point of view of the *behaver himself*. It is concerned with the person's own unique experience of himself and the world around him. For this reason it is sometimes also called the phenomenological frame of reference.

Some social scientists have carried on research and have developed theories in the external frame of reference; others have preferred the internal one. Both groups have provided us with important information about human behavior, and both have made significant contributions to the solution of some of our human problems. The adherents of one or the other of these frames of reference often state their positions with such vigor and determination that one might get the impression that one is right and the other wrong. A frame of reference, however, is never right or wrong. It is simply a matter of convenience. Observations made from any point of view may be perfectly true for that point of view. They may, however, lead to quite different conclusions or outcomes. For example, the farmer hears the weather report, "Heavy showers in the early afternoon" and says, "Good! That is just what we need!" The same report is a disappointment to children planning a picnic and a disaster to the manager of the baseball team or the operator of a carnival. Each of these people sees the event differently, but no one sees it wrongly.

Theories or frames of reference are only more or less appropriate for the problems we must deal with. Each has its unique advantages and disadvantages, its contributions and limitations, and each is more or less useful in helping us to deal with practical problems of behavior.

EXTERNAL FRAME OF REFERENCE

STIMULUS-RESPONSE PSYCHOLOGY

Within the external frame of reference, two great movements have grown up in American psychology. The first and still most widely used is stimulus-response psychology, also known as S-R, behavioristic or objective psychology by its various adherents. It is a point of view which seeks the explanations of behavior in the stimuli to which the organism is subjected. It is a way of looking at behavior familiar to all of us. We can see examples everywhere. Traffic stops when the traffic light changes. We eat when the food is set before us. We shake hands with the friend who holds out his hand. These are simple examples of the S-R principle in operation.

Looking at human behavior in this way has had tremendous influence upon every aspect of our lives. The S-R principle is as much a part of us as breathing. We learn very early that subjecting people to the proper pressures or blandishments often makes it possible to control and direct their behavior as we desire. This is true whether we are speaking of individuals or of nations. S-R is the approach we use most often in dealing with friends and relatives. It also is widely used in advertising and in selling, in friendly persuasion, and in more or less disguised techniques of threat and power. Behavioristically oriented psychologists base their investigations on the same basic principle. They approach their researches, however, with a good deal more care and control than the man in the street and devote their attention to exploring the nature and conditions of the S-R relationship at great depth and with much sophistication. Out of these studies have come understandings about human behavior that are of great significance to every aspect of modern society. Approaching human behavior in this way can also contribute much to the work of persons engaged in the helping professions.

THE PSYCHOANALYTIC CONTRIBUTION

Within the objective frame of reference a second great movement in psychological thought came into being with the influence of Sigmund Freud. It is probable that no other single figure has had so profound an influence upon current psychology. Freud and his contemporaries, and later his students, developed a theory known as psychoanalysis. This second great force in the external frame of reference immensely extended our understanding of the stimulus and its effects upon the individual in three important ways:

1/ Genetic principle. Freud and his followers pointed out the importance of the individual's history in determining his present behavior. To understand behavior, they said, it is necessary to understand not just the stimuli to which a person is currently being subjected, but all those stimuli which have acted upon him since the time of his conception. This idea, that each of us is the product of all his past experience, is commonplace for us today. We regard it as self-evident. When the idea was first developed, however, it had a tremendous impact on human understanding, especially in regard to our beliefs about the growth and development of children, the responsibilities of parents, and the goals and practices of psychological treatment.

2/ Effects of internal stimuli. A second major contribution of the psychoanalytic movement was the attention it called to internal stimuli affecting behavior. Freud and his students pointed out that people do not behave only in terms of those stimuli impinging upon them from without. Some of our most important behaviors, they said, are a consequence of stimuli arising from within the person himself. These include such stimuli as human values, wants, desires, and appetites. Other human behaviors are the result of needs for food, water, warmth, affection, and sexual satisfaction. The discussion of these matters had a tremendous impact upon thinking about human behavior at the time they were first advanced. Indeed, the bland assumption of Freud and his colleagues about the importance of sex in human behavior and the openness with which they discussed it was so shocking and caused such a furor in the prudish society of those days that many people, even now, are hardly aware that Freud ever made any other contribution.

3/ Unconscious stimuli. A third great contribution of the psychoanalytic movement was the attention it called to the importance of "unconscious" stimuli in the determination of behavior. They pointed out that not all of the stimuli to which the individual is reacting can be clearly perceived either by outside observers or by the individual himself. Many of the things which affect behavior exist at such low levels of awareness that persons may not be able to report them to other people when asked to do so. Thus, according to psychoanalytic theory, a man's unreasonable fear of dogs as a grownup might be the result of so traumatic an experience with a dog in childhood that he may be quite unable to recall it in the present. Everyone has many such concepts which he is unable to report on demand but which, nevertheless, have important effects upon his behavior. We have incorporated the concept of the unconscious so completely into our thinking about human behavior that it now seems an "obvious" fact of life. It is still an important principle that profoundly affects the work of persons in the helping professions.

Although we have been speaking here of S-R psychology and psycho-analysis as two great movements in the external frame of reference, it should not be supposed that these schools of thought exist as "pure cases." There are really a great many points of view among psychologists working in the external frame of reference. Some of these tend toward the stimulus-response view, some to the psychoanalytic view, and others to various combinations of these positions. All psychologists using the external approach, however, take the position of the outsider as their frame of reference for observing behavior. They interpret behavior as the resultant of the forces at work on the individual. Most of their study is designed to seek out these forces and to understand the nature of their impact. Their conclusions are based on careful objective observation and on the manipulation of the forces at work on their subjects. Over the years, psychologists have learned how to make these kinds of observations with great precision and have contrived ingenious devices for assuring that their observations are as accurate as can be. Out of their work has come a vast literature which has provided us with an understanding of the nature of man and his behavior. This literature is of great value in helping us find solutions to human problems. Like any frame of reference, it has its unique uses and its peculiar advantages and limitations. Before looking more closely at these, let us examine briefly the internal frame of reference.

INTERNAL FRAME OF REFERENCE

THE HUMANIST MOVEMENT

In recent years a third great movement has come into being in American psychology. This one is called the "humanist movement" or sometimes the "third force." It is a psychology that is deeply interested in the person's own experience, his internal life. It seeks understanding the nature of people's feelings, attitudes, beliefs, concepts, purposes, desires, loves, hates, and human values. Because these qualities are the very ones that most uniquely make us human, this psychology has come to be known as the humanist movement. Since feelings, values, beliefs, and purposes lie inside people and are not available for direct observation by outsiders, psychologists dealing with these matters are forced to operate from the internal frame of reference, also called the phenomenological frame of reference.

At the moment there is much confusion in the humanist movement because psychologists working in this area call themselves by a bewildering variety of names. This is quite likely to be the case whenever a new point of view comes upon the scene. As scholars from widely different backgrounds and experience delve into the subject, they create their own vocabularies and concepts. So, psychologists working in the humanist movement sometimes call themselves transactionalists, personalists, phenomenologists, self-psychologists, humanists, existentialists, or perceptualists. By whatever name, they all have much in common. All are concerned in more or less degree with attempts to understand behavior as the behaver himself experiences it.

Humanistic psychology is very largely the product of applied psychologists—persons engaged in one way or another with the practice of psychology. Most of its contributors have come from the ranks of social work, teaching, counseling, clinical or child psychology, and psychiatry. The influence of these kinds of workers on humanistic psychology has been so great that it has sometimes been called the "practitioner's" psychology. As we shall see throughout this book, it does have a special relevance for the work of those engaged in the helping professions.

PERCEPTUAL PSYCHOLOGY

The authors of this book regard themselves as humanists, and the particular orientation of that movement with which they are associated is called "perceptual psychology." This branch of psychology seeks to understand human behavior through the processes of perception—how things seem to the behaver at the moment of acting. It is a psychology which looks at behavior through the "eye of the beholder," from the person's own experience. The perceptual point of view is more explicitly set forth by Combs and Snygg in another volume, *Individual Behavior*.[1] Briefly, perceptual psychology takes the position that all behavior is a function of the perceptions existing for any individual at the moment of his behaving, especially those perceptions he has of himself and of the world in which he is operating. Each of us does at every moment what seems appropriate at that instant. When the nature of perceptions is understood, even the weirdest behavior becomes comprehensible.

It is no world-shaking idea that people behave in terms of how things seem to them. It is patently obvious. Nevertheless, it is the failure of people everywhere to comprehend this "obvious" fact which is responsible for much of human misunderstanding, maladjustment, conflict, and loneliness. Our perceptions of ourselves and the world have such a complete feeling of reality for us that we very seldom stop to doubt them. We accept the way things seem to us as the way things *really* are, and we behave accordingly. What is more, when others do not agree with us, we are likely to jump to the conclusion that either they are frightfully stupid or purposely not seeing the truth just to embarrass or injure us. What we regard as "firm conviction" in ourselves we may regard as prejudice in someone else. After shooting President Lincoln, John Wilkes Booth wrote: "I did not desire greatness. After being hunted like a dog through swamps and woods, wet, cold and starving, with every man's hand against me, I am here in despair. And why? . . . I have never hated nor wronged anyone." On his deathbed he still could say, "Tell mother . . . I died for my country." *Reality for each person* is what it seems to be for him. Our failure to fully comprehend that fact is perhaps the most important single cause of breakdowns in communication and the source of much conflict and human misery.

---

1. For a more extensive, systematic view of psychology from a perceptual orientation, the interested reader is referred to Combs, A. W. and Snygg, D., *Individual Behavior: A Perceptual Approach to Behavior*, New York: Harper and Bros., 1959.

According to perceptual psychology the individual's behavior is a function of all those perceptions existing for him at a given moment. The word "perception" is used by psychologists in this persuasion to mean more than "seeing." It refers rather to "meaning," the peculiar significance of an event for the person experiencing it. In this sense the behavior of a person at any moment is understood as the direct consequence of the field of meanings existing for him at that instant. This does not mean that all of the perceptions affecting behavior will be in such clear figure for the behaver that he could tell another person about them if asked.

At any moment the individual's perceptual field will contain some perceptions clearly differentiated from all others and toward which his behavior is directed. At the same time, there will also be in his field many other perceptions in varying degrees of awareness—all the way from those in very clear figure at the center of his attention to those perceptions so vague and undifferentiated that he would not be able to report them to us if we were to ask him. This sounds very much like the Freudian concept of conscious and unconscious awareness. In a sense it is; but perceptual psychologists prefer not to speak of "conscious" and "unconscious" because it gives the impression of two distinct conditions rather than varying levels of awareness at different degrees of clarity.

To understand the behavior of persons from the internal frame of reference, it is necessary to discover how things seem to them, especially how people see themselves and the world they are involved in. Things are not the same to the middle-aged, middle-class female schoolteacher and the ten-year-old schoolboy from the other side of the tracks. Events are different also from the point of view of management and labor, nurse and patient, counselor and client, parent and child; or from the point of view of Georgi Shlyapnikov, the brick mason in Mizhni Novgorod on the Volga in Russia and George Jackson, the brick mason in Kansas City on the Missouri River in the USA.

ADVANTAGES OF THE EXTERNAL APPROACH

A Helpful View of Causation

Each frame of reference, external or internal, leads to different conceptions of the causes of behavior and also to different ways of approaching the task of helping people. Seen from the external approach, behavior is understood as the resultant of the forces being exerted upon the individual, now in the present and from the past through the processes of learning or conditioning. The contributions of this way of viewing human behavior are tremendous for every aspect of our society. To deal effectively with the social, political, and humanitarian activities of the world we live in, we need the understandings about the relationships between people and their environments provided by objective psychology. It is important to know the nature of the forces exerted upon people and the kinds of actions these are likely to elicit. Such information provides the bases for our attempts to control and direct human affairs as individuals, groups, institutions, or governments. The things we decide to do in solving the problems of living—whether they be in social interaction, problems of labor and management, buying and selling, traffic control, or a thousand other situations in our society—are determined by what we have learned from the observation of people and their behavior. These observations may be obtained by scientists in controlled experiments or simply through the evidence of our own daily observations.

The genetic view of causation has helped us with explanations of how people *got* the way they are. It tells us, for example: "This child is a problem because he was rejected by his parents." "That worker is lazy because the union has undermined his desire to put in a full day's work." "That man is afraid because he has never cut loose from his mother's apron strings." "That woman is still trying to get over a broken heart." "The reason for the failure of those children is that they have grown up in a culturally deprived situation."

Out of careful observation of the effects of forces upon people, we are provided with important understandings of the dynamics of growth and change. This information in turn provides us with clues that we need for controlling and directing human destinies with greater efficiency. When we know how children learn, we can teach them more effectively. When we understand the effects of bad housing, we can construct better cities. When we understand the factors contributing to delinquency or psychosis, we can find ways of preventing them in the future. When we know what makes people angry, we can seek for ways to help them live in peace.

IMPLICATIONS FOR ACTION

A point of view about the causes of behavior does more than simply provide us with explanations. It points the way to methods of dealing with them. The external frame of reference begins with the belief that behavior is the result of the stimuli at work on the individual. This leads naturally to methods of dealing with people through the manipulation of forces acting upon them. This is usually accomplished through some application of techniques of reward and punishment, as when we seek to motivate children with ice cream cones or threaten the sinful with hell-fire and damnation. This is an important point for persons in the helping professions. If the methods people choose to help other people are dependent upon the views of causation they hold, it behooves helping persons to be keenly aware of the frames of reference from which they approach their professional problems.

APPLICATION TO MASS PROBLEMS

One of the special values of the stimulus-response approach to understanding behavior is its applicability to mass problems. Operating objectively, data can be obtained with or without the cooperation of the subjects. Once collected, the data can be accumulated in vast quantities, stored, and manipulated in infinite numbers of ways. This makes it possible to deal with aspects of behavior in large groups of people. It can help us, for example, take millions of men into the armed forces and distribute them quickly to the thousands of jobs required for operating a military machine. Or, it can help us select one thousand students applying for college entrance out of five thousand applications. It can tell us "what the chances are" that one event or another will occur if we do this or that. Such probabilities make prediction possible and so provide us with valuable guidelines for action. It cannot do this with absolute accuracy, of course, and some individuals are bound to be classified improperly. When masses have to be dealt with, this is part of the price we pay. Predicting human behavior is no easy task, and we need any help we can get.

We owe a great deal to the external approach for understanding behavior. We live with it so closely and use it so automatically in our daily lives that we are usually quite unaware of its existence as a frame of reference. It is there, however, and gives direction to our thinking and behavior as individual citizens whether we are aware of its influence or not. As professional workers, this is not enough. People who presume to help others cannot permit themselves to be governed by concepts whose implications they do not understand. Professional helpers need to be keenly aware of the frames of reference they use and of the directions these impose upon belief and action.

LIMITATIONS OF THE EXTERNAL APPROACH

THE STIMULUS QUESTION

One of the difficulties involved in the use of the external approach has to do with the fact that we cannot always know to what stimulus the individual is responding. For example, offering a child a handful of jellybeans the day before Easter will not create the same stimulus nor produce the same behavior as offering the same amount of candy the day after Easter, when he is surfeited with candy. The stimulus is not the same, and it may produce different behavior. While it is true that *most* of the traffic stops at the stop light, sometimes people don't! While we usually eat when food is put before us, sometimes we do not. A child we know screamed with fright when taken to the barber. When the barber removed his coat, then all was well. Without his white coat he was no longer a doctor to the child. The nurse who scolds her patient may believe she is teaching the patient not to behave in that way, but she may actually be teaching the patient to dislike nurses and hospitals. People are, indeed, affected by the things that happen to them. The nature of what happens to the individual, however, has to do with his own experience of the event and is not always apparent to the observer describing the situation from an outsider's point of view.

Ordinarily, there is likely to be some relationship between the stimulus and the experiencing of it by the behaver. As a consequence, explanations of behavior in terms of the observed stimuli often provide us with partly right answers to questions about behavior which can be expressed in terms of probabilities. We can then say, "The chances are that such and such will occur" or, "This result will occur in X percent of the cases." It is even possible, with a sufficiently large number of observations, to express these relationships in fairly reliable terms. When it is necessary to deal with large numbers of people or activities, such probabilities may be quite sufficient. For many workers in the helping professions who must be able to understand and predict the behavior of individuals, however, such "chances are" data will often not be enough. They will need to know what *this particular* child or patient *will* do rather than what *eight out of ten may* do.

ACCESSIBILITY OF INFORMATION

The need for knowledge about a person's past required by the objective point of view for understanding behavior poses another difficulty for the professional helper. Such knowledge is often difficult to acquire for all sorts of reasons: records may be lost, people who know or who have information may be unavailable, or there may be confusion about what really happened or what was really significant. In courts of law, for example, the credibility of witnesses is always a knotty problem and it frequently happens that several witnesses may provide quite different explanations of what "really" happened. Information may also be unavailable because the people who could supply the answers may resent a probe into their private lives and refuse cooperation. Even when information is provided, there is always the possibility that it may not be accurate. One of the authors, for example, had lived for years with a vivid impression of an event which occurred in his childhood. When he recounted the story recently at a family gathering he was told by his mother and father and others who had been there at the time that what he thought happened had not occurred at all!

SEDUCTION OF EXPLANATION

While the external approach to behavior can often be helpful to persons engaged in the various helping professions, the exclusive use of this approach can sometimes lead to a *cul de sac* in which explanation becomes a substitute for helping. There is a seductive feeling of accomplishment in discovering the answer to a puzzling problem in another person's behavior. It is easy to be carried away by this kind of exercise and to lose sight of the fact that it is still a long step from explanation to cure. Sociologists, for example, are particularly prone to analyze the current social scene. Having explained it to their satisfaction, they often leave us still without solutions. School psychologists frequently make reports to teachers which only tell the teacher what she already knew, albeit in fancier language. It is one thing to know that the derelict bum on skid row is a product of vicious social forces and quite another to do something about them. Effective helping is not accomplished when the helper knows the answers; it is achieved only with a change for the better in the lives of students, clients, or whomever it is we are seeking to help.

TENDENCY TOWARD "BUCK-PASSING"

The kinds of explanation provided us by the external approach to behavior also lend themselves to a game of "buck-passing" in which no one can ever be held responsible for anything. Since the causes of behavior are regarded as lying in the past, failures can be neatly charged off to what someone else did "back there." The college can blame the high school; the high school can blame the grade school. The grade school can throw up its hands crying, "What can we do with a child from a home like that?" But, alas, the poor parents, being low men on the totem pole, have no one to pass the blame to. They are stuck with the full responsibility for all of society's ills. If the historic view of causation is to be followed to its logical conclusion, however, parents, too, must be held blameless. The *real* villains are Adam and Eve, or the amoeba, depending upon which view of man's creation one accepts.

LIMITATIONS OF ENVIRONMENTAL TREATMENT

A further practical difficulty in the use of the external approach arises from its emphasis upon control of the stimulus as a means of changing behavior. If behavior is a function of the stimulus, it follows that in order to change behavior, it will be necessary to make some kind of change in the environment of the individual. But this is not always feasible. Even when the professional worker knows the stimuli to which an individual may be responding, it may not be possible for him to do anything about it. What, for example, can the school nurse do about the family of a child who feels unloved or unwanted while his parents teeter on the edge of divorce? Or what can a teacher do about a brutal or alcoholic father, or an immature, overanxious mother? The physician may know that smoking is dangerous for his patient but be unable to prevent him from getting and using cigarettes.

Generally speaking, the older an individual gets, the more difficult it becomes to affect his behavior by controlling the environment in which he is operating. The world of a helpless infant is a very small one, composed for the most part of his parents and the home he lives in. But, as he grows older, the world to which he responds grows ever larger and infinitely more complex; and by the time he has reached adulthood, the possibilities of controlling his behavior by attempting to control his world have become very slim indeed, if not altogether impossible. It is a comparatively simple thing for parents to remove dangerous objects beyond the reach of the toddler. Imagine the problems involved in trying to keep a grownup from finding the means to commit suicide if he really wanted to do it. Attempting to affect behavior through control of the environment rapidly loses its value as an effective tool for the helping professions by the time most people have achieved their adolescence. After that, it is necessary to find some other means to help.

It is apparent from the discussion in these last pages that the external approach is no panacea for the problems of the helping professions. Despite its limitations, however, it does provide important guides for workers in the helping professions when its possibilities and limitations are clearly understood. Fortunately, the advantages and disadvantages of the internal frame of reference neatly complement those of the external approach in such fashion that the helper knowledgeable in both frames of reference can greatly increase his chances for success.

ADVANTAGES OF THE INTERNAL APPROACH

CONCERN FOR THE INDIVIDUAL

While the external approach to behavior lends itself particularly well to the problems of large groups, the internal approach is particularly useful in working with individuals. The internal frame of reference, as we have seen, seeks understanding of human behavior from the point of view of the behaver himself. It looks for the causes of behavior in the individual's own feelings, attitudes, beliefs, understandings, values, perceptions of himself, and the world in which he moves. These are highly personal matters not readily available to examination by external techniques. They are the primary data of the internal approach.

Human attitudes, feelings, values, beliefs, and perceptions are the very aspects of experience which make us human. They are also the causes of our maladjustments and failures and the sources of our greatest joy and fulfillment. The problem of the helping professions is primarily a people problem. It is not surprising, then, that humanistic approaches to understanding behavior should have special values for the helping professions.

In the external approach, we observed the difficulties often encountered because the observed stimulus was not always what it seemed. For example, some teachers have handled the matter of cleaning the chalkboard erasers so that the children regard it as a privilege. Others have used this task as a punishment for misbehavior. To predict the behavior of a child who is asked to clean the erasers, therefore, will not be likely to be very accurate unless we know which of these meanings the task has for him. The perceptual psychologist believes it is not the stimulus which produces behavior but the meaning it has for the person on whom it is applied. This focus of perceptual psychology upon the perception of the stimulus rather than the stimulus itself often makes possible many more accurate predictions of the behavior of individuals.

Advantage of Immediate Causation

The external approach to behavior relies heavily on the genetic view of causation. The internal approach provides us with a current interpretation. Behavior is understood in terms of the ways people see themselves and the world in which they are operating now, in the present, at this instant. For persons in the helping professions, this is a concept of enormous significance!

For several generations, many have believed it was not possible to understand or help other persons without an exhaustive knowledge of his past history. But, if it is true that a person's behavior is a product of his present perceptions, then it should be possible to understand him and help him even if we do not know the full story of how he got this way! The social worker who knows that a child's misbehavior is the result of his feeling that people don't like him can understand his misbehavior even though he may have no conception of what it was in the child's world which produced this feeling. Better still, knowing that a child feels people don't like him suggests its own program of treatment. If he knows that a child feels people don't like him, there are things a helper can do for that child, even if he has no conception of what it was that produced this feeling in the first place. One of the things he can do is to try to find ways in which such a youngster can be placed with people who might like him. Even if this fails, the helper himself can provide some assistance by demonstrating his own liking for the child! As we have seen, workers in the helping professions must usually deal with their clients, students, or patients on an instant to instant basis.

An immediate concept of causation seems tailor-made for the helping professions. It provides a way of understanding behavior that permits action at once without the necessity for probing the individual's past or knowing the precise nature of all of the forces currently exerted upon him. This is a tremendously significant contribution to the helping professions. What it does for teachers is a case in point. For some time, teacher educators have demanded of teachers that they understand all their pupils. By this they usually mean an in-depth comprehension of the child's psychological make-up. The reasoning behind this impossible demand was that learning could best be adjusted to the individual needs and capacities of children only if teachers possessed the fullest possible understanding of each child. Such an expectancy for teachers has placed an intolerable burden upon them. A few elementary school teachers with small stable classes might hope to approximate this demand in the course of a year if they did little else. But what of the high school teacher with two or three hundred students drifting through his classes in the course of a day? Insistence upon understanding in the genetic sense of the term imposes a hopeless task upon most teachers. If, however, it is possible to work with a child and effectively understand him in the present, teachers are at once relieved of an impossible expectation and provided with vast new possibilities for successfully carrying out their tasks.

It should not be supposed from this discussion that we are denying the truth of the genetic principle that behavior is a product of the individual's past experience. That idea about behavior is just as true as it ever was. Generally speaking, the more data we have about any problem the more likely we are to be able to arrive at correct solutions. The point is that not all data is of equal value. What data is needed will depend upon what our goals are and how we propose to reach them. Knowing the details of a child's early life and the fact that he came from a broken home may tell us how he came to feel that nobody likes him today. Knowing his feeling about himself, there are things we can do to help him even if we do not know how he came to be in this condition.

IMMEDIATE GUIDELINES TO ACTION

It is interesting that most modern schools of psychotherapy are predicated upon this understanding that effective changes in behavior can be accomplished through helping clients directly in the present. The long, agonizing delving into the client's past which formerly was considered an absolute essential for effective treatment is no longer regarded so. One can see many instances of this in daily life. Nurses, for example, may help patients feel less depressed without knowing how they got so. Businessmen can aid employees to feel better about themselves and their jobs and still be quite unaware of the lives of their employees off duty.

One of the authors has often noted in his experience as a psychotherapist on a college campus that the clients who spend long hours exploring their past in counseling are, almost without exception, graduate students in psychology! From their studies, they know that behavior is a function of their pasts. When they come for therapy, then, they set about exploring it in detail. Clients who have not learned so thoroughly that their behavior is a function of the past spend very little time digging into it. They begin at once to explore their present feelings and perceptions. It even happens that they get well despite the fact that at the end of therapy the counselor may still not know how they became unhappy in the first place!

Because the immediate frame of reference does not impose upon the helper the necessity for searching, probing, diagnosing, and analyzing, it also facilitates the development of rapport and cooperative relationships. Working with people's immediate perceptions, how they feel, believe, think, and understand, is working with the individual's own reality. He is on his own ground in a subject matter he knows and understands. As a consequence, he is quite likely to feel much closer to the professional helper, more readily understood, and willing to enter into communication with him.

Perceptual psychology is especially valuable as a practitioner's psychology. Its principles are often deceptively simple. They have an "of course" feeling about them and often fit one's own experience so closely as to seem like one has always known them. This quality is very upsetting to some people who believe that what is simple must also be suspect as science. But the simple and the obvious can have vast implications. It is necessary to remind ourselves that simplicity is the *goal* of science. What could be simpler, for example, than the physical formula $E = mc^2$?

LIMITATIONS OF THE INTERNAL APPROACH

PROBLEM OF THE OBSERVER

Despite its values for the helping professions, the internal approach also has its limitations. Because it deals primarily with people's perceptions, feelings, attitudes, and beliefs, its data lies always inside the individual and is not directly observable or measurable. Thus, workers using the internal approach have a much more difficult problem of observation and data collection than if they used the external approach. It is a real advantage to be able to make simple objective observations of the stimuli to which a person seems to be reacting. Often such observations can be made by persons with comparatively little training or experience. It is much more difficult to discover the *meaning* of the stimuli to which a person is reacting as this appears in the peculiar personal world of the subject. This problem requires the examiner to be able to place himself in the subject's shoes or to be able to infer the nature of his internal world with some degree of accuracy. This is not always easy to do. Generally speaking, it calls for a great deal of understanding, personal discipline, and skill in human interaction for the making of valid observations. By contrast, observations can often be made in the external view by relatively untrained observers—even, sometimes, by machines. This dependence upon the skill of the observer can be overcome, but it nevertheless introduces additional possibilities of error in perceptual psychology and so complicates its uses.

The internal frame of reference is an individual approach to behavior. It does not lend itself effectively to dealing with large groups or with mass data. It is possible, of course, to acquire the data for mass problems by the examination of many individuals. The time and energy required very quickly makes this a highly expensive approach when applied to large populations. The accuracy of prediction sought in perceptual approaches is frequently not needed anyhow. There are many problems on the social scene in which we are not really interested in high degrees of exactness. It may not be important to know what Mrs. Brown, Mrs. Smith, or Mrs. Jones will buy as individuals, often it will be enough to know probabilities of what the women of the community are likely to purchase. For this kind of data we are probably much better off with the external approach.

COOPERATION OF THE BEHAVER

A further difficulty inherent in the internal approach is its frequent dependence upon the cooperation of the subject. A great many observations in the external frame of reference can be carried on without the cooperation or even the knowledge of the subject involved. Investigations into a person's past history through school and medical records, for example, can be carried on pretty much at the desire of the investigator, often without regard to the wishes of the subject. In the internal frame of reference, however, this is often not the case. Being concerned with deeper, more personal aspects of human experience, workers in the internal frame of reference must have much more contact with the person and may even need to have his cooperation. In psychotherapy, for example, it is first of all necessary for the client to be willing to subject himself to this experience. Until an alcoholic, for example, is willing to accept that fact that he is an alcoholic, there is very little that can be done to help him. This necessity for having the cooperation of the behaver also calls for a great deal more skill on the part of the helper. It demands a great deal of artistry in interaction with people and a large capacity for empathy and understanding.

LACK OF TESTED TECHNIQUES

A major problem with using the internal frame of reference at this time grows out of its comparative newness—that is, the lack of tested and proven procedures for measurement. Objective approaches for studying behavior have been in the process of developing for more than half a century. During that time, large numbers of ingenious devices for measuring behavior under many different kinds of conditions have been invented. As a newcomer to the social sciences, the internal frame of reference has not yet had time to develop such refined instruments of measurement. New frames of reference always call for the development of new devices for the study of its subject matter. Professional workers approaching behavior from this frame of reference, therefore, will often have to work with instruments that are still crude as compared to those in use in the external approach. Every new direction in science has this problem. Witness, for example, the struggles of scientists to develop new instruments like atomic reactors or spaceships. The lack of precise instruments will be overcome in time. Meanwhile, professional workers using this approach at this stage will often have to invent their own instruments of observation and measurement as they go along. When looked at one way, this may be a disappointment; when looked at another way, it is an exciting challenge.

WHICH FRAME OF REFERENCE FOR HELPERS?

As we have seen in this and in the previous chapter, the behavior of a professional worker, like everyone else, is determined by the perceptions he holds. Thus the frames of reference we choose to approach our problems inevitably impose directions upon us and determine the nature of the tools we use and the techniques we employ in carrying out our roles. Each of the frames of reference for understanding behavior has its advantages and its disadvantages. Each also commits the user to its peculiar philosophy, goals, and programs of action whether the helper is aware of these determinants or not. There is always a temptation to simplify our problems by forcing them into clearcut categories or dichotomies of black or white, right or wrong, for me or against me, and so on. This is true of frames of reference, also. It is necessary to recognize that different concepts may each be accurate in its own frame of reference. A theory or a frame of reference is only a more or less convenient way to look at a problem or to order a collection of data. The question we need to raise when choosing one is not, "Which one is right and which one wrong?" but, "Which frame of reference is most appropriate for the purpose we have in mind?" Using an inappropriate frame of reference may be like trying to dig a canal with a soupspoon or trying to eat soup with a steam shovel. Some theories are broad and encompassing, some are narrow and concerned with only a limited problem. A frame of reference or a theory is only a tool, and it is necessary to understand our tools and how they can best be employed. Our problem is not choosing a frame of reference that is somehow right in itself, but choosing one that is appropriate to the problems we have to deal with.

This is not to imply that we are advocating eclecticism. Not at all. The eclectic uses whatever works. Using what works is certainly desirable in the helping professions. Since people are not expendable, however, we cannot simply plant a new crop if we make a mistake in cultivating them. Practitioners in the helping professions must behave responsibly. It is not enough to try something because it might work. There is no place in these professions for doing things just "on faith." People are much too precious for that. Whatever is done must have the presumption of reason and the probability of success. To assure this, the beliefs of professional workers must be as clear and as consistent as possible, for these produce their behavior. This holds for frames of reference and theoretical positions. A well-understood frame of reference provides the worker with guides to action and makes his behavior more likely to be consistent and efficient. There is a vast difference between using frames of reference with full understanding of their ramifications, applied to conditions for which they are appropriate, and operating without such understandings on a philosophy of "doing whatever might work." This is the difference between a professional and a "tinkerer."

Generally speaking, professional workers will find the internal frame of reference more often appropriate for their problems than the external one. The helping professions by definition are concerned with human beings and their struggles for fulfillment as individuals. It is not surprising then that a humanistic psychology should seem to be tailor-made for the problems of the helping professions. The internal frame of reference seems so especially appropriate for the helping professions that the reader will find it given special emphasis throughout this book. It would be a serious error, however, to regard the two points of view we have been discussing in this chapter as contradictory or opposed to one another.

SELECTED READINGS

Starred entries indicate appearance in whole or in part in Donald L. Avila, Arthur W. Combs, and William W. Purkey, *The Helping Relationship Sourcebook* (Boston: Allyn & Bacon, 1971).

* Avila, D. L. & Purkey, W. W. Intrinsic and extrinsic motivation: A regrettable distinction. *Psychology in the Schools,* 1966, **3,** 206–208.

Bischof, L. *Interpreting personality theories.* New York: Harper & Row, 1964.

Bonner, H. *On being mindful of man.* Boston: Houghton Mifflin, 1965.

Bugental, J. F. T. (Ed.) *Challenges of humanistic psychology.* New York: McGraw Hill, 1967.

* Combs, A. W. Some basic concepts in perceptual psychology. Speech given at APGA Convention, 14 April 1965, Session #239, Minneapolis, Minn.

Freud, S. *A general introduction to psychoanalysis.* Garden City, N.Y.: Garden City Publishing Co., 1920.

Hilgard, E. & Bowers, G. *Theories of learning.* New York: Appleton-Century Crofts, 1966.

* Hitt, W. D. Two models of man. *American Psychologist,* 1969, **24,** 651–658.

Maehr, M. L. Some limitations of the application of reinforcement theory to education. *School and Society,* 1968, **96,** 108–110.

* Rogers, C. R. & Skinner, B. F. Some issues concerning the control of behavior. *Science,* 1956, **124,** 1057–1066.

Skinner, B. F. A case history in the scientific method. *American Psychologist,* 1956, **11,** 221–223.

Wann, T. W. (Ed.) *Behaviorism and phenomenology: Contrasting bases for modern psychology.* Chicago: University of Chicago Press, 1964.

3

Self-Concept: Product and Producer of Experience

The most important single factor affecting behavior is the self-concept. What people do at every moment of their lives is a product of how they see themselves and the situations they are in. While situations may change from moment to moment or place to place, the beliefs that people have about themselves are always present factors in determining their behavior. The self is the star of every performance, the central figure in every act. Persons engaged in the helping professions, therefore, need the broadest possible understandings of the nature, origins, and functions of the self-concept.

WHAT IS THE SELF–CONCEPT?

By the self-concept is meant all those aspects of the perceptual field to which we refer when we say "I" or "me." It is that organization of perceptions about self which seems to the individual to be who he is. It is composed of thousands of perceptions varying in clarity, precision, and importance in the person's peculiar economy. Taken altogether these are described by the perceptual psychologist as the self-concept.

Each of us has literally thousands of ideas or concepts about himself: who he is, what he stands for, where he lives, what he does or does not do, and the like. A particular person might see herself as Mrs. Sally Blanton—wife, mother, part-time social worker; American, white;

young; resident of Tampa, Fla.; measurements 34-25-34; good swimmer; poor tennis player. All these and many other perceptions or beliefs about herself make up the personal and unique self-concept of Mrs. Sally Blanton. To be sure, not all the concepts about herself are equally important to Mrs. Blanton. Some concepts of herself may be recognized as transitory. Others, like her concept of herself as a woman and a "Mrs.," are probably extremely important aspects of herself and are difficult to change.

Descriptions like those Mrs. Blanton has of herself serve to distinguish her self as unique from all other selves. But self-description does not stop there. We are seldom content with description alone. Even more important are the values a person places upon his various qualities of self. People do not regard themselves only as fathers or mothers, but as "good" or "bad" fathers and mothers. They see themselves not simply as people, but as attractive or ugly, pleasant or unpleasant, fat or thin, happy or sad, adequate or inadequate people. These, too, are perceptions of self and, taken together with the thousands of other concepts of self, make up the person's self-concept.

The self-concept, it should be understood, is not a thing but an organization of ideas. It is an abstraction, a Gestalt, a peculiar pattern of perceptions of self. Despite being no more than an abstraction, however, these ideas are terribly important for the person who holds them. They may seem only like ideas to outsiders but, for the person himself, they have a feeling of absolute reality. In fact the self-concept is even more important to its owner than the body in which it exists. The body, according to Earl Kelley, is but "the meat house we live in," the vehicle in which the self rides. We recognize the distinction between body and self when we complain that "the spirit is willing but the flesh is weak," or "I would have come to the meeting, Joe, but my old body let me down and I had to stay in bed with the flu."

This distinction between the self-concept and the physical self may be observed in other ways. For example, the self-concept may be defined in such a way as to include matters quite outside the skin. This often happens with respect to one's most cherished possessions. A man may regard his desk as so much a part of him that he treats interference with it as a personal violation. Consequently, his reaction to a secretary who has intruded upon his territory by disturbing things in or on the desk may be so angry and forceful as to bewilder her. She exclaims to the other girls in the office, "You'd think I'd wounded him, or something!" Of course, she had. What appears to be only a piece of furniture to the secretary seems to be an extension of self to the owner of the desk.

The extension of self is observable even more often with respect to persons or groups. Psychologists refer to this experience as a feeling of "identification." By this, they mean the feeling of oneness we have with those persons or groups who have come to have special value for us. The self of a father, for instance, may be extended to include his son or daughter. When they are insulted, he almost literally behaves as though he were himself offended. The feeling of oneness with those we love and cherish has been experienced by almost everyone. Sometimes it may be so very strong, in fact, that awareness of physical separation may be temporarily lost. In the following excerpt from a letter, a young mother describes this feeling with respect to her newborn child:

> When they brought my baby to me I unwrapped her and lay for a while in awe examining the marvelous way she was made. Then, after a while, I placed her on my stomach with her head between my breasts and lay there with a curious feeling of triumph and exquisite peace. Now and then I would raise the covers a little and peek down at her. As she lay there I honestly couldn't tell where she began and I left off. I remember I wept a little because I was so happy. I'll never forget the moment as long as I live.

While few of us are privileged to experience the depth of identification felt by this young mother, almost everyone has some feelings of identification with other people somewhere. It is one of those things that makes us human.

The expansion of self-concept also extends to feelings about groups. In fact, one of the reasons groups come together in the first place is to have the experience of oneness with each other. In becoming a member of a group, the self-concept is expanded to include the other members. Thereafter the individual begins to behave as though the members are an extension of his self. He speaks of "my gang," "my school," "my friend," "my church," "my neighborhood," "my state," or "my country." Depending upon how strong the identification, he behaves with respect to them as though they were part of self. He may even begin to call the members of his fraternity, church, or racial group "brothers" or "sisters."

THE SELF: CENTER OF THE UNIVERSE

For each person, his self-concept is who he is. It is the center of his universe, the frame of reference from which he makes his observations. It is his personal reality and the vantage point from which all else is observed and comprehended. We speak of things as "right" or "left," "near" or "far," and, of course, we mean from ourselves. The self is also used as a yardstick for making judgments. We regard others as taller, shorter, smarter, more unscrupulous, more handsome, faster, older, or younger than ourselves. As the self changes, furthermore, the yardstick changes and what we believe to be true changes with it. What is considered "old" is likely to be quite differently defined at ages six, sixteen, thirty-six, or sixty.

Generally speaking, we feel quite at home with "what is me." Toward what is "not me," we are likely to be indifferent, even repelled. Allport points out, for example, that when a person cuts his finger he may put it in his mouth and, in doing so, drinks his own blood without the slightest concern. Once the finger has been bandaged, however, any dried blood on the bandage is no longer regarded as "me"; a suggestion to lick the blood from the bandage would likely be regarded with revulsion. Similarly, everyone is continuously engaged in swallowing the saliva which collects in his mouth. This same saliva, collected in a glass and offered to the person to drink, is a very different matter indeed! Experiences consistent with the existing self-concept are accepted quite readily. They are treated as though they belong even when accepting them may be painful. A failing grade for a student who already believes he is a failure may not concern him at all. It only represents a further corroboration of what he already believes. It fits. On the other hand, incongruous experiences may produce feelings of great discomfort. When a man who believes he is highly attractive is told in no uncertain terms by a beautiful girl what a heel he really is, the shock to the self is likely to be considerable. Doctors and nurses often find it very difficult to get patients newly diagnosed as "diabetic" to care for themselves properly. Such patients often find it very difficult to accept this new concept of self and the use of insulin and dietary prescriptions they must follow. It takes time to assimilate their new definitions of self. The disturbing effect of inconsistent experiences will occur even if the new thought is something the person would like to believe. This can be observed in the embarrassment a person feels when after long periods of failure, he is told he has done something very well. He may even suspect that the teller is being sarcastic!

SELF–CONCEPT DETERMINES BEHAVIOR

The importance of the self-concept in the economy of the individual goes far beyond providing his basis of reality. Its very existence determines what else he may perceive. The self-concept has a selective effect on perceptions. People tend to perceive what is congruent with their already existing concept of self. People who see themselves as men perceive what is appropriate for men to perceive, while people who see themselves as women see what is appropriate for women to perceive. So it happens that on the way home from a party, Mrs. Adams may say to her husband, "John, did you notice what Helen was wearing?" John is quite likely to reply, "No, I didn't notice that." But, being a man, there were other things he noticed which, almost certainly, his wife will not think to ask him about!

It is notorious how a man's behavior may change when he puts on a uniform and becomes "a soldier." With this self-concept he is free to behave in ways he would not dream of as a civilian. Students have been known to fail in school because of unfortunate beliefs about themselves, as in this example reported by Coach Darrel Mudra of Western Illinois University:

> What a boy believes about himself is really important. We had a student at Greeley who scored in the 98 percentile on the entrance test, and he thought that he had a 98 IQ. And because he thought he was an average kid, he knew college would be hard for him. He almost failed in his first term. He went home and told his parents, "I don't believe I'm college caliber," and the parents took him back to school and talked with the college counselor. When he found out that 98 percentile score meant that he had a 140 IQ, he was able to do "A" work before the year was over.

Once established, the self-concept thereafter provides a screen through which everything else is seen, heard, evaluated, and understood. Architects do not look at buildings in the same way the rest of us do. Similarly, the view of the world is different as seen by dressmakers, plumbers, house painters, nuclear physicists, or people who see themselves as Russian, Chinese, white, black, Hindu, or Muslim. Each person perceives the world around him filtered through his own self-conceptions; and this occurs whether he is aware of what is happening or not. Even when the businessman goes on vacation, he may find it very difficult to forget his business. In any vacation resort, men can be observed by the hundreds seeking each other out to discuss the comfortable things of the world they know while their wives equally uncomfortable so far from home, find comfort in talking housewifely things with people they never knew before.

The psychological literature is overflowing with learned articles and research studies dealing with the effects of the self-concept on a great variety of behaviors including failure in school, levels of aspiration or goal-setting, athletic prowess, mental health, intelligence, delinquency and criminality, ethnic groups, the socially disadvantaged, and industrial productivity. In every aspect of human existence the self-concept exerts its influence upon what people do and how they behave. When we know how a person sees himself, then much of his behavior becomes clear to us and it is often possible to predict with great accuracy what he is likely to do next.

CIRCULAR EFFECT OF THE SELF-CONCEPT

The selective effect of the self-concept has another important result. It corroborates and supports the already existing beliefs about self and so tends to maintain and reinforce its own existence. This circular characteristic of the self-concept may often be observed at work in the problems of children in learning arithmetic, spelling, public speaking, physical education, history, music, or any of the rest of the school subjects. Take the case of reading, for example: It now seems clear that many children who cannot read are unable largely because they *believe* they cannot read. It is comparatively rare these days that the child coming to the reading clinic has anything wrong with his eyes. With modern methods of testing children's health, sight deficiencies are usually discovered routinely. Instead, the youngster who comes to the reading clinic is much more likely to be handicapped because he believes he cannot read. For one reason or another he has developed an idea that he is unable to read. Thereafter, he is caught in a vicious circle which goes something like this: Because he believes he can't read, he avoids it. In this way he avoids the very thing that would be helpful for him. Because he avoids reading, he doesn't get any practice and so he doesn't read very well. Then, when his teacher asks him to read, he reads very poorly and she says, "My goodness, Jimmy, you don't read very well!" This, of course, is what he already believed in the first place! Then, to make matters worse, a report card is often sent home telling his parents how badly he reads and so they, too, join the act confirming the child's belief that he is indeed a very poor reader. In this way a poor reader is frequently surrounded by a veritable conspiracy in which all of his experience points out his deficiency to him. This conspiracy, moreover, is produced for the most part by persons whose intentions were excellent. They *wanted* the child to be a good reader, even though the net effect of their pressures was to prove to him he was not.

The reader himself may be one of those thousands of people who believes he cannot do mathematics, make a speech, or spell. With such a belief, he probably shuns those occasions where it is necessary to use the skill and so avoids the opportunity to practice it. Then, of course, his failure experiences when he is forced to act corroborate what he already firmly believes! Many research studies are now available showing the effects of student beliefs upon achievement in a wide variety of school subjects. There is even evidence to suggest that the self-concept may be a better predictor of a child's success in school than the time-honored IQ score.

The self-perpetuating effect of the self-concept is by no means limited to success or failure in academic subjects. It extends to every aspect of human experience. The same dynamics may be seen at work in all walks of life. The juvenile delinquent, for example, who has come to believe that nobody likes him, wants him, cares about him, and who thinks he is not much good, often comes to the conclusion that other people are his enemies. Thereafter, he may find delight in confounding authority. He builds up his feelings of self-esteem and value by taunting the police, and enjoys finding ingenious ways of frustrating and embarrassing them. Such behavior is hardly likely to endear him to others. Almost certainly, it will cause others to behave toward him in ways which confirm and support his already unhappy views of himself.

Dr. Walter Reckless and his colleagues at Ohio State University carried out a series of studies on the self-concepts of delinquent and nondelinquent boys. Among their findings are the following: The 12-year old "good" boy in a slum area perceives himself as staying out of trouble, of his friends as keeping out of trouble, of himself as going to finish school, and of his family as a good family. The mothers of the "good" boys also had favorable perceptions and prognostications of their sons. On the other hand, the so-called "bad" boy, spotted by his sixth-grade teacher as headed for trouble and for dropout, has the opposite perception of himself. He perceives himself as headed for trouble, of his friends as delinquents, and of his family as a "bum" family. The "bad" boy's mother echoed his perceptions. In a follow-up study at the end of four years, these investigations found that the "good" boy was practically delinquency free, while 40 percent of the "bad" boys were in the juvenile court one to seven times.

Fortunately, the circular effect of the self-concept operates equally well in positive directions. Persons with positive self-concepts are quite likely to behave in ways that cause others to react in corroborative fashion. People who believe they *can,* are more likely to succeed. The very existence of such feelings about self creates conditions likely to make them so. The nurse who feels sure of herself behaves with dignity and certainty, expecting positive response from other people. To those with whom she works, this in turn calls forth responses which tend to confirm the beliefs she already holds. So, the circular effect of the self-concept creates a kind of spiral in which "the rich get richer and the poor get poorer." The self-corroborating character of the self-concept gives it a high degree of stability and makes it difficult to change once it has become firmly established.

SELF-CONCEPT AND SOCIAL PROBLEMS

The self-perpetuating characteristic of the self-concept makes it of special concern in attempting to deal with the great social problems of our time. Millions of people everywhere in the world are caught in a vicious circle in which their experience seems always to confirm their unhappy or disastrous concepts of self. "Like mirrors locked face to face, in an infinite corridor of despair," they are trapped in a way of life from which there seems no escape. Having defined themselves in ways that preclude much hope of success, they remain forever victims of their own self-perceptions. Believing they are only X much, that is all the much they do. Other people seeing them do only X much then learn to expect that much from them and describe them as "X much people" which, of course, only confirms what the person felt in the first place! Many Negroes, for example, have been so thoroughly brainwashed by generations of experience into believing that they are unable, incapable, and second-rate citizens that they often continue to behave so, even in conditions where it is no longer appropriate. Poverty-stricken men in Appalachia who have lived too long without jobs or hope for the future eventually give up trying altogether. White men who have grown up with serious doubts about themselves but feeling superior to "niggers" resist with violence ideas of social equality. Their self-concepts are so negative and their world so full of hopelessness that they must have some belief that makes them better than something. How to help these and thousands of other desperate victims of their own perceptions off the treadmill of self-corroboration is one of the great problems faced by our generation.

The self-concept also plays its part in the social and philosophical problems posed by our great international dilemmas. People who see themselves as Americans behave like Americans, while people who see themselves as Russians, Chinese, Japanese, German, British, or Ghanians behave in ways appropriate to their conceptions of themselves. So also, people who see themselves as Buddhists, Taoists, Jews, Moslems, or Christians tend to think and behave in terms of their beliefs. Sometimes diverse ways of seeing even create differences and misunderstandings where none really exist if it were possible to penetrate to the basic issues beneath the surface of differences. U Thant, as Secretary-General of the United Nations, once expressed this in a description of his own growth and philosophy which had brought him to a point where he could see himself as a "person in the world" rather than a representative of Thailand, his native country. Feeling so, he said that he could watch a wrestling match between a man from his own and a different country and rejoice for whomever won. For most of us, more is the pity, such a "citizen of the world" self-concept is still beyond our experience.

HOW THE SELF-CONCEPT IS LEARNED

The self-concept, we have said, is an organization of beliefs about the self. These concepts are learned in the same fashion in which all other perceptions are acquired—as a consequence of experience. Before a child is born, he has already begun to make differentiations about himself and the world he lives in. This process continues after birth. A very large part of the infant's waking hours are spent in continuous exploration. Everything is smelled, felt, tasted, listened to, and looked at. Very early he begins to distinguish between what is "me" and "not me." With continued exploration, these perceptions in turn become increasingly differentiated into more and more explicit definitions. As language use develops, it soon becomes possible to give "me" a name, and the whole process of differentiation and concept formation is immensely accelerated. Before long the child is in possession of large numbers of perceptions about himself and his world, and a sense of his identity emerges. He becomes aware of himself as a unique person of many qualities and values all together having a feeling of personness. A new self has come into being. Once established, this self will exert its influence on every behavior for the rest of its owner's life.[1]

Some of the things people learn about self are discovered from interaction with the physical world. From these experiences they learn how big or how little they are, how fast they can walk or swim, or where they are located in the space they live in. They also learn what they can lift or not lift, what they can control, what dangers they must avoid or protect themselves from, what things are good or enhancing, and thousands of other perceptions more or less useful for getting along in the physical world we all live in.

ROLE OF SIGNIFICANT OTHERS

Of much more importance to the growth of the self, however, are the concepts we acquire from interaction with other human beings. Man is primarily a social animal, and it is from experiences with other people that his most crucial concepts of self are derived. People learn who they are and what they are from the ways they are treated by the important people in their lives—sometimes called "significant others" by psychologists. From interactions with such people, each of us learns that he is liked or unliked, acceptable or unacceptable, a success or failure, respectable or of no account. We learn very little from unimportant people even if they are called teachers, parents, social workers, counselors, priests, or rabbis. Only the significant people have much effect on the self-concept. The nurse, for example, is not very disturbed by what the casual acquaintance says about her skill. She is very much concerned about what her supervisor or doctor has to say (providing, of course, that she believes they know their business). What is learned about the self is a product of the peculiar experience occurring in the private world of the individual. What he learns from any event may be quite different from the way it appears to the outside observer.

Because the self-concept is primarily learned from experience with significant others, it should not be assumed that this is simply a matter of what one is told by the important people in his life. So much of our daily interaction with one another occurs through verbal communication that

1. The full story of concept development and the growth of the self is a fascinating field of exploration far beyond the treatment possible here. Interested readers are referred to references listed at the end of this chapter for further introduction to this important field of study.

it is easy to fall into the belief that what people say to each other has immense importance. Sometimes, of course, it may. The effect of words does not lie in what was said, however, but how it was read by the hearer. Understanding this fact is especially important for persons in the helping professions because so much of these people's work is dependent upon verbal interaction in one form or another. Believing that words are terribly important or that any matter can be solved by talk can result in making the helper ineffective. Certainly, talking is one of the most valuable tools we have at our disposal for influencing the behavior of others, but it is easy to exaggerate its contribution. It is not enough to be told one is loved; it is necessary to *feel* he is loved, and by someone who matters. One need only remind himself how seldom he takes "good advice" from others. Telling may be a way of affecting a change in another's self-concept. It is by no means infallible and is often vastly overrated.

From whatever source the self-concept is acquired, what is learned is a matter of the individual's own experience, not what seems to some outsider to be happening to him. A parent who scolds a child for not doing well in school may do so with the best of intentions, hoping to motivate his child to greater effort. To the child the meaning of this event may only be that he is stupid, unacceptable, or not much good. This kind of unintended learning is called "incidental learning" by psychologists and is often far more important in determining behavior than what the counselor or teacher or social worker expected to convey. Children learn about themselves, for example, from the atmosphere of the classroom, from the moods of teachers, and from the overt or covert indications of success or failure implied by approval or disapproval of teachers and classmates. This unplanned learning is likely to be much more significant and permanent than what the teacher taught. The child in fifth grade who is reading at second-grade level has a daily diet of failure imposed upon him by the rigidity of a system which insists on teaching all children at a given level as though they were alike. In the face of this daily experience, telling him he is "a good boy" is like a drop of water in a dry lake bed. Or, trying too hard to teach the young mother all she should know to care for her sick child may result in convincing her how inadequate she really is.

PLACE OF TRAUMA IN THE GROWTH OF SELF

Many people believe the self-concept is primarily a product of the dramatic events occurring to the child in the process of growing up. This idea has come about very largely because of the concepts introduced to our thinking by Sigmund Freud and his students. As he listened to his patients retrace the steps of their growth and development in the course of psychoanalysis, Freud found them repeatedly bringing to light shocking events which had happened to them in the past. It was natural to assume that these events had had deep and powerful influences on the formation of personality and the creation of the problems his patients carried into adult years. This impression was further confirmed by the patients themselves, who frequently spoke of these events as having had a critical effect upon them.

In more recent years we have come to see the role of early trauma in a different way. We now understand that the most important changes in the self-concept probably come about only as a consequence of many experiences repeated over long periods of time. It is the little day to day things repeatedly chipping away at an individual's feelings about himself that produce the most permanent, pervasive effects on the self. A child learns that he is acceptable or unacceptable—not so much from the dramatic events as from the thousands of little every day nuances of attitude and feeling picked up from those about him, often so subtle and indistinct at the time they occurred as to make it quite impossible in later life for the grownup to put his finger upon the particular event which produced his current feeling.

If the self-concept is learned only slowly as a consequence of many experiences, why should we have the feeling that dramatic events in the past have so deeply influenced us? The reason seems to be that dramatic events are easier to recall and become symbols which crystallize and bring into clear figure the essence of a particular feeling. The event has tremendous significance, not because the experience was that crucial in its own right but because the experience became symbolic making explicit, many implicit feelings developed over a long period of time. Many a child has known the death of a grandfather with little or no feeling of loss, and many are quite unable in later days to remember the event at all. For the lonely, rejected child whose grandfather was an island of care and concern, the same event has a far different meaning. Looking backward down the years of our growth, dramatic events provide the hooks on which we can hang accumulated meanings. As a consequence the adult may recall how shy he was as a child and how devastated he was the day in third grade "when all the children laughed at me!" What makes the difference in human personality is not the trauma itself, but the multitude of other experiences which hammered and molded its meaning into being.

STABILITY OF THE SELF-CONCEPT

We have described the self-concept as composed of thousands of concepts of self varying in importance to the person. We have also observed that the core of the self-concept has a high degree of permanence and stability once it has become established. Unimportant aspects of the self can often be acquired or changed fairly quickly. These are generally peripheral aspects of the self, or matters of comparatively little concern. Thus, it may be possible to teach a person a game so that he comes to think of himself as a person who knows how to play that game. By taking a person for a ride in an airplane, we may produce a change in his self-concept to "one who has been in a plane." While these kinds of changes are comparatively simple to bring about, they are seldom enough to produce important changes in personality. Most of the truly important changes in the self-concept, such as those related to values, attitudes, or basic beliefs, occur much more slowly and sometimes only after very long periods of time. This is often very frustrating to those who like to help people quickly or easily. Frustrating as it is, however, we need to remind ourselves that this same resistance to change is also our very best guarantee against being taken over by a demagogue. It is a good thing people do not change easily!

Generally speaking, the more important the aspect of self in the economy of the individual, the more experience will be required to establish it and the more difficult it will be to change it. Fritz Redl once illustrated this slow development of individual feelings about self in the course of a lecture on juvenile delinquency. Delinquents, he pointed out, are not made by any one thing:

> It takes fourteen years to make a good delinquent. Before that you can't really be sure you have one. To make a good delinquent everything has to go wrong, not once, but over and over again. The home has to go wrong, the school has to go wrong, the church has to go wrong, the community has to go wrong, his friends have to let him down, not once, but over and over again. They have to make a habit of it! Then, after 14 years of that you may have a good delinquent.[2]

After fourteen years of such experience it is also understandable why it takes time to change such a child's beliefs about himself and the world.

2. From notes taken at Dr. Redl's lecture by A. W. Combs. Since Dr. Redl was speaking ex tempore, the accuracy of the quotation cannot be checked. The illustration, however, is superb.

SELF–CONCEPT AND SELF–REPORT

If the self-concept plays as important a role in the determination of behavior as modern psychologists believe, then members of the helping
professions must become sensitive to the self-concepts of their students,
clients, or patients, and must be skillful in helping them make changes in
their concepts of self. At first glance, understanding someone's self-concept would seem like an easy proposition; if you would like to know how
someone sees himself, why not just ask him? That seems obvious and
straightforward enough. Unfortunately, it is not that simple. How a person perceives himself is a very private matter, and what he is able to tell
you about himself will depend upon his willingness to reveal himself to
you. Even if he is willing, there is still a question as to whether he can
describe himself accurately to you on demand. It is important for members of the helping professions to have a clear understanding of the differences between a person's self-report and his self-concept.[3]

The self-concept is what a person perceives himself to be; it is what
he *believes* about himself. The self-report, on the other hand, is what a
person is willing or able to divulge, or what he can be tricked into *saying*
about himself when asked to do so. The self-report is a behavior; the
self-concept is a system of beliefs. Clearly, these matters are not the
same.

All behavior is affected in one way or another by the self-concept including what a person says about himself. This does not mean, however,
that the relationship exists as one to one or that the self-report can be
accepted without question as an accurate description of the self-concept.
What a person says about himself may or may not be what he truly feels.
Even with the very best of intentions, he may be unable to give an accurate description of himself because other perceptions interfere and
create a measure of distraction or distortion. Few of us, for example, are
ever very free from social expectancy. What we say about ourselves is

---

3. This is a matter currently in great confusion in the psychological literature.
Most of the studies presented in the literature as researches on the self-concept, when reviewed by the present authors through 1968, turn out, on closer
examination, to be in reality studies of the self-report. Purporting to be researches on the self-concept, they have utilized measures of the self-report
as though these concepts were identical. The undiscriminating use of these
terms is a great pity. Treating them as though they were synonymous has
immensely complicated the literature, and serious students need to be keenly
aware of this state of affairs in interpreting research findings.

affected by our awareness of what we are "supposed" to say. Little boys, for instance, must insist they hate school even though they would give their eyeteeth to go back the week after it is over. Adults are not completely free to express their true feelings about self because our society disapproves of immodesty. It is regarded as very bad taste to go around telling people how great you are! Some aspects of self may be unreportable simply because they are so threatening that they cannot be openly admitted even though they may be clearly apparent to others. Who has not seen such a person stoutly denying what all of his friends and acquaintances quite clearly know to be true? The healthiest of people do not always feel safe enough to reveal their deepest feelings to other people even under the warmest and friendliest of conditions with their sweethearts, wives, or psychotherapists. If these constraints on accurate reporting of self do not exist, there remain the further difficulties of lack of language to express feelings accurately and the willingness of the reporter to cooperate on demand. Requests for information which seem impertinent or "nosy" to the recipient are quite unlikely to produce accurate self-descriptions.

What people say of themselves may be accepted as interesting and informative data but not, without question, as an indication of the self-concept directly. This was clearly demonstrated in several researches carried out at the University of Florida. In one of these studies, sixth-grade children were asked to describe themselves. Without knowing what the children said of themselves, a group of trained observers were asked to rate the children with respect to the very same self-concept items. When the children's self-reports were compared with the self-concept inferences made by the trained observers, no significant correlation could be found between the two. In another experiment, teachers were asked to pick which of two descriptions best fitted each child in their classes. One of these descriptions was the child's self-report; the other was a self-concept description made by trained observers. The teachers overwhelmingly chose the trained observer's descriptions as most like the children they knew.

Because it exists inside the person, the self-concept is not open to direct examination by any means currently known to us. It can, however, be understood indirectly through a process of inference from some form of observed behavior, as was done in the experiments mentioned above. The rationale is as follows: If it is true that behavior is a product of the individual's perceptual field, then it should be possible, by a process of reading behavior backward, to infer from observed behavior the nature of the perceptions which produced it. This is, in fact, what all of us do with people who are important to us. We deduce what it is they are thinking and feeling from the ways we see them behave. The psychologist in his research and the helper in his professional role do exactly the same thing although perhaps with greater control and precision than the man in the street.

The question may legitimately be raised as to why inferences about the self-concept, made from observed behavior, are more acceptable indicators of the self-concept than a person's own self-report. First, the inferred self-concept is more accurate on theoretical grounds; it approaches the self-concept as an organization of *perceptions* which *produce* behavior rather than accepting the person's behavior as synonymous with self-perception. Second, it recognizes the existence of distorting factors in the self-report and attempts to eliminate as many of these as practicable. Among the distortions mentioned above, for example, making inferences about the self-concept can eliminate or reduce errors introduced by social expectancy, lack of cooperation of the subject, lack of adequate language, or the subject's feelings of threat. It may, of course, be true that the inference procedure introduces other errors in the perceptions of the observer, but that is a problem in every human observation which scientists must deal with no matter what the nature of the observations. It is incumbent on the scientist to approach his problem with maximum awareness of the factors involved and scrupulous attention to their effects.

A person's *real self,* of course, is measured precisely neither by the inferred self-concept nor the self-report. The question is, Which of these provides the closest approximation for the purposes we have in mind? Despite criticism of the self-report as a measure of self-concept, the self-report has value in its own right. What a person has to say about himself is valuable data. It is observable behavior. Like any other behavior, it is an expression of the subject's perceptual field at the moment of acting. Because of its symbolic character and the uses the behaver makes of it for self-expression, it has more than ordinary value for helping us understand another person. Employed as behavioral data, it may provide valuable clues to the nature of the self-concept which produced it when subjected to processes of inference. Often the self-report, despite its distortions, may be quite sufficient data for the citizen operating in daily life. The scientist, student of behavior, or practitioner in the helping professions, however, will generally need descriptions of self that are more carefully and more rigorously obtained.

SELF–CONCEPT AND THE HELPING PROFESSIONS

Any aspect of human personality which affects behavior so fundamentally as the self-concept must be of vital concern to workers in the helping professions. It is, in fact, their primary subject matter in whatever arena they practice their arts. Counselors, teachers, social workers, and priests are in the business of helping students, clients, and parishioners to explore and discover better, more effective relationships between themselves and the world they live in. Whether or not they are successful in the practice of their professions will depend upon the effects they have on the self-concepts of those who seek their help, for major principles of human personality structures cannot be set aside because they are inconvenient for helpers. If the self-concept has the central importance suggested by modern psychology, then those whose responsibilities require that they work with people can ignore it only at the risk of making themselves ineffective.

People do not leave their self-concepts at the door. They bring them right in with them everywhere they go. While signing the papers for his relief check the poverty-stricken head of a family is learning about himself. The child in school may be discovering more about himself in a given class hour than about the arithmetic lesson his teacher thinks she is presenting. What persons in the helping professions do or do not do, affects the helper's self-concept whether or not helpers are aware of their impact and regardless of what they might wish.

In a fascinating experiment in New South Wales, J. W. Staines found marked differences in the sensitivities of teachers to the self-concepts of children. This sensitivity was accompanied by greater evidence of growth in the children they worked with. What is more, Staines found that the self-concepts of children were affected whether the teacher was consciously attending to their self-concepts or not. In the conclusion of his experiment he says:

> The educational significance of the self is reaffirmed when it is realized that changes in the self picture are an inevitable part of both outcomes and conditions of learning in every classroom, whether or not the teacher is aware of them or aiming for them. They occur, as in A's class where the teacher deliberately included them in his teaching goals and adopted them in his methods accordingly, and they occur in B's class where the teacher aimed at orthodox goals and was ignorant of these correlative factors. Since both classes were reasonably typical and both

teachers recognized by their headmasters as competent teachers, it is reasonable to generalize and expect such factors to operate in all classrooms. (Staines, 1958)

Persons in the helping professions who ignore the importance of the role of self-concept in their patients, clients, students, or parishioners are in grave danger of defeating themselves. People's self-concepts will not go away because we wish it. To ignore the self-concept and its impact upon behavior seriously handicaps the helper's effectiveness. His position is as ridiculous as the man who says, "I know my car needs a carburetor, but I think I'll run mine without one!" Or the rocket launcher who says, "I recognize that gravity is a factor which affects our procedures, but let us launch this rocket without taking it into account!"

The self-concept is important to helpers for another reason. Students, clients, and patients judge the value of their experience with helpers from the frame of reference of the self-concept. What affects the self-concept seems relevant; what appears remote from the self seems irrelevant. If the time the student or client or patient spends with the counselor or teacher does not seem relevant to his self, it can safely be ignored. If the helper continually misses the subject's self, what he has to say or do only seems irrelevant to the helpee who sooner or later concludes that the relationship is a waste of time and, one way or another, physically or mentally departs the scene. People do not listen long to those who have no significant message. They also evaluate helpers in terms of this significance and report their findings to anyone else who may ask their opinion. Thus, the helper who ignores the self-concept and his effect upon it is quite likely to fail to help his client; he also creates a poor reputation for himself in the bargain.

CHANGING THE SELF-CONCEPT

Because the self-concept is learned, it can be taught. This fact provides the theoretical basis upon which the helping professions depend. The purpose of these occupations is to assist other people in exploring and discovering more effective relationships between themselves and the world. The subject brings his self to the relationship. Thereafter, whether anything of importance occurs will be dependent upon the kinds of experiences the helper is able to bring into being for his clients, students, and patients. Whether they are aware of it or not, helpers are engaged in a subtle process of teaching. Since new concepts of self are learned as a consequence of interactions with the helper, effective helpers must be significant people. They cannot be nonentities. One cannot interact with a shadow. The helping relationship is an active one, and a completely passive helper is unlikely to teach his client anything but his own futility. The personality of the helper must play a vital part in any helping relationship. It is the helper's use of his self which makes the interaction whatever it is to become. If a helper's self is to have such a significance, it must be involved in the dialogue.

Helping requires patience. A major task of persons in the helping professions is the facilitation of change in the self. A proper perspective of the dynamics and limitations of these changes can contribute much to the helper's own mental health and to the probabilities of his successful practice. For example, while peripheral and less crucial aspects of the self-concept like "I can't ride a bicycle" or "I am broke" can often be changed fairly quickly, important concepts of self like "I am a man" or "I am unwanted by everyone" are likely to change only very slowly, if at all. Generally speaking, the more basic and more fundamental or important the aspect of self we hope to change, the longer it is likely to take. Appreciation of this fact can forestall the setting of impractical goals and inevitable disappointment for the helper. On the one hand, it will make it possible for the helper to be far more patient and understanding. On the other hand, it can avoid almost certain frustration and despair over the outcomes of his efforts. The man in the street often assumes he can change others by doing or saying some simple thing and that will make all the difference; but helpers should know better.

Failure to appreciate the slowness of change in self may destroy the very things which helpers seek. This is especially true in the case of those most deeply hurt and in need of assistance. Persons who have been deeply deprived, for example, have a great void within which requires filling. Helping them is something like trying to help a person who has fallen deeply in debt. For a very long time all the money he makes must go just to keep himself solvent from day to day. All his efforts are spent in just trying to balance his budget. Until that is done, little can be used to get ahead. The matter is made more difficult by interest charges upon the old debts or additional withdrawals made from his account to meet new emergencies. It may take a long time to help such a person recover to the point where he can take some positive action on his own, and helpers may become discouraged and give up the effort. One may have to believe his efforts are worthwhile despite no tangible evidence for a considerable period of time. With deeply deprived persons, a single experience is rarely sufficient to make much difference.

Central aspects of self require time to change. Failure to recognize this fact fully may do more than simply make helping relationships ineffective. Because of the self-perpetuating character of the self-concept, the impatient helper may begin his task intending to help and end by making his client worse! Let us take one of the tough delinquents Fritz Redl tells us it takes fourteen years to produce.

Here he is—surly, angry against the world, feeling as a result of his long experience, "Nobody likes me. Nobody wants me. Nobody cares about me. Well, I don't care about nobody neither!" Now comes the well-meaning social worker who, with the best of intentions, says to him, "Eddie, I like you." Much to her dismay her friendly words may be met with a stream of profanity. The inexperienced social worker may be deeply hurt by this rejection and outraged by the violence of the child's reply. Why should the child behave in this way? He does so because, from his point of view, "you simply can't trust people who talk like that." All his past experience has taught him so. The social worker's words seem a mockery to the child. They appear like outright lies or, worse still, someone is making fun of him. Small wonder that he lashes out at his attacker and let's her have "what she deserves." Unless the social worker knows what she is about and possesses "the patience of Job," she may succumb to the "natural" thing and slap him across the mouth. This, of course, only serves to prove what the youngster felt in the first place—"You can't trust people who talk like that!" So, what started out as an attempt to help becomes shipwrecked by the helper's own lack of perspective about the self-concept, ends in disaster, and confirms the child's beliefs more deeply than ever before. Worse still, the experience may serve to increase his distrust of persons in the helping professions generally.

HELPING IS NEVER IN VAIN

A proper perspective on the nature of the self-concept and its capacities for change will do much more for the helper than keep him from errors of impatience. It can provide him with faith in his processes and protect him from unwarranted feelings of futility. Despite the high degree of permanence characteristic of its central aspects, the self-concept can be changed. Throughout life it is continually changing. This change, to be sure, is more rapid in the peripheral and less important aspects of self; but learning goes on continuously and even the central aspects of the self-concept may change as a consequence of experience over the years.

One example of this is the change in feeling about self which occurs from childhood to adolescence, to maturity and finally old age. Even very old people in retirement may sometimes make considerable changes in self-concept, for example, albeit not so easily as they did in their youth.

The more open an individual is to his experience the greater is the possibility for him to learn new self-definitions. This openness is likely to be greatest in childhood when there is less clearly differentiated organization in the individual's field and the self-concept is less set in exerting its selecting effect on new experience. This is one of the reasons why a heavy concentration of our efforts to improve the lot of the poor and the culturally disadvantaged must be directed at programs for the very young whose self-concepts are only beginning the process of definition and crystallization.

The importance of the helper in the life of his client is never entirely without meaning unless the helper makes it so. Life is not reversible; every experience a person has, he has had forever. One cannot unexperience what has happened to him! Every experience of significant interaction must have its impact upon those who were involved in it. For some this may have major importance; for others very little. Any meaningful experience or series of experiences may not be sufficient to produce the changes we hope for. But they are always important!

Persons in the helping professions may often be heard to complain that there is little they can do because they do not have control of the outside lives of their clients, students, or patients. They complain that their good offices are spoiled by the unhappy experiences visited upon their clients by bosses, parents, or society in general. As a matter of fact, even a holding operation may make a very important contribution. When everything in a child's life outside of school is teaching him that he is unliked, unwanted, and unable, a loving teacher, skilled in providing experiences of success, may make a world of difference. She may not be able to turn the tide of events completely. If she does no more than help such a child keep his head above water, however, the effect expended is surely not wasted. Teachers rarely get credit for this kind of help, but it probably occurs with far more frequency than any of us realize. Similarly, the social worker who helps a young delinquent stay only "as bad as he is" when everything else in his world is pushing him downhill can make a contribution of tremendous importance—even if he does not succeed in making him over in a more socially approved image.

Even when it is not possible to provide all that is required, helpers must not fall into the trap of thinking their efforts are futile lest they contribute further to the inadequacies of their clients and students. After all, because a child is rejected at home is no good reason to reject him in school as well! What happens to an individual outside the sphere of influence of the helper may operate in directions opposed to those sought by the helper. This does not mean that what the helper does is of no avail. At times it is even possible that what the helper does for his client may help his client change his world as well. Take the case of the child whose family is exerting hurtful influences directly contrary to what his teacher is trying to do for him at school. These conditions may seem so bad to his teacher that she exclaims, "What can you do with a child from a home like that?" It seems to her that all her hard won gains are negated by what happens to the child in his family setting. Such an attitude is most unfortunate. It overlooks the fact that a family is a dynamic unit in which each person interacts with all the others. What happens to any one member must have its effects upon everyone else. Let us take, for example, the hypothetical case of George Anderson who is driving his mother to distraction by his hostile behavior. Let us now suppose this child is fortunate enough in school to have a teacher who provides him some feeling of warmth, friendship, and experiences of success. When George goes home from school these days he feels better than he did when school was a more unhappy place. As a consequence he doesn't upset his mother, Mrs. Anderson, quite so much. In turn, Mr. Anderson, coming home tired from work, discovers his wife is easier to live with and his home is a more restful place. When Judith Anderson, George's little sister, claims her father's attention while he is trying to read the paper, instead of pushing her gruffly away, he makes room for her to climb in his lap and so Judith gains from her father a greater measure of the love and care she needs. Because of this, she feels better too. As a result, she feels less need to nag her brother George, as she usually does, and so we have come full circle! Every good thing a helper does for a client, student, or patient, he has done forever. It may not be enough, but it is never futile. There is always the possibility that someone else may contribute something elsewhere, and such cumulative experiences may in time be sufficient to provide the help which is needed.

The self-concept, we have said in this chapter, is the most important single factor affecting human behavior. In so little space we have had time only to outline the major principles involved in this vital concept. The self-concept and its functions lie at the very heart of the helping process. As a consequence a very great deal of the remainder of this book will, in one fashion or another, be devoted to the contribution it can provide for the thinking of persons engaged in the various helping professions. One can be of help to other people knowing nothing about this important aspect of human personality. A proper knowledge of the self-concept and of its dynamics in the production of human behavior and misbehavior, however, can add immeasurably to understanding people in need of help. It can do much more. It can provide the guidelines by which persons in the helping professions may direct their own behavior more effectively and efficiently, and so contribute with greater certainty to the health and growth of their clients.

SELECTED READINGS

Starred entries indicate appearance in whole or in part in Donald L. Avila, Arthur W. Combs, and William W. Purkey, *The Helping Relationship Sourcebook* (Boston. Allyn & Bacon, 1971).

Allport, G. W. Is the concept of self necessary? In Allport, G. W. (Ed.) *Becoming*, New Haven, Conn.: Yale University Press, 1955, 36–56.

Beard, R. M. *An outline of Piaget's developmental psychology for students and teachers*. New York: Basic Books, 1969.

Combs, A. W. & Snygg, D. *Individual behavior: A perceptual approach to behavior*. (2nd ed.) New York: Harper & Brothers, 1959.

Combs, A. W. & Soper, D. W. The self, its derivative terms and research. *Journal of Individual Psychology*. 1957, **12**, 134–145(b).

Coopersmith, S. *The antecedents of self esteem*. San Francisco: Freemen Press, 1967.

Gordon, C. & Gergen, K. J. *The self in social interaction. Vol. I: Classic and contemporary perspectives*. New York: Wiley, 1968.

Maehr, M. L., Menking, J. & Nafeger, S. Concept of self and the reaction of others. *Sociometry*, 1962, **25**, 353–357.

Parker, J. The relationship of self report to inferred self concept. *Educational and Psychological Measurement*, 1966, **26**, 691–700.

* Patterson, C. H. The self in recent Rogerian theory. *Journal of Individual Psychology*, 1961, **17**, 5–11.

* Purkey, W. W. *Self concept and school achievement*. Englewood Cliffs, N.J.: Prentice-Hall, 1970.

Purkey, W. W. *The search for self: Evaluating student self concepts*. Florida Educational Research and Development Council Bulletin, University of Florida, Gainesville, Fla., 1968.

Staines, J. W. The self picture as a factor in the classroom. *British Journal of Educational Psychology*, 1958, **28**, 87–111.

4

A Humanistic View
of Motive

Next to our beliefs about ourselves, perhaps no others are more important than those we hold about what people are like and why they behave as they do. These provide the bases for every human interaction. In fact, they do more. Involvement with other persons is such an important aspect in our lives that our beliefs about the nature of people and what they are seeking determines in very large measure our successes or failures in life. For persons in the helping professions, these beliefs are crucial. Throughout history, people have been intrigued by the problem of the nature of man and many hypotheses have been proposed. Each of these ideas has had its effects upon the generations which held them and many can still be observed in the thinking of people today.

OLDER CONCEPTS OF THE NATURE OF MAN

THE CONCEPT OF MAN AS BASICALLY EVIL

The Doctrine of Original Sin is a very old concept of the nature of man and is still widely held in some circles today. This doctrine maintained that children entered the world innately perverse. This purpose of life was to correct this evil and strive toward goodness. Similar to other ideas about the nature of man, this concept appears to have arisen from people's observations of themselves and of others. It could easily be seen that human beings were capable of both good and bad behavior. Since grownups used their own behavior as the criteria for judging others, the child who did not conform to the mature standards set by adults was considered "naughty" or "bad." And, since most children who behaved in approved ways managed to develop into satisfactory adults, it seemed evident that people grew better as they grew older.

At the time, parents, assuming that tendencies toward good and evil were innate, did not regard themselves responsible for the outcome of their offspring. They felt that since people were born with bestial tendencies, they had to be "saved," civilized, and made "good" through some form of external pressure. For many centuries this concept was also an important part of certain religious dogmas and so was given the additional authority of the Church. More recently it was even given the apparent endorsement of science. Darwin's concept of evolution, for example, seemed to give credence to the basic animal quality of man's striving. Freudian psychology also seemed to lend support to this view in its concept of the "id," defined as the basic primeval impulses in the organism representing its roots in the uncivilized animal world from which people sprang.

The concept of man as basically evil is very old. It has played an enormous role in our history. Even today the principles of this essentially pessimistic view of human beings are accepted by people in all walks of life, including some members of the helping professions.

Man at War with Himself

The concept of man at war with himself is even more common in current thinking. This view sees the individual as a kind of perpetual battleground on which both good and evil forces are constantly striving for supremacy. Such a concept seems to find support in the observations we can make of the behavior of people around us. People do indeed behave well, and they do indeed behave badly. Conflict, competition, and struggle seem to be going on everywhere. Reflecting on his own behavior, almost everyone can recall how he has struggled against temptation, felt grief or shame over a harmful action, or glowed righteously at fighting against an evil impulse. The man-in-conflict view seems to fit a great many of our experiences.

The concept of man divided has been held for many generations. It can be found deeply imbedded traditionally, extending back to earliest times—not only in our own culture but also in most others. It exists in the folklore, myths, fables, and traditions in primitive tribes and highly civilized cultures in every part of the world. In the Western world, of course, it has long been a classic concept of Judeo-Christian philosophy. It also derives support from much scientific literature. In theories of evolution, for example, it seems corroborated by such principles as the "struggle for existence" and "survival of the fittest." In psychology, the conflict philosophy has been given great impetus by Freud and psychoanalysts who often describe maladjustment as the outcome of a person's struggles between the primeval bestial impulses of the id and the higher, civilized functions of conscience in the "super ego."

SOME IMPLICATIONS OF OLDER CONCEPTS

Human nature as seen from these older points of view poses difficult problems for the helping professions. The original-sin and man-in-conflict views require working with an organism that can never quite be trusted. If the basic nature of man is evil, one is always confronted with the possibility of its reversion to bestiality the moment it is permitted to operate freely. Helpers proceeding from this frame of reference continuously struggle against great odds and their task is doomed to eventual defeat. Belief that the human organism cannot be trusted strictly limits the outcome of helping relationships and makes helper and helpee antagonistic, since each is intent on different fundamental aims.

If people are essentially evil, then the organism cannot really be trusted and our grip upon civilization is always a tenuous one. The organism must be regarded with suspicion, and the helper must always be on guard for signs of reversion to type, ready to head off such tendencies as they appear. The forces of darkness await only the relaxation of effort to come into control once more. With this view of man, the helping task calls for eternal vigilance and unremitting effort.

The methods required to deal with such perverse tendencies must, furthermore, be powerful ones. The task of saving people in spite of themselves calls for vigorous measures. Helpers operating from these bases are engaged in a work of utmost importance against insuperable odds. It is no wonder that persons growing up in such traditions often come to believe that there is something innately good about work and that discipline for its own sake is a wonderful thing. They operate on the philosophy, "if it's hard it's good for them." Confronted with an untrustworthy organism, helpers in this orientation are battling for the very salvation of the individual and the maintenance of civilization. This is a task that can brook no nonsense.

Such a philosophy calls for methods of helping people which rely upon various forms of control and direction—for example, rewarding the taking of right paths and punishing the taking of wrong ones. This results in a way of dealing with people which Combs and Snygg have called in another book, "the fencing in" approach, by which persons are guided more or less firmly toward chosen goals through the imposition or removal of barriers much like the rat in a maze or controlling traffic on a modern freeway complex. These controls may be physical (walls, traffic lights, or electric shocks) or verbal (prohibitions or threats). Motivation is regarded as a matter of manipulation of people from without, usually through some form of punishment or reward. Such punishments may range all the way from outright force and coercion to more subtle forms of disapproval and social rejection. Rewards may also vary from those which are material to human gifts of love and approval. All these methods are predicated upon a concept of motivation which calls for the manipulation, control, or direction of an organism regarded as essentially perverse.

ORIGINS OF MOTIVE

In more recent years, humanistically oriented psychologists have arrived at quite a different view of the basic nature of man. They agree with observers throughout history that man does, indeed, sometimes behave well and sometimes badly. They point out, however, that because man *behaves* so, it cannot be assumed that he *is* so. Because people behave in evil ways does not necessarily mean their basic nature is evil, only that its expression is evil in a particular instance. Who has not hurt or embarrased a friend at some time or another while intending to be especially nice to him?

Some of our former concepts of the nature of man arise from our assumption that, internally, man is what he seems to be externally. In trying to understand behavior internally, perceptual psychologists have come to a different conception of the basic nature of man. This, in contrast to the formerly accepted idea of man's basic nature, provides quite a different concept of motivation and therefore sets up a different program of guidelines for persons working in the helping professions.

In biology we learn that a basic characteristic of protoplasm is its "irritability," that is, capacity to respond. Awareness is thus a quality of life itself. The ability of organisms to react to events around them exists in all forms of life from the simplest to the most complex. This capacity to respond, furthermore, is not haphazard. It is response with direction. Haphazard or fortuitous response would quickly result in eliminating the organism from existence in the course of evolution. The response of an organism is not accidental; it is goal-directed toward fulfillment. Even the lowly amoeba moves toward food and away from danger, at least as far as it is capable of doing so. So, also, do all the rest of living things. Mushrooms turn away from light whereas sunflowers grow toward it. Wounded flesh heals. Animals mate and care for their young. Each life in its own peculiar way continuously seeks fulfillment as best it can. This search for fulfillment is characteristic of life itself. Its expression produces behavior that is forever dynamic and striving.

Man is not inert, not a thing, not simply an object willy-nilly at the mercy of his environment. He is a system that is aware and continuously in search of fulfillment. This is his birthright, his inheritance as a living creature. The dynamic, striving character of persons has its origins in the nature of life itself. Like all other forms of life, people begin their existence with a built-in motivation and thereafter make of it what they can within the limits of their capacities. In this process, it is even possible for man to create segments of his own environment.

The experiences of man's basic striving as they appear translated into behavior may seem good or evil to the outside observer. However, the search for adequacy is, of itself, neither good nor bad. That is a value judgment—not a matter innate in the fundamental nature of the organism. It is a social judgment about behavior made by persons observing it from the frame of reference of a particular culture. We cannot say that the organism itself is basically either good or evil. However, inasmuch as the stiving for fulfillment certainly seems to be a constructive force in human existence, there seems to be some justification for considering our basic drive more positive than negative.

THE GROWTH PRINCIPLE

The basic striving of organisms for fulfillment has been called the "growth principle" because the effect is to move them continuously toward health and growth so long as possible. This is true whether we are talking of the single cell like a paramecium or of the great organization of cells which makes up a complicated mammal like a human being. Growth is characteristic of the very essence of life and finds expression in all of its ramifications.

The growth principle is so important to the physiological well-being of people that the practice of medicine has been predicated upon it. The physician knows that it is not he who cures his patients; rather it is the patient who cures himself. When the body is invaded by germs, many forces swing into action to defend the organism by destroying or immobilizing the offending invaders. The doctor's task is to minister to this process. He assists the body in its normal strving toward a healthy condition. To this end, he may try to impede or destroy invading germs with medication, or he may resort to surgery to remove or repair a disabled organ. By prescribing rest, nourishing food, or proper innoculations, he may further assist the body's attempts to return to a state of health by building up its resources. Whatever the doctor does, however, is dependent upon the organism's own fundamental drive toward wholeness; the treatment methods he uses are designed to facilitate the growth process.

The growth principle does not operate in physiological terms alone. It is equally operant in behavioral matters. Not only do the cells or body seek fulfillment, but physiologically and psychologically the entire organism strives toward growth. People do not just seek to be physically adequate; more important, they strive for personal fulfillment. For the sake of psychological satisfactions, they will even gravely risk their physical beings. To have a feeling of importance or worthwhileness, they may even court death. Examples in everyday life may be seen in the professional football player, racing driver, test pilot, or astronaut to name but a few. Throughout history, heroes have gone to certain death for their fellows. In doing so the hero sacrifices his physical self to enhance another self more important to him: his self-concept.

NEED FOR SELF-ACTUALIZATION

We have seen in the previous chapter how the self-concept transcends the physical body. The fulfillment of self which human beings seek in the expression of the growth principle is actualization of the concept of self, not simply its container. As a consequence, people may strive very hard for self-enhancement, not only in the present but for the future as well. Many people spend large portions of their lives and fortunes seeking to perpetuate a favorable image of self in the minds of others, even after death. As another way of keeping the self as adequate and effective as possible, suicide is a form of self-enhancement. To achieve this end a man may kill himself today rather than suffer the humiliation he knows is coming tomorrow. For the Japanese nobleman, committing hari-kari guaranteed prestigious immortality.

The growth principle at work has also been called by biologists "homeostasis," the wisdom of the body and the drive to health. Among psychologists it has been described by Maslow as a need for self-actualization, by Allport as a process of becoming, by Lecky as self-consistency, by Festinger as dissonance reduction, by Frankl as a search for meaning, and by Rogers as a search for self-fulfillment. In their earliest work, Combs and Snygg described it as a need for the maintenance and enhancement of the self; in a later work it was described as a need for personal adequacy. By whatever name it is called, the principle refers to the striving of all human beings engaged in a never-ending search for personal adequacy or fulfillment.

Psychologists frequently classify the more common expressions of the growth principle in action as "need," and have sometimes attempted to arrange these in a hierarchy of value or motivating force. Maslow, for example, describes a hierarchy of needs beginning from the basic physiologic ones necessary for the preservation of the organism (needs for food, water, or shelter) through more social ones (needs to be loved, cherished, and appreciated) to high-level needs like the need for self-actualization. He also suggests that such hierarchies of need represent a kind of demand system in which the more basic ones must find some form of fulfillment before higher order ones can be achieved. This observation seems amply demonstrated at the lower end of need hierarchies. A man dying of thirst is in no condition to think nice thoughts, and people with empty bellies respond very badly to demands that they consider the fine points of democratic government.

The sequential demand character of such lists of needs does not hold so clearly in the upper levels of these hierarchies. The search of the organism for self-fulfillment may find expression in many different patterns for any individual at a given moment. A pattern may also be quite different from that of another person even under what seem similar circumstances to the outside observer. While the idea of a hierarchy of needs has merit as a way of thinking about the value of needs, the practitioner should not regard it as universal. The fundamental striving of the organism is for self-fulfillment. The specific needs man displays are the goals through which his search is expressed. These may shift and change as time and circumstances determine, but the reach for fulfillment of self goes on unceasingly.

IS HUMAN NATURE SELFISH?

No doubt it will appear distressing to some readers that the basic nature of human beings as we have described it here is a striving for self-fulfillment. Some may find it repugnant to think that human beings are perpetually intent upon self-actualization. They may ask, "Is human nature really so fundamentally selfish?" The answer is yes and no. There is no doubt that the basic drive for self-fulfillment is certainly a concern for self. We have also seen in the previous chapter how the self-concept is the individual's basic frame of reference. And in this sense, human beings would indeed appear to be selfish. The picture, however, is not nearly so bleak as it seems.

We have seen in the previous chapter that the self-concept is capable of considerable expansion. If a child is born with a basic drive for self-fulfillment and has good experience with the people about him, then little by little he comes to expand his self to include those people about him who are important to him. He comes to feel "one with" his parents first, then with his siblings, playmates, and friends. As he grows older, the circle of those he includes within himself may expand to include wider and wider groups of people. In time, he may come to feel identified with "my country" and "my school." In the case of saints, the feeling of identification may eventually extend to all mankind. In that state, the problem of selfishness has completely disappeared, for when the self is identified with all mankind then what one does for self one does for everyone, and what one does for everyone one does for self! The question of selfishness is a problem of exclusion or alienation. It is a matter of the *size* of the self. A restricted self is a selfish one; an expanded self is a saintly one. The basic nature of man is selfish only in the extent to which the self has failed to grow by identification with others. In a later chapter we will discover that persons who have most successfully achieved self-fulfillment are also generous, warm, public-spirited, concerned, and highly unselfish.

DETERMINING EFFECT OF NEED ON BEHAVIOR

How people behave at every moment of their lives is determined by the basic need of the organism for self-fulfillment. No one is ever free of the operation of the growth principle. It is a function of life itself and has its effect upon every act. It also determines what we are able to see, to hear, and even to think and believe. Men participating in food deprivation experiments, for instance, report that it is extremely difficult to think of anything but food as hunger and the need for food increases. Under these circumstances they report fantasies of food in almost everything they do. Off-hours are spent drawing up menus for Thanksgiving dinners, and the slightest stimulus in their environment is likely to start such thinking although it may have no relation to food whatever. Similar effects of need upon perception have been demonstrated in research investigations in a wide variety of areas of human activity. Quite aside from research demonstrations, all of us have had experiences in our own lives indicating how perceptions are affected by felt need. When a man feels in need of a new suit, he is much more aware of advertisements dealing with men's clothing. In the course of our insatiable attempts to satisfy need, certain goals and values become differentiated as leading to satisfaction. Others, which seem to us to lead to the frustration of need, become differentiated as negative goals, to be avoided at all costs.

Because of the selective effect of need upon perception, the behavior of people becomes quite predictable if we know the peculiar nature that the striving for growth and fulfillment takes in them. From his own point of view the individual is eternally striving to fulfill himself as best he can in the conditions he confronts. How he does this may not always seem intelligent, desirable, or appropriate to those who judge him, but his primary nature is essentially positive and predictable when seen from his own frame of reference. The juvenile delinquent who finds it impossible to gain status and prestige in a broken home, in school, or in a church which rejects him may discover that he can find at least partial fulfillment in a gang. There is, after all, prestige and status to be gained from stealing cars, flaunting the police, or getting involved in a "rumble." What seems to contribute to the delinquent's self-actualization is not what society thinks desirable, but what the delinquent who is doing the behaving or misbehaving thinks will lead to that end. Seen from his point of view, his behavior makes sense. It is even predictable.

An understanding of need can often cause the most puzzling and apparently confusing behavior to make sense. For example, some coeds on a certain college campus expressed extreme reluctance to using oral contraceptives despite their expectations to become involved in sexual relationships. On questioning by the physician, their reasoning went like this: If they took the pills they would obviously be planning on sexual activity, and this was considered improper outside of marriage and unacceptable to their concepts of self as "good" girls. If they did have sexual relations and weren't taking the pills, it would then be because they were "swept off their feet in a moment of passion." This was regarded as enhancing, even excusable, since it could happen to anyone!

MAN: A TRUSTWORTHY, PREDICTABLE ORGANISM

The need for fulfillment characteristic of all living things is but a single need with a single direction. This makes the behavior of human beings predictable and the organism trustworthy, providing we know the peculiar expression of need in a given person.[1] This is quite a different conception of the nature of man than that which sees people at war with themselves. From the person's own point of view, he always does what seems to him will lead to fulfillment at the instant of his behavior. Far from being at war with himself, he is an organized totality with direction and purpose. "But," one may argue, "that does not seem to fit my personal experience. I remember when I had to make this or that difficult choice and it wasn't easy at all. Is this not an indication that I was at war with myself?" Not at all.

Whenever we look at our own behavior, it is necessary to remember we are looking at it "after the fact." That is, we observe it like any other outsider. From this outside position there may appear to be simultaneously existing desires. This seems so only because the matter is being observed externally. At the moment of behaving, however, the individual does what seems to him *at that instant* most likely to lead to fulfillment and actualization. To be sure, he may have perceived it quite differently before or after the act. The illusion of conflict occurs because he is look-

---

1. This does not mean that every person is trustworthy in a moral sense. The authors, too, have been robbed, lied to, and deceived in their lifetimes. The point here is that there is nothing *innately* untrustworthy about people. The human organism can be counted on to behave in predictable fashion. If it appears untrustworthy, this judgment lies in the "eye of the beholder" who may not have enough data to make accurate predictions possible. Had the authors known enough about their deceivers, they could have predicted the times they were robbed and lied to.

ing at two different events separated in time. The reader may test this against his own experience if he desires. Take some instance where you may recently have "misbehaved." Now, looking back on this act from your present position, it may seem as though the act was stupid, undesirable, or perhaps, even morally wrong. Even before the act occurred, it may have seemed, as you contemplated its possibilities, unsatisfying or immoral. At the moment it happened, however, it seemed like a good thing to do. It appeared desirable and need-fulfilling, perhaps even necessary, to accomplish the purpose you had at that instant. While there may be occasional confusion about ways of achieving fulfillment, there is no conflict of motives. Fulfillment is the motive no matter how it is accomplished.

Individuals' basic drive for fulfillment is also characteristic of the societies they create to achieve their purposes. All kinds of groups—schools, clubs, communities, nations—are engaged in seeking fulfillment for their members. They are formed for this purpose. They thrive so long as they achieve it and are destroyed or disintegrate when they can no longer provide it.

MALADJUSTMENT—A PROBLEM OF DEPRIVATION

The striving of human beings for self-actualization goes on as long as it is possible to do so. The need is insatiable. As soon as a person has achieved one goal there is always another just beyond so that no one is ever completely fulfilled and the drive for self-actualization continues as long as he lives. For some people, unhappily, the force of this drive may be more or less permanently blunted or its direction diverted to unfortunate channels because of deprivation, fear, or despair.

The achievement of a satisfactory degree of fulfillment constitutes psychological health. Persons who are successful in attaining a measure of self-actualization are likely to be happy and contented with themselves and effective in their relationships with the world. People who are unsuccessful or frustrated in their attempts to achieve fulfillment become sick and maladjusted. Just as the body's failure to achieve proper growth and fulfillment results in physiologic disease, so, too, failure of the individual to achieve satisfactory fulfillment of self means ill health psychologically. Disease is the product of blocks to the physical organism's normal tendency toward growth and health. In similar fashion, maladjustment is a consequence of blocks to self-fulfillment. Psychological ill health is a matter of falling short, a lack of success in the striving for self-realization. The maladjusted are the frustrated ones, and the seriousness of their condition is almost directly a function of the degree of deprivation they have suffered. Most of us can put up with mild degrees of failure to achieve fulfillment. When failures become chronic or strike people in important aspects of self-structure, they soon become unhappy. If deprivations are serious or persist for long periods, persons may then become increasingly neurotic. Depending upon the degree of frustration, they also become discouraged, dispirited, angry, or hostile. Almost certainly, they frustrate other people as well. If deprivation is too great or too long continued, people at last feel defeated and without hope. When this happens they become burdens or dangerous to the rest of us, for these are the people who fill our mental hospitals and our penitentiaries. Finally, severe deprivation leads to depravity.

People are not "naturally" sick. We now understand that sickness and maladjustment are products of human deprivation, failure, and frustration. In earlier times we regarded criminality as willful immorality. Treatments devised for this condition were also appropriate to that belief. They were often unbelievably harsh and brutal. Today we have a more enlightened view and regard such persons as psychologically sick rather than inherently evil. Little by little we are also learning to extend this understanding to the problems of the less dramatically ill, to the poor, and to the victims of prejudice for whatever reason. At one time we could regard the problems of the sick and the deprived as inevitable expressions of the Will of God. We no longer regard them as inevitable, and if they continue to exist they do so not as the Will of God but the lack of will of man.

If the view of human nature which we have been discussing here is accurate, vastly different attitudes toward human frailty and error are called for. So many of us are quick to blame our fellow men for their derelictions and misbehaviors. We get angry at parents for what they do to children. We scorn our patients for the stupidities which made them ill, and blame teachers for their inabilities to cope with the children they sent to the counselor. We overlook the fact that, from his point of view, the behaver always does what seems to him to be reasonable, even necessary, under the circumstances. We forget that others have problems too, and that the ways in which they behave are outgrowths of those conditions. If, however, the basic character of man is striving for fulfillment, if every human being is forever engaged in a search for self-actualization in everything he does, if each human being is ceaselessly searching to become the best he can, who then, can we blame for what?

FREEDOM AND RIGHTS OF OTHERS

Up to this point we have spoken of the need of the individual to achieve his own fulfillment. But what of fulfilling the needs of the rest of society? The answer to that question is as follows: If a person is truly free to seek the fulfillment of his need, and if he is achieving a reasonably satisfactory degree of such fulfillment, he will behave in ways that also satisfy the needs of the rest of society. Why should this be so?

First, it is necessary to remind ourselves that all of us live deeply imbedded in a social structure. We have created a world that is so cooperative and interdependent that few of us could last but a few hours without the aid and assistance of other people. We are dependent on literally millions of people whom we have never even seen for the satisfaction of even our simplest needs. This means that successful fulfillment of any individual can only be achieved through some form of successful interaction with others. The self-concept itself is learned from the behavior of others toward us, and most of our satisfactions come out of human relationships in one form or another. Dialogue between the individual and his society is thus necessary and sensitive. Human maladjustment is a product of the breakdown of this vital condition.

We have already seen that selfishness disappears as people discover fulfillment. As the self expands, increasing numbers of other people are brought into its organization and treated as extensions of self. In the degree to which fulfillment occurs then, behavior of the individual becomes increasingly responsible. In fact, the dynamics we are describing are an essential pre-condition for truly responsible behavior. Irresponsible behavior is a consequence of the breakdown of dialogue, a feeling of alienation or lack of commitment to others. Since the self is learned from the feedback of others, its enhancement is dependent upon successful interaction. *Providing they are free to do so,* it follows that people can, will, *must* move in directions that are good, not only for themselves but for others as well. Persons confronted with this idea for the first time will no doubt find that it strains their credulity. It may even seem to be hopelessly naive. However, if the basic motive of the organism is a drive toward health, and if it is free to move, it must progress in healthy directions. The essential condition in the statement lies in the phrase, "if it is free to move." The drive toward fulfillment is innate. The conditions for freedom are not; they exist in the perceptions of the individual and in the world he must cope with. A stupid man is not free. Neither is one who is deeply deprived, unable to feel for others, or bereft of the tools required to deal with his problems. We shall examine the conditions for freedom at much greater length in Chapters 7 and 8. If creation of those conditions is in fact feasible, the concept that "when men are free they can find their own best ways" becomes a clearly defensible principle. What is more, if men are interacting openly and meaningfully with other people, the ways they find for achieving self-fulfillment will contribute to the fulfillment of all.

The growth principle can be counted upon to provide the motive power. The problem for helpers is to create the conditions for freedom to let the principle operate. Just as the physical organism will recover when we are skillful in creating the conditions that make recovery possible, so, too, will people behave more adequately when we have been successful in creating the kinds of conditions that help set free their striving for fulfillment. Just as the physician attempts to free the physical organism to move toward recovery and growth, the task of counselors, teachers, parents, psychologists, social workers, and all others engaged in the helping professions is to minister to human beings in such fashion that this basic drive may be set free to move the individual most effectively and efficiently toward his optimal growth in behavioral terms. If we are successful in creating these conditions, the individuals' own basic drive for actualization and fulfillment can be counted upon to move him in those directions.

SOME IMPLICATIONS FOR THE HELPING PROFESSIONS

PEOPLE ARE ON OUR SIDE

If it is true that human beings are implacably driven toward health and adequacy, it follows for the helping professions that we always have a powerful ally on our side—the person himself. The discovery that the human organism is trustworthy is good news for those in the helping professions. It means that the people who helpers seek to assist are not enemies perversely, stubbornly, or maliciously resisting the efforts of professional workers. Rather, they are deeply and fundamentally motivated by the need to be the very best they can as they see it. So, persons engaged in the helping professions are not dealing with unpredictable, fortuitous matters, but they can formulate ways of behaving with respect to their clients, students, and patients with real hope that these may result in certain and predictable outcomes. Helper and helpee are on the same side of the fence. They seek the same thing—fulfillment of the client. This makes the relationship a kind of partnership. Such a partnership, to be sure, might on occasion be uneasy or filled with pitfalls and difficulties. A partnership, however, no matter how uneasy, is far more likely to produce positive results than an open battle between enemies.

PEOPLE ARE ALWAYS MOTIVATED

Most people regard the problem of motivation as a matter of management or manipulation in order to get them to do the things they would like them to. Motivation is regarded primarily as a system of rewards or punishments designed to get other people to do "what is good for them," or to keep them from behaving in some fashion considered harmful or against the best interests of the motivator. In light of the growth principle we have been discussing in this volume quite a different view of motivation is called for.

People are *always* motivated if they are forever engaged in seeking self-fulfillment. Indeed, they are never unmotivated unless they are dead. To be sure, they may not be motivated to do what some outsider believes they ought or should. The little boy in school who pokes the pretty little girl in front of him during the arithmetic lesson is not very motivated at that moment to do arithmetic, but he is surely not unmotivated! In the light of our discussion of the growth principle, motivation is not a problem of external manipulations; it has to do with what goes on inside people. It is always there, "given" by the very nature of the life force itself.

Frymier and Thompson, in discussing the matter as it applies in education, have expressed it this way:

> This picture of motivation suggests that motivation to learn in school is something which students *have* or *are* rather than that which teachers *do* to help them learn. Studies now under way suggest that motivation to learn in school is a fairly *constant* factor. It is subject to change, but generally only slowly. Teachers *can* affect students' motivational levels, but over extended periods of time like a year; probably very little in a single day.
>
> Motivation to learn in school is a function of one's personality structure, his goals and values, his conception of self and others, and his attitude toward change. These aspects of human behavior are learned and they are subject to modification. Nevertheless, teachers concerned

about their youngster's motivations have to do much more than use a carrot on a stick or a paddle on the behind if they hope for significant changes in any way. (Frymier, J. R. and Thompson, J. H., 1965)

The task of persons in the helping professions then, is not a matter of motivating those they seek to help, but rather a question of helping them explore and discover new goals, new values, and new ways of seeing themselves and the world. This is a matter of giving motive new and more satisfying expression through broadening and changing perceptions.

Understanding human motives in the terms we have described here will also have salutary effects upon the helper's relationships with his clients, patients, or students. Rapport is likely to be much better. Helpers who can truly understand and identify with their clients will most likely be more compassionate, concerned, and sympathetic—thus, far more inclined to foster good communication. On the other hand, operating on the assumption that human nature is fundamentally perverse is apt to make the helper suspicious in his relations with helpees and might cause him to behave in terms of reward and punishment. When behavior is not understood in relation to the individual's fundamental need for fulfillment, it is likely to be puzzling, stupid and depraved to the outside observer. Such an attitude in the helper will not endear him to those he seeks to help.

The irate father who viciously beats his child may be a figure of loathing and contempt until we understand that his attacks on Jimmy are motivated by a desire to "make him a good boy!" His problem lies not in his motives, but in his ways of solving the problem! One can like a father who wants his son to be a good boy, but that father who seems viciously intent on destroying his son is in danger of being hated. The kind of relationship established with such a father will be dependent on the helper's beliefs about the father's motives. It is a hard task to build an effective relationship with people who seem antagonistic and condemnatory. People in the helping professions who find it necessary to begin by blaming those they wish to help may turn out to be their own worst enemies. They run the risk of having their own unhappy attitudes get in the way of accomplishing the very purposes they seek to fulfill.

In the view of motivation taken in this volume, the goal of the helping professions becomes a positive one of ministering to a trustworthy striving organism rather than of controlling a perverse, unpredictable one. It calls for methods of helping designed to encourage and facilitate growth, and provides assurance that if helpers are succesful in creating the conditions for freedom, then persons will move toward whatever degree of fulfillment is possible for them. The reader may recognize that this understanding of the nature of man is basic to the concept of democracy. The foundation of democracy is a belief in people—the concept that when people are free they can find their own best ways. This means that what helpers do in helping individuals to achieve freedom will, in the long run, also prove to be good for society as well. It is a comforting thought that the basic tenets of democracy are not just "nice ideas." They have roots in the fundamental character of life itself. Helpers need not be split personalities. The beliefs they hold for working with their students, clients, and patients can be consistent with those applied to guiding their own behavior and that of the societies in which they operate.

A PROCESS ORIENTATION FOR THE HELPING PROFESSIONS

If the fundamental drive of the individual is for self-fulfillment, it is not necessary for helpers to know precisely and in advance the specific goals to be achieved by those they seek to help. If it is true that "man will become the best that he can be, when we have found the ways to set him free," the helping professions need to direct their attention to the *processes* of helping rather than to the ends of the process. Helpers can thus rest secure that, if they are successful in creating the conditions for growth, the results will be as positive as current conditions will permit. This removes a tremendous weight from the shoulders of the helper. It means he does not have to be God nor must he know in advance exactly how his clients or students will emerge from the experience. Consequently, he can devote his full attention to the creation of the conditions for freedom, and rest assured that the end results will be positive if he is successful in doing so.

Unless helpers *believe* people are trustworthy, they do not dare trust them! Unless the helper is satisfied in his own mind as to the positive nature of man's striving, he cannot afford to risk permitting his helpees to make decisions. Indeed, if teachers, social workers, and clergymen do not believe their clientele can make good decisions, it would be downright unethical to permit them to take such risks. It takes a very certain belief about the basic nature of man to be able to sit by and watch a helpee make a decision different from one's own. Yet, this is the kind of assurance demanded for the truly effective helping relationship. To follow this line of reasoning to its proper conclusion, helpers must adopt a position which says, "if I truly created the conditions for freedom for my client, student, patient, worker, or parishioner, and he has arrived at a solution different from my own, then I must be prepared to examine my own position with care. It could be that I am wrong!"

The process orientation to the helping professions we have been discussing here is, in fact, the position taken by most of the modern approaches to the problems of helping others in a wide variety of areas. It finds its expression in open-ended approaches to social work wherein the social worker avoids permitting his client to become dependent upon him and devotes his energies toward helping his client find his own solutions to his problems. A similar approach is advocated for the clergy by experts in pastoral care. In education it is represented by student-centered concepts of teaching designed to encourage and facilitate the student's own search for meaning. In counseling it is represented by existential and client-centered approaches to treatment in which clients are aided to discover their own answers to problems in a relationship with a counselor especially trained to facilitate this kind of exploration. In supervision and administration, it finds expression in emergent concepts of leadership which stress the assisting and facilitating aspects of administration rather than control and direction. Each of these modern developments in the helping professions is predicated upon the assumption that the human organism is predictable and, provided it has the proper conditions for freedom, can be counted on to move toward desirable ends.

ROLE OF THE HELPER

The role of the helper deriving from the view of man we have described in this chapter is essentially one of ministering to people. It does not seek to direct or control its subjects but to serve the organism and to create the conditions most likely to set it free. It is a matter of manipulation of processes rather than of people. It is a question of aiding, helping, facilitating, encouraging, and assisting rather than forcing, coercing, cajoling, bribing, or exhorting persons to better things. It is a matter of working *with* the organism rather than against it, of seeing helper and helpee as teammates rather than antagonists.

If the concepts of human need we have been discussing in this chapter are true, it also follows that the goal of the helping professions must be need gratification rather than need frustration. It must be more. It must also contribute to fulfillment and actualization, to increased feelings of personal adequacy on the part of clients, students, and patients. The helping professions are serving professions concerned with giving and teaching rather than withholding and disciplining. Helpers in this sense must eschew conditions which humiliate and degrade the self, and actively seek methods of helping others sustain and enhance positive views of self. This may be accomplished by working with the environment of the helpee or through the peculiar relationships established between helper and client.

Working through the environment, the efforts of helpers may be directed toward changing the helpee's world so that it provides him greater freedom to explore and discover his maximum fulfillment. The social worker may do this by helping an unemployed man to find a job. The teacher may accomplish the same purpose by placing a child in a congenial group. The psychologist may accomplish a similar purpose by placing a child in a foster home. In each of the helping professions there are literally thousands of ways in which the world may be influenced to provide more positive freeing experiences for people. A major task of the professional worker is to use these resources effectively to serve his client's needs and to make possible the achievement of maximum fulfillment.

A second way in which persons in the helping professions may contribute to the freedom of those they work with is through the relationship with the helper himself. In the first chapter of this book we have seen that the essence of professional work is the effective utilization of the self as an instrument for serving others. It is through the use of this self that helpers establish relationships with others designed to provide the freedom in which they may explore and discover more effective relationships between themselves and the world in which they live. This is the same goal we have just been discussing for the helper's manipulation of the world for his client in the preceding paragraph. In this case, however, the helper is using himself. In many ways this is a far more difficult process than the manipulation of the external world; yet some of the helping professions, especially those with responsibilities for the ill and unhappy, are almost exclusively dependent upon the effective development of such relationships.

SELECTED READINGS

Starred entry indicates appearance in Donald L. Avila, Arthur W. Combs, and William W. Purkey, *The Helping Relationship Sourcebook* (Boston: Allyn & Bacon, 1971).

Aspy, D. N. Maslow and teachers in training. *Journal of Teacher Education*, 1969, **20**, 303–309.

Cantril, H. The human design. *Journal of Individual Psychology*, 1964, **20**, 129–136.

Combs, A. W. & Snygg, D. *Individual behavior: A perceptual approach to behavior.* (2nd ed.) New York: Harper & Brothers, 1959.

Festinger, L. Cognitive dissonance. *Scientific American*, 1962, **207**, 93–107.

Frymier, J. R. & Thompson, J. H. Motivation: The learner's mainspring. *Educational Leadership*, 1965, **22**, 567–570.

Maslow, A. H. *Motivation and personality.* New York: Harper & Brothers, 1954.

Maslow, A. H. *Toward a psychology of being.* Princeton, N.J.: Van Nostrand, 1962.

Rogers, C. R. A note on "the nature of man." *Journal of Consulting Psychology*, 1957, **4**, 199–203(b).

Rogers, C. R. *On becoming a person.* Boston: Houghton Mifflin, 1961.

* Snygg, D. The psychological basis of human values. In D. Ward, (Ed.) *Goals of economic life.* New York: Harper & Brothers, 1953, pp. 335–364.

5

The Crucial Character
of Meaning

In order to produce a change in a person's behavior it will be necessary, in one way or another, to effect some change in his perceptual field—his personal field of meanings. To do this successfully helpers need an understanding of the nature of personal meanings and the ways in which they change.

FACTS, MEANINGS, AND REALITY

By the term "meaning," perceptual psychologists refer not simply to what is seen or heard but rather to what is comprehended by the behaving person. The person's private world cannot be directly invaded or manipulated. No matter how strongly it may be bombarded from without, the feelings, attitudes, ideas, and convictions of which it is composed remain forever the sovereign possession of the person himself.

For the person who holds them, meanings are the facts of life. A fact is *not what is;* a fact for any person is what he *believes is so.* If Joe Green believes his boss is unfair, he behaves as though he were. Whether Joe's boss is *really* unfair in the eyes of other people has little or nothing to do with the matter. As Joe thinks, he behaves. He can only behave in terms of what seems to him to be the fact of the matter. So far as Joe's behavior is concerned, the "real" facts as they appear to an outsider are irrelevant and immaterial. Indeed, if we try to convince Joe that he is wrong, we run the risk of having him believe we don't understand him either!

Even the facts we accept and act upon from the outside world are no more than accepted meanings held by people we respect. The facts we listen to and act upon during a national political campaign, for example, are likely to be those propounded by the party we belong to or admire. "Facts" presented by the opposition are discounted, perhaps even derided. Even the simplest and most obvious facts about the world around us are only true for members of a common culture. So long as one stays in the same culture, a given fact may never be seriously questioned. But, let him but step outside his own culture and he will soon discover that many facts he considers to be reality have no validity whatever in the new setting. Even something so commonplace as a "table" may be called a different name in another culture. In fact, it may not even be regarded as a table at all. Instead it may be seen as a platform for dancing, a seat for the village chief, a bed to lie on, a roof for shelter from the rains, or a useless object to be used for firewood!

The idea that there may be many realities is very disturbing to some people. It is distressing to think that things may not be what they seem. The question of whether there is any "real" reality, however, has baffled philosophers for at least two thousand years and still remains an unanswered question. Fortunately, to understand behavior we do not have to get involved in the question of whether a reality is *really* there. It is enough to know that people behave in terms of their field of meanings. This *is* reality for them and determines the nature of their behavior. With that understanding, we can build a psychology and establish effective techniques for helping people to grow or to solve problems in satisfying ways.

The personal quality of meanings and the importance they have in the private worlds of individuals is of tremendous significance to workers in the helping professions. People's assumption that reality is that which they experience is the greatest single cause of human misunderstanding and conflict. The moment we understand behavior in terms of personal meaning, a great deal that was formerly puzzling or inexplicable becomes meaningful and reasonable.

Recently a student in one of our psychology classes questioned the following situation. "I just got a paper from home. I read where a man was arrested for shoplifting. He had a whole sack of things he had taken. When they searched him, he had a hundred pounds on him! How do you account for his stealing under these circumstances?" The student was obviously puzzled. To her something seemed strange about this situation. The instructor, too, was puzzled, for he could not grasp in the problem anything needing explanation. Here was a statement of fact. There is nothing puzzling about a man being caught shoplifting with a hundred pounds of loot. Why should this student be so frustrated and disturbed? Then, suddenly, he remembered that the student was from Jamaica, a British colony. "Pounds" in the eyes of the student did not refer to weight, but to money! At once, the problem was clear. Why should a man shoplift when he has more than two hundred dollars in his pocket? As seen through the eyes of the student, the problem was understandable. The puzzle was clear when the instructor was able to perceive the problem through the eyes of his student.

Because of the individual character of meaning, people fail to understand one another and pass each other like ships in the night. This is particularly true of persons raised in different cultures, but it is also true of persons with different experiences who are raised in the same culture. Witness the difficulties in communication for men and women; adults and teenagers; or persons of differing occupations, religion, and locality. Without an understanding of the unique meanings existing for the individual, the problems of helping him effectively are almost insurmountable.

MEANINGS ARE DISCOVERED

It should be understood that the meaning of any event does not reside in the event itself. A common error among teachers is to assume that meaning lies in the subject matter. Bruner, for example, has made a plea for educators to de-emphasize facts and emphasize meanings. Unfortunately, he sees meaning as a function of content and asks us to organize subject matter around meanings instead of facts. Certainly, it should be easier to learn meanings if subject matter is better organized; but it won't solve the problem because meanings don't lie in subject matter. Meaning is a people problem. It happens in persons. Development of meaning is a creative act occuring as a consequence of people interacting with the world they live in.

We have already seen how concepts of self are acquired as a consequence of experience in the process of growing up. This is how all meanings are acquired—through a process of differentiation. It is literally true that people do not get information from the printed page. Meanings are really discovered by the learner. Meanings are also highly personal. No two people can ever have precisely the same meanings, because no two people will ever have exactly the same experience. The meanings which a person has differentiated out of his experience constitute the universe as he knows it. This is his own personal reality, although certain aspects may resemble to some degree the field of meanings held by others.

THE ECONOMY OF MEANING

Stability of Meaning

If it were necessary for persons to discover meaning anew in every situation, few of us would ever get out of our infancy. It is a fact that meanings have a degree of stability that makes it possible to settle things in one area and so free the individual to devote his time and attention to other areas. The perceptual field is not a conglomerate of individual meanings. It is a Gestalt, an organization, in which some meanings develop an importance or centrality in the field around which other meanings can be organized. The most important of these fundamental meanings is the self-concept about which we have already spoken. There are other organizations within the field which provide additional orientation and direction in the lives of people because they afford a kind of reference point to which other meanings can be referred.

Some anchorages are aspects of the physical world; persons have learned that these possess high degrees of stability and so can be used as reference points for the interpretation of new experience. Among the most common of these is the horizon which serves to orient us with respect to distance and location. Others are the relative positions of earth and sky—the discovery that far objects are smaller than near ones, and that bright things are generally closer than far ones. For most of us these seem so natural we take them for granted. But we were not born with them. We learned them, and having discovered their stability came to rely upon them. For most anchorages concerning the physical world, this occurred so early in our experience that we can scarcely remember not having them. Their development can sometimes be seen, however, in the drawings of young children, who take many more liberties with horizons than adults. Grownups in our culture have learned very thoroughly that we write and read from left to right. As a consequence it sometimes happens that parents who do not understand what is going on may become distressed at finding their child in the early stages of learning to read and write is quite unconcerned whether he does it from left to right or right to left!

Anchorages exist not only in respect to the physical world of experience, but they also apply to personal, social, and political relations. Children, for example, may regard one or more parents as practically infallible referrents for what is or is not so. For many a young child, "My daddy told me!" is the absolute clincher—the quintessence of truth—in an argument. Later a teacher may achieve this position and "my teacher told me" may then become the ultimate weapon at the dinner table. Adults may also develop similar highly stable feelings about husbands and wives, religious beliefs, and even philosophies or forms of government.

Anchorages have great value in providing expectancies or handy frames of reference against which new experience can be quickly tested and judged. They can also cause great distress when eliminated from experience. Persons in complete isolation who are deprived of most of their ordinary links to life usually find this a most distressing experience. In experiments on sensory deprivation, for example, psychologists sometimes suspend subjects in water at body temperature with ears plugged and eyes blindfolded, which takes them almost completely out of touch with the familiar world. Cut off from the usual anchors to reality, most subjects under these conditions find it very difficult to concentrate and often experience wild delusions. Similar anxiety and distress, usually on a less intense scale, may be experienced by almost anyone when his anchors to reality are destroyed. The first reaction to the assassination of a beloved President or to the loss of a husband or wife may be to deny the fact entirely. Most of us experience anxiety on discovering that a firmly held belief is not true at all. Little children may cling to the idea of Santa Claus long after they have begun to suspect he does not really exist, and may become extremely upset at the efforts of others to deny his existence. One of the authors still remembers the terror he experienced as a young child when it was necessary to tap his spine as part of treatment for polio. The treatment took place on the dining room table. To this day, the author recalls most vividly the shock of realization that, "Daddy is holding me down and letting them do this to me!"

The anxiety experienced when anchorages are disrupted creates difficult roadblocks for learning. It is not easy, for example, for persons raised in deeply fundamentalist traditions to adopt ideas about evolution.

Overcoming prejudice and accepting the fact of race equality can be a disturbing and difficult adjustment for persons raised in conditions leading them to opposite conclusions. Anyone who has ever struggled with the problem of breaking a habit can attest to the anxiety when comfortable forms of behavior are interrupted.

Values, generalized attitudes toward events or persons, are organizations of meanings much like anchorages in their effects. Like all other meanings, they are learned from experience but, because of their generalized character, tend to add to the stability of the person's perceptual field. For the person who holds values, they also provide a frame of reference for experience—a kind of shorthand determination of the meaning of events for the behaver. Since behavior is always a function of the person's meanings, when a value has become a central stable characteristic it thereafter affects a great deal of behavior. This often makes a person's behavior so predictable that other people, observing its stability, develop an expectancy and sometimes can be heard to say, "Well, of course! What do you expect of Joe? You know how he is!"

So important is the stabilizing effect of values upon behavior that in time it can be said in truth of an individual that he becomes his beliefs. It lends consistency to behavior. This fact has tremendous significance for workers in the helping professions. In Chapter 1, we have already seen how the effectiveness of persons in the helping professions is a function of their beliefs. This relationship between values and behavior is equally true for the persons they work with. When a person believes differently, he finds his own ways of behaving differently. It follows that, if helpers can find ways to assist their helpees in changing their beliefs, a change of behavior will also occur in the process.

THE SELECTIVE EFFECT OF EXISTING MEANING

We have seen in previous chapters how people's perceptions are affected by need and by the self-concept. We now add a third factor—namely, the effect of the existing field of meanings on new experience. Meanings, once discovered, tend to be relied upon and are seldom questioned unless the person is forced to do so because new experience does not fit his expectations. Just as the self-concept once established thereafter affects whatever else persons may perceive, the field of meanings existing for a particular person has a similar effect. In part this is due to the fact that some perceptions cannot be made until others have preceded them—that is, some differentiations can only occur when those prior perceptions on which they are dependent have been experienced. Best examples of this relationship are to be seen in learning school subjects with highly sequential characters—for instance, mathematics. Here, concepts are built in step-by-step fashion. Before one can grasp more complex concepts, the simpler ones must first be perceived. In this fashion the existing field of meaning exerts a degree of control upon what further meanings can be readily acquired.

This sequential relationship of meanings is also involved in respect to many of the concepts people need to acquire in the processes of growing into effective adults. Piaget spent a large part of his career studying concept formation in children, and was able to map with high degrees of accuracy the step-by-step progressions by which the children he studied moved from simpler to more and more complex concepts. While the children often moved through these phases at varying speeds, the sequences of development were likely to be highly stable.

The difficulty of differentiating new and more complex concepts in advance of prerequisite ones is practically illustrated in the problems involved in educating children from deeply deprived backgrounds. Generations of inadequate diets, poverty-stricken conditions, unstimulating environments, and inadequate early schooling have made it gravely difficult for children in the deep South to handle the work required in public schools geared to teach the children of a more affluent white middle class.

In addition to the building-block kind of selection exerted by the perceptual field, the individual's need to achieve fulfillment itself exerts a selective effect upon perceptions. We have already seen how this occurs with respect to the operation of the self-concept. The need of the organism to achieve fulfillment, of necessity, requires a stable perceptual field. A field of meaning without stability, or quickly changing in major ways from moment to moment, would be disastrous. Without a measure of stability, fulfillment would be impossible. Accordingly, once differentiated, meanings persist in the individual's perceptual field and exert their influence by determining in part the meanings of new experience. Meanings, once discovered, tend thereafter to be given to similar events.

New experience which fits the existing organization is quickly and easily incorporated. It corroborates and reinforces what is already differentiated. When, however, new experience does not fit existing meanings, the behaver is confronted with a problem of disparate perceptions (called cognitive dissonance by some psychologists) and some adjustment must be made. Generally speaking, this may occur in one of three ways:

The new experience may be denied or ignored while the person clings to the old meanings he has previously held. Everyone is familiar with this kind of behavior either in himself or in others. Facts which do not fit existing patterns may simply be bypassed. Letters about overdue payments may remain unread. Warning signs may not be seen. Unacceptable evidence is simply treated as though it did not exist. Even when sufficient pressure is placed behind a new meaning in order that confrontation cannot be avoided, meanings can still be refused admission to the field by forthright rejection. Thus, Communists may be found denying the successes of capitalism in their fervor to expound the glories of their own positions. Similarly, organizations on the extreme right often seem blind to the most obvious facts of social interaction. Forced into integration, for example, the Ku Klux Klansman resists change in his belief system and digs deeper into his established position.

A second way of handling meanings which do not fit is to distort them so that they will. In this way the experience is neither ignored nor denied Rather, it is given a meaning which does not require reorganization of the existing field. This can often be observed in listening to a friend report on a movie he has seen. Instead of telling the story as we remember it he tailors it to fit his own experience, takes liberties with the plot, and even puts the dialogue in his own familiar ways of speaking. Additional examples may be seen in the common practice of rationalization wherein a good reason for behavior is substituted for the real one. "I bought it because my old car was beginning to use oil." "I really need to eat to keep my strength up." "She probably had a date already." "The speed limit on this stretch of road is absolutely ridiculous."

The third way of dealing with divergent meanings is to confront the new experience and make whatever changes are appropriate in currently existing meanings. This could result in acceptance or rejection of the new concept. Such actions, however, are taken on the basis of willingness to confront the matter at hand and subject the existing field of meanings to the new data. This way of dealing with new experience is probably healthiest in the long run. It is also the sort of thing one does in the discovery of meaning in the first place.

Actually, these three ways of dealing with new meanings are seldom found in isolation. More often than not, all three ways of dealing with meanings are likely to occur simultaneously when a person is confronted with a new problem. Depending on what seems to satisfy need most effectively, however, some will be ignored, some distorted, and some changes will be made in the individual's personal field of meaning.

THE CIRCULAR EFFECT OF MEANING

The process of discovering meaning from the world on the one hand and imposing meaning on it on the other produces a most important circular effect on behavior. Having acquired a particular field of meanings, persons behave in terms of this field and so become an expression of their beliefs. Such behavior, moreover, is likely to call forth from others the kinds of interaction which tend to corroborate the existing field of meanings. For example, the child who is afraid of the water may be so terrified in early attempts to swim that he behaves out of his panic and splashes water in his face, which frightens him more, and so proves what he already believed at the start. Similarly, what teachers or counselors believe about children or clients is likely to cause them to behave in ways which corroborate existing beliefs. The "incorrigible" boy is likely to be more carefully watched and restricted, thus producing in him a feeling that he is "being picked on"—a feeling almost certain to result in aggressive behavior and further defiance of authority figures.

The circular effect of meaning on behavior can also be observed in the braggart who, feeling unimportant, tells stories designed to build up his sagging self. This behavior is unlikely to make him very popular, and the behavior of others toward him only confirms what he already believes. In a very real sense, each person is his own project, or the architect of his own personality. Every experience a person has which produces a change in his meanings must have its effects upon his behavior, and so, changes the person himself. This is perhaps best seen with respect to the choices we make in life. Each choice both opens up new possibilities and closes others. The decision to become a priest makes it most unlikely that that person will become an engineer. At the same time, such a decision opens whole new areas for exploration and discovery of meaning that are unlikely to exist in similar degrees for the person who makes the decision to become an engineer. As Tillich has pointed out: "Man is his choices." He is also increasingly unique, for he acquires his field of meaning from his own individual experiences. Thereafter, his personal field of meaning causes him to behave in ways forever expressive of his unique personality. So, people become more unlike and more individual the longer they live.

LEARNING AS DISCOVERY OF MEANING

LEARNING—A HUMAN PROBLEM

It will be recognized that what we have been talking about as the discovery of meaning is, in fact, learning. Learning is the discovery of meaning. The problem of learning, modern psychologists tell us, always involves two aspects: One is the acquisition of new information or experience; the other has to do with the individual's personal discovery of the meaning of information for him. The provision of information can be controlled by an outsider with or without the cooperation of the learner. It can even be done, when necessary, by mechanical means which do not require a person at all. The discovery of meaning, however, can only take place in people and cannot occur without the involvement of persons. This is the human side of learning.

We are accustomed to thinking of learning as a yes-no question. We say of a student, "He learned it" or "He did not" as though it were an all-or-nothing matter. The discovery of meaning, however, is a more or less question, a matter of degree and kind of differentiation.

A great deal of what passes for learning is no more than the production of temporary awareness. As a consequence, students do not behave in the terms they set down on the test, nor do clients and patients do what they know they should. As a matter of fact all of us know a great deal better than we behave. The capacity to report back information acquired is but the initial step in learning—the first faint glimmering of meaning. Unfortunately, it can seldom be relied upon to produce a change in behavior the moment the necessity for reproducing it is past. Nevertheless, paper and pencil tests continue to be widely employed in our schools and are often exclusively accepted as valid indications of acceptable learning. The mischief produced by this misconception is incalculable and leads to the grossest kinds of inefficiencies and injustices for everyone concerned—students, teachers, and administrators alike.

The discovery of meaning has barely begun with simple awareness. If it goes no further than this, there is a serious question whether the effort is worth the result at all. Real learning—learning which makes a difference and which produces a change in behavior—calls for a deeper, more extensive discovery of meaning. It calls especially for the discovery of the relationship of events to the self, for truly effective learning is a deeply personal matter.

MEANING AND THE SELF

Whether or not any meaning is sufficiently important to exert an effect on behavior is a function of its relationship to the person's self. The possibilities of what *might* be perceived in any given experience are practically limitless. Confronted with an event, however, we do not perceive just anything; we perceive what has meaning to us. Perception is a selective process. We attend especially to those matters having a relationship to self or to some extension of self. Thereafter, its effect upon behavior will be a function of the further meanings it acquires in the perceptual field. Combs and Snygg have stated this principle as follows: *"Any information will affect a person's behavior only in the degree to which he has discovered its personal meaning for him."*

Let us take an example to see how this works:

At breakfast you read the morning paper's statistics on pulmonic stenosis. There have been thirty-five cases in your state during the last year. Will this have any effect on your behavior? Probably not. For most readers this bit of information is probably little more than a foreign language. It has little personal meaning and so affects your behavior very little. Later in the day you hear pulmonic stenosis mentioned and, because you have nothing better to do and a dictionary is handy, you look it up. You learn that this is a disorder of the heart having to do with a narrowing or closing up of the pulmonary artery. You continue to read and discover that this is a disorder with which some children are born. The information now has a little more meaning, and you may feel vaguely uncomfortable. Now, since most of the readers of this book are concerned with the helping relationship, let us suppose you are a teacher and hear that a child in a school across town is afflicted with this disorder. The matter is closer now to your personal concerns. As a consequence it has more effect on your behavior. Perhaps you pay more attention, listen more intently, and even kick around the matter of pulmonic stenosis in your mind.

Suppose that we now give this topic even more personal meaning. Let us say that you are a teacher who has just read these words in a letter from the mother of a child in your class. She writes you that her child has this disorder and will need to be operated on in the near future. She asks that you consider the child's problem in assigning her school tasks. This item of information now has a much more personal bearing and produces a number of effects in your behavior. Perhaps you write a note to the mother. You certainly discuss the matter with other teachers and are especially nice to this child. This is no longer mere "information." It is something which is happening to one of *your* children. Because the information has more personal meaning, moreover, your behavior is more sharply focused and more precisely oriented.

Let us go one step further now and assume that you have just been told by your doctor that your son or daughter has this disorder. Now, indeed, your behavior is deeply affected. All kinds of things occur directly related to your awareness of pulmonic stenosis.

To conceive of this matter visually, we might think of a person's field of experience as shown in Fig. 1. In the very center of this field are the person's concepts of self, all together called the self-concept. At varying distances from this center are his perceptions of the rest of the world. The closer events are perceived to the self, the greater will be the effects that such perceptions have in producing behavior. The farther they exist toward the periphery of the perceptual field, the less influence they will exert. Plotting our discussion about the concept of pulmonic stenosis from the paragraphs above, we might illustrate the relationships to self on the line A–E and represent them as shown below in Figure 1.

The closer events are perceived to the self, the more likely they will affect behavior in significant ways. This is a basic principle of learning. The problem of helping people learn, then, becomes a problem of moving information into closer and more meaningful relationships to self.

A SOURCE OF LEARNING FAILURES

The principle that any information will affect a person's behavior in the degree to which he perceives its personal meaning also serves to explain why a great deal of what we attempt to teach has such little effect. Students who do not see the personal meanings of events for them are likely to be unaffected by the learning experiences provided. For a very long time in all the helping professions, especially in education, we have been operating from an inadequate concept of learning. Most of the innovations we have tried have been derived from some form of stimulus-response psychology.

Seeing the problem of learning in this way leads logically and naturally to a preoccupation with manipulation of events outside the learner. The distressing thing about this is not that it is wrong, but that it's partly right.

S–R psychology has important contributions to make to the informa-

Fig. 1   Diagram for the Nature of Learning

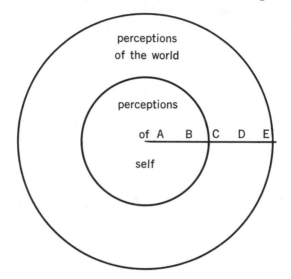

Pulmonic Stenosis

E. Reading the statistics.

D. Looking it up.

C. A child across town has it.

B. "My" pupil, Mary Alice, has it.

A. My daughter has it!

tion half of the learning equation. Through its application, we have indeed been able to improve our techniques to a high pitch of efficiency in the gathering and dissemination of information. Unfortunately, this very success leads us to a disastrous preoccupation with only half the equation. And, as a result of our partial successes, we are encouraged that the problems of learning might surely be solved if only we continue as we are doing with more precision more frequently, and with more intensity.

Accordingly, we are led to polish and repolish our techniques of providing information in the fond belief that if a little is good, a lot must be very much better.

Failure to deal with the second aspect of the learning equation explains why so much of what we have learned in school is forgotten. At one time, most of us learned the capital of North Dakota, the number of miles to the moon, the date of the Battle of Waterloo, and a million other such items of information. But where is it now? As a matter of fact, a great deal of what goes on in schools seems almost expressly designed to discourage the student's search for personal meaning while it concentrates almost exclusively on the ingestion of information. It is not unusual to hear a student complain that the teacher wasn't interested in what he thought, but only in what somebody had written in an assigned article. "Never mind what you think about that, Jimmy. What does the book say?" It is the failure of the student to discover meaning which accounts for the dropout. Students do not drop out because they weren't given information. They drop out because they never discovered what it all meant. And day after day, they found themselves swamped with information having little relevance either to themselves or the world in which they lived. It is very likely that our preoccupation with the information half of the learning equation is also responsible for some of the difficult problems of dehumanization, depersonalization, and alienation we have created for our young people.

KNOWING AND BEHAVING

There is a vast difference between knowing and behaving. Knowing comes from getting new information. Change in behavior comes from the discovery of meaning. Some of our most important learnings actually have nothing to do with new information but everything to do with the deeper and deeper discovery of the meaning of things we already have. Thousands of white citizens living in the midst of our "Southern Bible Belt" have been going to church for years. They have talked and sung for generations about the "Brotherhood of Man" with comparatively little effect on their daily behavior. Only recently have they begun to ask themselves if they truly mean it and only recently has it begun to show major effects on their behavior.

Most people in the helping professions are very proficient in the information half of the learning equation. They know how to give people information very well. Most failures in the helping professions occur, however, not because helpers are unskilled at providing information, but because of their lack of skill in helping persons discover the personal meaning of information for them. Our schools, for example, are expert at providing people with information. When it is time to think about improving schools it is often concluded that more information is needed. So, more is added: more subjects, more homework, more teaching machines, more audio-visual equipment, more languages, more math, more science, more physical education, etc. The list is practically endless. In recent years we have compounded the problem by turning our productive genius loose to devise a thousand new gadgets to gather and transmit information more effectively and efficiently than ever before! What might we accomplish with an equal effort directed at producing changes in meaning?

People's exposure to new information can often be greatly speeded up. The problem of changing meaning, however, is a slower, more difficult human task, which cannot be done by an outsider. It must be done by the learner himself. People need information, of course. The danger comes when we lose our perspective and expect that "telling" or giving advice is likely to result in permanent changes. People who do not perceive the relationship of events to self are simply unaffected by experience. The majority of Americans know there is a strong possibility that smoking will significantly shorten their lives. They have had access to innumerable "facts" about the matter. Yet, the behavior of many Americans clearly demonstrates that they do not really believe it. The act of smoking continues to be for them more self-enhancing than the possibility of developing lung cancer. Consequently, they manage to hold the facts at arm's length, to keep from perceiving the relevance to self.

When the chips are down, we all revert to what is personally relevant. The things we have learned but have not yet seen in relationship to self are quickly shucked off when school is out or the pastor is not around. Almost everyone knows what he *ought* to do. Misbehavior is usually the result of not wanting to do what one knows he should do because something else is more personally satisfying. Good examples of the reversion to what is personally significant can be found in the training of persons for the helping professions. It is fairly simple to teach beginners a new concept or techniques. They quickly come to "know it." A counselor, for example, learns several proper approaches to working with clients. He knows them, can pass a test about them, can even talk about them convincingly. Then he goes to work with a client and may behave as though he had never heard of the matter! Confronted with real problems, he does not have time to think about what to do. Instead, he does what comes naturally to him, the things most closely related to self and his past experience.

RELATION OF MEANING TO MEMORY, EMOTION, AND FEELING

MEMORY

The importance of personal meaning extends far beyond its significance for problems in human learning. It is also important for questions of memory, feeling, and emotion. When a person looks back at some event in the past what he remembers is not what really happened but that event colored by the meaning it had for him then or has now. He remembers what seemed to him at the time was happening or, even more inaccurately what it now seems to him must have happened! The memory of an event is thus a belief about it, not an accurate record of it. Any teacher who has ever given an examination is familiar with the maddening and sometimes hilarious meanings students retain from the most carefully planned lesson. Students do not recall what was said. They recall what they thought was said, what they comprehended. The crucial character of meaning in remembering may also be observed in counseling practice. Clients often spend long periods exploring memories of early life in the counseling hour and often in the course of these explorations may be observed to change their minds about events that happened in the past. They may be heard to exclaim, "You know, I don't believe it ever really happened like that at all!" "Guess I must have imagined that . . . ," or "Well, it really couldn't have happened like that. It must have been. . . ."

Additional errors in remembering may be produced by the selective effect of need, the self-concept, and the nature of the existing field of meanings—matters previously discussed in this volume. Because of these effects, memories may be distorted in ways more becoming to the reporter. Who has not been guilty of reporting what happened in the best possible light? And who has not embroidered his tale in a way that made him appear blameless, more righteous, brave, or smart? Memories may also be distorted in ways to make them fit the existing field. This occurs when persons remember what *must* have happened. Magicians make good use of this characteristic of human memory by purposely establishing in the mind of the observer a reasonable "set," so that what is seen later is interpreted in terms of what seems to the observer must have occurred.

These are serious matters for courts of law. The notorious inaccuracies of human memory make the "credibility of witnesses" an ever-present problem for defendants, lawyers, judge, and jury. Many courtroom rules of procedure so puzzling to the layman were really established as devices to assure the most accurate possible reports of exactly what happened in a given case. So, witnesses may be peremptorily told to "stick to the facts," and opposing counsel is given the right to challenge the introduction of opinion or conjecture if it seems prejudicial to his case. This is not just a problem for witnesses who might lie. Even under oath the story told by the most well-intentioned witness may be in error for any of the reasons we have already reviewed.

EMOTION

In the pulmonic stenosis illustration used earlier, we observed that the effects on a person's behavior increased with the closeness of meaning to self. The experience of emotion is also affected by the degree of personal meaning. For the psychologist, emotion is a state of acceleration. It is the response of the organism which makes it ready to act. Ordinarily, emotion is very low when one is sleeping with his "motor barely turning over." On awakening, more energy is required and the body processes become accelerated to adjust to greater demands. Emotion reaches its greatest heights in emergency situations where the self is in danger, as in anger or fear. Or, it is engaged in important enhancing experiences such as ecstacy or triumph. At such times the organism is capable of tremendous bursts of energy for short periods of time, but it is interesting to note that the physiologic effects accompanying emotion in all these forms are identical.

Emotion is an artifact of the meanings existing for the individual at any moment. Generally speaking, the closer the event is perceived to self the more intense the behavior and also the emotion experienced by the behaver. Emotion thus varies with the degree of personal involvement. We are not very affected by the death of a stranger, but are deeply moved by the death of a friend. The emotion we feel is a consequence of the relationship of the event to self. Note in the following illustration how emotion arises with increasing closeness to self. You are standing on the lawn conversing with a friend about snakes in a far-off country. (*There is not much reaction*). "I was just reading," says your friend, Ed, "that there is an alarming increase of poisonous snakes in Texas." (*"An alarming increase" is a little frightening anytime, more so if you live in Texas!*) At this point you are joined by another friend, Joe, who tells Ed he is mistaken. "The increase is not in Texas but right here in this state. And this county is one of the worst! (*Things start to pick up.*) As a matter of fact," he goes on, "I saw one in the lot next door just now." (*Acceleration increases.*) "Look out " shouts Ed. "You're about to step on him!" (*There is a surge to full power as you jump out of your skin!*)

The closer and more important the value of the event to self, the greater is the degree of the emotion elicited. The principle is true for happy and fulfilling events as well.

FEELINGS

The descriptions we give to emotional experiences are known as feelings. They might also be called personal meanings for that is what a *feeling* is—a description of the personal meaning of something to the behaver. When one says, "I love Mary," "I hate John," "I detest dogs," "I like good movies," "I feel hurt," "I feel disappointed, proud, amused, delighted," etc., he is expressing as best he can the personal meaning of those people or things for him.

Actually, of course, no one can ever express the full meaning of an event for him when he speaks of his feelings. The full meaning of the event involves the entire perceptual field of the speaker at the moment, and only a portion of that can ever be translated into words. One expresses himself with the best language at his disposal. We are all keenly aware of how poorly words express the full import of what we feel. What lover has not complained at the inadequacy of words to say all that he wished! So it is that while feelings are personal meanings, their expression in words is no more than an approximation, a representation of the meaning itself, a kind of shorthand to express a complex notion.

We have seen above that, with greater personal reference, behavior and emotion are more intense. So also is the feeling of personal meaning experienced by the behavior. One has little feeling at an isolated fact. The closer the fact comes to the self, however, the more personal meaning or feeling it acquires.

An understanding of this relationship of feeling and meaning is important for workers in the helping professions, for there is a common belief abroad that cognition and emotion, knowing and feeling, are unrelated entities. In the light of our discussion here, it must be clear that whatever meaning a person has, must possess both cognition and emotion in some degree. There can be no feeling except about something, and no knowing without some personal reference. So the counseling client who says, "I know it intellectually, but I can't do it" is telling us simply that what he knows is ineffective because he does not see it as related meaningfully to himself. To solve his dilemma, he does not have to know something else; he needs to discover the personal meaning of what he already knows. When he does, he will express it in feeling terms: "I feel that's what I should do," or "I believe I'll try that," or "I think that would be fun."

The Fetish of Objectivity

The attempt to treat knowing and feeling, or cognition and emotion, as though they were unrelated matters obeying different laws can only lead to confusion and misunderstanding. We do not experience cognition and emotion as separate entities. The only thing we ever experience is meaning, and meaning always consists of awareness with more or less personal relevance. Psychologically, emotion is understood as an indicator of personal involvement. Things which have no personal meaning arouse no emotions. In light of these facts, the fetish which some persons make over the necessity of objectivity becomes ridiculous. The fact is that one can only be objective about things that don't matter! What does not matter is worth no one's time or energy. Unless it matters, it is of no consequence. If it does matter, it matters subjectively.

Many advances have been made in the physical sciences through the application of what is sometimes called the scientific method, the attempt to make observations with complete objectivity. Because of the success of science, many people have attempted to translate these methods directly to problems of dealing with people. Unfortunately, the answers to human problems arrived at through complete objectivity frequently apply only to persons operating under laboratory conditions. They do not hold up for the man in the street, the child in the classroom, or the client in the counselor's office. Even the best of scientists are by no means completely objective.

Anyone who has ever worked with scientists closely can attest to the fact that they are by no means objective in respect to their theoretical positions which, after all, are what their observations are intended to lead to. Often they can be found defending their theoretical positions like a tiger defending its cubs. They treat attacks upon their theories as attacks upon themselves and, of course, in the light of what we know about the extension of the self-concept, this is literally true.

People do not behave in terms of ideas they do not care about. *Caring,* let it be noted, is what we mean by emotion. The discovery of meaning and its accompanying emotion lie at the very heart of learning. The practice of education, counseling, social work, or pastoral care which rules out feeling, of necessity, makes itself ineffective. The attempt to separate knowing from feeling or personal meaning is to make learning sterile. Humanism is not anti-intellectual. On the contrary, it seeks realistically to make intelligence functional. It is concerned about caring and personal meaning—not just because that is a nice way to live, but because it is the hard-headed, necessary road to producing the kinds of people we want and need.

The attempt to deal with people in purely objective terms may result in making the helper entirely ineffective. Some research on the helping professions at the University of Florida found that objectivity on the part of counselors and priests correlated with ineffectiveness! The counselor who attempts to deal with his client solely on the basis of "the facts" is bound to fail. So, also, the social worker or pastor who attempts to deal with a couple experiencing marital difficulties on a purely objective basis may only make himself futile.

SELECTED READINGS

Starred entries indicate appearance in whole or in part in Donald L. Avila, Arthur W. Combs, and William W. Purkey, *The Helping Relationship Sourcebook* (Boston: Allyn & Bacon, 1971).

Bartlett, F. C. Serial reproduction of picture material. In Bartlett, F. C. *Remembering* (Rev. ed.) Cambridge, England: Cambridge University Press, 1950, 177–178. Reprinted in Wrenn, R. L. *Basic contributions to psychology: Readings.* Belmont, Calif.: Wadsworth, 1966, 172–178.

Craddick, R. A. Height of Christmas tree drawings as a function of time. *Perceptual and Motor Skills,* 1963, **17,** 335–339.

English, H. B. Education of the emotions. *Journal of Humanistic Psychology,* Spring 1961, 101–109.

Heron, W. The pathology of boredom. *Scientific American,* 1957, **196,** 52–56.

* Ittelson, W. H. The involuntary bet. *Vogue*, March 15, 1952, 76–77, 127.

Ittelson, W. H. & Cantril, H. *Perception: A transactional approach*. New York: Doubleday, 1954.

Kolers, P. A. It loses something in the translation. *Psychology Today*, 1969, **2**, 32–35.

* Marshal, J. The evidence. *Psychology Today*, 1969, **2**, 48–52.

Schultz, D. P. *Sensory restrictions: Effects on behavior*. New York: Academic Press, 1965.

Wittreich, W. J. The honiphenomenon. *Journal of Abnormal and Social Psychology*, 1952, **47**, 705–712.

Learning as Meaning Change

The processes of helping must result in more effective and satisfying ways of behaving for clients, students, or patients. This calls for changes in personal meanings. Meanings, however, lie inside people and cannot be changed directly by outsiders. They can be influenced by events in the outside world though. To bring this about, helpers must be cognizant of the nature of meaning and the dynamics involved in changing it.

LOGICAL FALLACY

Many failures in helping people to change behavior occur due to a lack of understanding the relationship between meaning and behavior. Approaching the matter logically it would seem that if you want to change a person's behavior, you need to focus his attention on it, examine it carefully, decide what he ought to do instead, then go ahead and act on the decision. Unfortunately, this nice, logical approach only occasionally produces the kind of changes hoped for. Attempts to change behavior by dealing with it directly are only symptomatic approaches to working with people; they fail to deal with causes.

Why is this so?

The behavior we observe in ourselves and in others is only a symptom of what is going on within. The behaviors people engage in are not beginnings, but ends; they are not causes, but results.

In dealing with matters of human behavior and misbehavior, concentrating upon symptoms is an approach of very limited value. The at-

103

tempt to produce change by direct attack upon behavior is likely to be effective only under three kinds of conditions.

1/ If the manipulator's goals are short-term ones.   High-pressure salesmen, for example, know that people can sometimes be maneuvered into a momentary shift in behavior, and use this fact to their own advantage to get a customer to make a purchase or sign a contract if their only goal is to sign a contract in order to sell a product. Behavior can indeed sometimes be manipulated, but usually only for very short periods. Unless a more permanent shift in meanings enters the picture, people quickly revert to more accustomed ways of acting. For the salesman who is unconcerned about his customer's long-term satisfactions or his own future relationships with the customer, manipulating behavior in this way may be an acceptable way of dealing with customers. For persons in the helping professions, such short-term goals will seldom be sufficient.

2/ If the person whose behavior is to be changed can keep his mind exclusively on what he is doing.   It is sometimes possible to change behavior quite directly by "deciding" to do something differently. But unless changes also occur in perceptions, beliefs, desires, or some other personal meaning along with this decision, changing behavior this way is likely to be pretty inefficient. It may even result in such disastrous failures as to discourage further attempts at change altogether. This often happens when teachers' colleges attempt to teach students the "right" way to teach. If a method which the student is being asked to attempt fits him, his subject, and the situation in which he is working, he may be able to incorporate the idea into his belief system. He will then be able to carry it off with some hope of success. If, however, the method he is asked to try seems to him a mere technique or intellectual exercise, he will be able to carry it out only so long as he can keep his mind on it. So long as he has nothing else to think about and no emergencies or other unexpected events, he may be able to carry out his plan successfully. Unfortunately, this rarely happens. Classrooms can seldom be operated under such rigid controls. Consequently, the moment some unexpected event occurs and takes his mind off what he is doing, he is lost. Then, he tries to make sense out of his confusion by falling back on what he is thinking and feeling, or what he knows from previous experience. With his mind no longer on what he is doing, the methods he was trying almost certainly fail to work and, not understanding what has happened, the student concludes that the method is no good—that what was taught in teachers' college was "strictly for the birds." This conclusion is likely to be further corroborated by old-timers among the teachers around him who have been through the same experience. Few of us can change our behavior in really important ways by direct attacks upon the behavior itself. For really important changes it is necessary to deal with causes rather than symptoms.

3/ If the manipulated behavior fits the need of the subject. Behavior can often be changed directly by manipulation if it can be made to seem like an important contribution to the behaver's own needs and purposes. Examples of this principle can be seen all around us in the programs of advertisers who attempt to get people to behave in ways profitable for them. Advertising preys upon expressions of the basic need for adequacy as needs to be smart, loved, odor-free, masculine, attractive, in the social swim, or whatever. Since all human behavior is an attempt to satisfy the basic need for maintenance and enhancement of the self, manipulations which can be made to seem to the behaver as leading to those ends may, indeed, prove to be effective.

Attempting to change behavior by direct manipulation may be satisfactory for casual interactions with people in nonprofessional roles. It is hardly adequate for persons making a profession of helping, however. The attempt is likely to be highly frustrating for both helper and helpee. The helper is thwarted because the effects of his techniques are unpredictable, and the helpee is baffled because he cannot make them work. Since most helping professions are directly dependent upon the maintenance of effective relationships and open channels of communication between helper and client, such frustrations make direct manipulation of behavior of doubtful value.

Manipulative approaches to changing behavior have serious limitations for another reason. The goal of the helping professions is the production of persons capable of self-direction. Manipulation tends to defeat this purpose by making clients dependent upon their helpers—a condition directly contrary to the goal of self-direction.

Generally speaking, symptomatic approaches to helping are too imprecise or too long delayed for most professional use. If the helping professions have any excuse for their existence, they must operate in the most certain, predictable, and speedy ways possible. This is unlikely to be true when operating from a symptomatic orientation. Professional helpers must deal primarily with causes. This calls for attention to personal meanings and the production of changes in the perceptions of self and the world in those they hope to aid.

EFFECTS OF CHALLENGE AND THREAT UPON CHANGE IN BEHAVIOR

EFFECT OF THREAT UPON PERCEPTION

A most important factor affecting the discovery of meaning and its susceptibility to change is the experience of threat and its effects upon perception. These effects are of special importance for persons in the helping professions because they influence the perceptions possible and control the likelihood of change in ways of perceiving and behaving.

In an earlier chapter we have seen how the fundamental need of the organism for fulfillment has a selecting effect upon the person's perceptual experience. People perceive what they need to. This selective effect occurs whenever the person is confronted with events having special importance to him. The more important the relationship to self the greater the degree to which perception becomes focused. The closer it gets to Christmas, the greater the child's excitement. This focus of attention is especially active when people feel threatened, and the effects upon perception under such circumstances have extraordinary importance for persons in the helping professions.

Psychologists are aware of two effects of the experience of threat upon the individual. The first has been called "tunnel vision." When a person feels himself threatened, a narrowing of the perceptual field to the object of threat occurs. Almost everyone has experienced this phenomenon under frightening circumstances. Under the experience of threat what can be perceived is narrowed to the point where it is difficult to see anything but the threatening object—like looking through a tunnel. One of the authors recalls asking his daughter at the dinner table what she had learned in school that day. "Oh! Nothing!" she replied. "But was our teacher mad!" Under the threat of an angry teacher, little or nothing else made very much impression.

If threat is very great, attention becomes sharply focused on the threatening event, to the exclusion of all else. The child in school, for example, who feels threatened by his mother's being sent to the hospital is obviously in no condition to perceive the nuances of a Shakespearean line, the importance of the raw products of Arizona, or the implications of Constitutional law. Sometimes the narrowing effect of threat may even result in doing stupid things in an emergency. Once, in the midst of a party given by one of the authors at his home, a grass mat in front of the fireplace caught fire. Seeing this, the author picked up the rug, ran across the room to the front door, and threw the rug outside into the snow. When the excitement had quieted down, someone asked, "Why didn't you just kick it into the fireplace?" Why not, indeed? At the moment of the emergency, the only thing he could think of was to get the burning rug out of the house, and the simple solution of kicking it into the fireplace never occurred to him because his perceptions were narrowed to getting the fire out, not in!

The narrowing of perception effect of threat is equally operative when the feeling is only very mild. Combs and Taylor, for example, asked subjects to translate short sentences into a simple code. Some of these sentences were mildly threatening or unflattering. They found that, even under conditions of very mild degrees of threat, performance in translating was significantly disturbed. Nearly every subject made more errors and took longer to complete the code under conditions of very mild threat than when such threat was absent.

This restricting effect of threat on perception seems too important a factor to be overlooked in constructing an efficient learning situation. Indeed, it is exactly the opposite of what we hope to achieve in the helping professions. We do not want clients to be restricted in what they see. What we want is the broadest and richest experience possible. Narrowing of perception defeats the fundamental purpose of what the helping professions are attempting to accomplish.

A second effect of threat upon perception makes it even more important a factor in learning. When a person feels threatened, he is forced to defend the perceptions he already has. This effect of threat upon perception is extremely well-known to the man in the street, but it is truly amazing how little attention it has been given as a principle affecting learning. One needs only look about him to see numerous examples of the principle in operation. People in the midst of an argument do not seem to hear what others are saying. Children dig in their heels and refuse to cooperate. Grown men become stubborn. People resist what seem like perfectly clear demonstrations of how very wrong they were. Almost everyone is aware that when he feels himself threatened, his first reaction is to defend himself in every way he can. What is more, the greater the degree of threat to which he is exposed the more tenaciously he holds to the perceptions, ideas, or practices he already has. Under the experience of threat, people find it almost impossible to change. Thus, communication breaks down.

It is important to keep in mind that we are talking about an individual's experience of threat. Whether or not an individual feels himself threatened is a function of what he perceives. Whether an outsider observing the situation would agree that he is threatened is irrelevant and immaterial. Threat is a personal matter involving one's own unique experience with an event. A teacher may believe that she is not threatening a pupil when she grades his paper or corrects his use of language in the classroom. From her view, she is helping. Despite her evaluation though, the child may perceive it quite differently. The assumption that things look the same way to others as they do to us makes it impossible for us to understand the nature of what is going on in others' private worlds. This principle is especially important for members of the helping professions who are expected to help persons in trouble. People who feel deeply inadequate are generally extremely sensitive to further threats to self.

Obviously, events which force people into strongly defensive positions are not at all what we are trying to accomplish in the helping professions. We want to help people *change* perceptions, not defend those they already have. Anything that prevents the processes of change impedes the helping process.

Challenge

When subjected to what seem to be threatening situations, it may be observed that some people do not seem to be affected in the ways we have been describing. Some people instead seem to be challenged to do better work. What is the difference between threat and challenge?

People feel threatened when confronted with situations they do not feel adequate to cope with. People feel challenged when confronted with problems that interest them and which they feel reasonably able to handle. The behavior of the person who feels threatened is likely to be tenuous, unsure, inaccurate, and inadequate. He may even attempt to escape from the situation entirely in one way or another. In the same situation, a person who feels himself adequate to deal with the problem may not feel threatened at all. He may perceive it as challenge with important opportunities for enhancement of self. Therefore, he may meet such a situation with joy and vigor as a new test of adequacy.

The difference between a threatening and a challenging situation lies in the degree of adequacy an individual perceives himself to possess in relation to the situation confronting him. Again, it is necessary to remind ourselves that the distinction lies not in the eye of the outsider but in the eye of the beholder. The teacher encouraging the shy child to "share and tell" may feel she is offering him a challenge. From the child's point of view, he may be faced with a terrifying possibility of humiliation. The differences between the experience of threat and challenge are so important and the effect of these diverse experiences so great that every person in the helping professions needs to be keenly aware of them. A very large measure of the work of persons in these professions is based upon this understanding. A prime problem of helpers will be to find effective ways for challenging the persons they are trying to help, without threatening them.

COMPETITION: MOTIVATION OR THREAT?

The role of competition in motivating learning and behavior change is of special interest in considering the matter of challenge and threat. In our society, competition is almost universally assumed to be an excellent device for motivating persons to extend themselves in athletic events, business affairs, or getting an education. As a matter of fact, when understood in terms of the effects of challenge and threat, competition turns out to be a motivating force of limited value for some and downright destructive for others.[1]

We are very impressed by the competitive features of our society and like to think of ourselves as essentially a competitive people. Yet, the fact is that we are thoroughly and completely dependent upon the goodwill and cooperation of millions of our fellow men. Few of us could live for more than a very short time apart from others. Whether we like it or not, we are thoroughly and completely dependent upon others at every moment of our lives. In turn, thousands of other people are dependent on us. We are indeed "our brothers' keepers" as never before in history. Although it is true that we occasionally compete with others, competition is not the rule of life but the exception. Competition makes the news while cooperation supplies the progress. One needs but to reflect on his own past twenty-four hours to discover how overwhelmingly his behavior has been cooperative and how seldom competitive.

Examined in the light of our understanding of challenge and threat, three things become apparent about the effects of competition:

1. Portions of this section on competition have been adapted from Combs, A. W. The Myth of Competition, *Childhood Education*, 1957, **33**, 264–269, and are reprinted here with permission of the publisher. The Association for Childhood Education International, 1200 15th St. N.W., Washington 5, D.C.

1/ Competition has motivating force only for those persons who believe they have a chance of winning. That is to say it motivates those for whom competition is perceived as challenge. People do not work for things they feel they cannot achieve. They work only for things that seem within their grasp. It makes little difference how the situation looks to an outsider.

2/ Persons who are forced to compete and who do not believe they have a chance of success, are not motivated by the experience; they are threatened by it. Far from motivating people, competition under these conditions is quite likely to result in disillusionment and discouragement. People who do not see much chance of success cannot be inveigled into making an effort. They ignore the competition whenever they are able. Any teacher knows that those children who work for scholastic honors are the few who feel a possibility of winning. The competitors work like crazy while the noncompetitors go about more important business of their own choosing.

Competition is often treated as a means of getting people to extend themselves. Although it is thought to be a means of "challenging" people, it may actually be severely threatening. As we have seen, whether or or not competition is challenging or threatening will depend upon how the situation seems to the competitor—not how it seems to an outsider. Left to themselves, people will compete only rarely, and then only when they feel a chance of success. Forcing people to compete can only result in discouragement or rebellion. When the cards are stacked against us, we give up playing or start a fight with the people responsible for the stacking. Forced to compete against his will, a person may simply "go through the motions" of his job in a dispirited, listless manner, or break out in some form of opposition to his oppressors. Only they who have been fairly successful value competition so highly.

3/ When competition becomes too important, any means become justified to achieve the ends. The aim of competition is to win, and the temptation is to win at any cost. Although it begins with the laudable aim of encouraging production, competition quickly breaks down to a struggle to win at any price. When winning is not crucial, as in casual sports and games, competition can add excitement and fun and so serve a useful and satisfying function. Competition as a way of life is quite a different matter. The means we use to achieve our ends are always bought at a price. When victory becomes too important, students cheat on exams, athletic teams begin to "play dirty," and businessmen lie to their customers. That cost may be more than we want to pay. Price tags must be read not only in dollars and cents but also in terms of human values; broken bodies; broken spirits; and disheartened and disillusioned people who do not appear in the winner's circle, on the sports pages, or as guests of honor at the testimonial banquet.

Competition encourages lone-wolf endeavors, and lone wolves can be dangerous to a cooperative society. We need to be able to count on other people to seek our best interests along with their own. In the headlong rush to win, competition too easily loses sight of responsibility. It values aggression, hostility, and scorn. "Dog eat dog" becomes its philosophy. Too often the degree of glory involved for the victor is only in direct proportion to the abasement and degradation of the loser.

MEANING CHANGE AND PROBLEM-SOLVING

Learning occurs in the process of solving problems. Many of our schools and lecture halls operate in direct contradiction to this principle, as teachers and professors provide students with mountains of information about problems they do not have nor perhaps ever will.

Problems must precede answers. This is why giving advice is so seldom really helpful to other people, and why it is usually avoided in the modern practice of counseling, psychiatry, and social work. It is the active searching for answers to problems that helpers seek to encourage. They know that the process of searching for meaning may even be far more important for the growth of the individual than the answers he discovers.

There is a widespread belief in our culture that practice makes perfect. The proper road to learning, it is thought, is to provide people with the right answers and put them to work repeating them over and over until they have "learned" them. Donald Snygg once pointed out the fallacy of this notion:

> In 1929 Knight Dunlap demonstrated that one way to break habits was to practice them. He cured typists of their characteristic errors by requiring them to practice the error. He cured children of thumb sucking by requiring them to suck their thumbs. It is reasonable to believe that many children have been cured of piano playing by the same method; and it is quite likely that we have cured quite a few of arithmetic and reading! (Snygg, pages 80–81, 1966)

The prime situation for learning is not one in which the learner makes no mistakes. It is one in which the learner is helped to test his ideas under favorable conditions for their exploration, and in which he has opportunity to judge the likelihood of their success. In such a circumstance his mistakes may be far more valuable than his successes. It is the confrontation of problems which provides the stimulus for behavior change.

It is the task of helpers to assist individuals in confronting their problems, and to facilitate and encourage them in their active search for solutions. Psychologists have described this process as resolving dissonance, seeking self-consistency, discovering meaning, resolving tension, and the like. Such confrontations can be brought about in several effective ways.

1/ Creating problems for people.   This is a matter of creating predicaments. It may be done quite brutally or so subtly that the person who is being forced to confront the problems is not even aware of what has occurred. A judge may threaten a delinquent by ordering him to "shape up or go to jail." A teacher may find more subtle ways of confronting children with problems. She might, for example, encourage a group of children to put on a show. In doing so, she might confront them with the necessity for reading a part, writing signs and tickets, doing arithmetic to make change, developing a social organization, or a hundred other problems out of which the students may learn something of value about music, art, business, drama, or a whole gamut of human relations. In an even more subtle manner, a counselor may help his client little by little to uncover an idea so frightening that heretofore he has not been able to face with equanimity.

2/ Leading persons into situations where problems are bound to arise.   This is what the teacher does when she takes her class on a field trip. It is a technique also used by social workers when they send a person into a neighborhood they fully expect will shock, dismay, puzzle, or otherwise raise questions for a client. Problems requiring solution lie all about us. Arranging for confrontation with them often demands little more than going where they are. The most routine setting can sometimes produce great stores of problems if one waits long enough. A counselor knows that "All roads lead to Rome," and if he only listens to a client long enough, he will soon find himself face to face with a problem that must be dealt with. Group discussions provide extremely effective ways of creating problems for participants and are widely used by many of the helping professions for that purpose.

3/ Tapping the most fruitful source of predicaments found in the person himself. Human ambivalences and ambiguities are often the most poignant kinds of problems any of us ever face. Doubts, fears, conflicting desires, hopes unrealized, inadequacies discovered—problems like these can be the most painful of all and, of course, are the very reason for the modern development of some of the newer helping professions like counseling, social work, psychiatry, clinical psychology, and pastoral counseling. People's basic need for maintenance and enhancement of self requires that they engage in continuous search for meanings which will make possible the achievement of fulfillment.

The search for meaning goes on insatiably so long as life exists. People can, will, *must* explore meanings providing that (a) the goal seems important to them and (b) conditions allow them freedom to move. With such a motivating force, encouraging meaning exploration is not a matter that must be contrived, coerced, or carefully molded and directed. Encouraging people to search for solutions to their problems is not so much a thing to be taught as a process to be released. It follows, then, that encouraging discovery of meaning calls for the following situations: maximum flexibility for adjusting to individual needs, the widest possible choices for optimal maneuver room, and the greatest possible opportunities for freedom of exploration. If these conditions can truly be created, the individual's own need may be counted upon to do the rest.

LEARNING—AN ACTIVE PROCESS

Helping people discover new meanings is an active process. Until the learner *does* something with information, it is unlikely to affect him in any important ways. This is John Dewey's principle of learning by doing. Dewey did not mean that learning only occurred when there was physical activity involved although he certainly would have approved the value of such expression. His plea was made for psychological activity—doing something with concepts, whether in the personal confines of a single brain or climbing a mountain to see what was on the other side. Active involvement with new experience or new information is required. It is the dialogue which counts, the searching out of the relationship of events to the self. This is true whether we are talking about learning new ideas, a new job, or one's relationship to the social order in which he lives. Without commitment of the self to an idea, there is likely to be very little effect in behavior.

Effective learning is a product of dialogue with real problems. Problems may be faced when a lover is rejected by his sweetheart, an elderly man is forced to retire, one discovers he is overdrawn at the bank, a student fails the examination, or a million other possibilities. Problems may also be encountered symbolically through the media of language, art, or the whole range of modern electronic devices. It is probable, other things being equal, that symbolic confrontation generally has less impact or effect on the individual than real ones. On the other hand, symbolic confrontations have the advantage of keeping the person safe (while he thinks about murder, for example) and make possible a much wider range for exploration of meaning.

The value of action in learning has important implications for the permanence of learning and commitment of the learner. It is also fundamental to some of our great social problems. Whether learning will last and whether people can be counted on to support the values of our culture and behave responsibly toward it will depend upon the degree of personal involvement they feel toward what they have learned and toward the values of the society they live in. It is only what seems related to the self that affects the learner. What is perceived as "not me" can be safely ignored. Persons forced to attend to what is irrelevant soon find ways of escaping from such boring situations. They become the school dropouts; the counseling failures; the nonattending parishioners; and the "no show" at the clinic, community center, or public meeting.

Similarly, the values of a society are only likely to be adopted by and respected by persons who feel those values are personally relevant. After the Korean War, research on the young men who were captured by the enemy and successfully brainwashed showed them to be young people with little or no commitment to concepts of democracy or to those values generally supposed to be held dear in the USA. They were mostly young men from impoverished backgrounds who found themselves fighting in a war beyond their comprehension. It had no meaning for them personally. When it is necessary to argue with people whose beliefs are so strong that they are practically a religion and you have no personal commitments, you are a sitting duck to be changed. Ideas which do not seem personally relevant are unlikely to be defended when they are attacked. The only real defense against a committed man is a commitment of one's own.

IMPORTANCE OF FEEDBACK

For effective change in behavior, it is necessary that learners have continuous opportunities to observe the consequence of their acts. Seeing the results of meanings makes it possible to check the accuracy or appropriateness of perceptions and to correct faulty assumptions when necessary. Perhaps even more important, seeing the outcomes of new conceptions frequently has the effect of raising new problems to be solved. An act which does not produce the results expected by the learner immediately confronts him with a new problem. If he cannot see the outcome of his new meaning, he is left in the dark as to whether it needs further modification or not. Without feedback, new meanings are unlikely to be further stimulated.

Effective learning, whether it be in connection with shooting on a rifle range, selling a product, raising a child, solving arithmetic problems, or making love to someone, requires knowledge of results. Because this is so, much of the time and energy of helpers will be devoted to helping students and clients discover and deal with the consequences of their decisions. Sometimes they may do this by providing real opportunities to test out new meanings—as when a coach provides an opponent for a young boxer to test his new stance. Sometimes helpers can only wait while the client makes his own tests in the world he lives in. On occasion this may even require that counselors or teachers sit by quietly while a helpee tries for himself a solution that the helper knows in advance will probably not work. Not all feedback comes as a consequence of interaction with the real world. Much important information about the validity of decisions can occur through simple mental manipulation, and a great deal of the work of many helpers is directed toward helping clients or students "think about" the probable outcomes of one action or another during the helping relationship. This is one of the great values of language and symbols. Events can be manipulated and tested without the necessity for paying the penalties of full commitment to action.

EVALUATION

Most helpers are aware of the importance of a knowledge of results as a factor in learning. As a consequence, great stress is often placed upon evaluation. For some persons this concern sometimes becomes such a preoccupation that it blinds them to its proper place and function in the processes of learning. This unfortunate state is likely to occur when helpers forget that whatever benefits evaluation may possess, they must be assessed in terms of what goes on inside the person evaluated. Like every other practice in the helping professions, evaluation may be regarded in either way—from the point of view of the outsider or the point of view of the learner himself. When this fact is overlooked, helpers run the risk of making themselves ineffective or, worse still, of seriously interfering with the growth of students or clients.

Looked at externally, evaluation is usually accomplished by some form of comparison of performance with an external criterion, an amount of work to be done, right answers to be achieved, authorities to please, attention to capture, or contestants to be beaten. In the process, knowledge of results becomes much less important than success or failure. The purpose of evaluation thus becomes distorted. It is no longer used as important information for the learner, but as a prod to spur performance. It becomes a tool of the helper that is useful for manipulating or coercing the helpee and in the process' is very likely to fail to aid either party.

The effect of any information upon an individual, we have seen, is a function of its peculiar meaning in his private world of thinking and feeling. As a consequence the net effect of evaluation externally applied often boomerangs to destroy the very motivations it sought to produce. Who has not been seriously threatened by some evaluation made in good faith by a well-meaning outsider whose only thought was to spur us onward and upward? The effects of challenge and threat find clear application in respect to evaluation. Originally intended to challenge the subject, evaluation may be seen by him as threatening, and so will interfere with or destroy the very processes of learning it was intended to facilitate. The principles governing competition are also pertinent here, for the intended purpose of most evaluation is to induce the subject to accept the competitive challenge. He will do this only if he thinks he has a chance of winning; if not, the evaluation is unlikely to seduce him into making the effort. The fact that external evaluation is almost always accompanied either overtly or implicitly with judgments of goodness or badness, success or failure, and acceptability or inacceptability further complicates the question. Evaluations resulting in lowered self-esteem are seldom worth the effort. What derogates the self interferes with the process of learning, and so has little place in effective helping relationships.

Knowledge of results of most use to the learner are evaluations made by himself about how things are and where he is with respect to whatever goal he is moving toward. Everyone needs this kind of assessment to provide guidelines for action and information for further acting. Such observations made by the behaver himself are like looking at a road map. One sees where he is, where he still has to go, and what possible routes are available. The map tells him *where* he is, not *what* he is. This is the sort of evaluation most likely to be of use in helping relationships. There is a place for evaluative techniques in the practice of the helping professions, but it is important that persons presuming to help be clearly aware of the dynamics involved.

ACCEPTING RESPONSIBILITY FOR BEHAVIOR

Everyone needs feedback from the world he lives in. This is the data from which meaning is largely discovered. One of the most important sources of such feedback comes from the necessity to live with the consequences of one's acts. There is a limit to the value of consequences, of course. Not much is learned if the net effect of some behavior is the death of the behaver. People need protection from such drastic outcomes, but too much protection can be destructive of personality if not the physical self. One of the current ills of our public schools is the reluctance of teachers and administrators to let children live with the products of their behavior and misbehavior. This can often be observed in what happens to student governments. After much excitement in drawing up constitutions, the student government gets started and confronts the task of making regulations. With high enthusiasm the student body determines upon a new law, only to have it vetoed by the faculty. Somewhat chastened, they go back to try again, only to find that this law, too, is unacceptable. Small wonder, then, that students come to the conclusion that their student government is only a game. This attitude, of course, infuriates the faculty who say: "Look at that! They don't even treat their own student government as though it were serious! They have no sense of responsibility!" So, the brave new government deteriorates into a mockery of what was intended. How did this happen? It happened because the faculty was afraid to let its students make mistakes. They could not let the student body take the consequences of their own behavior and so robbed the whole experience of any important meaning.

Responsibility is learned from being given responsibilities. It is never learned from having them withheld. Like any other subject, it is learned from being given the opportunity to take the consequences of one's own acts in an atmosphere of safety. People cannot learn to be responsible if no one lets them have any responsibility. Failure to give people opportunities to experience responsibility makes them dependent and insecure. To overprotect people from life does them no favors. Quite the contrary, it robs them of the inner resources which can make their lives effective.

When parents and teachers become too fearful of making mistakes, they impose these fears on the children they live with. All too often the net effect produces a vicious circle. Because teachers and parents are afraid to permit children to take the consequences of their behavior, the children have no opportunity to be responsible for themselves. Later, when given responsibility by adults, they are likely to be frightened by it or unable to carry it out successfully. Either way the circle continues. If they reject the responsibility because of their anxiety, adults are likely to exclaim in righteous indignation: "Look there! I wanted to give him the responsibility but he wouldn't even take it!" Or, if the child accepts the responsibility and fails because of lack of practice, this simply demonstrates to the adult how incapable he is of handling responsibility. Either way the obvious thing to do, since the child is so inadequate, is not to give him responsibility. And so, we are back where we began. The effective discovery of personal meaning requires that this merry-go-round be broken by giving persons responsibility and *expecting* them to make mistakes. Anything less is self-defeating. Too much fear of facing the consequences can rob helpees of the very experiences they need to stimulate effective growth.

DISCOVERING MEANING TAKES TIME

It takes time to discover meaning. One has only to recall how long it took to learn some of his most important concepts in order to realize this. It is easy to forget this fact in the desire to help someone else arrive at the same conclusions. The teacher who took 20 or 30 years to learn his subject and who now believes he can teach it to a student in a few weeks or months has embarked on a frustrating course. There is a maximum speed for the discovery of meaning. How fast that will be depends upon a very large number of factors having to do with the nature of the individual, the subject under investigation, the student's previous experience, present circumstances, and so forth. The attempt to push the discovery of meaning too far beyond maximum speed may actually destroy the possibilities of the person's discovery of meaning at all. When people are pushed beyond the point where they believe they can effectively cope with events, the negative effects of threat increasingly enter the picture and destroy the possibilities for effective learning. Generally speaking the more important the meaning to be grasped, the slower the discovery of its significance is likely to be.

One thing required of helpers is the quality of patience. Many a helper has made himself ineffective in his zeal to move too fast in carrying out his functions. Persons being helped are often understandably anxious to get on with finding the solutions to their particular problems. They are often likely, therefore, to put great pressures on helpers to speed things up. It is, of course, incumbent upon helpers to aid in the quickest possible manner; but it is also necessary that helpers have a very clear conception of the goals, purposes, and dynamics of the processes they are engaged in.

There are limits to how much learning can be speeded. There is a vast difference between merely possessing information and being so aware of its meanings that one is able to behave in terms of it. It takes time to explore and discover these meanings. Attempts to bypass the process may only provide an illusion of aid which quickly breaks down when subjected to the test of application.

More often than not, the very best clues to maximum speed are provided by the persons being helped. As already seen in previous chapters, the individual's need for adequacy provides him with the motivation to move with dispatch when the way seems open for him to do so. Persons expert in the helping professions have long ago discovered this fact and have learned to work with, rather than against it, by following the lead of their subjects. They have learned that aiding in the discovery of meaning most efficiently is not so much a question of manipulating people as a matter of putting them in the way of discovering alternatives.

We have been speaking of the discovery of personal meaning. The word "discovery" needs special emphasis, for personal meaning comes about in just that fashion by differentiation of an idea out of the whole. To a very large extent the process of discovering meaning is one of letting it come, of making oneself receptive, and of appreciating new meanings when they appear. This takes time. Discovery of new meanings can even be seriously impeded by working too hard at it. Not unlike Archimedes, almost everyone has had the experience of working very hard at a problem and being unable to find the answer, only to have it come quite suddenly at a moment of relaxation while shaving, sleeping, or thinking of something quite aside from the problem he had been struggling with. Earlier in this chapter we have seen how the experience of threat or the concentration of attention tends to narrow perception to the object of threat or the event being attended to. Under these conditions, differentiations from a broader field of perceptions may be made temporarily impossible. This principle operates quite contrary to that held by some people thoroughly indoctrinated with the importance of work as the sole means to understanding. Apparently, some of our most important discoveries of meaning occur not when we are in the midst of the problem, but when we have laid it aside for a while. Vacations are not only fun—they can even be good for us!

Discovery of meaning comes about through a process of increasing differentiation of experience. Usually this occurs as a consequence of a series of slow steps in which one differentiation is followed by another and another until the new event is learned or its personal meaning discovered. This seems to be true even in those instances where insight has seemed to come about in a sudden flash of recognition—what the French call the "aha moment." Even in such instances, however, what appears to be a sudden flash of meaning usually turns out on closer examination to be but the final differentiation in a whole series of previous ones leading up to the final denouement by almost imperceptible stages. This is somewhat like finding the key piece in a picture puzzle which makes all of the surroundings comprehensible. Without the discoveries preceding it, finding the key piece would have been of little or no consequence whatever. Its extraordinary value is dependent upon the hard work that went before. So it is with the revelation of personal meaning. The fruit only comes when the ground has been plowed, when the seed has been planted, and when conditions favorable for growth have been established. In later chapters the nature of these conditions for facilitating learning will be explored in greater depth.

SELECTED READINGS

Starred entry indicates appearance in Donald L. Avila, Arthur W. Combs, and William W. Purkey, *The Helping Relationship Sourcebook* (Boston: Allyn & Bacon, 1971).

Bruner, J. S. The art of discovery. *Harvard Educational Review*, 1961, **31**, 21–32.

Combs, A. W. Counseling as a learning process. *Journal of Counseling Psychology*, 1954, **1**, 31–36.

Combs, A. W. The myth of competition. *Childhood Education,* 1957, **33,** 264–269.

Combs, A. W. & Taylor, C. The effect of perception and mild degrees of threat on performance. *Journal of Abnormal and Social Psychology,* 1952, **47,** 420–424.

Gibb, J. R. Defensive communication. *The Journal of Communication,* 1961, **11,** 141–148.

Ittelson, W. H. *The Ames demonstrations in perception: Together with an interpretative manual by Adelbert Ames, Jr.* New York: Hofner, 1968.

MacKinnon, D. W. The nature and nurture of creative talent. *American Psychologist,* 1962, **17,** 484–495.

McCandless, B. R. & Castaneda, A. Anxiety in children, school achievement, and intelligence. *Child Development,* 1956, **27,** 379–382.

Mouly, G. J. *Psychology for effective teaching,* (2nd ed.) New York: Holt, Rinehart and Winston, 1968.

Skinner, B. F. Why we need teaching machines. *Harvard Educational Review,* 1961, **31,** 377–398.

* Snygg, D. A cognitive field theory of learning. In W. B. Waetjen and R. R. Leeper (Eds.), *Learning and mental health in the school.* Washington, D.C., Association for Supervision and Curriculum Development, National Education Association, 1966.

7

The Limits of
Man's Becoming

Whatever helpers believe about the limits of human capacity must inevitably affect the goals they seek, the methods they employ, the respect they have for their clients, and even the amount of effort they are likely to expend in trying to be helpful. It is very well to know that such beliefs are desirable. To believe that people are fundamentally able sounds like a nice idea, but is it true? Can one really accept this concept with any degree of assurance that it can be supported by something more than wishful thinking? The answer is yes.

On examining human capacities, two aspects of behavior need to be considered: coping behavior and expressive behavior. One has to do with the ability of the individual to get along effectively in the world he is destined to live in—that is, how intelligently he can behave. This is a matter of efficiency, of being able to cope with life. But coping alone is rarely enough for any of us. We want more than to behave intelligently. We want also to achieve some measure of personal fulfillment from living. This is expressive behavior and represents the second aspect of capacity. It has to do with the person's own satisfactions from life. Capacity for intelligent behavior or coping is dealt with in this chapter. The question of personal fulfillment is reserved for the next. Of course, these aspects are always operating simultaneously and, though we separate them here for purposes of discussion, it should be clearly understood they never operate in isolation but always in dynamic interrelationship.

CAPACITY AND THE PHYSICAL MODEL

When we think about capacity for coping with the world around us, it is natural to do so in terms of our experience with our physical bodies. The physical model is always with us. Looking at ourselves, it seems quite obvious that we are severely limited by the nature of our physiology. There are limits to how far and how fast we can run, and these are likely to become more limited as we grow older. We need only get sick to observe how thoroughly an illness may impair effectiveness. Clearly, we cannot make our bodies do what our physiology will not permit. From such evidence it seems to be true that our capacities are dependent upon the hereditary characteristics with which we were born and the condition we have managed to keep ourselves in to the present. With this model continuously before us, it is not surprising then to assume that the capacity for behavior or misbehavior is limited in the same fashion as the body in which it occurs. This is the concept of human capacities most commonly held for generations. Until very recently, it was also held by most scientists who had studied the problem of human intelligence. Many psychologists are now taking quite a different view of the matter.

One of the most exciting discoveries of this generation is the idea that human capacity is far greater than anything ever thought possible. We are beginning to understand that we have been selling people short. We have believed that people are born with strictly limited capacities for behavior and that there was little or nothing anyone could do about it. No doubt many readers of this book have grown up with the firm belief that intelligence was inherited. Now we know that intelligence is something that can be created. The fascinating and outstanding thing about human beings is *not* their limitations, but their immense capabilities. Let us see why this is so.

It is true that our physical condition controls our physical prowess. But, most of the behaviors required for getting along effectively in the world we live in have little or nothing to do with the state of our physiology. They are matters of thinking, feeling, understanding, perceiving, and what we do or do not communicate to other people.

From perceptual psychology we learn that human behavior is a function of the person's field of meanings at the moment of acting. What controls behavior then is the perceptual field of the behaver. These perceptions, to be sure, occur in the physical body but are limited, if at all, only in small degree by its structure. Behaviors like thinking, loving, hating, wanting, creating, hoping, searching, and understanding or misunderstanding each other are matters of perception. They have little to do with the nature of the physical organism in which they occur. In fact, where the body itself goes and what it does is determined by the field of meanings existing for the self who resides therein. The body is the house in which we live. It is a mistake to regard it as synonomous with the person himself.

The physical body provides the vehicle for much behavior but does not explain it. The airplane is designed to fly. It operates only very awkwardly on the ground and not at all under water. Within the medium it is designed to operate, it has vast potentialities. Looking at a plane parked on the airport ramp, however, we cannot tell by an examination of its structure where it has been, where it is going, or even where it is now. So it is with human behavior. The body provides the machinery to go; where it goes and what it does after that is not decided by the machinery. And, a study of its physiology will not provide us with the understandings about behavior we need. It is true that we must have eyes to see. Thereafter, what is seen, what has been seen, and what will be seen in the future is no longer a question of the structure of the eyes alone. Perception is made possible, not explained, by the organism. The capacity for behavior or misbehavior transcends the organism in which it occurs. The body is not the controller of behavior, but the vehicle in which it occurs and capacity lies not in the structure but in the use to which it is put.

Human Beings Are Overbuilt

We are beginning to discover that the outstanding thing about the human organism is not its limitations but its potentialities. It is characteristically overbuilt! When an engineer builds his bridge, he designs it with a built-in "safety factor"—a degree of sturdiness many times what it is ever expected the structure will need to withstand. People are like that, too. Manifestations of physical effort far beyond normal expectation when required are not at all uncommon. In 1895 a great fire destroyed the Rotunda at the University of Virginia. During the fire students performed an incredible feat in rescuing a statue of Thomas Jefferson from the flames. Here is a description of the event from the *History of the University of Virginia:*

A few minutes before the explosion occured, the fine marble figure of Jefferson by Galt had been lowered by ropes to the level of a table hastily pushed forward to catch it. So great was its weight that this support at once gave way under it; but luckily the fall to the floor did not damage the statue. Turned over on its face, it was rapidly dragged to the door opening on the front stairway, and just as there began the attempt to pull it through this narrow exit, the explosion shook the whole building. "The statue," says Morgan P. Robinson, in his vivid description of the scene, "was gotten out on the staircase, and step by step, it was carried down the western stairs feet foremost. As the base of the statue was eased over each step, it would gather momentum, and gaining speed, would tear off the top edge of the next step, while, under the combined weight of the statue and twenty to thirty of the students, the whole staircase would tremble. It is conservatively estimated that it took from ten to fifteen minutes only to remove the statue from the library to the Lawn." (Vol. IV, page 260, Bruce, 1921)

Morgan P. Robinson, an eyewitness of the event, wrote

It is conservatively estimated that it took from ten to fifteen minutes to remove the statue from the library. Certain it is that it took a gang of workmen with rollers, jacks, and blocks, ropes, etc., half a day to remove it from the lawn to the museum where it was temporarily kept.

The plain fact of the matter is that most of us, in the course of our daily lives, use but a small portion of what is possible for the physical organism. We read every day of extraordinary feats of physical endurance: miners trapped in a shaft, sailors beating their way through a hurricane, athletes playing the game with a broken foot, persons surviving the horrors of a concentration camp. We also admire the courage of our friends as we observe their efforts to overcome adversity, to fight back to health after illness, or overcome what seem like insuperable odds. We recognize that if "the chips are down" we, too, could call on far more than we currently deliver. Indeed, it had to be so throughout man's history. The human organism could only have survived the course of evolution if it had within it the capacities to rise to emergencies.

We have seen in an earlier chapter how the basic need of the organism is a drive for fulfillment on which the physician depends to make us well again. Even in physical matters we have not yet learned how to use the fullness of that continuous force of physical health. American children continue to get taller and stronger. Life expectancy continues to increase. We have eliminated some diseases entirely and we have learned to control others so well that they rarely result in death. In recent times we have even learned to transplant organs from one person to another and still our scientists tell us we have not yet approached the upper limits of what is possible for human health and vigor.

In less physically related behavior the scope of human potentiality is even more extensive. People have been known to read a page at a glance and to perform prodigious feats of memory and perception. Human creativity goes on and on. Scientists continue to discover, painters to paint, and poets to write. There seems literally no limit to the possibilities people possess for thinking, feeling, loving, and behaving. People seem always to be rising to new occasions. It is commonplace in the business world to find that a man's behavior lives up to the promotion to which he has been raised. From everything we can observe, it seems clear that few of us ever remotely approach the potentialities for effective behavior which lie within us. Most of us use but a small fraction of our capabilities.

INTELLIGENCE AS FUNCTIONAL CAPACITY

Intelligence is the capacity of an individual to behave effectively and efficiently. This capacity may be looked at in two ways: ultimate capacity and functional capacity. *Ultimate capacity* is the maximum potential permitted by the physiologic make-up with which the person is born; it is what the individual could deliver if every condition of his life was maximally operative. *Functional capacity* is that behavior which a person can normally deliver when called upon to do so. This concept refers to the person's current capacity for effective and efficient behavior. It is also what we are referring to in this book when we speak of intelligence.

ULTIMATE PHYSICAL CAPACITY

To suggest that human capacities have no limits whatever is, of course, a ridiculous notion. Every animal is ultimately limited by the structure it possesses. Man, too, can do only that which the structure he inherited will permit. Physiologically, these limits are comparatively narrow; psychologically, they are far greater. We need, therefore, to distinguish between physiological and behavioral ultimate capacities. In Fig. 2 we have done this. We have represented the potentials for physical activities by a dot-dash line rising in a fairly smooth curve at one end of the continuum, and leveling off at a height fairly well above the base line. The levels at which people are able to engage in their day-to-day activities

Fig. 2   Diagram of Physical and Behavioral Potentials of Human Beings

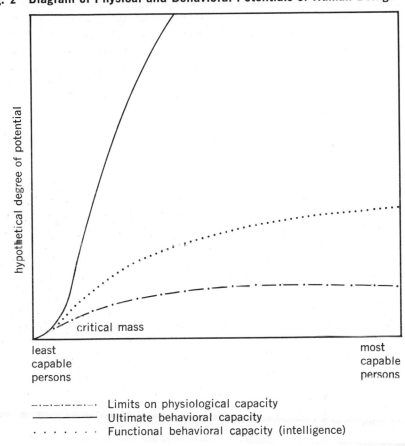

least
capable
persons

most
capable
persons

—·—·—·—·—·   Limits on physiological capacity
——————————   Ultimate behavioral capacity
· · · · · · ·   Functional behavioral capacity (intelligence)

lie somewhere between this line and the base of the chart. While persons may occasionally, under extraordinary circumstances, come close to the ultimate level, usually their physical activities are much lower.

ULTIMATE BEHAVIORAL CAPACITY

Turning to the question of behavioral capacity, we find a curve of quite different shape. There are, of course, a comparatively small number of pitiful souls born into the world with such inadequate physiology or nervous systems as to be severely handicapped behaviorally as well. Some of these, such as the "crib cases" in our institutions for the mentally retarded, are destined to live out their lives as little more than human vegetables. Others, like those less severely limited by brain damage or in-utero or postnatal failures of organ development, manage to cope more or less successfully with life but are destined to limited behavioral success because of their physical problems. These are people whose behavior is seriously impaired by physical deficiencies. They are represented on our diagram at the extreme left of the ultimate behavior curve. For most of us, fortunately, the picture is quite different.

We have described human behavior earlier in this volume as the product of the person's perceptual field. Given the machinery for perceiving, even in fairly limited degrees, the behavior possibilities thereafter are almost astronomical. Once a person possesses eyes or ears that are in reasonably workable condition, the possibilities of what he may see and hear are no longer restricted by physiologic endowment in the same fashion that physical activity is. The situation is like that in a nonlinear rather than a curvilinear equation. We can draw an analogy with the problem of lift in an airplane wing which rises in a smooth curve as speeds increase until it reaches the speed of sound. Once through the sound barrier a new equation is required, and a new set of conditions must be dealt with. This opening up of a new world of conditions is not uncommon in physical science. It is represented, for example, in the critical mass required for an atomic explosion. Up to a point the atomic pile reacts in smooth predictable fashion until the critical mass is reached; then a whole new set of conditions comes into being. Something like this is involved in the question of ultimate capacity for behavior. Given the critical mass to make perceiving possible, what the organism makes of it after that is no longer a function of physical conditions. To represent this diagrammatically, ultimate capacity to behave is represented in Fig. 2 by the dotted line which begins to rise smoothly to the critical mass, then zooms off the chart to heights unknown. Almost literally, perception transcends the organism in which it occurs.

INTELLIGENCE: THE CAPACITY FOR EFFECTIVE, EFFICIENT BEHAVIOR

Intelligence, as we have used it in this volume, refers to the person's functional capacity—his ability to behave effectively and efficiently. It refers to what behavior a person can deliver when he needs to. This functional capacity is represented in Fig. 2 by a solid line which begins at a very low level for those persons severely handicapped physiologically at the left-hand side of this diagram and rises to the heights achieved by the most brilliant persons on the right-hand side. With the most handicapped, at the origin of the curve, functional intelligence is severely limited by physiologic factors, but the curve rapidly outstrips physiologic capacity. It never remotely approaches ultimate behavioral capacity, however, even for the most brilliant persons. Because of the almost limitless possibilities for human perception, none of us ever achieves more than a very small portion of what is possible for us. The matter of a person's ultimate behavorial capacity is, therefore, a matter of little or no practical significance. No doubt there are limits to ultimate behavioral capacity, and someday we may discover what they are. When we do, we will no doubt also discover that these limits differ from person to person. But, since none of us ever remotely approaches these limits, what does it matter? The ultimate behavioral possibilities with which we are born are, for most of us, a purely academic question.

Our use of the term "intelligence" as synonymous with functional capacity is congruent with current thinking of many psychologists. They have not always defined intelligence in these terms, however. Originally, psychologists used the term to refer to ultimate capacity. Using it in this way, intelligence was regarded as fixed and immutable, as something derived primarily from one's heredity and open only in limited degree to change from environmental forces. Since the human organism is so vastly overbuilt, and ultimate capacity is so seldom ever achieved by anyone, psychologists have increasingly defined intelligence in terms of functional capacity. This is a much more relevant and useful concept for the helping professions. A person's current capacity for effective and efficient behavior is what most people mean by "intelligent behavior" in daily communication. It is also what intelligence tests are designed to measure. Its production is the goal of education and of the helping professions.

Defined as the capacity for effective and efficient behavior, intelligence is not an hereditary problem nor is it a static, unchangeable potential. Rather, it represents a comparatively low level of achievement with vast possibilities for improvement. It is interesting that this was the position taken by Alfred Binet, originator of the first intelligence tests. He declared:

> Some recent philosophers appear to have given their support to the deplorable verdict that intelligence of an individual is a fixed quantity— we must protest and act against this brutal pessimism—a child's mind is like a field in which an expert farmer has advised a change in the method of cultivation with the result that in place of desert land we now have a harvest. It is in this particular sense, the one which is significant,

that we say that the intelligence of children may be increased. One increases that which constitutes the intelligence of a school child, namely, the capacity to learn, to improve with instruction. (pages 54 and 55, Binet, 1909)

Unfortunately, Binet's warning was largely overlooked by many psychologists for a good many years after his death, and it is only recently that intelligence is once again being regarded as a broader human function capable of change. J. P. Guilford, for example, in his studies on the nature of intelligence, describes it as made up of at least one hundred and twenty qualities. Of these, he tells us that our schools and our intelligence tests have only been dealing with eight!

We will not stop here to review all the research which leads to the conclusion that capacity for behavior can be created. The evidence is so extensive and varied as to call for a book in its own right, which J. McV. Hunt has already done superbly well in a volume called *Intelligence and Experience*. We heartily recommend this book to readers interested in pursuing the evidence for intelligence change in greater detail. In concluding his scholarly review of the data, Dr. Hunt has this to say:

> It is highly unlikely that any society has developed a system of child rearing and education that maximizes the potential of the individuals which compose it. Probably no individual has ever lived whose full potential for happy intellectual interest and growth has been achieved. Various bits of the evidence reviewed hint that if the manner in which encounters with the environment foster the development of intellectual interest and capacity were more fully understood, it might be possible to increase the average level of intelligence within the population substantially. In view of the interaction between genotype and environment, it would be probable that individual differences would be increased, and that the biggest gains would occur in those genotypes with the highest hypothetical potential. There would be, of course, a long step between learning how to effect changes in child rearing and getting them adopted by the culture, but learning how is the first step. The hope of increasing the average level of intelligence by proper manipulation of children's developmental encounters with their environments, a hope which becomes reasonable with the evidences surveyed here and with relinquishing the assumptions of fixed intelligence and predetermined development, provides a challenge of the first order. It has great implications for human welfare as the growth of technology in western culture demands a higher and higher percentage of people who can manipulate symbols and solve complex problems. In this challenge the theory of man's nature and the fate of his welfare are obviously intertwined.[1]

1. J. McV. Hunt—INTELLIGENCE AND EXPERIENCE Copyright © 1961 The Ronald Press Company, New York (p. 346).

The importance of this concept for workers in the helping professions can hardly be overestimated. The idea that human capacity for behavior is not so fixed and immutable as we have thought in generations past, but that it is open to change and development is a concept of tremendous significance. It means the potentialities of most people extend far beyond anything we have ever dreamed.

WHAT INTELLIGENCE TESTS MEASURE

In the light of our discussion of the capacities for intelligent behavior, what is it that intelligence tests measure? For many years these tests have been used for the determination of human potentialities and are often regarded by the public and some users of tests as infallible indications of a person's possibilities. Most of the early intelligence tests were manufactured by persons operating in terms of the generally held belief that intelligence was quite static. Intelligence was regarded as a general capacity of the organism, primarily obtained from heredity, which established an upper limit on intelligent behavior. People might fall short of their possibilities; they could never rise above them. The early test-makers tried to measure this ultimate potential.

Since ultimate capacity is not open to direct measurement, the intelligence test-makers had to find another way of arriving at their estimates. They did this by making an assumption that all persons taking the test had had an equal opportunity to learn the material it contained. If everyone had an equal opportunity to learn the material, it was believed, then those persons who did better must have already possessed a greater innate capacity. Great pains were taken by some of the best test-makers to include in their tests only those items which were as common and as nearly culture-free as possible. Others, unfortunately, were not so careful, and the tests they produced deviated widely from the original assumption. In any event, operating on the equal-opportunity assumption, test-makers were really producing achievement tests, or tests constructed to measure how much of a given body of material a person had acquired.

Over the years since the great surge of popularity of these tests, we have come to understand that the basic assumption on which they are constructed is no longer tenable. It is totally unacceptable in the light of our discussion in this volume on several grounds. We would, for example, deny the fundamental assumption of equal opportunity. If behavior is truly a function of the private world of perceptions for each individual, there can never be common experience for any two people even in the same externally observed situation. Even in a family of identical twins, apparently treated identically, twin A's experience is largely created by twin B and twin B's is supplied by twin A! We have also maintained in this chapter that ultimate potentiality, at least at this stage of our knowledge, is so vast and its limits so ill-defined as to place it beyond current reach of measurement. Even if this were not the case, however, the attempt to measure ultimate human potentiality would not interest us much because the matter is essentially academic insofar as the helping professions are concerned. If no one ever comes close to ultimate potential, we do not need to know what it is. What interests us, practically, is a person's functional capacity for two reasons: It is a far more useful concept, and there is something we can do about it.

Although we have rejected the basic premise of intelligence tests, it should not be supposed by any means that such tests are without value. As tests of achievement, they can have real value in telling us where a person is with respect to a given body of information. In the degree to which they have been carefully constructed, they can also give us an indication of a person's current level of functioning. That, of course, is valuable information. We have seen that intelligent behavior is a function of the extent, richness, and availability of perceptions in the perceptual field. Intelligence tests can sample that field and give us an estimate of a person's current status in respect to whatever it is that the test samples. Since each test samples what its makers thought was important, we shall, of course, have to ask ourselves whether those matters are appropriate for the purposes we have in mind. Having settled that, we shall also have to determine whether the sampling is adequately done. After that, there still remains the question whether the persons taking the tests are truly free to deliver the sample at the time and place of testing.

DETERMINANTS OF INTELLIGENCE

Given a reasonably adequate physiology to start with, what, then, will the capacity for intelligent behavior depend upon? It will depend upon two things: the meanings a person possesses and his freedom to use them.

In an earlier publication, Combs has stated: "How intelligently a person is able to behave at any moment will be dependent upon the richness, extent and availability of meanings in his perceptual field." This is to say that the capacity to behave effectively and efficiently requires, in the first place, that the behaver possess the necessary or appropriate meanings for the situation which confronts him. A person with a rich and extensive field of perceptions will have vastly more possibilities for behavior than the person whose field of meaning is meager. The richer the field of meanings, the greater the potential for effective behavior. But mere possession of a rich and extensive perceptual field alone is not enough. It is also necessary that meanings be available for use when they are needed. One is likely to appear stupid to himself and to others if he cannot recall a person's name when the occasion arises. Every student knows that in the final analysis his intelligence is measured by what he is able to deliver on the examination. In the remainder of this chapter, let us examine some of the determiners of the breadth and depth of meaning. We shall leave the question of psychological freedom for the following chapter.

What factors determine the extent and richness of an individual's perceptual field? In earlier chapters of this volume we have already considered three very important determiners of personal meaning: the effects of need, the self-concept, and the existing field of meanings. Let us take a moment to review the major effects of these before adding to the list of meaning determiners.

EFFECT OF NEED

The need for fulfillment exerts a selective effect upon all the individual's experience, and so determines in large degree the kinds of perceptions likely to exist in his perceptual field. People perceive what they need to perceive. Because the operation of human need is insatiable, people are continuously searching for means to achieve its satisfaction. The mere fact of searching is quite likely to contribute to the richness of the field of meanings.

The selective effect of need, however, is a two-edged sword. The same search for need satisfaction which contributes to enriching the field can also result in restricting it. We have seen how the experience of threat, for example, may produce tunnel vision and so concentrate the person's attention that he is not open to wider experiences. This is a matter of great concern to persons in the helping professions especially, for many of the persons they seek to help either are, or have been, more or less seriously threatened. The effects of need may thus contribute to the extent and richness of perception; or, because of its attention-focusing power, it may have the reverse effect, blinding persons to experience and making it impossible to take full advantage of opportunities offered them.

THE SELF-CONCEPT

Because the need of the organism is always to achieve maximum enhancement, the self-concept exerts a most important determining effect upon the richness and extent of meaning. Like the effect of need, the self-concept may open whole new worlds of experience for individuals. It may also close off great areas of meaning, depending upon the nature of the self-definitions involved and the circumstances to which people are exposed.

EFFECT OF PRIOR MEANINGS

The need of the organism to maintain and enhance its organization produces a field of meaning with a high degree of stability in which new meanings are interpreted in light of what has gone before. In this way a selective effect is imposed upon new experience which could result in vastly enriching the field. On the other hand, existing meanings may have the effect of restricting possibilities by denying or distorting meanings antagonistic to those already in existence; or, by focusing attention on the further development of existing meanings, they may produce such preoccupation as to preclude paying attention to a wider field of events.

AGE

Another factor determining the breadth and depth of meaning is age. Developing a field of meanings takes time. Other things being equal, older persons, having experienced more, are likely to have more extensive fields of meaning. People have to have lived long enough to have had some kinds of experiences, especially those dependent in sequential fashion on earlier ones. Despite the doubts of young people, there really is some advantage in experience. The mere fact of living longer means more possibilities for experience but, of course, does not guarantee them. As we observed in the paragraph above, existing meanings in a person's field may restrict his further possibilities for perceiving. This often happens when older persons become unable to accept new meanings, and may produce the generation gap so distressing to young and old alike.

PHYSICAL CONDITION

We have already observed earlier in this chapter that the ultimate capacity of some unfortunate individuals may be seriously impaired by inadequate physiology. Fortunately, this seems to be the case for comparatively few. However, the state of the physical organism also has its effects upon functional capacity, even in the case of persons whose ultimate capacities are quite sufficient for living effective lives. The acuity of a person's sight, hearing, touch, smell, and taste certainly have their effects upon the nature of his experience. These are our "windows on the world"—the machinery through which interaction may occur.

The physical vehicle we ride around in also has its effect upon meanings through the feedback it produces in the reactions of other people. The experiences of a beautiful young woman are quite different from those of her less attractive sisters. Similarly, the physical prowess which makes a young man a football hero may bring him vastly richer meanings than those he might have had without his magnificent physical condition. Feedback of a less happy nature is received by adolescents with acne or handicapped persons. Their physical conditions impede full participation in the life around them and distort other people's reactions to them.

Other aspects of physical health may also have their effects, although not perhaps so obviously at first glance. Whatever reduces body vigor may impair the possibilities of experience. Meanings are acquired from interaction. Whatever impairs the possibilities of interaction, then, may interfere with the discovery of meaning. Because a sick and lethargic child does not get involved in school or play with his peers, the meanings he develops may be limited by this fact. Almost everyone has had the experience of feeling "too tired to care" or so ill that all he wanted to do was sleep. So, almost anything that reduces the body's readiness and capability for involvement may reduce experience. These reducers include such things as malnutrition, focal infections, illnesses of various kinds, glandular disturbances, injuries, or the like. Any of the physical factors we have been mentioning may reduce or modify the amount and kinds of meanings which an individual may possess. It should be clear, however, that this is not necessarily so. Some persons with severe impediments, like Helen Keller, for example, manage to develop breadth and depth in their field of meanings despite their physiologic limitations.

It is even conceivable that some handicaps might enrich the field of meanings, making a person more sensitive in some ways than his more fortunate fellows.

OPPORTUNITY

The extent of a person's meanings are affected by every aspect of environment, particularly by the people with whom he comes in contact. The meanings existing for people in the North and South are by no means the same. People who live in the mountains, the plains, the seashore, the river valleys, the desert, or piney woods have different kinds of experiences and different kinds of meanings as a consequence. The interactions people have with the world around them and the people in it create private worlds of meaning and feeling and, in turn, determine the intelligence with which people may operate.

The effect of opportunity on personal meaning begins as early as life itself and continues as long as a person may live. Because of the selective effect of existing meanings upon subsequent ones, the earliest development of meanings is particularly crucial in the development of intelligence. In recent years we have become keenly aware of the plight of many children raised in poverty-striken areas of the nation where there is little opportunity to broaden experience beyond the deadly, daily grind of keeping body and soul together. Many of these children have had no opportunity to experience even the most common events in the lives of their more fortunate fellows—like seeing a cow, using a telephone, learning to swim, riding a bicycle, writing a letter, or counting money. Millions of children raised in such circumstances grow up with sadly restricted meanings and are inadequate to cope with the world in which they have to move. This often results in a dreadful vicious circle continually corroborating itself. With inadequate perceptual fields to cope with the complexities of life, such children are often doomed to failure unless they are very lucky. Because they are stupid, they cannot cope with life. Because they cannot cope, they continue to be deprived and produce for their children in turn the same dreary existence which so warped them in the first place. With a new awakening of conscience, we are beginning to find ways of breaking into this vicious cycle. Federal, state, and privately supported programs designed to cure the ills of poverty, to improve education, to provide employment, and to eliminate the degradation of prejudice are increasingly being instituted to enrich the lives of children caught in these traps. In doing so, we are also increasing the capacity of children for more intelligent, effective, and efficient behavior in the future.

Some most significant research has been carried out in recent years by psychologists investigating the effects of enriched experience on the growth and development of intelligence in very young children. In one of the most important of these, Ira Gordon taught new mothers how to stimulate their babies by using ordinary materials which might be found in even the most poverty-stricken home. He was able to show at the end of a year that these efforts did, indeed, raise the intelligence levels of the children as measured by standard tests. In working with older retarded children, S. Kirk demonstrated that important gains in intelligence levels could be brought about for many children originally diagnosed as mentally retarded by means of broadening opportunities provided by experience in nursery school. The work of these researchers, corroborated by that of many others, leaves little room to doubt that the provision of enriched opportunity can create markedly improved capacities for effective behavior.

The meanings one has are functions of his opportunities. Without opportunity, meanings may be restricted or distorted so that effective behavior becomes well nigh impossible. The principle is nicely illustrated in the report of a colleague about his experience working with children from upper-middle-class homes compared with those in a poverty-stricken slum area. One of the problems he presented to these children went as follows: "You are all alone in an empty room of a deserted house. Up against the ceiling out of your reach is a balloon with a ten-dollar bill attached to it. How would you get it down?" Many of the children from upper-middle-class homes, he reported, had great difficulty in finding a solution to the problem and many gave up with the problem still unsolved. On the other hand, children from slum neighborhoods frequently solved the problem with great dispatch. "I'd break the window," they said, "and throw the glass at the balloon!" For these children, windows were not inviolate. They were something to be broken if need be. For the upper-middle-class child, windows had quite a different meaning which did not make them available for solving the problem.

The primary purpose of schooling is to provide children with opportunities to gain deeper and broader meanings of the world in which they live. Children deprived of schooling or given inadequate schooling have far less opportunity to develop the richness and extent of meanings necessary to live fully effective and efficient lives. The development of meaning is a problem of interaction between the individual and his world. Whatever reduces the opportunities for such interaction must have its effects upon the individual's functional capacity.

EFFECTS OF VALUES AND GOALS

The extent of a person's meanings will also be determined by the interests he develops and the values and goals he seeks or avoids. The things one believes to be important have vital effects upon capacities to perceive. They select what further perceptions are likely to occur. A businessman known to one of the authors once drove himself to the brink of ruin for failure to decide what was important. He had a small machine shop. After World War II, when the Government was "tooling up" the armed forces again, hundreds of contracts were available for all kinds of things the Army and Navy needed. This was a golden opportunity. Time after time he said yes to the contracts offered him and then scurried around to get the machinery to produce them. At the end of the year he had doubled his plant capacity. He was tooled up to make hundreds of needed items. But soon the contracts began to run out and all those machines had to be kept running. He was tooled up in all directions without rhyme or reason and had to dash about trying to find contracts whereby he could keep his machines running. The poor fellow exhausted himself and finally landed in a mental hospital while his business sank into bankruptcy.

The goals we seek and the values we ascribe to, have inevitable effects in determining the nature of the field of meanings and, thus, behavior. The decision to go to college, for example, opens a whole new world of possibilities for the student on the one hand; on the other, it closes doors and makes certain kinds of experiences more unlikely. The decision to enter a college of engineering makes it very unlikely that the student, if he is successful, will find himself happy as a migrant farm laborer. Similarly, the decision to become a fisherman takes a man out to sea. This will bring him very different kinds of experiences than those of his brother who decides to become a coal miner. People's interests will affect the extent and character of meanings they acquire. Persons interested in baseball go to baseball games; those interested in art go to museums. These interests even determine such simple matters as the pages one looks at in a newspaper.

LIMITS OF CHANGE IN CAPACITY FOR EFFECTIVE BEHAVIOR

The variations in the breadth and depth of meanings people possess vary tremendously. At one end of the scale is the restricted perceptual field of the severely mentally retarded child who spends his life in the fetal position in which he was born. Further up the scale are the people who manage to "get by." That, in itself, is no mean feat in the kind of world we live in. The richness and extent of meanings needed just to safely navigate in a city like New York or Los Angeles, for example, are considerable. Most people, somehow, manage to develop meanings taking them far beyond such minimal levels, and some become truly remarkable. At the top of the scale the perceptual fields of some of our most gifted people are often so rich and extensive that they can range over vast areas of human understanding.

The breadth and depth of meanings for any person is probably in a continual process of change. The perceptual fields of some become more fertile and extensive throughout their lives. For others, the growth of meaning seems to grow by fits and starts. For still others, unhappily, the field of meaning may become less rich and extensive with time.

A glance back to the determiners of effective behavior we have been discussing in the last few pages will make it clear that all of these, but one (time), are open to considerable amounts of change. One can do little to manipulate age. That usually has to take care of itself. The rest of the determiners, however, lend themselves to manipulation. The capacity for effective behavior can be created, and these are the variables through which it can be accomplished. They are also the subject matter of the helping professions, the dynamics by which the professions can hope to reach their objectives.

To this point we still do not know the upper levels to which intelligence can grow. Whatever those upper limits are, the attainment of them will, almost certainly, be brought about as a consequence of our learning how to deal with the determiners of behavior we have listed above and such others as we may discover in the future. We are still a long way from knowing how to create intelligence with skill and certainty. In our discussion of these determiners, some of the guidelines are apparent, however. There is much we can do with what we already know. In addition, we need to press forward the frontiers of our knowledge. A great deal more research is necessary to help us better understand these determiners and to find effective ways of putting that knowledge to work.

One place we can look for clues to that research is in the lives of gifted persons. In the past, we have been accustomed to looking at such people as happy accidents of heredity. Many persons in the helping professions spend much time and energy trying to find these people and provide them with special nourishment and stimulation. If it is true that intelligence can be created, however, these are no happy accidents. Rather, they represent our crowning achievement—the people with whom we have already been especially successful! Our problem is not to find and coddle them. It is necessary to find out how we produced them so that we can set about producing more of them as rapidly as we can! The study of their growth and development should provide us with important clues to how we may repeat the process with others.

There is another side to this coin. Determiners not only control what is possible, they also limit possibilities. In this discussion of intelligence, we have discounted the severe limitation of heredity thought to govern behavior by previous generations but it should not be supposed that there are no limits at all to concern us. Men are always hindered by ignorance and indifference. Failure to use the information we have can result in limiting intelligence severely. Despite our current knowledge about the effects of deprivation on the children in our ghettos, for example, thousands of children continue to grow up handicapped by their experiences. This happens not because we are unaware of some of the things which must be done; it happens because we are unwilling to do what must be done.

Even with the best of intentions, however, the determiners would still exert a limiting effect upon intelligence. A child growing up with a restricting self-concept is just as severely limited as though he had been born that way. We have also seen that, once established, the self-concept tends to resist change and that the circular effect it exerts upon selection of perceptions causes it to corroborate itself. Similarly, restrictions upon the full development of the physical organism, impoverished environments and lack of opportunities, inhibiting goals and values, or the effects of threat upon perception can all produce seriously limiting effects upon intelligence. What is more, these limitations may be so very difficult to eliminate that we do not have the time, energy, or economic wherewithal to deal with them. There are indeed, limits upon the growth of intelligence, and functional limits can be as formidable as hereditary ones. They have the advantage, however, that being functional there is something we can do about them.

If intelligence is a function of the breadth and depth of meaning, in order to create intelligence we need to expand and deepen the individual's perceptual field. To do this effectively, it will be necessary to deal with both aspects of the problem. Helpers will need to find ways of reducing or eliminating the limiting effects of determiners on the one hand and ways of maximizing their positive contributions on the other. This is a matter of learning and teaching. For the learner, it is a question of enriching and expanding his field of personal meaning. For the helper, it is a task of creating conditions, of providing the kinds of experiences that make enrichment possible. In later chapters we will look more closely at how this is accomplished.

SOME IMPLICATIONS FOR THE HELPING PROFESSIONS

We began this chapter by calling attention to the research finding that effective helpers are persons who have strong beliefs that their clients, patients, and students are essentially able. From our explorations in this chapter it would appear that those concepts are not unfounded. Capacities for effective behavior are far greater than most persons suspect. Better still for the helping professions, the determiners of capacity lie to a very great extent within our control. This is a very exciting idea for the helping professions. It means that professional helpers are not mere victims of human intelligence, but creators of it! It means that clients, students, and patients have tremendous capacities for growth and health, and that there is something that can be done for almost everyone.

It makes a great deal of difference whether one approaches his job believing that it is only a holding operation with little or no likelihood of success, or that it is one of vast possibilities. For generations many teachers have believed, for example, that there was really very little they could do to increase a child's capacities. The beliefs they had about the children they worked with severely limited their expectations both for the children and for themselves. All too often, both parties fulfilled those expectations. No one enjoys feeling futile. A point of view about human capacities which places many of the controls within the teacher's hands therefore opens whole new vistas. They can approach their jobs with hope and rest assured that what they do is significant. For teachers sincerely committed to their professions, this knowledge can prove a great challenge and satisfaction. For teachers not so committed, it can be deeply threatening. It means that failures cannot be blithely charged off to heredity or to what someone else should have done. One's effectiveness in the profession is laid at his own doorstep.

Effective helpers will need to be knowledgeable about the determiners of capacity we have been discussing in this chapter and elsewhere. These factors will become the tools of their trade. The success or failure of counselors, teachers, nurses, social workers, and others in the professions will be in part dependent upon their success or failure in dealing with them. Helping people develop richer and more extensive fields of meaning will make it possible for them to cope more effectively with life and to behave in more intelligent fashion. But the mere possession of such a field is not enough. There must also be freedom to use the meanings people have. This is the problem of the next chapter.

SELECTED READINGS

Starred entries indicate appearance in whole or in part in Donald L. Avila, Arthur W. Combs, and William W. Purkey, *The Helping Relationship Sourcebook* (Boston: Allyn & Bacon, 1971).

Bettelheim, B. Where self begins. *Child and Family*, 1968, **7**, 5–12.

Birney, R. C., Burdick, H. & Teevan, R. C. *Fear of failure.* New York: Van Nostrand, 1969.

Bugental, J. F. T. (Ed.) *Challenges of humanistic psychology,* New York: McGraw Hill, 1967.

* Combs, A. W. Intelligence from a perceptual point of view. *Journal of Abnormal and Social Psychology,* 1952, **47,** 662–673(b).

Getzels, J. W. & Jackson, P. W. *Creativity and intelligence: Explorations with gifted students.* New York: Wiley, 1962.

* Gordon, I. New conceptions of children's learning and development. In W. B. Waetjen and R. R. Leeper (Eds.). *Learning and mental health in the school.* Washington, D.C., Association for Supervision and Curriculum Development, National Education Association, 1966, 49–73.

Herman, Sister Mary. Self concept of the Negro child. *Catholic School Journal,* 1966, **66,** 62–63.

Hunt, J. McV. *Intelligence and experience.* New York: Ronald Press, 1961.

Hunt, J. McV. The implications of changing ideas on how children develop intellectually. *Children,* 1964, **11,** 83–91.

Kvareceus, W. C. Poverty, education and race relations. In W. C. Kvareceus, J. S. Gibson & T. J. Curtin (Eds.) *Poverty, education and race relations: Studies and proposals.* Boston: Allyn and Bacon, 1967, 3–10.

* Purkey, W. W. *Self concept and school achievement.* Englewood Cliffs, N.J.: Prentice-Hall, 1970.

8

Freedom and Self-Actualization

How well people will be able to find fulfillment in the lives they lead will be dependent in part upon possession of an adequate field of meanings. This will provide the potential for effective behavior. By itself, an extensive field of meanings, however, is still not enough. A person must have, in addition, the freedom to make the most efficient possible use of his meanings. Sometimes this freedom may be impaired by forces outside the person in his physical environment, or hindrances may be created intentionally or accidentally by people. More often, restrictions upon freedom have their origins within individuals themselves. This is psychological freedom having to do with the extent to which a person is open to the development of new meanings and how able he is to make fullest use of his field of meanings. A very large part of the work of persons in the helping professions will be devoted to assisting others to free themselves from these internal impediments.

The question of intelligence and psychological health are often spoken of as if they existed at opposite ends of a continuum. Critics of education, for example, have sometimes asked, "Do you want to educate for knowledge or adjustment?" The attempt to separate these matters in such an either-or fashion can do much damage to our understanding of the problems of human beings. Truly intelligent behavior cannot be so neatly segregated. It requires both the capacity to cope with life and the freedom to operate effectively. Knowing and feeling are closely interrelated, and knowledge without personal relevance is unlikely to be very effective. In recent times many scholars have devoted their attention to the study of self-actualization, what man could become if he were maximally free to use his potentialities to the utmost. They ask, "What would such a person be like?" and "What can we do to help people achieve these exalted ends?" Though scholars have approached the study of self-actualization from different orientations, there is general agreement that people with much psychological freedom are also most likely to have attained high levels of self-actualization. Three factors, in particular, play important roles in the determination of psychological freedom and self-actualization: self-esteem, openness to experience, and the capacity for identification.

SELF–ESTEEM

The basic tenet of democracy has been stated in these terms: "When men are free, they can find their own best ways." But what is a free man? A man with a full belly? A man without problems? A man with no pressures? Free to do as he pleases? When such things are achieved, a man is still only part way there. People need more; they need the freedom to *become*. Scientists who have written about the nature of self-actualization are generally agreed that one characteristic of such fortunate persons is the possession of a high degree of self-esteem. They see themselves in essentially positive ways.

It would be hard, indeed, to overestimate the importance of a positive view of self for effective behavior. The self is the center of a person's existence, his frame of reference for dealing with life. Persons who approach their problems with an air of "can do" are already far ahead of those who begin with a "can't do" attitude, expecting defeat. With a positive view of self one can dare, be open to experience, and confront the world with open arms and quiet certainty. Negative views of self may lock a person in a vicious circle in which his efforts to deal with life are always too little, too late, or inappropriate.

Bolstering Effect of a Positive View of Self

The self is the most important instrument we own with which to cope with the world. Whatever its nature the self-concept goes along. Even a poor, ragged, unhappy self must be dragged by its owner into everything he does. A positive self has vital effects on a person's efficiency on the one hand and his freedom to confront new matters on the other. Having a high degree of self-esteem is like owning a stout ship. With a sturdy vessel under foot one may go sailing far from shore. When one has doubts about his ship and concern about its seaworthiness, he must play it safe and stay close to harbor. Self-esteem is like that. It is a firm foundation from which to deal with the problems of life with security and sureness.

Free people, the studies show, see themselves as liked, wanted, acceptable, able, dignified, and worthy. Feeling this way about themselves, they are also likely to have deep feelings of personal security which make it much easier to confront the emergencies of life. They feel about themselves that they are people of dignity and worth, and they *behave* as though they are. Rogers has pointed out that one of the characteristics of healthy personalities is a trust in the organism. With greater feelings of certainty about themselves, people can trust their impulses more. They experience their selves as trustworthy and dependable.

A positive view of self provides a great inner strength from which a person may deal more effectively with the exigencies of life. Whatever makes the self smaller or meaner, on the other hand, undermines confidence and produces fear and withdrawal. Even an event so traumatic as war is dealt with in terms of what a person has come to feel about himself by the time the event occurs. H. B. English, for example, speaking of the behavior of the people of Coventry during World War II says:

> Rich and poor alike were reduced to a common level. Now, who, do you suppose most steadily endured the deprivation of destroyed homes, of loss of the conveniences of modern life—heat, light, running water? *Mass Observation*, a sort of public opinion poll which asks no questions but seeks to record what people say in public places, was on the spot to find out. It was the desperately poor people who were driven to panic by loss of their tragically meager belongings; the well to do, though they had lost so much more, had far greater fortitude in the emergency. (See H. B. English's *Dynamics of Child Development*, page 193.)

The persons with a long history of success contributing to positive views of self were best able to cope with trauma. Those with a history of failure were unable to handle emergency situations.

The assurance-producing character of a positive view of self can also be observed in the behavior of children with positive and negative views of self as they confront the problem of what to do about poor schoolwork. When examiners asked children with positive views of self and history of success in schoolwork, "What can you do about it if you have a bad grade in spelling?" (arithmetic, social studies, or whatever) the children suggested all kinds of possibilities: "Study harder," "Ask my teacher," "Ask my mother to help me," "Practice," "Try to find out what I'm doing wrong," etc. When the same questions were asked of children with negative self-concepts and histories of failure, the reply was, almost without exception, "Nothing!" They regarded the matter as hopeless, the problem insoluble.

People with high self-esteem are also more likely to be independent, autonomous agents. They do not need to go with the crowd. Because they have "trust in the organism," they can stand on their own two feet. They resist the surrender of integrity involved in dependent relationships. Their dependence is on themselves. If the self is sufficiently strong, there is no need to rely on the decisions of others when such reliance is not appropriate. Strong, positive feelings about self make possible independence and autonomy on the one hand and effective cooperation on the other. The man with high self-esteem maintains his independence. Because he believes in himself he can move in directions of his own choosing when the group or society are following a course he does not approve of. He feels no need to slavishly follow group wishes to attain fulfillment. With trust in himself he can afford to depart from group norms and ignore group pressures. The same feelings of self-esteem also make it possible for him to be a more effective cooperator when that is appropriate, for he can enter such relationships without a feeling of self-surrender. Cooperation, for him, is no capitulation of self, but a self-investment, a manifestation of psychological freedom.

THE RICH GET RICHER

It is characteristic that the self-concept tends to corroborate itself. The person with a positive self is thus in the most happy position of having his efforts to deal with life reinforce the positive feelings he already possesses. The feeling of "can-ness" loads the dice in favor of its owner and makes success more likely. It is notorious, for example, in the field of athletics that once a record has been broken by someone it is quickly equalled by others. Coach Darrell Mudra, one of the nation's most successful college football coaches, reports an amusing example of the effect of a positive view in the following incident:

> We had a wrestler at Adams State College when I was there who was confused about the quality of his opponent. There were two boys named Martinez in one of our meets. One was a great wrestler and one was a

poor wrestler. The one our boy was wrestling was really the good one, but he thought he was wrestling the poor one. Our boy was just an ordinary, average wrestler but he went out there and tore the boy up. After the match, we rushed down to the locker room to congratulate him. He was standing on the bench there and we were telling him about how great it was. He was really puzzled. When he finally became aware of what had happened, he fell off the bench! Now, if he had really known, I am sure he would have been pinned in the first period. But because he didn't know he performed at a level that was not thought possible. Think of how surprised the other wrestler was to have this boy come out there like a tiger! [1]

We have already observed how the experience of challenge or threat is a question of feelings of personal adequacy. People who see themselves in positive ways live in a less threatened world, and more of their experience is likely to seem challenging to them. They can risk involvement. They can dare to try. They may even find joy in the confrontation of problems. They can enter into effective dialogue with life. In his studies of self-actualizing persons, A. H. Maslow has observed that such people show much more expressive behavior than coping behavior. That is to say, much more of their behavior is directed toward simply being who and what they are than designed to "deal" with life. What is more, the expressive behavior of such people is much more effective in coping with life than the coping behavior of their less fortunate fellows. Such a relationship with the world is the very essence of psychological freedom. It is also the essence of creativity. We have already observed that a positive view of self makes daring and personal involvement more likely. These things, with the tendency to expressive behavior which Maslow reports, lie at the very heart of creative behavior. Persons with positive views of themselves can afford to be free spirits. Indeed, anything less would be a negation of themselves. Creative is what they are; it is not a problem to be worked at.

Persons with positive views of self tend to behave in ways that result in experiences of success with the world and with the people in it. The feedback they get from the world in turn makes them far more likely to be happy and effective in their personal and public lives. This success serves to build a person's feelings about himself still higher. The circular effect is equally true in the opposite direction. Persons feeling inadequate

1. Reprinted by permission of Dr. Mudra from an original manuscript in preparation at the time this volume went to press. Dr. Mudra has recently joined the faculty at Western Illinois University, Macomb, Ill.

behave in ways which tend to confirm their own inadequacy. People who see themselves in positive ways have a vast advantage in life and far more possibilities to live happy and effective lives than their fellows.

In summary, a positive view of self contributes to psychological freedom. It provides its possessor with a firm platform from which to deal with life, and makes more likely his effective and efficient interaction with it. What contributes to self-esteem makes intelligent behavior more likely; what destroys or "derogates self is stultifying and stupefying."

A positive view of self is learned; and being learned, it can be taught. It comes about as a consequence of successful experience with the world. People learn that they are liked, wanted, accepted, and persons of dignity and integrity because they have been treated as such. They see themselves as able because they have experienced success. Self-esteem is a consequence of successful living. Lack of self-esteem, on the other hand, is a product of failure, a falling short. Generally speaking, whatever undermines self-esteem or self-integrity interferes with psychological freedom and reduces the likelihood of effective and satisfying behavior.

THE FALLACY OF THE VALUE OF FAILURE

Many people believe that failure is good for people, a valuable stimulant for growth. This idea seems to have arisen from the observation that people are often strengthened by the experience of solving problems. That, of course, is true. The observation has been pushed much farther, however, so that many people believe quite firmly that problem-solving is not only good, but also that extensive failure is a strengthening thing. They adopt the attitude "if it's hard, it's good for them," and honestly believe that the experience of failure builds character, courage, and stimulation to succeed. From what we now know about self-actualization and the development of supremely healthy people, such an assumption is not only false but also downright destructive!

Earlier in this volume we have described psychological illness as a problem in deprivation, a failure of the organism to be able to achieve fulfillment. Failure psychologically is like disease physiologically. We do not say about diseases, "Let us give these diseases to children as soon as possible!" Rather, we say, "Let us keep this child from getting diseases just as long as we possibly can." Or, alternatively, we may say, "Let us give him the disease in such an attenuated form that we know he will be successful with it." This is what we do with an innoculation or a vaccination, because we know that the body is strengthened by a *successful* experience with the disease. Then, when the real thing occurs in the future there will be more resistance to it. The same principle holds for psychological disease. A diet of failure is destructive to human personality. People learn they are adequate and able from having success experience. The best guarantee we have that a person will be able to deal with exigencies in the future is that he has been essentially successful in the past. Even the self-made man who beats his chest and proclaims to the world that he came up the hard way overlooks the fact that he became a self-made man by being successful. He became what he is today, precisely because he was successful in avoiding failure!

Positive effects of feelings of success and negative ones from experiences of failure are beautifully illustrated in the following report from a nursing supervisor:

Louise was in her second year as a sophomore in our College of Nursing program when she was assigned to my instruction. She was the motherless daughter of a small town general practitioner. Her older brother was a medical student and progressing well.

Her intellectual test scores placed her as "barely able" to achieve in college. The previous year she had failed the first semester of the sophomore year. She decided to repeat that semester the following year. She attained a "D" grade. Her evaluation gave little hope for her success. The instructor in effect was saying, "I tried, but I couldn't find enough evidence on which to base a grade of F."

Louise was very plain, the only student who insisted upon wearing her mousey brown hair in a net. She had "I can't succeed" written all over her face. She trembled when asked to recite formally or when asked a question informally.

I felt, as her clinical instructor, that the patients would suffer if Louise's assignments were too difficult. I felt she would make mistakes, possibly drastic ones, and I did not want that burden. Looking back, I never thought I was providing success for Louise by giving her patient assignments she could handle. I never thought of Louise in that way at all. I was concerned with myself and the patients for whom my students were caring.

The other instructors were interested in Louise's progress. As the weeks passed, I proudly related how well she could perform with her simple assignments (four to six months behind) and that her trembling had stopped. She could smile and relate to others more freely.

I was told by my superiors, however, that I was handling the situation terribly. (This was damaging to my self-concept, I realize.) The only way to approach extremely weak students like Louise, they said, was to give them the roughest assignment possible for that level students, supervise them heavily, collect the data to fail them, show them where they have failed, write it up and put an "F" on the evaluation.

They convinced me! I did a bang-up job and you know what? Louise behaved true to her perceptions. She blundered miserably, made hair-raising mistakes and failed.

I did such a good job. I was praised highly. Louise did not return this past September. And I feel like a failure knowing that I am a part of Louise's nightmare of failure.

It is very dismaying to observe how our society believes in the value of failure. When modern educators suggest eliminating failure from the classroom, they are often met with storms of protest from parents and the community who fear that this would destroy the very basis of our public schools. There is no word in the vocabulary of the English language that distinguishes between the act of failing and judging it "non-negatively" and non-critically. The very word *failure* is derogatory, implying a sense of "no goodness," that one is vanquished, defeated, and inadequate. A person learns very early that if an act does not reach its expected or desired outcomes, then he is a failure. Nursery school children, for example, are often delighted with the successes of their friends and point out with pride—"Yeah, Jimmy does it gooder 'n me." Very shortly, however, he learns to call this state of affairs "failure," with all its connotations of personal inadequacy.

What makes a thing failure, it should be understood, is what the person believes about it. If a child believes he has failed, it does not make much difference whether other people think so or not. He behaves in terms of what he believes. A society that does not distinguish between "non-accomplishment" and "failure" runs a serious risk of demoralizing and discouraging vast numbers of its populace.

Rejecting the value of failure does not require that people always be coddled and protected from difficult kinds of experience. Not at all. People like to work hard when the goals are worth it and when the tasks are perceived as possible. They enjoy being challenged. It is the experience of long-continued threat that produces destructive outcomes and feelings of inadequacy and failure.

Failure, we need to remind ourselves, is debilitating and weakening. Because it is, it needs to be eliminated from human affairs as best we can. Success experience, on the other hand, is the key to further success and a strengthening, buttressing force in human personality. Every human being, of course, will confront, at one time or another, both kinds of experience. The problem for the helping professions is to understand the dynamics of these experiences sufficiently to assure that long-term effects on human beings are positive rather than negative.

SELF-ESTEEM IN THE CLASSROOM

The effects of self-esteem upon the success of students at every level of education have now been documented in hundreds of researches. The evidence is clear that what students believe about themselves has its accompanying effects upon how well they learn. This is true whether we are talking about beginning matters such as reading and spelling, or highly complex ones such as advanced mathematics or success in a chosen vocation.

SELF-ESTEEM IN INDUSTRY

The effects of self-esteem extend far beyond the classroom. Some of the most interesting examples of the effects of positive views of self are to be found in experiments in modern industry, where attempts to improve the feelings of self-esteem in employees have often resulted in surprising improvements in worker productivity and decreases in labor turnover, grievances, and absenteeism. An early classic in this field were the Hawthorne studies at Western Electric. In these studies a group of women, specially picked for an experiment, were given successive privileges and incentives—and with each addition their production rate rose. Then, when all these things were taken from them, production went up again! Apparently, the boost in self-esteem which these women experienced because they were part of an experiment and so "important to the company" was more significant in their performance than the incentives consciously applied by the researchers. This sort of response to improvements in self-esteem has been found so frequently in other settings both inside and outside industry that it has been given the name "the Hawthorne effect."

More recently, the Harwood Corporation took over a plant in distress and instituted a systematic program designed to improve the self-esteem of its workers. Careful records were kept concerning the effects of this program and the following are some of those listed by the firm's research team:

> For the past decade—during which the participative approach had its widest application—employee turnover at the plant has dropped to under 6 percent annually. In the apparel industry generally (in which most employees like those at Harwood are women), an annual turnover of 25 percent is rated excellent. According to the best available in-

formation, the Harwood plant has the lowest turnover in the entire apparel industry. Worker productivity has been rated by visiting engineers as the highest or in the highest bracket of any plants in the United States. The wage scale is higher than that of any competitor in this segment of the industry. Harwood has grown faster than any of its competitors and is now the largest firm in its field. By any or all of the factors that constitute organization effectiveness—performance, profits, employee earnings, worker satisfaction, and emotional well-being—the success of the Harwood plant is notable.

In addition to these notable gains in productivity, the research team reports the following outcomes with respect to the human questions involved in labor-management relationships:

> An intensive review of relevant documents leads to one conclusion —explicit, unimpeachable, and incontrovertible; they do not contain a single complaint, grievance, or reference of any kind concerning the company's participative management practices; its approach to group problem-solving and goal-setting; or its experiments designed to learn more about the value of democratic practices and the process of creating a desired kind of organization life.
>
> Not once in 20 years of bi-weekly grievance meetings, in which some 900 different grievances were filed, have the issues of "manipulation," "manipulative democracy," "democratic participation," "involuntary manipulation," "worker participation," "experiment," "intimidation," or "coercion" ever been raised or the company's participative management approach ever been challenged—not by any union member, not by any union official, not by any grievance committee, not in any of the seven union contracts signed since 1946. . . .
>
> In addition, union officials who were directly involved at that time were recently asked if they could remember any protests against "the company's continued experimentation," "involuntary manipulation" or "democratic management practices." None could.[2]

SELF-ESTEEM IN ATHLETICS

The importance of self-esteem, sensitivity, and identification seems equally important in what may at first glance seem a most unlikely area —college football. Coach Darrell Mudra once made the astonishing statement that there is no place for competition, as it is presently conceived by many coaches, on a football team. What is truly essential, he says, is teamwork. And this in turn is dependent on the feelings of players about themselves and their sensitivity to each other. It is these qual-

2. Reprinted by permission of Dr. A. J. Marrow and the editors of *Trans-Action* from Gomberg's "Fantasy." Sept./Oct. 1966.

ities, he feels, above and beyond the possession of basic skills which make the difference between a winning and a losing team. The following are a few quotations from Dr. Mudra's provocative creed:

You might say that our system is player centered, rather than system centered. There is nothing mysterious about the split-T or a Pro Offense, or a Wide-tackle Six, or about any other system in football. The magic lies in the players and that is why we have become player centered. . . . We start with nothing definite, but have a very general system in mind. We would like to have all of the coaches and all of the players determine what we are going to do. When we work out our blocking assignments, we do this in small groups. The tackles may work in one group, and the backs in another group, and the ends in another, etc. What they work out may not be as technically precise as the assignments the coaches would develop. However, what they work out they are usually able to learn and execute well. This results in more effective individual and cooperative performance. The success of the play is dependent upon what the players follow with conviction, not upon what the coaches know but perhaps have not been able to communicate totally.

It is the contention of the writer that competitiveness, as competitiveness is generally conceived, is not a natural but rather a learned attribute which, in some situations, may impede rather than promote growth. The innate drive for self actualization is many times greater than the learned competitive drive which men have acquired in a competitive culture. Man does not strive to become better than his fellow man; he strives to become the ultimate of his potentialities.

It is important that the old ideas of competition be replaced by opportunities for identification. When a player views an opponent's performance in the old traditional competitive way, he may not be able to perceive the significant aspects of the performance because his antagonistic feelings may block them out. When an opponent or team mate makes a great play, shouldn't it be gratefully accepted as an opportunity to learn a new technique? During the Mineral Bowl game we played last year, the coaches sent 13 plays into the game and the quarterback used only one of them! He emerged as the leader and assumed the responsibility for calling plays. When we sent in a play, we sent it in as a suggestion and he knew that he could shake off any play he didn't want to use. Our quarterback earned the right to lead the team. We feel that the players will work much more effectively when they are involved. They have more equity in making each assignment succeed if they help decide what it is going to be.[3]

Such ideas about how to run a football team must surely seem heretical to many people if it were not for the fact of Dr. Mudra's remarkable

3. Mudra, D., *op. cit.*

record. His nine-year record, compiled on four different campuses, shows 74 wins and only 14 losses. Two of the wins came in championship post-season bowl games!

The relationship of self-esteem to success and maladjustment to failure provides a major guideline for the helping professions. Self-fulfillment, the avoidance of deprivation is needed for helping. To accomplish this the helping process must result in increased self-esteem. This calls for helpers skilled in facilitating the growth of a positive view of self in students, clients, patients, and parishioners. The production of self-esteem is the prime goal of the helping professions, and ways of bringing it about are the major processes by which these professions operate. What might it mean, we can ask ourselves, if we were truly successful in bringing about important increases in self-esteem for persons in all walks of life? The possibilities stagger the imagination! If we could accomplish this, even in part, for the discouraged, the defeated, and the deprived, we would change the very fabric of the society we live in.

OPENNESS TO EXPERIENCE

A second characteristic required for maximum freedom and self-actualization is openness to experience. This has to do with a person's ability to perceive the world. It is the capacity to confront what is, to enter into a transaction with it, and develop new meanings as a consequence. Highly self-actualizing, fully functioning personalities seem able to deal with the world with a minimum of distortion. They are able to look at themselves and the world about them openly and without fear. They tend to see themselves accurately and realistically.

Psychologists have sometimes called openness to experience "acceptance," by which they mean the ability to confront what is—whether it be in self or the outside world. It should be understood that the word *acceptance* used in this way does not mean "giving in to" or "being resigned to." Rather, the term means being open to, or willing to confront. It is possible for a person to accept the fact that someone dislikes him, for example, without necessarily agreeing that he is, therefore, totally inadequate. Persons in the helping professions are often called upon to accept the fact of a client's misbehavior without rejecting the client. Acceptance, used in this way does not imply agreement with or powerlessness to change.

The first requirement for being able to deal with the world or with one's self must be the capacity to perceive it, to enter into dialogue with it. Whether this is possible will be in very large measure dependent upon a person's feelings of self-esteem. Highly self-actualizing persons find acceptance easy. Deeply deprived and maladjusted people often find it difficult if not impossible to achieve. This relationship of openness to self-esteem was measured in a simple experiment carried out by one of the authors. All of the sixth-grade children in a school were given standard tests of adjustment. On a list of things "Boys and Girls Sometimes Do" they were also asked to indicate those items which were true of themselves. All of the items on the list consisted of behaviors chosen because they were probably true of every child, but somewhat unflattering to admit. Some samples: "Sometimes I have lied to my mother," "Sometimes I forget to brush my teeth on purpose," or "Sometimes I have been unkind to animals." When the results of the two tests were compared, it was discovered (as predicted) that the better-adjusted children said more of the unflattering things were true of them than did the maladjusted ones. One little boy with the highest adjustment score in the school agreed that nineteen of the twenty unflattering items were true of him.

Highly self-actualizing people have such a degree of trust in themselves that they are able to look at any and all data without the necessity for defending themselves or distorting events in ways they would like them to be. Lack of acceptance is a major characteristic of neurosis and shows itself in myriad forms—from the inability of the young child to accept his baby brother, to the middle-aged philanderer unable to accept the evidence of his advancing age, to the mother unable to accept herself in the housewifely role. Persons with extreme inabilities to accept reality terminate in our mental hospitals and are described as "out of touch with reality."

SELF-ESTEEM AND OPENNESS

The walls people build to keep others out also keep them in. The protections set up to avoid injury also have the effect of destroying openness to new experience. It has been repeatedly demonstrated in research and in clinical practice that feelings of self-acceptance are prerequisite to being able to accept other people. A weak, defensive self or one repugnant to its owner provides a poor basis for constructive feelings about other people. We have already seen how the self-concept tends to produce behavior which corroborates itself. Persons who reject themselves are very likely to reject other people as well, and so contribute to closing themselves off from the very experiences which might in the long run solve their problems. This relationship between self-acceptance, acceptance of others, and openness to experience was beautifully illustrated by two severely handicapped young women known to one of the authors. Two girls, each seeking entrance into a graduate training program in clinical psychology, came to the author's office on successive days. Because the office was on the third floor, each of the girls had to be carried up for an interview. The first girl was a hard and bitter person. She was an attractive girl so far as her features were concerned, but her dour, angry, defiant stance spoiled what good possibilities she had. Her attitude at once repelled her audience. In the course of conversation the author said, "I wonder if you have given any thought to the degree to which your handicap. . . ." That's as far as he got. She snapped, "I don't have a handicap!" Unable to accept herself, she was also unable to deal effectively with herself or others. The second girl had the same condition, but what a difference! She was not as physically attractive, to be sure, but had a much more open, feminine personality—a person one felt immediately drawn to. The author said the same thing he had said to the first young woman, but this time was allowed to complete his sentence: "I wonder if you have given any thought to the degree to which your handicap might make it difficult for you to work in this field?" This is what she replied.

> I have thought a lot about that. You know, in addition to polio I had TB some years ago. At that time I laid on my back for two years in a hospital and had lots of time to think. It seems to me that experience could be helpful. You know, I kinda feel that somebody who has gone through this much will be better able to understand other people who have suffered.

One person was able to accept herself and hence was able to accept other people; the other, unable to accept herself, was rejecting the world as well.

Persons with high self-esteem, able to accept themselves, are also able to accept other people; this makes effective interaction with others much more likely. Because they believe in and trust themselves, they can act with high degrees of autonomy. They are freewheelers and are able to move off in new directions, which is what is meant by creativity. People open to experience enjoy exploring. They are neither thrown by their experience nor defensive against it. Being more open to experience, they have a wider selection of data from which to draw their solutions to problems. With more data they are likely to find better answers, and this in turn makes possible more effective and efficient behavior, which is what we mean by intelligence.

NEED AND OPENNESS

The need for self-enhancement generally keeps the individual continuously searching in his world for new ways of achieving greater self-actualization and has the effect of opening him to experience. The need for self-fulfillment may operate, however, to discourage openness, depending on how things seem to the behaver. This personal character of need fulfillment is often a great frustration to persons engaged in the helping professions. The kind of openness needed for self-fulfillment as seen by the helper may not at all be seen that way by those he would help. So, the nurse who is anxious to improve the patient's diet suggests new things the patient should eat; from the patient's view these suggestions may not seem only unappealing, but even repugnant. Similarly, it is the job of teachers to open students' experience so that they will have the necessary equipment to deal with life in the future. For the student concerned only about the satisfaction of his present needs, however, these attempts of the teacher may appear to be meaningless in terms of his goals.

VALUES AND OPENNESS

Each of us behaves in terms of what seems to him important or unimportant. Although the possession of values always has the effect of both opening and closing avenues of experience, some values and attitudes are much more likely to produce openness than others. It has been said, for example, that a genius "is a guy who gets into trouble for the sheer joy of getting out again!" Certainly, a person who values solving problems is much more likely to have new experience than one who avoids them. Creativity calls for breaking with tradition, going out in the blue, trying one's wings, breaking out of the established ruts. It is also likely to be accompanied by a certain amount of disorder. In school, for example, a creative class will probably not be a quiet one, and a rigidly ordered class will not be a creative one. So, a teacher who places too much value on order, procedure, custom, tradition, and the "right" way may actually impede openness in her students.

The attitude that it is good to look and fun to try, in itself, is almost certain to lead an individual into circumstances where his experience will be broadened and deepened. Certainly it will be quite different from that of someone who has the attitude that you must not look or that "only the experts can have good ideas." One of the characteristics of persons who have achieved a high degree of self-actualization seems to be what psychologists call a "toleration of ambiguity." That is to say, such people seem to have an attitude that it is "all right" to live with an unsolved problem. Less fulfilled persons often find the confrontation with problems that do not have immediate solutions unbearable and so may be led to adopt any solution, even a bad one, in order to solve the problem.

Encouraging Openness

Openness to experience is learned. Acceptance is acquired from having been accepted. It follows that rich opportunities are called for in which individuals can explore and test themselves in safety. Such openness comes from opportunities to get involved in events. Like learning to swim, however, one needs sufficient help to be sure that he doesn't drown. On the other hand, one can *never* learn to swim if he doesn't go near the water. Openness to experience comes about as a consequence of being sufficiently secure where one is. He is then able to branch out into new events with courage and determination. This provides us with a guiding principle for the development of openness.

A large portion of the time and efforts of persons in the helping professions will be directed toward aiding clients, students, and patients to develop greater openness and acceptance. Much human maladjustment is the product of failures of acceptance; the work of counselors, psychiatrists, social workers, and all those persons who work with the mentally ill will, of necessity, be determined by the principles affecting acceptance and openness. So will the efforts of other professionals working with quite normal people. Openness to experience is a major factor in intelligence and so must play a very important part in the efforts of all those concerned about the effective growth and development of other people. It plays an especially crucial role in the behavior of parents and teachers who are responsible for the education of the next generation.

Unhappily, well-intentioned attempts to motivate others often boomerang to produce quite opposite effects. Parents who are too anxious for their child to do well may urge him to do better so strenuously that the child may learn from the experience only that he is not very acceptable as he is. A steady diet of this sort of thing can quickly cause a child to feel inept and inadequate. Such negative effects of attempts to motivate are often seen in especially painful form in the treatment of persons with handicaps. Children are often subjected to much advice designed to get them to extend themselves, to rise above their difficulties. Notable examples like Teddy Roosevelt, Franklin Roosevelt, Abe Lincoln, Glenn Cunningham, and even The Ugly Duckling are frequently pointed out to them as models to follow. This, in effect, is asking the child to concentrate his major efforts in life upon his weakest point! Few adults would readily be willing to accept such a concentration of energies for themselves. The principle of challenge and threat is important here. If a handicap is minor and can be approached by the person as challenge, such motivating efforts may prove salutary. But what happens to the person with a major handicap which cannot be overcome? Continuous urging to perform the impossible is enough to discourage the strongest person. In the long run it is likely to produce a twisted, unhappy, defeated human being.

A review of the factors affecting openness and acceptance discussed above will provide a number of effective principles giving direction and suggesting techniques by which persons engaged in the helping professions can carry out their functions with increased likelihood of success.

FREEDOM AND IDENTIFICATION

Intelligent behavior requires a transaction with life, the ability to enter into a dialogue with people and events, to commit one's self to involvement. Meaning, we have seen, comes about as a consequence of the discovery of the relationship of events to self. A self which remains aloof must, of necessity, make itself less effective. A self incapable of commitment is walled-off from experience. Its field of meanings is the poorer, and its potential for effective behavior is reduced. A rich field of meanings is the product of a self in active transaction with the world. Whether a person is able to enter into such transactions and how satisfying they are likely to be, will depend upon the degree of identification he feels with events and people in the world he lives in.

Humans are social beings. The degree to which they are able to attain fulfillment is dependent upon how successfully they are able to work out effective relationships with the other people who make up the society or culture in which they live. We are so very dependent upon other people that some measure of successful interaction with them is essential to life itself. Satisfying human relationships are not just a nice idea; they are vital to living. Experiments with monkeys deprived of opportunities to interact with other monkeys demonstrate that such isolation causes them to grow into distorted, maladjusted personalities. Raised out of touch with each other, they frequently cannot even be induced to mate. Apparently, they do not know they are monkeys without experience with others which helps them discover who and what they are. Similarly, people become human through human interaction. Feelings of identification contribute to that process and so to the humanization of persons.

All of us live in a world of people. People are by all odds the most important aspects of our world, the sources of most of our satisfactions and frustrations. In fact, other people are the only really important ingredients of life. Physical things, whether they be money, cars, or clothes, only gain meaning and importance when they are shared with other human beings. Without personal reference they are nothing. It is in the nature of our relationships with others that freedom and personal fulfillment are determined.

IDENTIFICATION WITH IDEAS

Identification is important in affecting behavior not only with people. It is equally significant with respect to ideas. We have already observed the intimate relationship of the self-concept and learning. Whether any information is likely to result in changed behavior will be dependent upon the closeness with which that information is perceived to the self. Ideas incorporated into the self-structure can be counted on to determine future behavior. There is simply no learning of consequence without involvement of the person in the process. Ideas by themselves are mere illusions. It is only in persons that they come alive, and only through the personal discovery of their relationship to self that they affect behavior.

Real learning and the richness it bestows upon life comes about only with self-involvement. Persons who will not or cannot enter into dialogue with ideas are cut off from experience, hemmed in, and inhibited from comprehension. This principle was vividly brought home to one of the authors of this book while visiting a museum with an artist friend. The author was working hard at trying to understand some modern paintings, but getting absolutely nowhere. Then his friend said to him, "Stop working at it. You are looking at it from afar, groping for it at your fingertips. Let it come to you. Try to be with it. Let yourself get involved. Let it flow into you." Looking at the painting in this way, the author almost at once experienced a whole new relationship with paintings. He discovered a new beauty, meaning, and sensual delight as he let himself "be with it." Instead of *looking at* the painting, he learned to enter into a *dialogue with it* and so opened a whole new world of experience for exploration. The self at war with experience is shutting itself off from meaning, reducing psychological freedom. The self capable of entering interaction with ideas or concepts is opening and expanding its world, simultaneously broadening its base of operations and increasing its chances for the achievement of self-fulfillment.

Nowhere is this relationship between the self and ideas so important as in education. It is a major purpose of schools to bring students into effective relationships with the accumulated experience of other human beings. How successful they are in accomplishing their task will be dependent upon how well they succeed in inducing students to invest themselves in the processes of learning. We have all had the experience of being or not being "with it" in school. We learned little or nothing in those classes where, for some reason, we refused to invest ourselves in the learning process. On the other hand, we can remember that, in those classes where we worked hard, interacted with our classmates, and the like, we learned a great deal. And it made no difference whether our interest came from within or was the result of an inspiring teacher or exciting subject matter. Once invoked, we were with it, and we learned. What was learned was also far more likely to be retained and acted upon. People do not sabotage their own projects. It is only those projects people feel no sense of identification with that are ignored or active, are only fought against.

IDENTIFICATION AND SELF-ACTUALIZATION

Deep feelings of identification with other people seem to be a major characteristic of highly self-actualized persons. The possession of these feelings in turn produces interactions with their fellows which corroborate and strengthen existing beliefs. Broad feelings of identification, for example, make it possible to put much more trust in others. They contribute a sense of sureness to one's transactions. Relationships with others can be entered into much more openly and freely. When one is certain of his welcome, he is free to walk more boldly and dares to do or say what other less certain persons could not risk. Interactions with others can thus be entered with an *expectancy* of success. Because they feel they belong, broadly identified persons establish relationships with other people as though they were members of the family rather than strangers. Fulfillment comes much easier to persons capable of such involvement. The feedback they experience from these interactions is also more supporting and enhancing than that of less self-actualized persons.

A sense of oneness with others is likely to produce in its possessor a deep compassion for people. Others quickly discover this fact and are led to respond in kind. They also discover that deeply identified persons are highly responsible and trustworthy, for what they do for others, they do for themselves and vice versa. As a consequence they are likely to respond to them warmly and openly. Because broadly identified persons are less threatening, other people can afford to relax their defenses and enter into more responsive relationships with them. This was so frequently true in the lives of some of the self-actualizing persons Maslow studied as to sometimes become an embarrassment. Because they were warm, open, compassionate, and understanding, they tended to attract people with problems and so found themselves at times surrounded by unhappy persons in need of help! In the eyes of others, self-actualized persons are perceived as warm, friendly, responsible, and trustworthy people. Because they are so experienced, they are highly attractive to others. From the behavior of those about them, in turn, they learn they are liked, wanted, respected, appreciated, and loved. This makes it possible for deeply identified people to be more so than ever in a rising spiral which represents the very essence of psychological freedom.

Deep feelings of identification are also likely to contribute to more intelligent behavior. With positive feelings toward others, persons can approach relationships with an expectancy of success. With a feeling of oneness they have little to fear and so can commit themselves to interaction with no holds barred. Persons without such feelings operate under great handicaps. They must deal with others as strangers, or enemies, rather than as comrades or friends. Accordingly, they tend to approach interactions with hesitation. Expecting resistance, they are very likely to get it and so defeat themselves almost before they begin.

IDENTIFICATION AND PSYCHOLOGICAL HEALTH

A major characteristic of the psychologically ill is a lack of identification. Time after time persons who come to psychological clinics; persons who seek the help of counselors, social workers and priests; persons who run afoul of the law or enter our mental hospitals, turn out to be persons with deep feelings of depersonalization or alienation. They feel cut off from their fellow men. Far from feeling free, they feel themselves bound in by life, constricted and unable to achieve fulfillment. They become the loners, the not free, the driven, hostile ones who cannot achieve identification, and solve their problems by withdrawal from or rejection of involvement. In the kind of world we live in, it is almost impossible to achieve a satisfactory measure of self-fulfillment without identification. We live in a "people" world; without effective involvement with people we are lost.

It is probably no accident that the very best cure we have been able to find for juvenile delinquency is marriage. Of all the things associated with delinquents who improve, getting married seems more effective and more certain than any other one thing that we know about. When you have somebody who cares, somebody to live for, somebody to share things with, you are provided a measure of relief from the boredom and feelings of alienation which lie at the basis of much delinquent behavior.

Many of the great social and personal problems of our time are brought about by the terrible dehumanizing forces we have set loose in our midst. We have created a society in which millions of people feel they are of little account. The net effect of many of our technological innovations has been to depersonalize individual human beings and make satisfying human interrelationships increasingly difficult to achieve. A very large part of the activities of persons in the helping professions will be directed toward helping people discover and enter into new and more satisfying relationships between themselves and other people.

The problems of alienation and loneliness, of course, exist at every level of our social structure. They are especially poignant with respect to the young. Many young people grow up with deep feelings of alienation from the society they live in. Many are desperately lonely and find themselves at loose ends without satisfying commitments. We cannot afford this waste. On humanitarian grounds the loss in human potential involved in this rejection is tremendous. The loss in human happiness is even greater. If it is not enough to be concerned about the matter because we love and respect our young people, there is another very practical reason why we had better be interested. It is downright dangerous not to be concerned. These are the citizens of tomorrow.

Psychological freedom is a function of identification. Identification in turn is learned from the experiences people have with the significant others in their lives. The feeling of oneness must be discovered. It cannot be given. It comes about as a consequence of personal discovery that some idea, some person, some thing is deeply enhancing or fulfilling. Those are matters helpers can do something about.

SELECTED READINGS

Starred entries indicate appearance in whole or in part in Donald L. Avila, Arthur W. Combs, and William W. Purkey, *The Helping Relationship Sourcebook* (Boston: Allyn & Bacon, 1971).

Allport, G. W. *Pattern and growth in personality.* New York: Holt, Rinehart and Winston, 1961.

* Combs, A. W. What can man become? *California Journal for Instructional Improvement.* 1961, **4,** 15–23.

Courson, C. Personal adequacy and self perception in high school students: A study of behavioral and internal perceptual factors. *Journal of Humanistic Psychology,* 1968, **8,** 29–38.

Crutchfield, R. S. Conformity and character. *American Psychologist,* 1955, **10,** 91–98.

Jourard, S. M. *Disclosing man to himself.* Princeton, N. J.: Van Nostrand, 1968.

* Kelley, E. C. The meaning of wholeness. *ETC: A Review of General Semantics,* 1969, **26,** 7–15.

Maslow, A. H. Creativity in self-actualizing people. In H. H. Anderson (Ed.) *Creativity and its cultivation.* New York: Harper and Brothers, 1959, 83–95.

* Maslow, A. H. The creative attitude. In R. L. Mooney & T. A. Razik (Eds.) *Explorations in creativity.* New York: Harper and Row, 1967, 43–45.

Perceiving, behaving, becoming: A new focus for education. 1962 Yearbook, Association for Supervision and Curriculum Development, National Education Association, 1962.

Redl, F. & Wineman, D. *Children who hate.* Glencoe, Ill.: Free Press, 1951.

Rogers, C. R. *On becoming a person.* Boston: Houghton Mifflin, 1961.

9

Goals and Purposes
of Helping

Goals and values are major determinants of human behavior. What helpers believe about the ends to be sought and the dynamics by which those
ends are to be achieved inescapably determines what they do or do not
do, in whatever form the helping role may be practiced. Beliefs about
goals and values also determine the helper's success or failure. It makes
a difference how one behaves as a teacher—whether he believes his purpose is to mold children in the proper directions or to help them grow.
Similarly, a counselor will behave quite differently toward a couple considering divorce, depending upon whether he believes his proper function
is to keep the couple together or to help them find their own best solutions to their problems.

A helper's conceptions of the goals he is seeking to accomplish have
inexorable effects upon his behavior. This will be true whether he is
clearly aware of them or not. Even dimly held conceptions have their
effects upon what helpers try to do. Goals and purposes determine action. Vaguely held goals are like sailing through fog; with luck, one can
sometimes make harbor. When purposes are confused or inconsistent
the situation is much worse. Then it is like sailing with a dozen captains,
each with different ideas; if one lands at all, he is lucky.

People are far too precious to be dealt with in such fashion. Persons
who enter the helping professions automatically assume the responsibility for making certain that what they do will more than likely contribute
positively to the lives of students, clients, or patients. This cannot be a

"maybe" question. Helping must be as predictable a process as the helpers can make it. It is important, therefore, that persons in training for the helping professions develop clear, accurate concepts concerning the goals and purposes of the profession. This requires that the helpers' goals and purposes be (a) supported by basic psychological thought, (b) internally consistent among themselves, and (c) demonstrably effective when applied to practice. In the remainder of this chapter, let us examine some aspects of the goals and purposes of helping that are consistent with the humanistic approaches to behavior taken in earlier chapters.

WHO NEEDS HELP?

In the complex world we have created, people—ourselves and others—are the most important problems we face, and each of us solves these problems more or less successfully. While some people solve them much more effectively than others, no one is immune from problems and almost everyone at some time or other is likely to find himself in need of aid. Some fortunate people see themselves in highly adequate ways, and they behave so. They are regarded by those around them as successful people, and so are given the acceptance and approbation of the societies in which they live. These are the happy, self-fulfilling ones. They seem to have it made. But human need is insatiable. Even the most highly self-actualized persons continue to be in need of self-fulfillment to the end of their days, and that can only be achieved with the help of their fellow men.

Persons less fortunate see themselves in more tentative fashion. Despite their doubts and fears, however, they manage to behave in ways that are generally acceptable to society and reasonably fulfilling for themselves. This is the position most of the readers of this book are probably in—that is, at a point somewhere between illness and health.

Other people, still less fortunate, see themselves in much more negative ways. These are the sad, unhappy ones who nevertheless manage to cope with life in ways acceptable to those around them, even if the struggle often provides them with little personal satisfaction. The world has many such, apparently successful, but personally unfulfilled people. Many examples of these unhappy people who come to mind are in the entertainment world and are frequently in the public eye. But success in the public eye and deep feelings of deprivation in private life are to be found in every walk of life. They may be observed in the driven industrial magnate, the wealthy suicide, or the beautiful and charming divorcee. One can even find them among his friends. These are the people who seem to the outside world successful and effective, but confess in private to feelings of frustration, deprivation, or alienation.

Sometimes the personal doubts of "partial achievers" may even provide the stimulation to drive them to truly exceptional accomplishments, as in the case of an artist like Van Gogh or an emperor like Napoleon. Persons in this condition often surprise us because, as members of society, we observe from without, and from that point of view they seem to be acceptable, effective persons. Then, one day we discover what terrible loads they have been staggering under, and we are amazed that they could have gotten along so well. The human race is tough, and what an individual can stand before showing signs of his pain to outsiders is often beyond belief. It is from this group of personally unhappy, but fairly successful, copers that most of the clients of counselors, pastors, and social workers come.

The most pitiful of those who need help are the ones for whom both sides of the equation are negative. They see themselves as inadequate, unfulfilled, and deprived; they are also regarded by the society in which they live as inadequate, unacceptable, despicable, and perhaps even dangerous. These are the desperate ones who see no hope for themselves and cannot cope successfully with the world they live in. They are the ones who cause parents and teachers trouble, who (in their adult years) find themselves on relief or fill our jails, our mental hospitals, and our institutions. It was, in part, to relieve society of the burdens produced by these kinds of people that the development of some of the more recent branches of the helping professions came about. But even if the helping professions did not help society solve its problems, there would still be ample reasons for their existence on purely personal and humanitarian grounds. Life is just better when people care.

CHANGING GOALS OF THE HELPING PROFESSIONS

Most of the helping professions originally came into being for rehabilitative reasons. Guidance programs in the public schools, for instance, were at first seen as a means of dealing with the "sore thumbs," the academic or psychological cripples. They were developed at first to work with those youngsters who were unable, for one reason or another, to fit into the usual molds. The task was to fix up and patch up, to deal with the misfits, the casualties of the system. Most of the helping professions began with this rehabilitative emphasis. Even the oldest professions, like teaching and the clergy, in the beginning, had a major desire to "save" their subjects—in one case from stupidity, in the other from sin.

Later the helping professions became increasingly interested in the problems of prevention—that is, in keeping people from getting sick. After one has gotten into difficulties, rehabilitation is always more difficult and expensive than staying out of trouble in the first place. This phase in the development of the helping professions was immensely stimulated by the development of such social sciences as anthropology, psychology, and sociology, which provided clues to how people got into difficulties and so opened the way to more effective diagnosis and prevention. The invention of psychological tests provided an additional tool by which workers might discover persons in need of help. The creation of the "guidance counselor" in our public schools was one of the products of the testing movement. Today, school counselors do very much more than administer psychological tests. But in the early days of this profession, tests were the guidance worker's major tools and gave him his primary reason for being.

Expanding the purpose of the helping professions from rehabilitation to prevention also expanded the clientele immensely. The sick are comparatively few; the potentially sick includes all of us. As a consequence, all helping professions have grown tremendously with the adoption of the preventive goal. Society looks with ever-increasing hope to the helping professions for the prevention of human distress and failure. Education is newly esteemed for what it can do in the prevention of cultural deprivation. Counseling and guidance are regarded as important services for *all* children. Psychotherapy is now such an accepted device for preventing illness that in some circles it has become quite fashionable to have been "analyzed." Social workers are no longer restricted to working with the poor or the maladjusted; we are increasingly recognizing their value for social planning and for the operation of a wide variety of agencies devoted to helping people individually or in groups at every level of the social order. We have even seen the development of new helping professions almost exclusively designed for the preventive problem, for example, in public health nursing or some aspects of social group work.

Change in our conceptions of the purpose of the helping professions has not stopped with prevention. Our new understandings of human capacities and the studies made in recent years on the nature of self-actualization have opened whole new vistas to the helping professions. Our new conceptions of human capacity make it clear that man's potential is vast beyond belief. The research on self-actualization provides understanding of the nature of man's becoming and points the way to the goals by which it may be achieved. The more we study human potential, the more apparent it becomes that the ultimate goal of the helping professions must lie in self-actualization and fulfillment. It is not a matter of patching up the failures or even preventing affliction, as important as these undoubtedly are. It demands a forward press, a reaching for the heights, and the fullest possible realization of self for not just a few, but for everybody!

In Chapter 4, we defined health as the achievement of fulfillment, and illness as a problem in deprivation. The healthy organism is free to operate at its maximum levels, to realize its ultimate potentialities. Illness, on the other hand, is the product of the frustration of fulfillment, of the organism's failure to achieve acceptable levels of actualization. The goal of the helping professions in these terms must be the development of the highest possible levels of personal fulfillment in its clientele. To accomplish this end, it seeks to encourage and facilitate the exploration and discovery of more effective and satisfying relationships between self and the world.

Fig. 3   Diagram of the Helping Problem

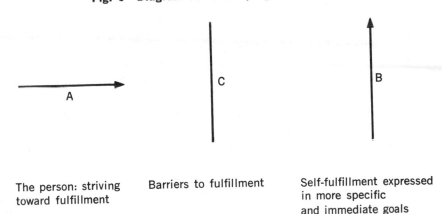

The person: striving toward fulfillment

Barriers to fulfillment

Self-fulfillment expressed in more specific and immediate goals

THE BASIC DYNAMICS OF HELPING

The fundamental strategies of helping are always directed toward one or more of three prime targets represented diagrammatically in Fig. 3: the person (A), the goal (B), or the barriers (C). At any moment we choose to look in on the state of a person's being, we will find him in some kind of goal-related behavior and striving for something, even if it is only to continue his nap. How well he will be able to achieve his goals at any moment will depend upon the resources he has within him to bring to bear upon his problems at that instant. This, as we have seen in Chapter 7, is a function of the richness and extent of his perceptual field. The goal toward which the person is striving is always the goal of self-fulfillment; but, of course, this goal is defined in many different terms, shifting and changing from time to time as need satisfaction requires. Human problems arise when the striving of the organism is in some fashion impeded by barriers to the achievement of fulfillment. These barriers may exist in the world outside the individual, or they may exist in his own perceptual structure. In seeking to help their clients, students, or patients, members of the helping professions may direct their energies toward any of these aspects of the problem singly or in combination.

All of us have experienced the doctor-patient relationship, which medical model involves a person who knows (the doctor) and a person who does not (the patient). We automatically call this model into play when it is necessary to be helpful to someone else. Unfortunately, it is likely to be ineffective because the model is inappropriate for describing the helping relationship. Helping people to change their perceptions of themselves and the world requires a different kind of model from that required to change the physical body. Human behavior is a function of how people perceive. Changing behavior, therefore, requires a change in perception. But perceptions lie inside people and are not open to direct manipulation by outsiders. Thus, helping another person change behavior involves a relationship directly opposite that of doctor and patient. In the helper-helpee relationship it is the *helpee* who knows and the *helper* who does not; the *client* has the crucial information and he must do the changing. The diagnosing and prescribing techniques used by the doctor in helping his patient are only occasionally likely to be successful when problems are psychological rather than physical.

Helper and helpee both want the same thing—increased fulfillment for the client or student. The motive power is inherent in the person and it is the task of the helper to contribute however he can to setting it free to operate. He does this by attacking any of the phases of the helping process outlined above. He may do it by manipulating the environment to which the helpee is exposed, or by seeking to bring about changes in the subject's personal organization of meanings.

PERSONAL OR ENVIRONMENTAL APPROACHES

Helping functions can be instituted in either of two ways: by concentrating on the cnvironment or on the person's own field of meanings. Each has its unique possibilities and limitations already discussed in Chapter 2. The first of these alternatives, of course, is the simpler one; unfortunately it is also restricted in its possibilities. Trying to change a person's behavior by making a change in his world may be comparatively simple with a very young child whose world is not very big, but changing the world of a grownup who is free to go where he pleases in the community is quite a different matter. Using the environmental approach, it will be necessary for the helper to know a great deal about the forces causing his client to behave as he does. Since the behavior of the individual is a consequence of *all* the forces exerted upon him throughout his history, this is a stupendous task. To know all about the forces exerted upon the individual is patently impossible. Fortunately, it is also not necessary, for the forces acting upon people are by no means equal in importance. By selecting those forces most directly affecting pertinent meaning the helper may reduce the amount of needed information to workable size.

If environmental approaches are to be helpful, it will also be necessary for the helper to understand the nature of the subject's current field of meanings sufficiently to make a prediction concerning the probable effects of whatever environmental change is contemplated. It is necessary that the teacher understand the way in which a child perceives his world. For instance, a teacher who insists that a pupil "stand up and give his report" should be confident that this will produce a positive rather than a negative outcome for the youngster. It is not enough to make a change in environment with a vague hope that it "might" be helpful. Since it is the meaning of the experience for the person which makes the difference, the use of environmental techniques in helping must be predicated upon a high degree of sensitivity in the helper.

Generally speaking, the older a person gets the less possible it is to be of much help to him by controlling the world he lives in; instead we must depend more upon producing some change in his perceptual world, the world of his thinking and feeling. The helping professions, for the most part, must depend upon inducing some changes in people's meanings by the use they make of themselves in interaction with their subjects. Professional helping is primarily a relationship in which the helper has little to sell but himself and his interaction with those he seeks to assist. It is this relationship upon which the process of helping depends. The essence of effective professional work is the effective use of the helper's self. This calls for the development of a high degree of sensitivity to individual personal meanings.

BUILDING PERSONAL RESOURCES

One way of helping is by building up the helpee's resources, his ability to mount the necessary effort. This is a matter of increasing human potential. The greater the strength the person can call upon when needed, the better will be his chances of success in the dialogues of life. This is the condition the physician seeks when he prescribes rest or a diet. It is also the goal of the teacher in providing information and success experience, or what the counselor hopes to convey in expressing his faith in his client.

Whatever increases a person's intelligence places him in more favorable stance for dealing effectively with events. This is, in fact, the major purpose of our educational system. Increases in human potential are also created by strengthening factors contributing to self-actualization. A positive view of self provides a firm foundation for interacting vigorously and assuredly with life. The same is true for feelings of identification. People who feel they "belong" are in far stronger positions to deal with life than those who do not. Factors governing intelligence and self-actualization thus provide the helper with important clues to ways in which he can contribute to the growth resources of those he seeks to assist. Careful examination of the practices of social workers, counselors, teachers, or any of the other helping professions will quickly make it clear that most techniques these persons use contribute in one fashion or another to increasing the strength of their clients. Whether their users intend it so or not, the net effect of many of their functions is to increase intelligence, create a more positive self, or increase feelings of identification.

REMOVING BARRIERS

The goals of helping can also be achieved by removing the blocks which lie in the path of the person's striving. The helper, by removing the block himself or having it done by others, might do this *for* a person. How it is done will depend, among other things, upon the nature of the blocks and the skills of the helper. If the blocks occur in the exterior world, it may be possible to remove them physically. Quite different kinds of approaches are necessary when blocks are conceptual or attitudinal and so lie inside the person. In this instance, removal of blocks will require the active participation of the helper.

The principles governing the experience of challenge or threat are pertinent for dealing with barriers. Obstructions perceived as challenging may be confronted as fascinating problems whereas barriers perceived as threatening may be terribly frustrating and even destructive. Many helpers' efforts in all of the helping professions are therefore devoted to aiding clients to perceive the barriers they confront in less threatening terms. Sometimes a barrier can be surmounted, for example, when a child learns to handle a mathematical function he previously could not. Sometimes barriers may be changed in such a fashion that coping with them becomes possible, or sometimes they may simply have to be accepted and lived with.

A case in point involves one of the authors' clients who, in middle age, married a bachelor who had lived all his life with his mother. The couple moved in with the old lady who immediately began a campaign to make life miserable for her daughter-in-law; but she was so clever about it that her son was never aware of what was going on between the two women when he was not around. The poor bride was trapped in a situation which her husband could never be expected to understand and she had no way to deal with her mother-in-law. After struggling with her problem for months, she became quite ill and sought help in therapy. During the course of counseling she carefully considered the possibilities of doing away with the old lady, but decided that was no solution because it would mean the end for her too. At long last she decided, "I'm thirty years younger than she is. I'll wait her out!" Having accepted the necessity to live with the barrier and having found a way to cope with it, her neurotic symptoms disappeared and she found herself able to tolerate her problem. Sure enough, a few years later the old woman died and left her daughter-in-law triumphantly in charge of the scene.

CHANGING GOALS

The problem of encouraging growth may also be attacked through a change in goals. A person, finding himself blocked in one direction, may find it possible to solve his problems by turning to another field of endeavor. Many efforts of social workers, for example, involve helping clients to find greater fulfillment through changing goals. Sometimes this is necessary because the world a person lives in has changed and personal striving must also change to adjust to new circumstances. Examples of this may be observed in trying to find new jobs for Appalachian coal miners no longer needed in the coal fields. Sometimes clients may be helped by changing goals to more appropriate or attainable ones. So, a mother demanding that her child become what she wishes may be helped to live more happily with her family by accepting her daughter's goals.

The discovery of new goals is not simply a device for solving existing problems; it is also a way of *creating* problems and so leads the way to further growth and development. For generations good teachers have been engaged in the business of helping students discover new goals worth striving for. In this fashion, lives may be greatly enriched and possibilities for fulfillment enormously expanded.

HELPING: A PROBLEM IN LEARNING

In essence, helping is a learning process. When helping is successful, the student, client, or parishioner has learned a new and better relationship between himself and the world in which he lives. Likewise, unsuccessful attempts to help may result in learning a poorer, less effective way of living. Whatever happens, the person being aided learns something from the experience—even if it is no more than the idea that the helper is not much help to him. The helping process is an experience in problem-solving.

Learning, we have seen, always has two aspects: the acquisition of knowledge or experience and the discovery of its meaning. So, the helping professions provide their subjects with information and experience in the particular realms with which they are concerned. This is what the teacher does in providing the student with information about a subject. It is what the social worker does when he introduces his client to a new group setting and so provides new experiences of other people. Similarly, the counselor interprets a psychological test for his client, a nurse shows a new mother how to bathe a baby, and the priest or rabbi interprets the Holy Scriptures for his flock.

Helping does not stop with the provision of information. It requires the discovery of meaning as well. It is only when the individual has discovered the personal meaning of information for himself that it can be expected to make a change in his behavior. Almost anyone can provide other people with new information or experience. You don't need a professional just to give information. In fact, with our shiny new hardware we can often do this better without intervention of a human being at all. Problems of humanization and personal discovery of meaning will not be solved by computers or gadgets. They must be solved in the final analysis by human commitment and involvement, in interaction of persons with persons. The discovery of meaning is a human problem and requires a person who is willing and able to use his self to stimulate and encourage growth in the self of another person. In this area the helping professions make their most unique contribution.

THE COMMON PURPOSE OF HELPING

The goal of the helping professions is self-actualization, and the purpose of the helping profesions is to assist people to achieve it. This goal is the same for every form of the helping professions whether it be counseling, social work, pastoral care, nursing, teaching, or any of the dozens of other specialties currently recognized in the field. While practitioners may behave in many different ways to assist people in achieving self-fulfillment, the goal remains the same for all. A number of research studies are now available demonstrating this fundamental unity. In a study of the beliefs of psychotherapists, F. E. Fiedler found that experienced psychotherapists—no matter what school of thought they were working in—were closer together in what they believed constituted a good helping relationship than were beginning therapists and expert therapists in the same school of thought. Apparently, as they became more expert in their professions, they grew closer together, which would seem to suggest that there is probably a "good" helping relationship toward which people move as they become more expert. Even more intriguing, Fiedler found that the "man in the street" could describe the good helping relationship about as well as the experts! Apparently there is a "good" helping condition which all of us are vaguely aware of even if that is not our primary business. In a similar experiment, R. W. Heine came to the conclusion that there is probably only one basic psychotherapy and that all therapists approach that common principle in more or less degree. This is not so surprising. After all, if the basic nature of people and the laws of behavior are stable, one would expect expressions of these basic principles to show commonality. Arising from common bases the principles governing the operation of effective helping relationships *ought* to be similar.

The process of helping is a process in problem-solving that is governed by what we know of the dynamics of learning. Helping people discover more effective and satisfying relationships between themselves and the world is an exercise in learning. In that sense all helpers of whatever school are fundamentally teachers. Some persons will no doubt recoil from the thought of helpers as teachers. What they do seems so different from the kinds of teaching they have observed or experienced. This is probably because they are accustomed to thinking of teaching as "telling." The technique used by helpers in the one-to-one relationships of counseling, for example, seems a far cry from such procedures as lecturing, assigning, evaluating, rewarding, and punishing. Teaching seems to them to be synonymous with controlling, directing, and even coercing people. Such practices, to be sure, are employed by some teachers. Many modern teachers, however, regard them just as distastefully as they are seen by colleagues in the other helping professions. There is little reason to suppose, however, that learning which occurs in the classroom is basically different from that which occurs in the varied relationships of any of the other helping professions. All are concerned with learning. Each hopes to assist the student or client to learn a new and better way of dealing with himself and the world about him. The distinctions we formerly made between the tasks of the teacher and other persons in the helping professions no longer seem tenable in the light of these understandings. The best teachers in our schools today are a far cry from the forbidding, authoritarian stereotypes characteristic of a generation ago. Helping people learn is the basic problem of the helping professions, and helping people learn is precisely what we mean by teaching. In a very real sense, then, every therapist is a teacher and every teacher is in some degree a therapist.

It may appear to some readers that emphasis upon the common character of the various helping professions is like "straining at a gnat." The point, however, is important. It will often be necessary for two or more helpers to work together with a particular student or client. Without a clear understanding of commonalities, effectiveness can easily be destroyed. It is a disaster for a student or client to find himself caught in the cross fire of helpers at war with one another. In a team or institutional setting, helpers must often work together and it is important that they recognize and appreciate their common goals and purposes. Unhappily, this is often not the case. Teachers and counselors, for example, sometimes deal with each other as antagonists rather than co-workers. Some counselors may delight in gossiping about the terrible things that parents and teachers have done to the children they are working with. And there are teachers who regard the work of counselors as unwarranted invasions of their own prerogatives and speak with disdain of "headshrinkers." Such attitudes are not only bad for the subjects who are supposed to be helped, but they also seriously undermine the *esprit de corps* of the institution itself. Helpers who treat each other with disdain are unlikely to be able to work together in effective ways. They, themselves are in need of help.

Persons in the helping professions always need to be keenly aware of the distorting effects of their own self-concepts. Like everyone else, helpers behave in terms of their beliefs. As a consequence, misunderstandings arise from each profession's belief in the importance of what it is doing. What others are doing then seems to be less important or less valuable because it is less understood. This can sometimes get to be so bad that particular expressions of the helping professions may turn into cults with firm beliefs that they themselves are "the chosen ones." These attitudes may be further institutionalized with elaborate entrance ceremonies designed to maintain the "purity" of the profession. When this happens the various branches of the helping professions may find themselves working at cross purposes when they ought to be working in close conjunction in order to be of maximum assistance to to those they seek to help. To avoid this kind of internecine warfare, it is important that persons in the helping professions understand the basic commonality of their tasks and learn to appreciate the work of others in the helping professions with sympathy and understanding. The goals of the helping professions are so great and the need of clients, students, and patients so insatiable that no branch of the profession can hope to make the helping process its exclusive prerogative. The professions must work in concert. This requires beginning with a proper appreciation of their common purpose. Some training institutions have taken the lead in this direction by developing programs in which persons aspiring to various aspects of professional work begin their education together.

HOW HELPING PROFESSIONS DIFFER

People in the professions who understand the common purpose of help-ing are more likely to work well together. People who properly respect the ways the professions differ will be more likely to aid their clients. The problems of helping people are immense, and their peculiar areas and needs for help are so diverse that many helping professions have come into being.

THE AREA OF HELP

One way the professions differ is in the area of fulfillment they seek to provide. The physician and nurse are concerned with problems of physi-cal health. Teachers specialize in knowledge, understanding, and growth. The social worker exerts his primary efforts toward social adjustment and welfare. Counselors seek better personal fulfillment for their clients, and the clergy are concerned with the relationship of their parishioners to questions of morality and the Divinity. These are not so much differ-ences in kind as they are differences in aspects of concern. Large areas of overlap exist from profession to profession. While each has an area of particular responsibility, they can hardly avoid being concerned with other areas as well. The human personality is a whole and can rarely be dealt with a piece at a time.

In the early days of the development of the helping professions, vari-ous branches sometimes sought to establish exclusive domain over the right to practice in one aspect or another. Some psychiatrists, for exam-ple, at one time hoped to define the practice of psychotherapy in such a fashion as to make it the exclusive prerogative of the medical profession. After years of effort, however, it became apparent that counseling and psychotherapy cannot be defined in ways that do not involve what thou-sands of others in the helping professions do or, even, what people gen-erally do in daily life. If warm, friendly talk or the giving of advice were made the exclusive property of a particular profession, few of us, whether professional or not, could long remain out of jail!

THE PERSONALNESS OF EXPLORATION

A second way in which the helping professions differ is in the "personal-ness" or closeness of the matters explored to the subject's self. This closeness to self is sometimes referred to as "depth." It may help to picture the matter as shown in Fig. 4.

Fig. 4 The Personalness of Exploration

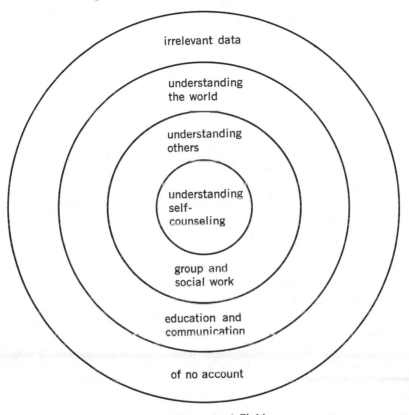

The Perceptual Field

The goal of the helping professions is aiding people to explore and discover more effective and satisfying relationships between themselves and the world. In Chapter 5 we have seen that effective learning consists in the personal discovery of meaning for the learner. To accomplish its purpose the helping process must assist its clients to bring events into closer terms with self. Not all meanings are equally important for people, and the relationship a person needs to discover between them and self will occur at varying levels of relevance. In Fig. 4 these are diagrammed on a line running through the center of the concentric circles representing various levels of relationship of events to self. Events at the center of the person's experience are perceived as having deep and important relationships to self. Events perceived on the periphery have little or no relationship and are as a consequence perceived as of small account.

In order to live effectively, a person needs to discover personal relationships with at least three major areas of events: the world of knowledge, other people, and the discovery of his own very personal self. These areas are represented in Fig. 4 by a series of concentric circles. On this scale we can plot very roughly the general areas of the various helping professions. The peripheral ring of the scale represents an area not regarded by any of the helping professions as their primary concern except, of course, that any information first coming into a person's field begins at the periphery. Somewhat closer to self is the world of information, the accumulated culture of society. This is the area of primary concern to education and teaching. It is the purpose of education to help students discover the personal meaning of the world in which they live. Still closer to self, each of us needs to discover effective relationships in living with other people. This is the area of the helping professions such as social work, human relations, and group psychotherapy or counseling. At the very closest points to self are the relationships we have with those who are closest to us—our husbands, wives, children, or closest friends. It also includes the personal discovery of who we are, what we are, and what we want and hope for. These are highly personal matters and are the areas with which the counselor and psychotherapist are primarily concerned.

By the term "depth," psychologists refer to the relationship of events to the core of personality, the self-concept. In our diagram, then, the practice of counseling generally concerns itself with very deep aspects of personal exploration, social work, and group work with less central matters, and the teaching of subject matter with more peripheral questions. It should be clearly understood that the distinctions we have made here are matters of convenience only and represent but general areas of concern for each of the helping professions. In the final analysis, all the professions, if they are to be effective, are concerned with helping their clients, students, and patients discover increasingly closer relationships of events to self.

In this process, they will necessarily be involved with matters falling in other areas than that of their primary designation. Modern teaching, for example, requires a great deal more than attention to the relationship of the child to the world of knowledge. Teachers are also concerned about the relationships of children to each other and with the growth of the child's concepts of self. Similarly, counselors will often find it necessary to assist their clients in understanding the meaning of events outside the central core of concern about self. People are always unitary. They cannot be divided neatly into segments. It is the whole self which behaves or misbehaves, and each of the professions must deal with the whole self. The distinctions we have made are merely areas of responsibility that are generally assigned to each of the helping professions in common practice.

A comprehension of the relationships diagrammed in Fig. 4 may also be helpful in understanding some of the differences in procedures employed in various professions. It helps explain, for example, why counseling techniques are more likely to be "nondirective" than those of teaching. There is good reason why this is so. When the problem is one of helping a student to discover the meaning of the outside world and the accumulated culture, there is much a teacher can tell him. The information required to make an effective adjustment to society and the world of people, however, is far less in control of the helper than is the case in education or teaching. The discovery of effective relationships with society and other people calls for a good deal more personal involvement on the part of the subject and considerably less information which can be provided by the social worker, group therapist, or human relations counselor. Finally, in matters relating to one's deepest self there is very little really helpful information which can be supplied from outside. Accordingly, the counselor or psychotherapist must, of necessity, be much more nondirective than the teacher for the very simple reason that the information his client needs to explore is already very largely in his client's possession and there is little of any great value which the counselor can add.

THE NUMBERS TO BE HELPED

Helping professions are also different in respect to the numbers of persons with whom they operate at any one time. The teacher or pastor may be working with hundreds or even thousands, social workers typically work with much smaller groups, and counselors work with only one. While the basic principles of the helping professions remain the same in all of these cases, clearly, the methods helpers use to assist their students and clients must vary with the size of the group they are dealing with.

PERSONAL AND INDIRECT APPROACHES

Finally, there are important differences in the helping professions that are dependent upon the intimacy of the relationship between helper and helpee. Some professions, like counseling and social work, rely very heavily upon the personal dialogue established between counselor and client. The helper seeks to bring about some change in his client's meanings as a direct consequence of that interaction. He uses himself as the prime instrument of the helping process. Teachers, too, may have such close relationships with students, but the sheer numbers they have to deal with will usually call for less intensive relationships. In the classroom, teacher influence is more often exerted through such devices as manipulation of events, the setting of problems, introductions to new experience, or the shifting about of student membership in various kinds of groupings.

Some helping professions rely very heavily upon intimate personal relationships. Others do not. Quite obviously, the relationships between helper and helpee must become much less intimate when the major thrust of the helper is to accomplish his purposes by various forms of environmental manipulation. Some persons engaged in the helping professions may operate indirectly in still another sense. The supervisor or administrator, for example, may not deal directly at all with the persons he seeks to help. Rather, he must often exert his helping function through one or more third parties. This is the consultant role and calls for helping persons the consultant may never have met and never will see.

SOME ETHICAL CONSIDERATIONS

The task of helpers is to provide the conditions which will set free the client's own need for self-fulfillment to achieve its optimal expression. This is a process of problem-solving and learning in which the helper serves as catalyst (to set events in motion) and teacher or guide (to assure the process has maximum opportunities for producing positive growth). The specific ways in which this process is brought about will differ from one branch of the helping professions to another but, whatever the branch, the moral responsibility of the helper is the same—that is, to assist his clients in the quickest, most effective ways possible. It is cruel and inhuman to permit people to suffer a lack of fulfillment any longer than absolutely necessary. Persons in the helping profession must always, therefore, employ the most efficient ways possible to help their clients achieve maximum growth and health. It is not enough for a helper "to do his own thing" because it is his thing to do; he must be keenly aware of his personal assets and limitations and those of the peculiar branch of the helping professions with which he is identified. This is essential for all helpers. It is especially pertinent for those working with clients in trouble or suffering deprivation.

The responsibility of helpers goes further. It is not enough to understand himself and his branch of the profession. Helpers must see themselves and their professional efforts in the broad perspective of the whole helping process, including a proper appreciation of the contributions of other branches of the profession. Clinical files bulge with unfortunate cases of persons who did not get the help they needed because the helper they chose was either too enamored of his own special competencies or too ignorant of the possibilities inherent in other aspects of the professions to make proper use of them. It is clearly impossible for each person in the helping professions to be competent in all others. The truly effective practitioner is aware of the resources of his community and is free to use them. Among those resources are the other helping professions. In addition to their own specialties, it is therefore necessary that helpers have an understanding of the potentialities of others and the will to make maximum use of them.

SELECTED READINGS

Starred entries indicate appearance in whole or in part in Donald L. Avila, Arthur W. Combs, and William W. Purkey, *The Helping Relationship Sourcebook* (Boston: Allyn & Bacon, 1971).

* Bergin, A. E. Some implications of psychotherapy research for therapeutic practice. *International Journal of Psychiatry.* 1967, **3**, 136–150.

Bills, R. E. About people and teaching. *Bulletin of the Bureau of School Service,* College of Education, University of Kentucky, Lexington, Ky., 1955, **28**, 1–77.

Brammer, L. M. & Shostrom, E. L. *Therapeutic psychology: Fundamentals of counseling and psychotherapy.* Englewood Cliffs, N. J.: Prentice-Hall, 1960.

* Buhler, C. B. Human life goals in the humanistic perspective. *Journal of Humanistic Psychology,* 1967, **7**, 36–52.

Combs, A. W. Counseling as a learning process. *Journal of Counseling Psychology,* 1954, **1**, 31–36.

Fiedler, F. E. A comparison of therapeutic relationships in psychoanalytic, non-directive and Adlerian therapy. *Journal of Consulting Psychology,* 1950, **14,** 436–445(a).

Frank, J. D. *Persuasion and healing.* Baltimore: Johns Hopkins Press, 1961.

* Rogers, C. R. The interpersonal relationship in the facilitation of learning. In R. R. Leeper (Ed.), *Humanizing education: The person in the process.* Washington, D.C.: Association for Supervision and Curriculum Development, National Education Association, 1–18, 1967.

Rogers, C. R. *Freedom to learn.* Columbus, Ohio: Merrill Publishing Co., 1969.

Strunk, O. *Religion, A psychological interpretation.* New York: Abingdon Press, 1962.

10

Developing Understanding

All workers in the helping professions begin their tasks from observations of their students, clients, or patients. These observations can be made in either or both of two major frames of reference: From the external point of view we can develop understanding *about* people, what they are like as seen by the outside observer; from the internal frame of reference we can understand the individual through his own eyes, from his point of view. Each of these modes of observation has its unique values for the professional worker and he must learn to use them appropriately.

Careful observation of people under more or less controlled conditions will often be sufficient to make it possible to deal with them in groups, or to provide valuable guidelines for ways to control and direct their behavior. More often, helpers will need to understand the meanings of things in the peculiar private world of those they must work with. They need somehow to reach inside the skin of the helpee, to see through his eyes and appreciate his feelings, attitudes, wants, goals, and desires. This calls for something more than objective accuracy. It requires subjective sensitivity, or empathy—the capacity to place one's self in another's shoes, to perceive as he does.

For the helping professions dependent upon developing relationships between helper and helpee, the quality of empathy in the helper will be *sine qua non*. Educators of counselors, social workers, teachers, nurses, and the clergy agree on the importance of sensitivity in candidates for those professions. The crucial character of empathy as a factor in successful practice of the helping professions has also been demonstrated repeatedly in research. Everyone, of course, has some measure of sensitivity to his fellows. Without this, no one could exist for very long in modern interdependent society. Some people have developed a high degree of empathy as a normal part of their growing up. These are the lucky ones. Others have to sharpen up their capacities either by accident or by design in the course of training for or experience in the professions. Because the matter is so important for workers in the helping professions, this chapter is devoted to an examination of sensitivity and ways in which it may be acquired.

IMPORTANCE OF SENSITIVITY

The first requirement for developing sensitivity is that *you must want to develop this quality*. This seems so obvious as to hardly need mentioning. But obvious things are often the most difficult to perceive. We do not lack for data about people and their behavior. We live immersed in such data every hour of our existence. We need but open our eyes to see and our ears to hear, and other people will be willing and eager to impress upon us their personal interpretations of man and the world. We are surrounded by people clamoring to be heard, often desperately seeking to be understood. But what we see and what we hear is largely dependent upon what we believe is important. It is possible to live in the midst of events and never know they exist until they are brought into figure by a change in need. One can drive past a house a hundred times and never really see it until it is necessary to call on someone who lives there. The teacher preoccupied with "getting the lesson across" may miss completely what her students are really comprehending. Perception is a selective process. What is perceived depends upon the need of the observer. Unless it seems important to understand someone, it is practically certain he will not be understood.

Fortunately, the development of sensitivity does not require the learning of a new skill. Most of us are already sensitive to those people who seem important to us. Even little children are keenly aware of the feelings and attitudes of the adults who surround them and may be heard warning one another: "Watch out for Daddy! He's angry!" For little children and grownups the development of such sensitivity is a matter of survival. On the way from childhood to maturity, however, most of us discover that it is not necessary to be sensitive to everyone, but only to those who have important roles with respect to us. So we continue to be sensitive to our sweethearts, our bosses, supervisors, or those in positions to help us or harm us. Conversely, we may lose sensitivity for the feelings of those unimportant or subservient to us. Learning to be more sensitive is not a question of learning something new; it is a matter of learning to do explicitly and frequently what we naturally do implicitly and occasionally. It would seem that ought to be easy enough. All that is necessary is to decide what is really important and then go ahead and do it. Unfortunately, it is not that simple because of the following three major difficulties.

1/ CORRECTNESS OF ONE'S PERSONAL VIEW

The way in which things seem to each individual has such a complete feeling of reality that one seldom questions it. It seems to be the way things are and is accepted as the plain "fact of the matter." It is rare indeed to question our own experience. Because our own experience seems so right and so "so" it is difficult to understand the world of another without making an effort. It is even more difficult when his reality seems contrary to our own. Then we are faced with the distasteful possibility that we may be wrong. The development of sensitivity requires an understanding of this characteristic of our own perceptions and a willingness to accept the reality of another's perceptions as real *for him*. For example, while visiting a ward in a mental hospital one day a patient tore open his shirt and rushed up to one of the authors. In obvious pain he exclaimed, "Doctor, there are fourteen devils on my chest! They are stabbing me with spears! See them?" Of course, the author did not *see* them, but it was clear the patient *felt* them. So, he replied, "No, Joe, I don't, but I can see that you feel them. I am sorry about that." Had the author scoffed at the devils the patient saw and felt, he would simply have demonstrated how little he understood. But, by being willing to accept the patient's reality as being real for him the doors of communication were kept open and it was possible to maintain the rapport necessary for long hours of further discussion. Fortunately, it is not necessary to give up one's own reality to understand that of another. All that is required is a willingness to recognize that someone else's ways of perceiving are equally real to him.

2/ CULTURAL PRESSURE FOR OBJECTIVITY

A second hindrance to developing sensitivity arises from the highly materialistic culture in which most Americans are raised. Objectivity is in our blood. We are a nation of contrivers and experts at controlling the physical world. Our country's history began with conquering the wilderness. We are all immensely proud of our great corporations, monuments to our skill and proficiency in the making of "things." This emphasis upon things and their control is further reinforced by the Protestant ethic of our religious tradition with its emphasis upon making ourselves be good. (See doctrine of original sin concept discussed in Chapter 4.) It is still further expressed in our worship of science. We are all impressed by the marvels of science, revere its objectivity, and confidently expect its methods to provide us with answers to every problem. These cultural pressures cause the external view to come naturally to us. The logic of "getting the facts" seems irrefutable.

So deep is all this in our background that it is hard for most of us to give up the idea that a fact is real. It is difficult to conceive that a fact is only an idea existing in the minds of men. We have a cultural suspicion of the subjective. The development of sensitivity, however, demands a willingness to relinquish objectivity when it is not appropriate, and accept the subjective experience of people as valid data for human behavior. That is a difficult thing for most people to do.

3/ THE EFFECT OF FOCUSING ATTENTION

Only one thing can be in the forefront of attention at a time. It is impossible to examine both the leaf and the tree simultaneously. Preoccupation with one set of events precludes attention to others. While visiting a school near the end of the day, one of the authors wandered into the classroom of a teacher who had clearly been having a bad time. Not wanting to upset her further by getting up and walking out immediately, he sat down to wait the few minutes remaining until the bell would ring. As the youngsters were filing out of the room he walked to the teacher's desk with the intention of saying something friendly and apologizing for coming to her room at such an inopportune time. Just as he reached the teacher's desk a little boy entered the room, handed the teacher a note, and left. The teacher took one look at the note, threw it on the desk, and exploded in anger. "How could anybody be so impossibly picayune?" she exclaimed. "Honestly, what does he think we are? Haven't we got enough to do?" The author was completely in the dark as to what this was all about, but it was clear that the teacher needed to talk it out. As she did so he could not help but see the note which was lying on her desk. It said, "At the end of the day all window shades should be half-drawn" and was signed by the principal. How did this breakdown in human communication occur? Here is how it happened. This was a brand new school and the principal was proud of it. That noon he had gone out to lunch at the Rotary Club. Driving up to the front of his building on the way back, he noted that window shades were at varying levels across the front of the building. "Wouldn't it look nice," he asked himself, "if all the shades were at the same level at the end of the day?" So he went to his office and wrote the note to his teachers. The object he had in mind seemed so important to him that he never gave a thought to how it would seem to his staff!

Most breakdowns in human communication occur in just this fashion. Because communicators are preoccupied with what seems important to them, they fail to communicate with others. The teacher preoccupied with covering the subject will not understand the students she is trying to teach. The counselor preoccupied with what his client "ought" to do may impose his wrong solutions because he did not really hear what his client was saying. Learning to be more sensitive requires a commitment to its importance. Freud told us long ago that we never do anything unless we would rather. What we think, what we hear, who we listen to, and even what we see are determined by what we feel is important.

Unless we value sensitivity and understanding, it is not likely to occur. Yet it marks the difference between good and poor professional workers. In researches at the University of Florida on good and poor nurses, teachers, counselors, and even Episcopal priests, one outstanding quality associated with good professional workers was sensitivity to the meanings of those they worked with. Effective professional workers were concerned with how things were from the point of view of those they worked with. If sensitivity is not sufficiently valued by helpers, it is most unlikely to occur and the effectiveness of the helper will be diminished.

READING BEHAVIOR BACKWARD

Basically, the problem of developing sensitivity is a question of learning to read behavior backwards. According to perceptual psychologists, people behave as a function of their perceptions. If this is true it should then be possible for us to understand how people are perceiving by working backward from their behavior. When we see a child drink, we can infer that he felt thirsty. When we see a player duck the ball thrown at him, we can infer he was afraid it was going to hit him. If a person's behavior is a function of his perceptions, it follows that, if we observe his behavior carefully, it should be possible to reconstruct the feelings, attitudes, purposes, in the perceptual field of the behaver.

This is the procedure that everyone uses quite automatically in dealing with other people. The teacher, for example, observes a child who is not reading very well. As she watches him behave, she asks: "Now what is his trouble? How is he seeing what he is doing?" She formulates inferences as she makes her observations. "Does he understand the sound?" she wonders, and then tests this hypothesis by further observation of the child's behavior in reading various materials especially selected to test that hypothesis. As a result she may decide that he does hear the sound and makes a new hypothesis: "Perhaps he is not distinguishing between A and O, T and TH." Then she tests this hypothesis, perhaps through the use of diagnostic tests. Eventually, by a process of observation, inference, and test she may arrive at an understanding of how things are with the child, and therefore be in a position to help him perceive more adequately in the future.

The same procedure is used by the administrator seeking to understand what is "bugging" the people on his staff. He tries to grasp how things seem to them and repeatedly tests his inferences against further observations. For most of us "getting the feel" of other people in this fashion is not something new. Everyone has had experience in making inferences about the perceptual world of others. The problem for the professional worker is not a matter of learning to do something new, but of learning to do more effectively and efficiently what he now does accidentally, crudely, and occasionally.

Reading behavior backward is also what the psychologist does in studying behavior, but usually with greater care and precision than the man in the street. It is also the way in which professional workers develop sensitivity and acquire the characteristics of empathy. The technique consists of making and testing inferences against the yardstick of externally observed behavior. The worker observes the behavior of his client and, reading behavior backward, makes inferences about the kinds of perceptions that might have produced the behaviors observed. These are then checked against subsequent behaviors and inferences to determine their reliability and predictability. Through such a process of continuous observation-inference-test-observation-inference-test over a period of time, the helper is able to come closer and closer to the probable state of a person's perceptual field.

Can Inference Be Scientific?

Some objective psychologists take exception to the use of inference as a technique for understanding behavior. They feel it is too subjective, too open to possibilities of error and distortion introduced by the person doing the observing. Their concern is certainly a valid one. The use of self an an instrument for making observations does, indeed, add a possible source of distortion not present in more mechanical ways of observing and recording behavior. This does not warrant rejection of the method, however, if the sources of error can be controlled.

All sciences are dependent upon the making and testing of hypotheses. To control the accuracy of this process, scientists have invented tests of validity to be applied to the testing of hypotheses as follows:

1. Feelings of subjective certainty. Does the hypothesis seem reasonable and accurate to the possessor?
2. Is the hypothesis consistent with all the known facts? Does it fit? Does it provide an adequate explanation of all the data?
3. Will it stand the test of mental juggling? Will it still ring true when confronted intellectually and subjected to the impact of other concepts, explanations, or suppositions?
4. Will it predict? Using the hypothesis to make predictions, will these predictions be borne out in fact?
5. Is the hypothesis acceptable to other workers, especially recognized experts? Have other persons come, preferably independently, to the same conclusions?
6. Is the hypothesis internally consistent? Does the hypothesis stand up when various interpretations are made to confront one another?

The products of all the sciences (including the physical sciences which we are accustomed to regarding as the essence of accuracy and precision) are, in the final analysis, dependent upon one or more of these tests in establishing what is "fact." Perceptual psychology is subject to the same requirements. The tests listed above are used to determine the acceptability of inferences about human behavior in the same basic fashion as the astronomer tests his inferences about a new galaxy or the physicist tests his inference about quantum theory. The making of inferences, in itself, is not unscientific. The way in which they are made and tested may be unscientific, however. Every science, including the science of behavior, is dependent upon inference to extend its horizons beyond the immediate and the palpable. To reject the use of inference would seriously hamper our attempts to understand people. Our problem is not to reject inference but to learn to use it properly.

LEARNING TO LISTEN

Since behavior is a product of human perceptions, people are always telling us how things are with them through the ways in which they behave. Children do this in their play so much that psychologists have learned to use play both as a diagnostic device to explore how children are thinking and feeling, and for treatment in helping them change their perceptions of themselves and the world. One need not be a mind reader, for example, to get the message about how a child feels as he watches him lambaste the "baby brother" doll or flush a drawing of the teacher down the toilet! The behavior of adults is equally revealing. Most of us soon get to know what to expect about our friends, neighbors, bosses, or enemies as we have opportunities to observe them in action. Children, too, can read the behavior of adults, and they do it even when adults are doing their best to hide their feelings. In the psychological clinic, for example, rejecting mothers are often heard to exclaim: "Why does he keep asking, 'Mama do you love me?' I keep telling him I do, but he keeps on asking till it nearly drives me crazy!"

Philip Jackson, in an interview study with teachers, reports how teachers use fleeting behavioral cues to tell how well they are doing their jobs. Here are a few excerpts from those interviews.

> *Interviewer:* How can you tell when you are doing a good job?
> *Teacher:* Oh, look at their faces.
> *Interviewer:* Will you tell me more about that?
> *Teacher:* Why, sure, they look alert; they look interested; they look questioning—like they're ready to question something. They look like they're anxious to learn more about it. . . . At other times, you know you haven't done a good job when they look blah or look disinterested or I-don't-care attitude, well, then I feel bad, you know, I've done a bad job.

Another teacher says:

> "The reaction, I think, of the children, and what they seem to have gained from it. Their interest; their expression; the way they look."

Still another says:

> I can tell by the way they sound. There is a sound that you can tell and you can tell when they are really working.

Interviewer: You mean the sound of the room in general?
Teacher: The sound of the room in general. Now it doesn't always have to be a quiet sound—it can be a noisy, buzzing sound and you're still doing a good job and everybody is working.
Interviewer: But can you tell?
Teacher: I can tell. You can feel it.

And still another says:

It's the easiest thing in the world. You know you're missing at the first yawn. Teaching and learning, if they're not enjoyable and fun, are both very difficult to accomplish. When the kids aren't having a good time, if they're not paying attention and sitting up, that's it—a theatrical sense is something you can't learn, but a good actor can sense his audience. He knows when a performance is going well or not going well, simply by the feeling in the air. And it's that way in the classroom. You can feel when the kids are resistant.[1]

ATTENDING TO MEANINGS

Developing sensitivity is a matter of listening to *meanings* rather than observing behavior. Psychologists have sometimes called this "listening with the third ear." It is a matter of seeing behind what people are saying or doing to the meanings or perceptions producing their behavior. Every behavior is in some measure expressive of perceptions, but behaviors resulting from very strong feelings are almost impossible to dissemble. The very attempts which others make to hide their feelings only serve to reveal them more. Like the comment of Hamlet's mother, "The lady doth protest too much, me thinks," our suspicions are aroused by overdone behavior. A counseling client of one of the authors once said it this way: "Sometimes when I am talking to you I try to keep you from really knowing. I act like a mother bird defending her nest by pretending she has a broken wing to lead you away from what I don't want you to see. But you know, you always know."

An important technique of counseling, called by Carl Rogers the recognition and acceptance of feeling, is, in reality, the response of the counselor to the client's perceptions. Using this technique the counselor listens carefully to his client, penetrates to the meaning (feeling) being expressed by the client, and tries to express this clearly and sharply for

---

1. From P. W. Jackson, *Life in classrooms.* New York: Holt, Rinehart & Winston, 1968. Reprinted with permission of the author.

him. Note how the counselor does this in the following excerpt from an interview with a woman in marital counseling:

> *Client:* He does things like that all the time. I never know what he is going to say. When we are out with our friends he thinks it is very funny to tell them about something that I did that he thinks stupid. Sometimes I just want to crawl under the rug.
> *Counselor:* You feel pretty humiliated and ashamed. I can see how you might.

Such concentration of attention upon the person's meaning is characteristic of effective helpers. One can hear it in use by the teacher who says, "Jimmy, I can see you are very angry at Paul. I can understand that, but you must not hit him with the shovel"; or the nurse who says to her patient, "I realize you are not sure you can do it, Mrs. Smith. I know it will not be easy for you."

The kind of intensive listening required for the helping professions is not a passive process. It is an active one. It calls for sharply focused attention and keen interest in the words and behavior of others. This is quite different from much of the conversation which characterizes our daily lives. Indeed, for most people real listening is a seldom used art. The purpose of much conversation is not to hear what the other person has to say, but to enjoy the opportunity to express one's self. Listening in on the conversation at a tea, cocktail party, or casual conversation on the street, it quickly becomes apparent that no one is really listening. The speakers are amusing themselves while the audience patiently, or not so patiently, waits to get the floor to tell about his operation or his trip to San Francisco. To find a good listener is often difficult—so much so that good listeners are often described by others as wonderful conversationalists!

LISTENING IS THERAPEUTIC

The importance of listening extends far beyond its value for aiding in understanding other people. The experience of being listened to is often therapeutic in itself. Growth in others may be facilitated by a sympathetic listener even if he does little else. In this sense every human being who has ever listened patiently to the problems of another is as much a helper at that moment as those who claim impressive titles by reason of position or academic degrees. One of the authors once knew a man whose life experience clearly demonstrated the significant role of the sympathetic listener. Most people who interacted with this man came away from the experience feeling much better and looking much brighter than they did when they first began speaking with him. And, almost without exception these very same people would say something as follows: "Oh, what a fine guy he is! He's one of the most interesting people I have ever talked with. I could talk to him all day!" From these comments, one would think he must have been a very dynamic person. But, as a matter of fact, he was never responsible for more than 5 or 10 percent of the conversations he engaged in. He was actually very shy and retiring, albeit most sensitive and empathic.

A good portion of the training of persons in the helping professions is given over in one form or another to developing sensitivity. Student teachers, for example, are required to spend long hours observing children and their teachers with the intent of improving abilities to see and hear what is really going on in the classroom. Counselors, social workers, and clinical psychologists engage in practice sessions with real or actor-clients while supervisors attempt to help them see ever more clearly what their patients or clients are truly expressing. One technique devised by counselors for teaching beginners to listen is the Listening Game which some readers might like to try. In a group session, it is agreed by all the participants that no one may speak until he has first stated the gist of what the previous speaker had to say in a fashion satisfactory to the previous speaker. It is fascinating how the application of this rule slows down the conversation! Most people playing this game quickly discover that listening is, indeed, a difficult art, and they are chagrined to discover how little they normally hear of what is being expressed by those around them.

USING THE SELF AS INSTRUMENT

In Chapter 1 we have seen that effective professional work is dependent upon the skillful use of self as an instrument for carrying out the helping task. Understanding of others is also dependent upon the use of the helper's self for the making of inferences. This use of the self as instrument, however, is a two-edged sword. Properly used, one's own experience may be very helpful in understanding others. It may also lead one badly astray! Scientists in all fields must calibrate their instruments in order to assure the most accurate possible measurements. They adjust their voltmeters to 0 position before reading the strength of the current, and carefully balance their scales before using them to weigh things. In similar fashion the human instrument can be calibrated to provide increasingly accurate inferences about what goes on in people. It is a matter of choosing a reliable instrument to start with and using it thereafter with care and discipline according to the basic rules which science has provided for the making of observations and checking reliability. The physical scientist does this with his instruments but human beings have to do it to themselves. This requires discipline and control.

USING EXPERIENCE AS DATA

The most obvious and meaningful source of information for the making of inferences is our own experience. Each of us has had intimate involvement in the growth and development of at least one person. This is important data and its proper use can add immeasurably to our understanding of others. Even the suffering we have endured can help us understand and sympathize with others who suffer. But not necessarily! The effect is not automatic. One needs but to look about him to observe in the lives of friends and acquaintances how hardship, segregation, or tragedy have made some persons angry, hostile, and closed-off from their fellows while others seem to have become increasingly warm, gentle, and understanding as a consequence of what they have been through. What seems to make the difference is the individual's ability to accept or be open to his experience. An attitude of defensiveness prevents experience from getting through and adding to sensitivity. Persons who have been too deeply hurt build walls around themselves for self-protection. Such walls serve to protect the individual from interaction with others but, unfortunately, they also prevent him from getting through to them.

Intimate experiences wherein one has an opportunity to communicate with others deeply and meaningfully add much to the capacity of individuals to act sympathetically with others. They provide the raw material from which understanding is built. Research evidence shows that persons who have not been loved are incapable of loving. Similarly, acceptance of others is related to acceptance of self. Apparently one needs to have experienced a human feeling to be able to truly grasp its meaning for another. This does not mean that in order to understand another it is necessary to have experienced the same event that he did. That, of course, is always impossible. What *can* be experienced in common are the meanings of events, feelings, attitudes, beliefs, understandings, or concepts. Therefore, since the authors of this book are males, they cannot experience childbirth. They can and have, however, experienced with their wives the joys, anxieties, fears, and fulfillment of childbirth, to say nothing of their common experience of the problems of parenthood.

It is probable that any peak experience in which an individual is living and participating "to the hilt" contributes something significant to his capacity to interact with life and with others. Having felt the glory of a sunset, one can know much better what it means to another. Having won, lost, loved, hated, and suffered disillusionment or triumphed over adversity, these qualities of living can make one more alive. Intimate experiences wherein one is able to communicate heart to heart with another, for no matter how short a period, extend and increase one's capacity for understanding.

Having lived and experienced is by no means a guarantee that we will understand other people better, however. Delinquents and criminals have often suffered, but because of this they are not necessarily abler to deal with people. Quite the contrary, they regard most people as their enemies! The divorcee might say: "I know all about men. I've been married four times." But she leaves much to be desired as an expert in marital affairs despite her extensive experience! Experience provides us with a reservoir of data about human behavior but, unfortunately, it is not always so neatly labeled that we can clearly distinguish what is trustworthy and what is not.

To make the best use of experience, we have to use it—not as fact but as data. We need to use it for what it is worth, at the same time avoiding the error of assuming it is infallible simply because it is our own. This means we have to explore it, examine it, and test it against the experience of others and against the harsh realities of life. In this way we can define experience, eliminate its errors, and in the long run contribute more effectively to the satisfaction of our own needs and those about us.

POSTPONING PERSONAL NEED

Developing sensitivity requires a willingness to postpone immediate need satisfactions in the interests of another. This is often difficult, for our own ways of perceiving and thinking have such a feeling of "goodness" or "rightness." So strong is the tendency to impose our own structure on events that a conscious effort is required to set them aside even for a little while. An outstanding art teacher of our acquaintance once illustrated this very nicely. The evening before class, she spent many hours working out a new project. The next day she waited for an appropriate moment to tell the class about the exciting project she had worked out for them. Everyone in the class was busy and interested in what he was doing, and for a long time she had no opportunity to break in. Finally, she started to tell them about the new project but no one paid any heed. After several attempts to capture their attention she said to them wi some irritation, "I guess you just don't want to hear what I have ranged for you!" This brought no response from anyone. Everyone c tinued with the projects they were already engaged in except for one la who could always be counted on for some kind of a comment. He re plied, "Not today, Mrs. Smith." She told us some time later, "You know I was really kind of hurt. I thought it was a wonderful idea and I had worked so hard getting it ready! Somehow, though, my good sense managed to prevail and I set my own idea aside for a later occasion." Often it takes a real wrench to break loose from our own predilections to follow the thinking and needs of others.

Even psychiatrists and clinical psychologists, presumably well-trained in making careful diagnoses, have been known to describe their clients as having the psychiatrist's or psychologist's own personality problems. Freud, too, observed that we seldom recognize a problem in others that we have not wrestled with ourselves. The ability to set aside personal need is probably dependent in very large measure upon the degree of fulfillment the helper himself is experiencing in his own life. Sensitivity to others is a difficult skill to display in the absence of some positive personal satisfactions. The capacity for self-abnegation is a quality of persons who are achieving some measure of self-actualization. Inadequate and threatened persons must be so continuously on guard against the world that there is little time or inclination remaining to be much concerned about others. Only a free self can give itself. An important prerequisite for the development of sensitivity, therefore, is the opportunity for fulfilling experiences in the life of the helper himself.

The personal discipline required for the development of sensitivity is greatly facilitated by the possession of a deep conviction that "I, too, could be wrong!" Nothing gets in the way of empathy more than the bland assumption of infallibility. It is absolutely essential that counselors, social workers, and clergymen working with persons in serious trouble understand that there is literally nothing a person (including one's self) might not do if exposed to the right combination of unhappy circumstances. Uncomfortable as it may be, belief in one's own fallibility makes the development of empathy and honest sympathy with others much easier. When one understands that a fact is only a belief shared by those we think are important and may or may not "really" be true, the recognition of one's own fallibility is also much easier to accept.

VALUE OF A READING PROGRAM

Another valuable source of understanding is one's own reading program. Whatever provides us with insight into the nature of people and their problems, hopes, and desires may contribute greatly to the development of sensitivity, either as general background for interpretation or, more directly, as participation in human experience. In this connection, one naturally thinks of the professional and scientific literature available in the various social sciences; of course, these materials are invaluable for persons working in the helping professions. Out of such reading the student may acquire the setting or backdrop against which the understanding of a particular individual may be seen with greater clarity and richness. A program of reading in the social sciences, however, is by no means enough to develop adequate sensitivity for persons in the helping professions. Scientific material is usually objective and descriptive. It presents human beings as they are perceived by the outside observer. Much of it is also couched in statistical or normative terms descriptive of populations rather than individuals. People engaged in the helping professions, therefore, must usually acquire subjective understanding from other sources or from their own experiences.

A fruitful source of subjective understanding of other people is to be found in the nonscientific literature available to us. It has often been said that our best psychologists are poets and novelists. In a very real sense, this is true. While scientists are highly skilled in providing us with understandings of people in normative, statistical, and abstract terms, poets and novelists are far superior in helping us grasp the essential humanity of people. Through drama, poetry, autobiography, and novels it is possible to expand our experience vicariously. We can enter the world of seeing and feeling, believing, hoping, trusting, caring, loving, and hating in more or less degree as these are experienced by other people. As we give ourselves up to the spell woven by these kinds of writers, we can be for a time what we are not, never have been, or perhaps never could be. With James Agee we can experience something of what it means to have "A Death in the Family," even if we have never had one. With Malcolm X we can feel something of what it is like to be black and to grow up in the slums of a city. Through literature we can experience the frustrations and power of being a President, the growth of intelligence with Helen Keller, or the pitiful searching of a Marilyn Monroe. The world of literature provides a vast treasure chest of experience that is invaluable for persons in the helping professions. The understanding, empathy, and capacity for a deep sympathetic identification with others which the poet, dramatist, and author put down on paper are the very same qualities which persons in the helping professions must actively put to work in carrying out their respective functions.

BEING IN THE STREAM

The tendency to structure the world is always with us. Much of our time is spent impressing meaning upon life and forcing it into some mold, category, or classification. Without this we could not exist. Yet, often it destroys what the experience otherwise might have to give. Looking at the abstract painting the novice asks, "What is it?" The artist looks and "lets it come to him." Stereotypes about "What Negroes are like" distorts or destroys the opportunity to know a man whose skin happens to be dark. It is sad to be so firmly the prisoner of our preconceptions. Fortunately, the capacity for openness we possessed as children can be recaptured if one is willing to be in the stream and let it convey the message it has.

This demands an openness to life, a willingness to walk with others in their perceptual worlds. It requires a temporary giving up of how things seem to us and an active effort to enter into the world as it is seen through the eyes of others. So it may be possible to experience new things which have been there all along. This happened years ago to one of the authors at Christmas time when he was working in New York City. For many years he had passed through the Grand Concourse of Grand Central Station several times a day. Then, one evening standing in line for tickets he became aware of an English gentleman just in front of him, apparently newly arrived in the United States, who stood entranced, looking up at the ceiling and murmuring, "Incredible, simply incredible! Magnificent!" At this the author looked up too, and discovered to his astonishment that indeed it was. He had seen the beautiful ceiling for the very first time!

People in the helping professions may often be observed in efforts to "get with it." The kindergarten teacher may literally get "down to the child's level" by stooping beside him or sitting on a child-size chair. An attempt is made to be congruent with events to let them tell their story. Counselors do this as they listen with understanding to a client describe some behavior which the counselor may personally feel is repugnant. Such openness is almost childlike in character. It is a kind of naïveté, a wide-eyed wonder which permits the world to come in, to be whatever it is.

Steeping one's self in human experience is one means of developing the sensitivity of the instrument we have to work with. Like everything else, however, there are limits. Not all experiences are equally valuable. To make a cult out of "steeping one's self in life" or a way of life out of "daring to be different" can have the effect of drastically narrowing experience rather than expanding and enriching it. Every generation has seen groups set out to make themselves different, only to find themselves soon trapped in some banal conformity.

Development of sensitivity cannot become a lifetime task. Being sensitive to those we love or are deeply identified with may be possible without great expenditure of energy or of discipline and control of self. The extension of sensitivity to those we do not have such close association with is a much more difficult matter which most professional workers have to work at. Good helpers find that their jobs are likely to be draining and exhausting. As a consequence, like everyone else, they need opportunities to charge their batteries, to find satisfaction and renewal which make it possible to return to the task refreshed and able to give it the energy and attention required.

The self can be made into an effective and reliable instrument for understanding and helping others. Like any other, however, the human instrument requires continuous checking and calibration. Most physical instruments become less accurate with time and use whereas the human instrument can actually improve itself. Human organisms tend to become increasingly sharper, stronger, and more effective with use. So, the self can be made an ever more effective and sensitive instrument with exercise and discipline.

SPECIAL SOURCES FOR DEVELOPING SENSITIVITY

As we have suggested earlier, people are always telling us how things seem to them if we can develop the sensitivity to hear what it is they are expressing. Since all behavior is the external expression of the individual's internal thoughts and feelings, every behavior can tell us something about how things are with another individual. However, not all behaviors are equally fruitful in helping us understand another's internal world.

Some behaviors may tell us a great deal about a person; others may tell us very little. Some, like the behavior of young lovers, may be purposely contrived to mislead observers. Some behaviors are readily available to casual observation as, for example, a man's behavior in the checkout line at a supermarket. Others can be observed occasionally, only under special circumstances, or through some device which will permit invasion of the person's private world in spite of his wishes.

OBSERVING

A good deal of sensitivity can be acquired by simply looking receptively. We have already seen that this is an active process of "reading behavior backwards." The choices people make are not haphazard. They have meaning to the individual. So, the kind of car one drives, the sort of house he builds, the care he gives his yard, the clothes he wears, or the pictures he paints all have something to say about the behaver.

What is observed when watching others is also dependent on the intent of the observer. What is seen is likely to be what one is "set" or "expects" to see. Idly watching, one may see almost nothing. "Girl-watching" may be simply an act of appreciation. Watching a movie or TV show may be escape or amusement. Watching an antagonist may be purely defensive. If looking is to be utilized for increased sensitivity, it must be directed beyond surface manifestations to the nature of personal meaning existing for the behavior we observe.

Every science must begin its work from disciplined observation, and most training programs for the various helping professions include extensive practice in observing. The approach to making observations advocated by these programs will depend upon the general frame of reference stressed by the trainers. Those operating from an objective orientation emphasize careful reporting of precisely what was done by the subject. Looking at people in this way the observer carefully records the moment to moment activities of the persons he was watching. Here, for example, is part of a report made by a young social worker:

Time: 3:30 P.M., January 4, 1968.
Place: Third Avenue Playground.
When I arrived, Mr. Albert pointed out Jimmy Christianson to me. He is ten years old but seems small for his age. He was dressed in blue jeans, sneakers and an old brown zipper jacket with a big tear under the left arm. He was sitting on the bench along the first base line with four other boys waiting his turn to go to bat. Jimmy kept swinging his feet

back and forth and gripping the bench with his two hands as he did so. He seemed pretty excited about the game and kept yelling, "Sock it to 'em, Eddie! Attaboy!" to the boy up at the bat. Every once in a while he would turn and say something to one of his bench mates but I could not hear what it was he said. Once, when Eddie swung and missed, Jimmy groaned and hid his face in the back of the boy next to him. Then he picked up his first baseman's glove, pounded his fist in it and yelled, "That's O.K., Eddie! Let 'em have it!"

The purpose of such detailed reporting is to teach the beginner to make careful observations and to see precisely what is going on with a minimum of distortion. Observations made with such care and detail are usually more valuable for the discipline they demand of the learner than for daily use in the helping professions.

More often the helper will need to make his observations in a subjective frame of reference and approach his task holistically. By operating in this way, he is less concerned about recording precise details, and devotes his attention to those aspects of special significance in understanding the behavior of the subject from his own point of view. It involves steeping himself in the experience and making and remaking hypotheses consistent with the behavior observed. In this fashion he seeks to build a picture of the world as it appears to his subject—the ways in which the subject sees himself and the peculiar searching and strivings which motivate him. Here is a sample from the report of a beginning teacher:

When I arrived at Miss Anthony's class on Tuesday, the children were in the middle of a project running a store. Leslie was in a group of three who were supposed to be making a big sign for the store front. They had a large sheet of paper on the floor and were drawing on it with crayons. Like his behavior on the playground yesterday, Leslie was very bossy, continually telling the other two children what to do, how to do it and constantly criticizing them. He seems to need to be always the center of attention. It's as though, for him, imposing his will on the other children is far more important than the production they are working on. When the teacher came close at one point he ran to her and pulled her by the hand to come see their sign, but even as he did so, he managed to stand directly in front of the other two kids so they were pretty effectively blocked off from the teacher. From the look on his face you could see he was eating up every word of praise the teacher said like it was "Manna from heaven." He seems to have a terrible need for attention at all times. Even the way he poises his body seems to be saying, "Please, please, please, look at me! Give me! Pay attention to me!"

ARTISTIC PRODUCTIONS

Among the most revealing sources of data about the internal world of people are the artistic productions which they attempt. When painting, drawing, or acting, people bring into play their own experience and so reveal it to others who have the eyes to see it. No two actors ever perform a role in precisely the same way. Each gives the part his own peculiar twist which may reveal as much about the actor as the part he is playing. Similarly, the things people draw and paint may provide important clues to their internal states of feeling and being. The paintings of patients in hospitals are often used by psychologists to aid in understanding the mentally ill. Children's artistic productions are studied by teachers for the information they provide about what they are thinking and feeling.

Useful as artistic materials may be for providing clues about the feelings and attitudes of others, interpretations from such materials can by no means always be accepted at face value. The value of fantasy for most of us is that it provides opportunities to let ourselves go, to express ourselves uninhibitedly. As a consequence, what is presented in fantasy may be only a caricature or exaggeration of personal feelings represented in much greater force than it truly signifies in a person's economy. It is even possible that what seems to be expressed in a picture may have nothing whatever to do with the individual's feelings at all. The story is told, for example, of the little boy whom everyone was concerned about because all of his drawings were done in jet black. What seemed to his teachers an indication of depression and despair turned out to be nothing of the kind when they asked the child, "Why are all your pictures so black?" He replied, "Because I sit in the last seat and when the crayons get to me only the black ones are left!"

PERSONAL DOCUMENTS

Written productions are among the most fertile sources of material for understanding others. Unlike observations of behavior or inferences made from what people have to say, which must be caught "on the wing," written material can often be held and studied for comparatively long periods of time. As a consequence, personal documents can often help us catch the flavor of people in a way that nothing else can. Teachers often use written assignments, for example, as devices by which their understanding of children can be increased at the same time they are checking the student's progress in English and spelling. Here, for example, are poems written by two ninth-graders. The first provides us with a forceful insight into the meaning of an automobile to a young adolescent boy. The second provides a charming and poignant picture of the sadness of a broken love affair for a young girl.[2]

DRIVING A CAR

When I get behind the wheel
    I feel different;
When I touch the key
    And hear the hum of the engine
I feel like popping the clutch
    and digging.
When I touch the accelerator
    I feel as if I am in a rocket
Heading nowhere.
    I love to tinker with an "eight"
    And see what makes it purr.
When I drive a car
    It seems as if I am floating
On a cloud.

THE RING ON THE LITTLE GOLD CHAIN

It's odd how when you return his ring
You start remembering everything;
You both were always so carefree and gay,
Loving each other in your own little way.
You recall when he said you were his girl,
And how he had set your heart in a whirl.
You remember his ring that you wore on a chain
And how your heart sang when you heard his name.
You smile when you think of how you would fight.
Then kiss and make up the very next night.
You think of the days when you walked down the street
And everyone said, "My! Don't they look sweet?"

2. The authors regret that the young poets' names are unknown. The poems were shared with us by a teacher from a collection that has been accumulated over the years.

But it's all over now; what's done is done;
They say to stop crying and start having fun;
But you know there will always be a small pain
When you think of the ring on the little gold chain.

When available, personal documents such as letters, diaries, and auto-biographies are equally valuable in helping us to understand the internal world of others. As for any of the sources of data we use for making in-ferences about the private worlds of others, however, it is especially necessary to beware of accepting such personal documents as one-to-one expressions of what the individual is truly thinking and feeling. Of course, they may be. But, when writing such materials, people are seldom unaware of a real or potential audience and so may intentionally or un-intentionally write for a desired effect on the reader. This is particularly true of autobiographies written for posterity, or letters written for a spe-cial purpose—but it may be equally true of diaries.

PROJECTIVE TESTS

Psychologists have devised hundreds of tests for exploring various as-pects of the internal life of persons, based upon the "projective hypoth-esis" that whatever response a person makes to a situation must inevi-tably be a product of the peculiar meanings existing for him at that mo-ment. Projective tests, therefore, provide the subject with some sort of problem or situation to deal with. His solutions to these problems can then be carefully studied for indications of his motives, feelings, atti-tudes, hopes, desires, and personal ways of seeing self and the world. The projective tests now available cover a wide area. Some are formal de-vices with carefully worked out methods of scoring and administration. Others consist of little more than pictures to be responded to, or a set of instructions to be carried out. Some are pencil and paper tests; others require some form of acting out. The variety is almost limitless and new ones are being invented continually. Many are used not only for practical diagnosis but also as research instruments for investigating aspects of personality theory, human motivation, and learning.

A commonly used projective instrument for exploring children's per-ceptions about school, for example, are various types of "picture story tests." In this test a child might be shown a picture of some school situa-tion as, for example, a little boy seated alone in a classroom with his head in his hands. The child would then be asked to make up a story about this picture telling what was going on at the present time, what led up to this situation, and what probably happened afterward. From the child's responses the psychologist is then able to determine something of the nature of his probable attitudes toward himself, school, teachers, classmates, and the like.

Another commonly used projective instrument is the Sentence Completion Test wherein the subject is given an uncompleted sentence with the instructions to complete it. Here are some samples:

Fathers usually ——————————————————.
My teacher ————————————————————.
Children should never ———————————————.

Other projective tests may ask persons to tell what they see in ink blots, to draw pictures of some sort, to provide a proper ending for an incomplete story, to act out a dramatic event, to play a role in a discussion, or to freely associate to a set of stimulus words. The list is nearly endless, but this is not the place for an exhaustive review. Interested readers may want to investigate this important area of psychological knowledge elsewhere.

Most projective tests require a high degree of professional training and skill for interpretation plus a strong sense of professional ethics, especially since many of the projective devices are intentionally designed to mislead the test taker. Often they are presented as tests of imagination, skill in storytelling, or the like. As a consequence the subject may be tricked into revealing aspects of his personal life that he would not be willing to reveal if he knew what he was doing. This kind of invasion of privacy cannot be taken lightly and raises important ethical questions for the users of projective instruments.

SENSITIVITY TRAINING

A comparatively new development in the training of persons in the helping professions is the use of sensitivity training groups to help beginning workers increase their sensitivity and capacity for entering into empathic relationships with students, clients, and patients. Such groups are usually composed of five to ten persons under the leadership of a trainer or leader skilled in group techniques. Sometimes these groups are called sensitivity training; basic encounter groups; T-groups; or, simply, discussion groups. All have the common objective of aiding group members in one fashion or another to explore themselves and their ways of perceiving other people. When well-conducted, they can prove of great value in the training of helpers. Unfortunately, it is not always easy to predict the probable outcomes of participating in sensitivity groups. When a new technique for working with people appears on the scene, for a time it often becomes a fad because all kinds of people experiment with it for all kinds of purposes. And this has happened with group processes. Many persons of widely divergent levels of competence and responsibility have experimented with leading sensitivity groups with equally divergent results. Some participants in these kinds of groups have also found the experience so exhilarating and satisfying that they become "encounter buffs" seeking out such experiences at every opportunity. Others have been deeply shaken by their experiences and retreat to lick their wounds in isolation. As a consequence, at this point the matter is in great confusion.

There is no doubt that group experiences can be of tremendous value in the development of sensitivity. In time, all this experimentation will no doubt lead to clearer understanding of the dynamics of encounter groups so that they may be used with increased skill and greater certainty of positive outcomes. In the meantime, helpers need to recognize that the terms "encounter," "sensitivity," or "T-group" are blanket terms which cover a broad spectrum. They must also realize that while group experiences can be extremely useful devices for the development of sensitivity and empathy, they need to be chosen with care and discrimination. How helpful a group is likely to be, will depend primarily upon the philosophy held by the leader, the purposes he has in mind, and the skill and experience he has demonstrated in previous sessions.

FRINGE BENEFITS OF THE CAPACITY FOR EMPATHY

The increased humanity and sensitivity to others that comes about as a consequence of intimate interaction with others is also one of the fringe benefits for workers in the helping professions. Helping others is actually a two-way street. One cannot successfully enter deeply and meaningfully into the life of another person without having that experience affect one's self as well. With tongue in cheek, someone once described psychotherapy: "when two people get together to help each other!" The joke is probably true.

Helping relationships seek to create circumstances for the helpee in which he can drop his normal defenses and participate openly and freely in exploring himself and the world in which he lives in ways not possible to him in his usual life situations. When successfully accomplished, the experience is provided for *both* parties—helpee and helper. The creation of such conditions for one's client, student, or patient calls for sensitivity, openness, and empathy on the part of the helper himself. These kinds of relationships entered as part of his professional role provide the helper with the same kind of warm and intimate relationship with another as they do for the person he is trying to help. So, the practice of sensitivity contributes to the capacity of persons in the helping professions to be ever more sensitive in the future. In this way, effective practice in the helping professions provides its practitioners with the rare privilege of engaging in work resulting in a continuous process of personal growth.

SELECTED READINGS

Starred entries indicate appearance in whole or in part in Donald L. Avila, Arthur W. Combs, and William W. Purkey, *The Helping Relationship Sourcebook* (Boston: Allyn & Bacon, 1971).

* Aspy, D. N. How did he get there? *Peabody Journal of Education.* 1969, **47**, 152–153.

Axline, V. *Dibs: In search of self.* Boston: Houghton Mifflin, 1964.

Ball, G. Speaking without words. *American Journal of Nursing.* 1960, **60**, 692–693.

Combs, A. W. The personal approach to good teaching. *Educational Leadership*, 1964, **21**, 369–378.

Courson, C. The use of inference as a research tool. *Educational and Psychological Measurement*, 1965, **25**, 1029–1038.

Gillham, H. L. *Helping children accept themselves and others.* New York: Bureau of Publications, Teachers College, Columbia University, 1959.

Ginott, H. *Between parent and child: New solutions to old problems.* New York: Macmillan, 1965.

Gordon, I. J. *Studying the child in school.* New York: Wiley, 1966.

Rogers, C. R. *On becoming a person.* Boston: Houghton Mifflin, 1961.

* Rogers, C. R. The interpersonal relationship in the facilitation of learning. In R. R. Leeper (Ed.), *Humanizing education: The person in the process.* Washington, D.C.: Association for Supervision and Curriculum Development, National Education Association, 1–18, 1967.

Williams, T. R. The personal-cultural equation in social work and anthropology. *Social Casework*, 1959, **40**, 74–80.

11

Establishing Helping Relationships

The goal of helping processes is the production of more effective and satisfying relationships between the helpee and the world he lives in. This is brought about by a process of exploration and discovery of new meaning, a process also called learning. The helping professions did not invent it. What helpers have to offer is themselves and their know-how about the dynamics of learning which may serve to make the process more certain, more speedy, and more satisfying for those they seek to assist.

GENERAL APPROACHES TO HELPING

The helping process must deal with three aspects governing learning. First, the conditions for confrontation must be brought into being. An atmosphere which makes exploration possible must be established. Second, clients must be brought into dialogue with some new experience. This might be in the form of interaction with the helper, an encounter with some aspect of the outside world, or the acquisition of some new information through reading, talking, or other form of communication. This is the information phase of the learning process. Third, the helpee must discover the personal meaning of his new information or experience for himself. This is the most crucial stage and the aspect in which helpers need to exert their greatest skill. Almost anyone can provide new information or experience. The special contribution of the professional helper, however, lies in his unique ability to deal with the first and third learning stages. In approaching this task, three general possibilities are open to him: authoritarian, laissez faire, and democratic.

An *authoritarian* relationship is one where some individual is clearly in charge. The leader has almost total responsibility for what takes place —such as making the rules, applying rewards and punishments, and generally determining what transpires. In its extreme form the leader is boss and is expected to know what is best for everyone. Followers are expected to do what they are told.

A *laissez-faire* structure is one in which no one assumes responsibility for leadership. Each person "does his own thing." If there is a designated leader, he takes a "hands-off" attitude and contributes nothing but his presence.

A *democratic* relationship is one characterized by mutual and developmental responsibility. Each individual is encouraged to participate in terms of his talents and contributions. The leader offers guidance and understanding, and moves with the help and desire of each participant. It is a situation characterized by mutual faith and trust, with all participants willing to let others make their own decisions and even, sometimes, to trust others to represent them by delegating authority to others.

Many interesting studies have been conducted to ascertain the differential effects of these organizations upon the behavior of participants. R. Lippitt and R. K. White, for example, have found that groups operating under authoritarian leadership were quite efficient in carrying out their tasks. When leaders left the group, however, group members became confused and at a loss as to what to do next. They had learned to rely on the leader for the answers to their problems. The permissive, laissez-faire groups were poorest of the three types investigated. Group members were characterized by frustration, discontent, and boredom. They had no models to emulate and no quarter from which to receive help. As a consequence, such groups soon disintegrated with little or nothing accomplished. The democratic organizational structure seemed most productive in these experiments. Participants became more involved and creative, and were generally more interested and willing to take more active responsibility.

The laissez-faire type of organization has little to offer the helping professions. Helpers, after all, are not expected to be inactive like bumps on a log. Their special skill is presumably related to actively aiding their students, clients, and patients. Most helpers operate in terms of the authoritarian approach studied by Lippitt and White or the democratic one. Of course, these rarely appear in practice as pure cases. Helpers are hardly ever entirely authoritarian or entirely democratic; rather, these categories represent ends of a continuum along which practices can be observed to lean more or less one way or another.

OBJECTIVE-INTELLECTUAL ORIENTATION

The authoritarian approach might also be called the objective-intellectual orientation because it arises out of a logical attack on the helping problem. It deals with the problems of helping others in the same fashion as one might tackle a question in mathematics. One examines the problem objectively, determines the nature of the components, decides upon desirable goals, examines how to get there, and then sets about accomplishing the task. This is a logical, straightforward, objective approach, also called the "scientific method." It is the avenue most often used for dealing with just about everything we encounter in our world.

Applied to helping relationships, the objective-intellectual approach leads to various devices for controlling and directing behavior. The helper entering the helping relationship with this philosophy is cast in the role of the expert, the one who knows. His task is to diagnose the problem, manipulate events to the discovery of a solution, and guide the student or client to a proper plan of action. Almost of necessity, counselors operating from this frame of reference become probers examining, sometimes openly, sometimes subtly, into the client in a search for the reasons for his behavior. Teachers using this road to helping are likely to be preoccupied with questions of assigning work, testing, and grading, and exert themselves to make sure their students arrive at the "correct" answers.

The objective philosophy also makes helpers into explainers, experts in delineating how things got this way. They become expert diagnosticians of persons, events, or the social scene. This is often a fascinating intellectual exercise for the practitioner and a quest full of surprises and puzzles to be solved. People who do it well are often highly admired. It can even become so pleasant a pasttime that social workers, counselors, and psychologists especially, may get lost in the process and assume, when they have done it cleverly, the problem of helping has been dealt with, too. School psychologists, asked to study a difficult child, for example, have sometimes been known to report their findings to a teacher in magnificent technical prose which, when reduced to simpler language, simply confirmed the teacher's belief that the child was a difficult problem.

The objective philosophy is also likely to make the helper an authority figure. His approach to the problem of helping calls for imposition of the solutions arrived at as a consequence of his explorations and diagnosis, rather than that of the student-client. This manipulation may take the form of attempts to control the client's environment or to change his behavior, beliefs, or goals more or less directly.

There can be no doubt that an objective-intellectual approach often gets results. It also affects the helper by making him the expert, the man with the answers. That can be a terrible responsibility because a person who presumes to provide the answers must be right. Mistakes cannot be tolerated and so the helper adopting this philosophy assumes a dreadful burden. It is also likely to give him a very heady feeling of power and importance, an image encouraged by many professionals through the cultivation of an air of aloofness and an aura of magic about their practice.

GROWTH PHILOSOPHY

An alternative path to the solution of human problems concerns itself more with persons than ends. The helper does not devote his energies primarily to the diagnosis of problems and the formulation of answers to be applied to them. Instead, he actively involves himself in the processes of searching. He perceives his role as facilitator, helper, assister in a cooperative process of exploration and discovery. Problems are not approached from an external orientation; rather the helper "gets with it." He enters an encounter with his client or student that is designed to help him explore and discover more effective relationships between himself and his world. The helper is less concerned with ultimate answers than with creating the conditions in which they can be most efficiently discovered. His expertise rests, not so much in knowing answers as in the processes by which they may be brought into being.

The helper operating in this frame of reference neither accepts responsibility for the solutions his client may arrive at nor for knowing what they "should be." He does accept responsibility for creating conditions which will be truly helpful in assisting the client's own search for self-fulfillment. To this end he enters a dialogue with him to seek effective solutions to problems and more adequate perceptions of self and the world.

Such a relationship casts the helper in quite a different role from the intellectual approach. It demands that he be helper, assistant, and colleague in a cooperative search. His role is congruent with, rather than external to, the helpee's condition and purposes. As a consequence, he can be more friendly and the relationships established can exist on a man-to-man basis of effective human interaction. Such a definition of his role will also result in different perceptions of the helper by his clients. They are likely to see him as a less fearful object, a nicer person, and more of a human being. Because his role does not require him to have the right answers, moreover, the helper can be far more relaxed and authentic. He does not have to play a role. He can be who he is.

Whatever does or does not happen in the helping relationship will be a product of the interaction established by the helper. The kind of interaction will be determined by the basic philosophy with which he approaches his task. One's fundamental beliefs have a way of showing. Helpers cannot decline to work in any of the general approaches discussed above. In spite of themselves they will choose, and their behavior will make it quite clear which one they adhere to. Helpers can continue to explore both points of view in depth to the point where they have made a personal commitment to a position, somewhere on the continuum between the two extremes, in which they can operate comfortably, effectively, and authentically. Like the students and clients they work with, helpers, too, will behave more successfully when they have discovered the personal meaning of concepts for them.

THE STRUCTURE OF HELPING ENCOUNTERS

Helping relationships are special ones. They differ from the kinds of relationships people encounter in most of their daily lives. Most ordinary experiences are dialogues in which both parties are seeking personal enhancement. In the helping relationship, one party determines to set aside his own needs temporarily to help another. This, in itself, makes the helping relationship distinct from ordinary ones and perhaps an entirely new experience for some people seeking help. Because of their special goals, helping encounters are also characterized by special kinds of processes which may not be found in the daily experiences of the persons who are seeking aid. For these reasons, people entering the helping relationship must be helped to understand its nature and ways of functioning. The process of helping clients and students to discover what the helping encounter is like and how to use it most effectively is sometimes called "structuring the relationship." Helpers accomplish this by the ways they behave.

The helper is not a passive object in the helping relationship. What happens will be largely determined by what he makes possible. There can be no relationship with a nonentity. Helpers have to *be* somebody, and what they do or do not do gives direction to the process of helping. The very choices they make in responding to students or clients communicate messages about the relationship. The teacher who ignores a child's behavior is not inert. She is teaching that child something about himself and his place in the class. He may learn from being ignored to be patient, what is the "right" way to behave, that his teacher doesn't like him, or a hundred other possibilities. The message communicated by a teacher's behavior is real to the child and helps establish the nature of the dialogue whether the teacher wishes it so or not.

As partners in the helping encounter, helpers determine its directions. They do this in three important ways: by serving as models for their clients, by pointing the way to the most fruitful paths of exploration, and by suppressing or extinguishing less profitable routes. How they do this will in turn be dependent upon the helper's own perceptions of his role and functions.

THE HELPER AS MODEL

Persons in the helping professions expect to exert their influence as significant others in the lives of those they work with. The more significant they become the greater the degree to which they will be regarded as models by their students and clients. This will occur whether or not the helper is pleased to play this role. We do not use the word "model" here in the sense of exact patterns established for clients to emulate, although that too may occur with some helpees. We use the term, rather, to imply an example of personness, of authenticity of behavior in the helper himself congruent with the positions he takes with his student or client, so that he does not appear to deny in his own behavior what he seems to be espousing for others.

Helpers cannot escape being models. What they do indicates so much more clearly who they are that what they say will often not be heard. The helper who advocates doing what he is unwilling to do himself is unlikely to be very convincing. This is not to suggest that helpers must be paragons of virtue—only that one of the best ways to convince other people that a given bit of behavior is worthwhile is to see it manifest in the helper's own behavior.

It is fruitless, for example, to tell a young person that he shouldn't smoke or drink while the helper has a cigarette hanging out of his mouth and a glass of liquor in hand. The helpee may never drink or smoke, but it will not be because of that helper's influence. Parents often violate this principle in regard to aggressive behavior. Everyone wants to raise children who are able to stand up for themselves. On the other hand, few parents want them to be openly hostile or unnecessarily physically aggressive. So, when a child is observed fighting with another, especially if he is picking on someone smaller than himself, the parent tries to stop him. How does he go about it? He often gets angry, rushes into the fray, smacks the child, and threatens severe punishment if he is caught fighting again. And this is supposed to teach the child not to be aggressive!

THE HELPER AS REINFORCER

The kinds of relationships established by the helper will be determined in large measure by what he reinforces. One of the oldest psychological principles about learning is that people tend to learn those things which result in some kind of reward. Everyone has a need for self-enhancement, and what is experienced as enhancing is likely to be sought on other occasions. The professional helper, whether he be teacher, counselor, social worker, supervisor, or whatever, has importance simply because of his position. What he rewards, consequently, has special significance for those with whom he works. Whatever the helper reinforces in the helping dialogue, therefore, tends to structure the relationship. From the feedback he obtains from the helper, the helpee learns how to use the helping relationship.

The helper may employ reinforcement quite openly so that both he and his client are aware of what is happening—for example, a teacher might say: "That's right, Jimmy," or "That's the way! You're doing very well." On the other hand, reinforcement may be so subtle that the helpee is not consciously aware of what has happened. This can occur when, out of all the responses made by the student client, the helper consistently rewards a given type and so encourages the helpee to continue in that direction. It is a natural thing to pursue rewarded directions, and persons can often be "conditioned" quite unconsciously to new ways of responding. If people react more favorably to the politeness and respect of a "Please, sir," a child soon learns to use that method of getting a response, even though he would be quite unable to tell you he had made that discovery. To structure the relationships provided for their clientele, it is necessary for helpers to have a clear conception of the nature of the helping process and what needs reinforcing. This is not always easy. Sometimes what a helper reinforces may be so very subtle that it is not apparent to the helper himself. Many a counselor has had the unhappy experience of reassuring a client with the intent of strengthening his confidence only to find he has produced a transference and made his client dependent upon him. To avoid this kind of error, helpers will need to be deeply sensitive to the meaning of their own behavior as seen through the eyes of clients. Otherwise, they may find themselves structuring the encounter in ways they had not bargained for.

THE HELPER AS EXTINGUISHER

Helping relationships can also be structured by extinguishing behavior. This may be accomplished by direct suppression of a helpee's acts—for example, a teacher might say: "That's wrong, Joe. Try again." Or, a social worker might suggest to his client, "I don't think that will work." The structure of the relationship may also be defined by simply ignoring the client's explorations in undesirable directions. Behavior which does not result in some form of feedback is very soon discarded as many parents and teachers have long since discovered. Expert teachers, for example, handle many behavior problems by simply ignoring them. They know that without some reinforcement the behavior is likely to quickly spend itself. Similarly, many problems between parents and children could easily be avoided if the child's misbehavior were calmly ignored.

It makes a difference what the helper responds to. As a significant other, whatever the helper does or does not do conveys some sort of message to the student or client with whom he is working. The choices he makes in reacting to his client or student are important. The meanings he communicates occur whether he wills it or not. They are the feedback from which the helpee learns about himself, and express in more or less subtle ways the approved or disapproved uses to be made of the relationship. If helpers are unaware of these interactions, they run the risk of behaving irresponsibly and of making the helping professions fortuitous. To meet the obligations they have assumed as helpers and to raise techniques above the level of mere accident, helpers must be keenly aware of the impact they have upon their clients, they must be clear about the kind of relationships they hope to establish, and they must be capable of expressing that understanding in their professional behavior.

LIMITS IN THE HELPING RELATIONSHIP

Every life situation has limits. This holds for helping relationships as well. People need limits. Few of us could live without them. Knowing the boundaries of a situation provides a feeling of security and so has the effect of creating freedom. The traffic light on the corner limits freedom in one sense, but its existence makes it possible for people to go where they desire in safety. The amount of freedom we have is often determined by our willingness to give up some degree of autonomy in one area for the greater good of increased freedom in another. We live surrounded by limits of many kinds and become so used to them that the first thing most people do on entering a new situation is to begin testing the limits. Students do this the first day of class when they ask the teacher: "How many books shall I read?" "Do you want the papers in on Tuesday?" "How long do I have to get ready for my presentation?" They also ask each other: "Do you think he means it?" "What kind of a guy is he?" People begin any new situation by searching out the boundaries. They cannot deal constructively with events until they know what they are.

The establishment of clear limits is particularly important for children, who need to know limits because a very large part of their growth is accomplished by pushing against them. In this way they find out what they can and cannot do. Substitute teachers know how avidly children pursue the question of what this new person is like, what she will stand for and what she will not, whether she means what she says, knows whereof she speaks, and the like.

Laymen have often mistakenly believed that "experts" in human behavior advocate that some relationships should be completely free of limits. Many parents and educators have labored under this misconception, probably because of confusion over the term "permissive" and the strong advice of child care specialists to give children greater opportunities for self-directed activity. However, no professional person in his right mind has ever advocated that the rearing of children, or any human relationships, should be without limits, because no human being could exist very long without them. The important question is not *whether* limits but *what* limits, and the answer must be decided in terms of their effects on the persons they are applied to.

Effective helping relationships need limits. These are established by the person in charge whether he be counselor, teacher, priest, nurse, or whatever. They should also be made apparent as clearly and as quickly as practicable. The sooner they are understood the sooner both helper and helpees can proceed toward more creative and fruitful endeavors. Sometimes this may be accomplished by stating limits outright at the beginning of the relationship. Most helpers, however, have learned by sad experience that this seldom works very well. In the opening sessions of a helping relationship the statement of limits will frequently not even be heard. Upon settling into a new situation, people are confused and a little suspicious and therefore often fail to hear what is said. Furthermore, they are likely to be trying to see if what the helper is saying matches what he is doing and so miss many of the words being spoken.

Generally speaking, the establishment of limits is best accomplished by the factors mentioned above—the behavior of the helper and what he responds to or ignores. Limits are best established not by what people say but by the things they do or do not. Most persons learn very early the superiority of action over words, and consequently discover the limits of any helping situation primarily from their own experience of it. Even so, they may need to re-explore them now and then if for no other reason than to assure themselves they have not changed. Where young children are concerned, it may even be necessary to provide reminders of what the limits are so long as the relationship exists.

STABILITY OF LIMITS

It is important that the limits of helping relationships be stable. If limits keep shifting, people don't know how to respond. They become upset and perform very badly. They also begin to mistrust the helper and any hope of being of some use to the individual seeking help then vanishes. If limits are consistent, people can adjust to almost anything. One of the authors recalls overhearing three little boys discussing their next year's teacher at the end of the term. One of them asked another, "Who you got next year?" "I got Miss Johnson," he replied. "Oh, I feel sorry for you. She's terrible!" Then he went on in great detail about how bad Miss Johnson was. The third child finally ended the conversation saying, "Yes, she's bad. So okay! You'll get used to her!" This is true. People can adjust to almost anything if it stands still. It's the ambiguity, the contraditions that drive people wild and keep them constantly re-examining the limits. An outstanding characteristic of most good teachers is their ability to establish limits quickly, quietly, and firmly. Their students soon settle down to work. Poor teachers, on the other hand, are unsure or vacillating. Students spend hours testing their limits.

While limits need to be stable, it is not necessary that similar limits be held by all helpers or that all helpees be treated alike. Stability is not rigidity. The important consideration is that the limits fit the helpee and be fair and helpful for the persons they seek to help. People differ, and any attempt to treat them all alike must necessarily be unfair to most of them.

CREATING AN ATMOSPHERE FOR CHANGE

To bring about change in behavior requires changing personal meanings. But this is no simple task, for perceptions lie inside people and are, consequently, not open to direct manipulation. To change behavior it is necessary, somehow, to involve the behaver in the process. In one way or another, he must be induced to explore and discover new meanings with respect to himself and his world. A person's self, however, is precious. It cannot be heedlessly placed in jeopardy. The turtle cannot go anywhere until he sticks his neck out. He will not stick his neck out unless there is something out there he wants and he feels it is safe outside. In similar fashion the self can only be committed when there seems some likelihood that commitment will result in a measure of fulfillment and that the self will not be damaged in the process. This is true for everyone, especially for those sick and inadequate persons whose selves are so threatened that they must be continually maintaining and protecting themselves from further destruction.

To bring about changes in meanings, persons in the helping professions need to be skilled in creating the kinds of atmospheres that will make self-involvement likely. Generally speaking, this calls for atmospheres in which a person feels: (a) that it is safe to try, (b) reassured that he can, (c) encouraged to make the attempt, and (d) satisfied to do so. How well this occurs will depend upon the helper's understanding of the dynamics of the learning process and the goals and values which seem to him important in creating helping relationships. These must be such that his clients perceive the processes he creates as promising fulfillment on one hand and safe enough to risk encounter on the other.

Removing Barriers to Involvement

Many of the helper's efforts in whatever branch of the helping professions he belongs to will be devoted to removing the barriers which lie in the path of the subject's commitment to the process of helping. The creation of a freeing atmosphere is in part a matter of the client's finding promise of satisfaction. It is also a matter of eliminating as nearly as possible the blocks that lie in the path of the client's innate need to move toward health. This is accomplished by sensitivity to the nature of such barriers and a systematic attempt to find ways of removing them. The following anecdote illustrates how this was first learned by one of the authors of this volume.

During the Great Depression of the thirties, one of the authors was employed as a school psychologist in a large high school in a northern city. He was also faculty adviser for the HiY, a service club for boys. The school had a regulation that any money obtained from students by a service club during the year had to be returned to the students in some form before the end of the year. One year the club came to the end of the year with $35 in the treasury. What to do with it? The club held a meeting to decide.

Somebody suggested giving a party for the school. Another said, "Well, it ought to be for everybody." The adviser said, "Let's see if we can figure out a way of getting everybody into the act." Someone else suggested, "Well, we could have a dance. But if we do have a dance, the people who can't dance won't come." Then another person said, "Well, maybe we could have a dance that everybody will come to." That was a novel idea and the question immediately arose as to what kind of dance it could be. Somebody came up with the idea, "Let's have a square dance." Since this was a large city high school and nobody knew how to square dance, so far as anyone knew, this met the criterion.

Then somebody said, "Even if we have a square dance, some people won't come because they don't have the right clothes." The reply: "Well, this is a country dance; we won't let anyone in who looks too sharp!" And that was adopted as policy. Somebody else pointed out, "Well, they won't come if they aren't able to get a date," and somebody else countered, "We could make it stag. We could let the boys in one door and let the girls in the other on opposite sides of the gym, and nobody would know who had a date."

Then somebody suggested: "Some people won't come because they won't have enough money and after the dance was over they would want to buy something to eat for the girl they were with." So it was decided, "Let's feed them at the dance." A committee was set up to enlist the aid of mothers in baking cakes and another to make a deal with a soft drink distributor. After all this, someone said, "We've still got a problem: Some won't come because they can't afford it." After much figuring on the cost of the band and an estimate of how many people would come, the price of the dance was finally set at eight cents.

Many people had doubts whether such a program would succeed and said, "It will never work!" When the night of the dance finally came, the largest crowd turned out that had ever been in the gymnasium since the school was built. In fact, so many people came that nobody could dance!

A similar technique can be applied to any helping relationship. It consists in systematically searching for the barriers to commitment and eliminating them from the scene. Sometimes they may be attitudinal, physical, inherent in the structure of the relationship, and in rules and regulations or administrative machinery. They may even be found in the helper himself! The authors have successfully applied the method to problems of counseling, psychotherapy, teacher education, group process, and consulting relationships of many varieties. Not all blocks are easily removed, of course, and some may have to be lived with. The device has value, however, in putting the finger on critical blocks to the helping process and in helping to create more effective atmospheres.

CHALLENGE AND THREAT IN THE ATMOSPHERE FOR CHANGE

To a very large extent, creating the proper atmosphere for learning is a matter of dealing with challenge and threat. As we have observed in earlier sections, people feel challenged when they are confronted with problems which interest them and which seem to lie within their capacities of solution. People feel threatened, on the other hand, when they are confronted with problems they do not feel able to deal with. To produce the kind of atmosphere usually needed for the helping process generally requires the production of challenge and the avoidance of threat.

This is not to suggest that behavior cannot be changed by threat. It can, of course. People *do* learn from such experiences. As we have seen, however, the effect of threat is to narrow perceptions to the threatening object. What is learned, therefore, is likely to be highly specific. It is likely also to be of a negative character—learning what *not* to do. Thus, by spanking him, a child may be taught not to cross a street; by fining him, a grownup may be taught not to speed, at least, when there are police officers around. When the goal is simple and clearly defined, threat may, indeed, result in learning. It is a technique widely used by persons in authority for thousands of years. Because a device will sometimes work however, there is no good reason to adopt it as a general principle for continuing action. Helpers' tools must be used with precision and must be applied to the problems for which they are uniquely appropriate. This is especially true in the use of threat, for the effects of threat on learning extend far beyond directly observable results. To operate without awareness of these may only destroy with one hand what is so carefully built with the other. Health for most clients is achieved from attainment of positive goals rather than negative ones, from things to be sought or attained rather than avoided.

The specificity of goals required for the utilization of threat as a device for encouraging learning is seldom appropriate for the helping professions. The learning of subject matter, solving of personal problems, or achievement of maximum self-actualization can rarely be defined in precise terms. Quite the contrary is called for. Goals like these require openness to experience and freedom to depart from minutiae. The purpose of the helping professions is to expand, to open up, to encourage exploration and discovery. These ends can rarely be achieved by experiences of threat. Most helping relationships require the careful elimination of threat. To get a mouse out of a mousehole one does not poke at it with a broomstick. It is necessary to entice him out, to make it more desirable outside than in. The same is true for clients. Confrontation of a broader world generally calls for relationships with helpers who are friendly representatives of the outer world.

Even where the specific and negative aspects of threat can be overcome, its use in the helping professions would still be limited for still another reason: the destructive effect of the use of threat on the helping relationship itself. Most of us do not take kindly to people who threaten us. Threatening people are regarded with suspicion, and what they have to say is generally heard with reservations if, indeed, it is heard at all. Most people respond to threat by resistance, suppression, negativism, or rationalization—responses unlikely to enhance the relationships between helper and helpee. Most helping relationships are deeply dependent upon establishing rapport between helper and client. Whatever destroys this capacity for dialogue interferes with the process.

PUNISHMENT AND THE HELPING RELATIONSHIP

The effects of the experience of threat are especially applicable to the question of the use of punishment as a device for improving human behavior. Behavioral scientists of many persuasions (Skinner, Combs, Mouly, Gladstone), even those who disagree on many other matters, have expressed grave doubt about the appropriateness of punishment as a technique in the facilitation of behavior. B. F. Skinner, for example, writing on the subject of punishment felt it necessary to subtitle his discussion "A Questionable Technique." There are two major questions with regard to the use of punishment: First, there is reason to doubt that punishment works, in anything more than temporary and superficial fashion; second, the technique often causes side effects whose negative consequences far outweigh any positive results.

In discussing the question of punishment, it is necessary to differentiate between punishment in a physical context and punishment in a social one as, for example, where a child might be punished, by a hot stove, or by an angry parent. In the physical context, when a child touches a hot stove, the consequences are usually no more involved than some slightly burnt little fingers. This is an objective, unemotional encounter with life, with causes and consequences clear even to a small child. A person, unless he is very ill, cannot remain angry or hold a grudge for long against a stove, and he certainly can't gain revenge on the punisher with much satisfaction.

Punishment, inflicted upon one human by another, is something else. That involves much subjectivity and emotion. Furthermore, the reasons for the punishment are seldom clearly understood, the justification is usually questioned, and retribution is a likely possibility. Punishment in a social context is a questionable technique, indeed!

Does punishment really do what we want it to—that is, teach people to be better human beings? The answer seems to be that if it teaches at all, it teaches only what *not* to do. What is the best or right thing to do is still open to question. Because it deals with behavior directly, punishment only treats symptoms. One of the authors is acquainted with a little girl in his neighborhood who presently knows two words. The first is "Jo Jo," the name of her dog, and the second is "No!" which needs no explanation. This child is not unlike many who are glutted with no's and don'ts, but starved for do's and yeses. When punishment is used, only a part of the job has been done. There remains the more important task of teaching a person what is the good thing to do.

The effect of punishment, more often than not, is only temporary. In most instances it has only short-term effects in regard to stopping bad behavior. At the time punishment is administered, the culprit may stop what he is doing, especially if he is a small child being physically restrained by an adult. But, there is every reason to believe, both in terms of scientific research and common observation, that the behavior will be manifest again. This can be illustrated by an incident occurring in the neighborhood of one of the writers.

One of the authors lives in a typical housing development, with rows of houses back to back, small yards in-between, and each house with double sliding glass doors facing his neighbor's double, sliding glass doors. The children who live directly behind the author's house had a habit which greatly infuriated their mother. When they wanted to play with the author's child, they would come to the double glass doors, yell, bang on the doors, and stare into the house. The irritated mother would often scold the children for this, telling them that it wasn't nice to stare into people's houses or to make a commotion around their doors and windows. But the scoldings had little effect and the children continued to make their presence known to the author's child in the same delicate manner.

One day the irritated mother waited until her children were engaged in the familiar act of attracting the attention of the author's child. Then she came flying across the yard, stick in hand, and proceeded to whale the daylights out of her offspring! What a scene—children crying, stick cracking, and the mother screaming!

The mother made it clear that this was only a sample of what would happen if she ever caught them bothering their neighbors in that manner again. Furthermore, in the future they were to wait for the author's child to come out to play, and not go after him again. That was that! The children had been punished and that act, that exact, particular bit of behavior had been stopped. The children have never since come to the backdoor, stared into the house, or called for the child. Now, they come around to bang on, stare into, and scream through the *front* sliding glass doors! At least the children's mother is happy because "What you can't see or don't know won't hurt you."

The most significant arguments against the use of punishment, the authors believe, are not with regard to whether it works, but in connection with the side effects that accompany its use. There are many such side effects, of which the following are samples.

1/ Punishment of any kind generates many negative responses.   Persons who are punished become fearful, anxious, and hostile, and because of these feelings often engage in "displacement"—that is, striking out at others in retaliation for the pain and embarrassment they have suffered. Such behaviors are certainly not socially facilitating, and it is doubtful that anything of value can be learned under such conditions. The results are seldom any better for the administrator of the punishment either. Punishment is a vengeful kind of human response made in the heat of anger and frustrated emotion. A helper can accomplish very little under these conditions, and they often have a snowballing effect. The more a person is punished the more frustrated and hostile he becomes. This causes him to strike back even more forcefully, thereby causing the punisher to become more frustrated and angry and to punish harder and with greater furor—hardly a pleasant or fruitful human experience.

2/ Punishment often is extremely difficult, especially for young children, to associate with the undesirable behavior *rather than with the child's* self.   It is easy for a child to mistake badness in the self rather than in the act for which he is being punished. It is a simple thing to believe that it is "me," not my behavior, that is bad. This is likely to happen particularly when the punishment for a single act is prolonged over a period of time, as when someone is given the "silent treatment" for long periods after he has committed an undesirable act, or when a child is told, "Wait till your father gets home. You'll get it then!"

3/ Punished behavior can generalize to desirable behavior.   Without realizing the consequences, behavior that is inappropriate at a certain age or time is often punished when it will be quite desirable at another age or time. The result is that individuals inadvertently are made incapable of performing highly desirable and, in many cases, absolutely necessary human acts. This is a consequence of punishment that can be detected in the life of every human being, to one degree or another. The following is a specific example familiar to one of the authors. One Christmas some parents decided that a nice gift for their three children would be a set of illustrated Bible stories. The set was beautiful, elaborate, expensive, and contained 24 volumes. It was accompanied by a wooden bookcase. The set was presented to the children on Christmas Day. The thought behind the gift was commendable and the gift was a fine one indeed—but not for these children, at the time the set was given. All three children were much too young to appreciate such a fine gift and were unable to care for it and use it appropriately. Nevertheless, on Christmas Day the children were shown the set, told it was theirs, and then, as quickly, told they were not to handle it! If they wanted to use it or see some of the pictures, they would have to call on one of the parents who could handle the books.

One can guess what happened. It was too much to expect that a child could understand how he could own something and yet not be allowed to touch it. So, time and again, one child or the other attempted to take a book from the case, and each time they did so, the mother or father would punish the child. Of course, each time such an incident would occur the severity of the punishment would also increase.

Thus, for a period of from one to three years, depending on which child was involved, his major encounter with books and religious material occurred under the stress and emotional turmoil of a situation in which he was yelled at, smacked, and generally dominated by an angry, reprimanding parent.

One can easily anticipate some of the questions these parents will be asking in a few years. "Why doesn't my son like to read? We have always had lots of books in the house." "Why is it so hard to get these kids to go to church? They have been surrounded by religious ideas since they were tiny children!"

This kind of association may happen as the direct result of punishment for behavior that is bad at one time, but good at another. Sex-training, for example, is one area in which this frequently occurs. Why not? How could it be otherwise? For years we punish, condemn, or manifest embarrassment at every response a child makes which has the slightest sexual connotation. Then, when he has reached some magical age, or joins in the communion of matrimony, he is expected spontaneously to be an accomplished lover!

The use of punishment for controlling misbehavior is at times inevitable. Sometimes the consequences of the act that a person is about to perform are so dire that there may be no time for another alternative. Sometimes certain behavior must be stopped in the quickest way possible. As a tool for the helping professions, however, punishment generally leaves much to be desired. While it may, on occasion be necessary to employ it, helpers need to be fully aware of the dynamics involved in its use and especially with the meanings it creates in the experience of the subject lest helpers destroy with the left hand what the right is trying to build.

The purpose of helping relationships is the stimulation and encouragement of growth. This is an internal matter, occurring from within. It calls for encouragement and stimulation rather than threat and coercion. To grow a healthy plant we get the best possible seed we can find and plant it in the best possible soil available. We provide it with optimum conditions of light, moisture, temperature, and the nutrients it needs in order to grow. After that, we get out of its way and let it grow. In similar fashion the helping professions approach the problem of growth by creating conditions of maximum freedom for clients, parishioners, students, or patients. The very first step in this process is the provision of an atmosphere which makes the exploration of personal meaning possible.

HELPING BEGINS WITH ACCEPTANCE

A major requirement for the creation of an atmosphere for change is acceptance. We defined this earlier as willingness to confront, to enter into interaction with whatever is necessary to assist the process of growth. Growth cannot proceed from where people are not; it can only occur from where people are. Accordingly, the atmosphere for helping must start from a base which accepts the person as he is and where he is. As we are using the term here, acceptance has nothing to do with approval or disapproval. It has to do only with willingness to face facts, to begin where persons are. The student, client, or patient is accepted as who he is, what he is, and how he feels without judging or valuing.

The experience of being accepted has important values in reducing the feeling of threat and so making possible more open approaches to examining self and the world. The counselor, for example, "accepts" unjudgmentally his client's expression of hatred for his brother, and thus makes it possible for his client to look at his feelings. A teacher may accept the error of the student without judgment as simply a matter of fact. This makes it possible for student and teacher thereafter to find a better solution. The pastor, too, accepts the "sin" of his parishioner as understandable and so makes it possible to talk about and find more effective ways of behaving. In the following report a nurse describes the value of acceptance for one of her patients.

While making the rounds of my floor, I saw a woman patient start to cry. Her face just crumpled in spite of what seemed to be great efforts to maintain composure. I went into her room and stood by the bed; her eyes were closed with tears running from under the lids. She seemed to sense my presence for she took my hand and held on to it with a very tight grip. I waited, for I didn't wish to pry, yet felt that this was not a casual thing which was occurring. For several minutes I stood there while she cried silently. After a time, she told me why she was crying. She had had surgery three days previously; her physician had just told her that she had inoperable carcinoma. She had been given the hope that a relatively new antimetabolite might offer relief, longer life, and, she hoped, a cure. Her choice was to accept the risks inherent in the treatment or to refuse. She was also trying to decide what to tell her husband and son. There was nothing I could offer her except myself as a person to listen; her decision had to be hers. I stood and listened while she cried and talked.

The knowledge I had about the course of her illness, the new treatment, the support she would need from her family, physician, other people, none of this was what she needed. The need at this moment was for a fellow human to listen to her. I felt that I was such a person, one who could listen. Her world had turned inside out and upside down. She was the very attractive wife of a successful businessman, the mother of a handsome son, an interesting, vital, well-educated woman who was having to accept the fact that she was facing invalidism, prolonged illness, and death. She said that she was not a woman who cried easily, yet she seemed to accept a nurse as a person with whom she could cry; by some very great effort she regained her composure before her son and husband came to visit her.

For many persons in need of help the very experience of being accepted is, in itself, a most important release from the negative effects of threat.

Without acceptance or the will to confront, very little can happen in the helping relationship. People cannot go forward if they are not open to experience. The treatment of an alcoholic, for example, must begin with the alcoholic's acceptance of the fact that "I am an alcoholic." The student must begin with the recognition that he doesn't know and that there is a question to be answered. The mother who believes that a neighbor's reports about her child's misbehavior "can't be true" is unlikely to be very effective in bringing about a change in her child. Change begins with the recognition that a problem exists.

Since the way things seem to each of us has such a feeling of reality, it is easy to reject the reality of others and demonstrate a lack of acceptance in relationships. Helpers have been known, for example, to reject the surly, unmannerly delinquent upon very first contact with him. He has grown up in a world which largely rejects him and comes in with a chip on his shoulder. In his world toughness and defiance are the ways to prestige and status, so he slouches in his chair and snarls his reply to questions. Such behavior can be infuriating to the helper who does not understand his business, and it seems "only natural" to lash out and demand that the subject "Behave yourself! Be polite! Sit up and pay attention!" From the point of view of the delinquent, such behaviors are not only undesirable, but being polite in the world he lives could ruin him! Even from the helper's own point of view such demands do not make much sense. These are the kinds of behaviors we *hope for* from this subject *when he gets better*. To demand such behavior of him now is like a doctor saying to his patient: "Go away and get better. Then come back and I'll help you!"

To begin the helping process with a denial of the way things are is hardly likely to create an atmosphere for facilitating change and growth. Nevertheless, with the best of intentions many helpers fail to be effective by closing the doors to consideration of events at the beginning of a conference. A child who expresses a shocking or naughty attitude may be told, "Why, Jimmy, you mustn't feel that way!" And so, his feelings, the very things he must explore to get over his difficulty, are barred from examination. Before one can examine his feelings he must be allowed to have them!

Freeing atmospheres provide the stage on which exploration of self and the world takes place. For effective practice a large portion of the helper's attention and efforts will need to be devoted to the creation of atmospheres which make exploring possible and encourage students and clients to make maximum use of relationships. When this is done well, the need of the individual for adequacy can be counted on to supply the impetus for movement. In this chapter we have pointed to some of the factors helpers will need to consider in the creation of proper conditions for growth. For the helper's own growth as a professional worker, attention to the atmospheres he creates must be a continuing matter of concern so long as he remains in the helping professions.

SELECTED READINGS

Starred entry indicates appearance in Donald L. Avila, Arthur W. Combs, and William W. Purkey, *The Helping Relationship Sourcebook* (Boston: Allyn & Bacon, 1971).

Amos, W. E. & Orem, R. C. *Managing student behavior.* St. Louis: Green Publishing Co., 1967.

Aspy, D. N. The effect of teacher-offered conditions of empathy, positive regard and congruence upon student achievement. *Florida Journal of Educational Research*, 1969, **11**, 39–49.

Ausubel, D. P. A new look at classroom discipline. *Phi Delta Kappan*, 1961, **43**, 25–30.

Ginott, H. G. *Between parent and teenager*. New York: Macmillan, 1968.

Premack, D. Toward empirical behavior laws: I, Positive reinforcement. *Psychological Review*, 1959, **66**, 219.

Risley, T. R. Learning and lollipops. *Psychology Today*, 1968, **1**, 28–31.

* Rogers, C. R. The characteristics of a helping relationship. *Personnel and Guidance Journal*, 1958, **37**, 6–16.

Sarason, I. G. Verbal learning, modeling, and juvenile delinquency. *American Psychologist*, 1968, **23**, 254–266.

Skinner, B. F. *Science and human behavior*. New York: Free Press, 1953.

Truax, C. B. et al. Empathy, warmth, genuineness. *Rehabilitation Record*, 1966, 10–11.

Webster, S. W. *Discipline in the classroom*. San Francisco: Chandler, 1968.

12

Aiding the Search for New Meaning

To aid in the search for new meanings, helpers must do more than remove the barriers to involvement; they must assist their clients in the active process of discovering meanings more likely to lead to self-fulfillment than those they have had before. This calls for special attention to those experiences leading to increased capacity to cope with the world and to self-actualization. These are the primary questions: How can I aid my client to extend and enrich his field of meanings? How can I help him feel a broader, deeper sense of identification? How can I encourage him to see himself in more positive terms? How can I contribute to the capacity of my client for openness to experience? The answers helpers find to these questions provide fruitful clues to the construction of effective helping relationships.

POSITIVE SELF AND THE SEARCH FOR MEANING

The self is the primary subject of learning. Whatever threatens its dignity and integrity is likely to impede the helping process by creating an atmosphere which forces the defense of self and disengagement from the encounter. On the other hand, the search for an adequate self is insatiable, and helping relationships which seem to contribute to this end will more likely be sustained and meaningful. Learning is a personal affair and whatever dehumanizes people tends to get in the way of effective learning and self-actualization. The atmosphere for exploration must reassure the person that he can value and respect the self and permit it to enter the process. To bring this about, the helper must value the self of the person he works with.

The self cannot be forced into learning; it must be encouraged to it. A positive view of self is a priceless resource for learning. Because it is, its production becomes a major goal of helpers. Since the self is learned from experience, what happens in the helping dialogue must provide persons with positive experiences of self. It must help them feel they are liked, wanted, acceptable, and able to deal with themselves, their fellows, and the world in which they live.

Providing people with positive experiences of self is not always an easy thing to do. Much of the world we have created has very dehumanizing effects. The provision of positive experiences of self often runs counter to some of society's most valued modes of operation. The helping relationship must, therefore, be a special one, a kind of microcosm that is quite different from the person's normal experiences in every day life.

Unhappily, the things we do to help other people, even with the best of intentions, often backfire because they are seen by those we would like to help as self-negating or degrading. This forces them to protect themselves by resistance or by dropping out of the relationship entirely. Schools do not intentionally create dropouts. They may, nevertheless, produce them because they want so much what is good for youngsters. Too much wanting can cause teachers to behave in such coercive ways as to create deep feelings of inadequacy and despair in the minds of students. Who among us has not encountered a well-meaning friend who told him what to do? More often than not, such advice turns out to be quite useless and only contributes to further misunderstanding.

Only a strong self can risk hazardous involvement for any length of time. Hence, whatever causes a person to feel that his self is less good, less valuable, or less acceptable is likely to interfere with effective learning. Helpers must behave in ways that provide those they want to help with strengthening, positive views of self. Such concepts of self facilitate the process of exploration and discovery. In fact, they do more. Adequate views of self are the very goals of the helping professions. It makes little sense to operate in ways that make the eventual goal more difficult. The helping process, itself, must begin by providing the most adequate experiences it can for its clients, students, and patients.

IDENTIFICATION AND THE ATMOSPHERE FOR LEARNING

Learning is essentially a social process. Most of the important learnings we have are achieved as a consequence of some kind of interaction with others. Despite the admonitions of generations of teachers that children should "work alone," students show great ingenuity in finding ways to work together because they know it is better that way. It is a mistaken notion that learning is a solitary matter best achieved in isolation from others. The most important aspect of our world is people, and it is with and through people that our most important learnings are achieved. This is true even for the learning of highly abstract intellectual concepts. It is far more so with respect to learning the things we need to know about how to get along with each other and how to achieve maximum fulfillment.

Identification with others is important to the learning process not only because it provides interaction and stimulation, but also because it makes it possible for persons to explore more widely, to adventure more daringly, and to be more creative and less hesitant in their approach to life itself. Deprived persons do not make good explorers. Persons without feelings of oneness with other people are likely to be so very busy erecting and maintaining their defenses that they have little time for the kind of exploration and discovery that lie at the very heart of the process of discovering meaning.

The Freeing Effects of Caring

The atmosphere most conducive to learning calls for feelings of identification between helper and helpee. To serve as significant others in the lives of those they seek to aid, helpers must commit themselves to the process. They must care. Carl Rogers has postulated that an essential characteristic of the helping relationship is "unconditional positive regard" on the part of the helper. The importance of this factor has been demonstrated repeatedly in his research and has been corroborated further in the researches of Carkhuff, Aspy, and Truax among others. People do not identify very long with persons who reject them or treat them as unimportant. Being loved is immensely releasing, and the loving and caring attitude of helpers, in itself, provides an important ingredient for the facilitating atmosphere.

The need for love in human interrelationships has been described by writers universally. It is known to artists, poets, novelists, philosophers, psychologists, anthropologists, and the clergy as a major factor in the success of human interaction. For those who have experienced its power for fulfillment, writers are not needed to emphasize its values. Yet the place of love in the helping professions is often ignored in favor of "being objective." Love is approached, if at all, with apologies, fear, or shame. Even to talk about "liking" is sometimes regarded as though it were not really relevant to the helping process. This was beautifully expressed in a letter written by a fifth-grade boy after his teacher permitted the class to hold a free discussion which got around to the question of love. Next day the little boy wrote

> Dear Miss Jones:
> It sure surprised me when we talked about love in our class yesterday. I learned a lot of things. I learned how people feel about each other. It sure surprised me when we talked about love. I never knew you could talk about things in school that you didn't get grades for!

What a pity that such an important factor in human life is often not regarded as part of the curriculum!

Love in its sexual connotations or in a maudlin sense, of course, has no place in a professional helping relationship. But love in the sense of human caring, of concern for each other, is a basic element of helping. It contributes directly to the processes of communication and is a major characteristic of the self-fulfillment that the helping process seeks to produce.

If helpers do not care, they run grave risk of defeating themselves as professional workers or, worse yet, of interfering with the growth of those they seek to help. This does not mean that helpers have to love everyone. Some people are not very lovable and no one can turn feelings on and off at will. What is required is that helpers deliver the very best professional relationship they are capable of. That, in itself, is a kind of caring. If helpers can love their charges in addition, that is like icing on the cake and a further assurance of the likelihood of success.

Stronger, wider ranging personalities are products of deep feelings of oneness with the rest of mankind, and the production of such feelings of identification is a major goal of counseling and psychotherapy. It is equally important in institutions like our public schools. A threatened child does not learn well. A child who does not like his teacher begins with a severe handicap. A deprived self is so busy filling up its wells of inadequacy that time cannot be spared for broader, richer voyages of exploration and discovery. People are much more likely to learn from people they like, respect, and feel "one with" than they are from those who seem dangerous and remote.

SELF–DIRECTION AND THE DISCOVERY OF NEW MEANINGS

SELF-DIRECTION AND INDEPENDENCE

The goal of the helping professions is the production of free and intelligent persons who are capable of behaving effectively and with personal satisfaction. It is not enough that they behave in these ways only when they have to. We must be able to count on them to behave in these ways under their own steam as free and autonomous agents. Whatever increases dependence and interferes with independent self-direction, therefore, gets in the way of the helping encounter.

Instead of strengthening the self, dependence requires surrender. The giving-up of one's body is sometimes necessary in the interest of physical health. Entering a hospital for an operation, for example, one expects to surrender his body to the skilled hands of others. This can be helpful when other persons can do what needs to be done. In the growth of self, however, surrender is seldom likely to be helpful because the self can rarely be changed by outsiders directly. The actualization of personality can only be accomplished by the person himself. He must sooner or later take charge of his own salvation. Too great a dependence on the helper gets in the way of the free atmosphere desired for effective helping.

In early forms of psychotherapy, clients were often encouraged to become almost totally dependent upon the counselor or therapist. This process, known as "transference," was considered a necessary and valuable stage in the process of helping. More recently, theories of therapy have generally rejected the development of deep transference as more of a hindrance than help. Most counselors prefer to avoid the development of dependence in favor of practices which respect the dignity and integrity of the individual, and encourage the assumption of responsibility for the guidance and direction of his own destiny.

No matter what intimate relationship one may develop with another person, no one can ever know the nature of problems facing a self better than its possessor. Only he is in possession of the full range of data. The person is always the world's greatest expert on his own experience. An outsider, no matter how skillful, can never be more than an amateur when it comes to knowing another person's self. This is why the answers that persons find for themselves are so often likely to be superior to those suggested by well-intentioned outsiders. The atmosphere for helping must therefore discourage dependence and encourage the development of self-direction.

Unfortunately, the development of an atmosphere which encourages self-direction is often not easy. It is such a simple, natural thing to create dependence in others. The persons one seeks to help may even encourage it. This is especially true of desperate and unhappy persons who are often quite willing, even anxious, to let someone else solve their dilemmas. Helpers with the best of intentions can easily be seduced into developing dependent relationships. Our own perceptions of things have the feeling of "of courseness" about them, even a kind of simplicity which can lead one into believing that surely they must be similarly appropriate for others. It can seem so very much quicker to tell another the obvious answers. It may even seem cruel and heartless to permit him to flounder about in search of his own solutions. So, quite without malice, but rather with generosity and goodwill, the helper may spring forward to tell those he would like to help the answers to their problems and, in so doing, may create dependence and destroy self-direction in the very persons he seeks to help. Persons skilled in the helping professions have generally learned to avoid "telling" and "advising," not only because their advice may be wrong but because the telling itself may create dependence and interfere with the processes of self-propulsion.

AUTHORITY IMPEDES INDEPENDENCE

Too great a reliance upon authority tends to undermine a person's confidence in himself. It gives him the feeling that all the good answers are held by the authority figures; therefore he may wait for them to supply answers, or spend his time in efforts designed to coax, trick, or threaten persons in authority into sharing their wisdom with him. The effect of reliance upon authority is to destroy initiative and gets in the way of the kind of active search for solutions necessary for effective helping relationships. But reliance upon authority is easily learned, while taking charge of oneself is often a slower, more tedious process. In the famous Lippitt and White studies on democracy and autocracy, children quickly adapted to a shift from democratic to autocratic atmospheres and let the leader make the decisions. Changes in the other direction were much more difficult. Children accustomed to autocratic groups only learned to take responsibility for running groups democratically over an extended period of time. Independence and self-direction grow from within. Authority can be imposed from without. Since the goal of the helping professions is the production of independent, self-directing persons, the role of authority in the helping professions is usually antithetical to the processes these professions seek to engender.

Because it is nice to be needed and wanted, it is easy for helpers to be seduced into dependent relationships. Persons in need of help are likely to look upon their helpers as rather special people. This is a pleasant feeling for helpers too; in fact, it is so pleasant that it is tempting to continue the feeling and so, quite unconsciously, contribute to the further dependence of the persons one seeks to help. People in the helping professions, like everyone else, have a basic need for the enhancement of self; but this satisfaction should not be realized by weakening those they seek to help. The helping atmosphere must be one which provides the client with experience which reassures him that he can deal with life. It must provide him with the feeling that good and useful answers to his problems can be found in himself. To accomplish this end, the authority of the helper must generally be held to a minimum.

Preoccupation with the Past

A further interference of authority with the free atmosphere required for helping is often found in the preoccupation of helpers with the past. If learning is conceived as the acquisition of right answers, it follows that persons in need of help should be provided with these as quickly as possible. Furthermore, where else should one find the right answers than in the experience of persons in the past? Thinking this way about learning inevitably leads the helper to a preoccupation with the information aspects of learning and to heavy reliance upon history or the solutions others have found for their problems. This procedure usually fails for at least three reasons: First, one's own problems always seem unique; secondly, the answers others have found rarely fit our own problems because the circumstances we confront are different or times have changed; thirdly, even if the answers others have found are appropriate, they are likely to seem so only after completion of one's own explorations. The fit of answers is discovered in the process of exploring problems. Too much preoccupation with information or the experience of others may have the net effect of short circuiting or turning off the helping process.

ENCOURAGING ACTIVE SEARCHING

The search for meaning is an active process; it cannot be accomplished standing still. The helping encounter must actively encourage the process of searching. This condition is achieved in part by an attitude of fearless looking, that "it is good to look and fun to try." It may be provided in the form of success experience or the discovery of challenging problems. It may be acquired "by osmosis" from the attitudes and behavior of the helper. Whatever contributes to the feeling that "anything can be looked at" is likely to be helpful. On the contrary, whatever prevents such an attitude gets in the way of effective learning.

The helper's sensitivity is an important factor contributing to the searching attitude. The experience of being understood by another is an indication that the self is comprehensible and acceptable. When an understanding teacher says to the student, "I can see that really bothers you, Jack," he may be doing more than providing simple acceptance. He may also be helping to eliminate the student's feelings of shame and humiliation which prevent him from making an effort. The point is well illustrated in the comment of a "problem child" after spending three months in the class of an especially accepting teacher. The child said of her teacher, "Well, she makes you feel all *smo o o oth* inside and you aren't afraid to answer or ask questions or to try even if it is hard things." Interaction with an empathic person may be more than releasing; it may possess an important positive thrust as well.

Counselors stress the importance of remaining unshockable in order to create this kind of feeling. In this way they can provide an example which says to the client: "I am not afraid to look. What you fear is not so terrible that it cannot be faced." This attitude is particularly necessary in counselors, for the persons they work with are often in difficulty precisely because they feel unable to face what seem to them terrible truths about themselves. In the practice of psychotherapy, it is a common thing to hear clients say, "If people ever really knew . . . !" With persons so fearful of looking, it is especially necessary to create an atmosphere which reassures them that they are understandable and that the matters they fear can be dealt with.

Such encouragement is needed in other helping professions as well. We have succeeded, almost everywhere, in erecting an incredible number of barriers to involvement—attitudes or practices which say to people: "Watch out!" "Don't look at that." "That is forbidden" (or inappropriate, or nasty, or unacceptable). Teachers in school do this when they say to the child: "I'm not interested in what you feel about that. What does the book say?" We do it with children in our families when we teach them the "right," "nice," "proper," things to do, think, and feel. We do it with each other when we change the subject because "we would rather not think about that." Even as a society, we become highly skilled in simply not seeing what lies before our eyes—for example, the sick, the slum, the Negro, the prisoner, or the fact that other countries and other cultures do not see things as we do. A major task of the helper, no matter what branch of the profession he may be engaged in, must be to overcome the negative effects of such built-in resistance to looking.

RESTRICTING EFFECTS OF EVALUATIVE PROCESSES

Many barriers to exploration masquerade as aids to learning. Devices established ostensibly to motivate people turn out, instead, to get in the way of learning. Perhaps the worst examples of this process are to be found in overemphasis on evaluation. Educators, for example, begin with the assumption that people need to know where they stand. Surely, no one could take much issue with that! They also believe that people need to be motivated to do their very best. Accordingly, a grading or marking system is introduced to do two excellent things: to let people know where they stand and provide a system of rewards and punishments to spur them on. The theory sounds unassailable, but all too often it fails in practice. In the first place, it frequently evaluates people who neither want nor need it—at least, not in the terms provided. For some, grades become the goal of learning; students sometimes give up their own goals for the meaningless symbols of grades. For others, grades appear irrelevant, a waste of time, to be dispensed with a minimum of involvement. Thus, the marking system, which set out so bravely to bring about involvement in exploration, often ends by diverting, restricting, narrowing, or even shutting off completely the very events it was designed to encourage.

Evaluation can be important and helpful. It is not a good thing in itself. It has to be used with accuracy and precision with reference to the needs, purposes, and perceptions of those to whom it is applied. Like the doctor choosing a drug, the helper in human affairs must be aware of the side effects involved in the measures he uses to help his clients, students, or patients. Without such awareness he may become his own worst enemy. It is no accident that psychotherapists generally eschew making evaluations and judgments in counseling practice. They do this because they have discovered from long experience that evaluating tends to destroy rapport, creates resistance, and generally interferes with the free atmosphere that is so essential for encouraging discovery of personal meaning.

FEAR OF MAKING MISTAKES

One of the most certain destroyers of the atmosphere for exploration and discovery is the terrible fear of making mistakes. This fear is often held both by the helpers and those they seek to assist. Many helpers, filled with the milk of human kindness, try to keep their students, clients, or patients from making mistakes. With the best of intentions, they point out the horrible pitfalls along the way, or seek to protect the client from them. Sometimes they may even punish helpees to make certain they do not fall into error. Unfortunately, a rejection of mistake-making can often destroy the very things that both helper and helpee are seeking. The atmosphere for helping must encourage looking. A fear of mistakes has quite the opposite effect; it discourages searching and exploration, no matter what the intentions of the helper. People who are afraid to make mistakes are afraid to try. And, when people are afraid to try, the very wellsprings of creativity and innovation are dried up.

It is, of course, necessary to protect young children from making certain kinds of mistakes, like running out on a busy highway, but over protection can get in the way of the helping process. Protecting people too much from error can run the risk of cutting them off from challenge. An important source of learning is met in the necessity for taking the consequences of mistakes. A consultant arrived at a school shortly after the election of a new student body president took place. He found the administrators and teachers in a high state of indignation because the students had just elected a youngster who vigorously campaigned for office on a platform he obviously could not deliver. He promised his constituents such things as no detention halls, every Friday afternoon off, free dances every week, and a dozen other equally unlikely benefits. The faculty was so incensed by the young man's election that they were seriously considering invalidating the election. They asked the consultant if he did not feel that this action should be taken. He disagreed and pointed out to the faculty that, with the best of intentions, they were about to rob the students of a valuable lesson in practical democracy. How else can one learn the value of a vote? What better way to learn the importance of a careful choice of leadership than having to live for awhile with a bad one you elected yourself? Counselors and social workers call this "confrontation with reality." They recognize its value. Instead of overly protecting their clients from making mistakes, they seek instead to help them explore and discover the meanings to be gained from such experiences.

Giving people the right to make mistakes is not just a question of deciding to do so. Whether a helper is able to permit the persons he works with such freedom has to do with his own feelings and beliefs about the nature of people. From a number of researches on good and poor helpers we know that one of the characteristics of good ones is a belief that the people they work with are able. If one believes people are able, he can let them. If he does not, then it will be necessary for him to protect the people he works with from their folly. Indeed, he would be operating quite unethically if he did not! Deciding to let people make mistakes cannot be done without an honest belief in the capacities of people to survive the process and arrive at their own best solutions.

POINTING THE WAY FOR STUDENTS, CLIENTS, AND PATIENTS

The specific ways in which a particular helper goes about working with the students, clients, or patients he intends to help will be largely dependent upon his personal philosophy of the helping process. If the helper's prime adherence is to an objective-intellectual frame of reference, then aiding helpees to discover more effective ways of behaving will involve three major steps: making a diagnosis, deciding on a plan of action, and putting it into effect. Much of the helper's efforts will be directed toward manipulating and controlling the forces impinging on the student-client. Like controlling the flow of current in an elaborate electrical system, he mans the switches obstructing and facilitating the movement of the current to realize the goals he deems appropriate. Operating this way the concern of the helper is with facts, forces, and events; and by his behavior he turns the attention of the helpee to these matters. "What happened?" he asks. "What did you (or he or she) do?" In spite of himself the philosophy to which he is committed turns attention to objective questions. The helpee, perceiving this interest, assumes that is the proper area of exploration and tries to explore the "facts" with which he is confronted. Sometimes it works. Sometimes the student does not have to really understand, but only pass the examination; or the client does not need an important change in his values, but only sufficient knowhow to accomplish a momentary end. Not every aspect of life requires deep personal changes in meanings, and such approaches to helping may therefore be enough.

If it is deeper meanings which the helper hopes to change, they cannot be dealt with so directly. Manipulations of the helper must be channeled, not toward attempting to control behavior but rather toward controlling the circumstances of the encounter. The concern of the helper is less with facts than with meanings, less with the manipulation of forces, and more with the nature of the relationship. Attention is directed toward establishing conditions for effective exploration of meaning and teaching the student or client where to look for the most efficient discovery of new meaning.

Meanings are the building blocks of helping, the materials for the construction of a more effective self. To this end the efforts of effective helpers must be directed toward concentrating attention on personal meanings. In doing this the helper points his subject toward the areas of exploration most likely to be profitable for him in solving whatever dilemma he may be confronted with.

The specific techniques which helpers use to induce exploration of meaning will vary widely from one type of helping profession to another. It is a highly individual question dependent in part upon the helper's beliefs about people, the goals he perceives as appropriate for the helping process, the kinds of persons he works with, settings in which he operates, the kind of techniques he has learned to use and how he sees himself. With all these variables affecting choices, the methods used will be highly individual. A detailed discussion of them is beyond the province of this book. We can do little more here than point out a few examples of how some helpers concentrate attention upon personal meaning in several of the professions.

POINTING THE WAY IN COUNSELING

Meanings are matters of belief, values, attitudes, conceptions, and judgments. Accordingly, one way counselors assist their clients is to point the way to those significant factors for consideration. This is accomplished in the counseling dialogue by holding them up for examination. In the following excerpt from a counseling case, note how the counselor bypasses the factual content of what his client is saying to respond to the personal meaning she is expressing. The young woman in the case came for help because of her deep distress over a shriveled hand birth defect.

Y. W.: I thought that—well, what I am trying to say is that I would try to push it off and I found that I couldn't.

C.: You found that that was impossible.

Y. W.: I thought that they were just being sorry and were trying to make up by giving me things.

C.: They were sorry—

Y. W.: (*cutting in*) That was no good. It did no one any good.

C.: You don't want people to feel sorry for you.

Y. W.: Never! I never want that!

C.: I see, Although you didn't want people to feel sorry for you, you felt you got it anyhow.

Y. W.: Yes, people didn't say anything but I could feel it. I used to wonder what would happen in a group if someone actually said something about it. It frightened me so. I think that I wouldn't know what to do. I am afraid of what they might do. I would rather not have my parents know what happens sometimes. Better that I know it just myself than all three of us.

C.: You prefer that they not know about it.

Y. W.: They must have known when I was little. In those days it didn't matter to me. I remember one instance when I went home from school—the only instance that I ever told them how I really felt. That was the time when I packed up here at school and took a train home. I just couldn't stand it any longer and called them up and told them I was coming home. I should never have done it. Some of the girls said something, and it got worse and worse until I couldn't stand it any more. So I went, and I was sorry I did.

C.: You feel that that was a mistake.

Y. W.: I don't know what happened. When I was on the train—I remember I called them and told them I was coming home and then on the train I decided that I would not tell them anything. I'd make up some other story about something else. I was riding home from the train in the car when Mother said, "Is it about your hand?" And then I told her about it. I just broke down and told her. That was the only time.

C.: M-hm.

Y. W.: Afterwards I told them that I wanted something done. Something just had to be done! I had an appliance made, but it didn't work. I gave it up after awhile and never mentioned it again. They didn't either. They didn't know the other times. I don't think there is anything to be gained now by telling them.

C.: So this has been a kind of secret that everybody knew, but nobody talked about.[1]

---

1. From the *Case of Edith Moore* by Arthur W. Combs. Reprinted by permission of the publisher from Snyder, William U., *Casebook of Non-Directive Counseling*, Boston: Houghton Mifflin Co., 1947.

In counseling this technique is sometimes called "recognition and acceptance of feeling." It could equally well be called recognition and acceptance of personal meaning, for that is what feeling is. The use of the technique by the counselor has the effect of focusing the client's attention upon his personal meanings rather than upon the factual material that he is expressing.

POINTING THE WAY IN ADULT-CHILD RELATIONSHIPS

Haim Ginott in a delightful book for parents has recommended a similar technique to improve communication between parents and children. Here, for example, are some sample conversations he reports between children and parents:

> When a child comes home with a host of complaints about a friend or a teacher or about his life, it is best to respond to his feeling tone, instead of trying to ascertain facts to verify incidents.
>   Ten-year old Harold came home cranky and complaining.
> *Harold:* What a miserable life! The teacher called me a liar, just because I told her that I forgot the homework. And she yelled, My goodness, did she yell! She said she'll write you a note.
> *Mother:* You had a very rough day.
> *Harold:* You can say that again.
> *Mother:* It must have been terribly embarrassing to be called a liar in front of the whole class.
> *Harold:* It sure was.
> *Mother:* I bet inside yourself you wished her a few things!
> *Harold:* Oh, yes! But how did you know?
> *Mother:* That's what we usually do when someone hurts us.
> *Harold:* That's a relief.

>   *From general to specific.*—When a child makes a statement about himself, it is often desirable to respond, not with agreement or disagreement, but with details that convey to the child an understanding beyond expectation.
>   When a child says, "I am not good in arithmetic," it is of litttle help to tell him, "Yes, you are pretty lousy with figures." Nor is it helpful to dispute his opinion or to offer him cheap advice: "If you studied more, you would be better." Such hasty help only hurts his self-respect and the instant lesson only decreases his confidence.
>   His statement, "I am not good in arithmetic," can be met with earnestness and understanding. Any of the following would do:
>   "Arithmetic is not an easy subject."
>   "Some of the problems are very hard to figure out."
>   "The teacher does not make it easier with his criticism."

"He makes you feel stupid."

"I bet you can't wait for the hour to pass."

"When it is over, you feel safer."

"Exam time must be extra tough."

"You must be worrying a lot about failing."

". . . worrying about what we will think."

". . . afraid we'll be disappointed in you."

"We know some subjects are not easy."

"We have faith that you'll do your best."

A twelve-year old boy related that he almost "dropped dead" when father talked to him with such understanding after he brought home a failing report card. His inner reaction was, "I must live up to my father's faith in me." [2]

POINTING THE WAY IN SCHOOL

Teachers also accomplish a similar kind of focus with comments like the following:

"I can see that you feel very angry at Jimmy, Billy. I can understand how you might feel that way but you're not allowed to hit him."

"How do you feel about the poem, Helen?"

"Do you think the court was justified in the ruling?"

"What do you think is the purpose of the procedure?"

The success of a helper in pointing the way to the significant questions for his students or clients in this fashion will, of course, depend upon his sensitivity to the internal world of the persons he is working with. To be able to respond in the ways we have been illustrating above calls for a kind of empathy with the helpee, the capacity to "listen with a third ear." By concentrating attention on personal meaning the helper is really telling his client where he needs to look to find the solutions to his problems. When consistently treated this way the student or client soon learns to look in these places for himself without the guidance of an outside person. Where group discussion leaders have used this technique, after a few sessions group members can be observed responding in these ways to each other quite without any special instruction to that end. Concentration upon the personal meaning of events makes it possible to penetrate to the heart of events in much of human activity. It shucks off interminable description or preoccupation with unimportant details and so makes it possible for helping relationships to move forward with dispatch.

2. From Ginott, H. G. *Between parent and child.* New York: Macmillan, 1965. Reprinted by permission of the publisher.

SELECTED READINGS

Starred entries indicate appearance in whole or in part in Donald L. Avila, Arthur W. Combs, and William W. Purkey, *The Helping Relationship Sourcebook* (Boston: Allyn & Bacon, 1971).

* Carkhuff, R. R. and Truax, C. B. Toward explaining success and failure in interpersonal learning experiences. *Personnel and Guidance Journal,* 1966, 723–728.

* Combs, A. W. Fostering self direction. *Educational Leadership,* 1966, **23,** 373–387.

Frank, J. D. *Persuasion and healing.* Baltimore: Johns Hopkins Press, 1961.

Frankl, V. E. *Man's search for meaning: An introduction to logotherapy.* Boston: Beacon, 1963.

Fromm, E. *The art of loving: An inquiry into the nature of love.* New York: Harper & Row, 1956.

Jackson, P. W. *Life in classrooms.* New York: Holt, Rinehart & Winston, 1968.

Jourard, S. M. & Lasakow, P., Some factors in self disclosure. *Journal of Abnormal and Social Psychology,* 1958, **56,** 91–98.

* Kelley, E. C. *Another look at individualism.* Detroit, Mich.: Wayne State University, College of Education, 1962.

Moustakas, C. E. *The authentic teacher: Sensitivity and awareness in the classroom.* Cambridge, Mass: Howard A. Doyle Publishing Co., 1966.

Roberts, W. Believing is seeing. *Saturday Review,* Oct. 19, 1968, 62.

Truax, C. B. & Wargo, D. G. Psychotherapeutic encounters that change behavior: For better or for worse. *American Journal of Psychotherapy,* 1966, **22,** 499–520.

13

Communication

Learning always has two aspects: exposure to some new experience and the discovery of its meaning. The new experience required for learning may occur as a consequence of the interaction of a person with some aspect of his physical world. But of far more importance to most of us are those interactions we have with people and what is communicated by them. A very large portion of our lives is spent trying to communicate with our fellows in one fashion or another. While everyone engages in these attempts more or less successfully, the processes of communication are especially important for the helping professions. They are the primary tools of the trade. What happens in the interactions of teacher and pupil, counselor and client, priest and parishioner, supervisor and worker will be very largely dependent upon the communication skills of the helper.

How successful helpers are in creating effective relationships with their clients will depend on the beliefs they hold about the nature and processes of communication and how effectively they are able to invest themselves in the dialogue. Most breakdowns in communication come about because of faulty assumptions on the part of communicators. It is, therefore, imperative that helpers carefully examine their beliefs about this vital aspect of the helping task.

COMMUNICATION: A FUNCTION OF COMMON MEANINGS

When we think of communication, most of us think almost at once of words, of talk. Communication, however, is much more than a matter of words. The development of language was one of man's great accomplishments and makes possible more effective communication of meanings. But even as we admire this accomplishment, it is necessary for us to keep in mind that words are no more symbols which make possible the transmission of meanings. In themselves they lack the impact to produce the changes in meanings necessary for changed behavior. We are all familiar with the fact that the behavior of many of our friends and acquaintances is vastly different from the things they say. Many a teacher has been dismayed at the glibness with which his students are able to say the "right" things even while they behave as though they had never heard of them. Indeed, words are extremely valuable vehicles for the transmission of information, but they do not represent true communication all by themselves.

Communication is a function of common meanings, the overlapping of the perceptual fields of communicator and communicatee. It is a matter of acquiring common "maps" so that the meaning existing for one person may exist for others as well. Communication is thus a problem of shared experience. Whether it is successful will be dependent only in part upon what is said or happening outside the individual. More importantly, effectiveness will be determined by what goes on inside the persons involved in the peculiar world of meaning which makes up their perceptual fields.

When meanings overlap we have the feeling of understanding or of being understood. When meanings fail to overlap, communication breaks down and misunderstandings occur. A teachers' college dropped the name "probationer" for students getting practical field experience when it was discovered that some people in the communities they served thought the students were just out of jail. Breakdowns are also amusingly illustrated in the *faux pas* which children make on test papers in school or the reports they make to adults of their experiences in the world. We are amused when the child tells us "God's name is Harold" because in Sunday School he prayed, "Harold be Thy name." Or when he tells us he sang in church about "the consecrated cross-eyed bear!" Failures of common meanings which leave us standing on a freezing street corner for a half-hour because the friend we were supposed to meet thought we said 2:45 instead of 2:15 are much less amusing. They can even be disastrous for the world when nations misunderstand each other so badly that they go to war.

What Is Communicated?

What is communicated is not what is intended but what is comprehended. Here, for example, is what one child comprehended from the "Pledge of Allegiance." When asked to explain the pledge word by word, it came out something like this:

"I give a lot of money to the old soldiers for the flag of the United States and the flag holder on which it stands, one country under God, that you can't take apart, where you do as you please—just you and me and for everybody else!" The proper data with which helpers need to be concerned is not what they are saying or doing but what their clients are perceiving in the relationship.

The fact that words do not mean the same things to all people is a common observation. The fact is so important in human affairs as to have resulted in the science of semantics, which was developed to provide us with a better understanding of the importance and use of words. A well-known semanticist, S. I. Hayakawa, points out that words do not only differ in the *content* of their meaning, but that they also differ greatly in their accompanying *emotional impact*. Such words as "pretty" or "ugly" do not describe only an objective quality of appearance; they also carry connotations of "goodness" or "badness," of attraction or repulsion, of positive or negative. Descriptive words like "democrat" or "republican" are always associated with feeling tones which are likely to be far more important than the factual circumstances they describe. Even the simplest of words we use in daily life have emotional attachments. This is especially true when words are concerned with questions of belief, values, attitudes, feelings, emotions, or any number of abstractions. The meanings attached to words do not remain static. They shift with changing times and places. The connotations of words like "sex," "pill," "moon," "black," and "pot" are notorious examples of how word meanings have changed in recent times. Each of these words has meanings unassociated with them a generation ago.

To be unaware of changes in meanings can create important misunderstandings. One of the authors recently witnessed a very heated argument between two young lovers because of the failure of one to recognize that a common word had taken on a new meaning. The word was "commitment." Traditionally this word has often referred to something one had to do against his will. The dictionary definition, as a matter of fact, still carries this connotation. Recently the word has taken on a very different meaning. It has come to mean that one is dedicated to a cause, has devoted himself body and soul to some idea or person. The quarrel began because the young man had assimilated this new connotation while the young lady still interpreted the word as meaning an obligation, a task one was forced to do. Consequently, when the young man said he was committed to his love, she flew at him indignantly, asking, "What do you mean you're committed? I'm not going to force you into anything!" And a serious argument began. A break of irreparable proportions might well have materialized between these two young people had there not been someone near to clarify the problem. Wars have resulted from similar failures to agree on common meanings.

The concomitant meanings attached to words have sometimes been known as "incidental" learnings in traditional psychological thought. They often create annoying problems for research workers because they introduce factors into experiments on behavior that are not easily controllable by the experimenter. Often they interfere in what would otherwise be uncomplicated, clear-cut objective experiments. For the professional helper the "incidental" aspects of words will often be far more significant than the words themselves. To be unaware of this impact may make the helper ineffective, no matter how good his intentions.

In some helping situations the words used between helper and helpee may even be of no consequence whatever. The fact of communication, of engaging in a human interaction with another person, may, itself, be the important facet of the helping relationship. Man is an intensely social animal and often a very lonely one, even when surrounded by thousands of other people. Accordingly, the very fact of being able to get through to someone else may fill a very important need. This is especially true for those afflicted with deep feelings of alienation. Almost everyone has had the experience at some time or other of sitting next to a stranger on a train or plane and being surprised at the depths and extent of feelings communicated by his seat mate. In such instances the stranger could not care less what advice you have to give him. He has chosen to talk precisely because he will not have to listen to advice. What he seeks is the experience of release in telling his story to someone—anyone! All he needs is a willing listener.

NONVERBAL COMMUNICATION

Because of the importance of language in daily life, most of us are keenly aware of the verbal exchanges we engage in. But communication occurs without words, too. Even at a very great distance we can spot our friends by the way they walk or the gestures they make. We are continually bombarded by bits of information concerning the people and the world around us quite without reference to words. Who has not spoken to a friend by a look? Shrugged his shoulders in resignation? Made a face at an enemy? Or conveyed the concern he felt by a touch of the hand? These nonverbal communications may even be a far more powerful means of conveying meaning than a book full of words.

While traveling to Washington with a friend, one of the authors experienced an interesting illustration of a nonverbal, deeply meaningful communication with a total stranger which occurred in the twinkling of an eye. As they walked down the aisle after the plane had landed, the author glanced at a young woman seated next to the window holding her baby. She was slowly moving her nose back and forth through her baby's hair. As the author passed she glanced up, met his eye and in a flash a deeply meaningful experience was shared. As they descended the steps from the plane the author's friend asked, "Do you know that girl?"

"Never saw her in my life before," the author replied.

"Well! She certainly talked to you!" exclaimed the friend.

"Yes, and I talked to her, too!" said the author.

The young woman was caught in the act of smelling her baby's head, a meaningless gesture to most of the passengers debarking. But, she was thoroughly enjoying the experience, for there is something very special about the smell of a baby's head. It is a sensuous, loving experience that the author, too, had known with babies of his own. So, in an instant two strangers shared a deeply meaningful experience and never a word was spoken.

A very great deal of what transpires between teacher and student or counselor and client will be dependent upon the nonverbal aspects of the relationships they engage in. The beliefs of helpers are conveyed to helpees despite the words they use. This fact has been repeatedly demonstrated in research on the helping professions. It has also led educators responsible for the training of workers in the helping professions to concentrate greater and greater attention on beliefs students hold, the sensitivity they develop, and the relationships they create with those they seek to help. It is these factors which determine in large measure the nature and effect of what is communicated in the helping dialogue.

RESPONSIBILITY FOR COMMUNICATION

When understanding fails to come about in human interaction, it is common to blame the other fellow. If he does not understand, it is easy to point out, "We told him what to do!" This neatly places the responsibility for communication on the receiver, the communicatee. It also absolves the helper of blame. He can wash his hands of the affair and continue to feel successful no matter how great a disaster he has produced for his client. Such a procedure is comfortable for the communicator, to be sure, but not very helpful—especially not for persons engaged in the helping professions. Communication is always an interaction, and the responsibility for its breakdown must lie with the participant assuming the helping role. Having held himself out as able to help, it is up to him to deliver. Responsibility for communication lies always with the communicator, not the communicatee.

If others do not understand us, that is our fault and not theirs. If the reader of this book does not understand what the authors are saying, then we haven't said it well enough for him. If the person in the receiving role accepts some responsibility for listening carefully or trying to understand what is being conveyed, that, of course, is immensely facilitating. It cannot, however, be *demanded* or even expected by the helper. A major goal of helping is freeing people so that they will be able to enter into effective dialogue. It is part of the helper's job to find ways of helping his charges confront the world despite their fears and anxieties or outright resistance. The creation of openness is, in itself, a goal of the helping process. It is unfair to ask as a condition of helping another that he already have achieved the very goals the process is designed to produce!

COMMUNICATION MUST BE RELATED TO NEED

How well helpers are understood will ordinarily be a function of three major questions:

1. The relationship of information to need.
2. The relationship to existing information in the perceptual field.
3. The openness of the field at the moment of communication.

In Chapter 4 we already observed the effects of need on perception. The principle is simple enough! Other things being equal, we perceive those events we need to perceive. Examples of this principle may be found in our own experience. Although we may pass a street innumerable times, we do not perceive its location until it becomes necessary to find the home of a new friend there. Ads for new cars are bypassed until we begin to feel that the old car is getting a bit shabby. Despite daily familiarity with the principle in practice, however, it is easy to overlook its role in communication.

Need exerts a selective effect on what is perceived. People take in what information they need to absorb. The rest is likely to leave them unmoved if they perceive it at all. This fact creates a great problem for educators, who must provide information and experience for students who will not need that information for years to come. It is a comparatively easy thing to teach a person what he currently wants to know, but it is much more difficult to get him to comprehend what he "may need some day." This is one of the reasons why many teachers enjoy teaching the "gifted" students who are already interested in and eager for academic information. It is far more difficult to teach such material to children coming from disadvantaged backgrounds, or to find teachers willing to work with such children. Not much teaching is really required to work with people who have a clear-cut need.

It takes real genius to communicate where need is not so patently evident. A major portion of the time and efforts of good teachers must be devoted to creating needs even before information is provided. This is what the first-grade teacher does when she sets up a store in her classroom. In the course of running the store the children develop many needs to know. They need to know about money because they have to make change. Spelling is important because they have to make a sign. They must know how to read in order to understand the label on the bottle. It is necessary that they know how to get along with others, for running a store and selling its goods requires cooperation. Some people, who do not know any better, regard such teaching activities with suspicion. It's too much fun! Though it may look like play to outsiders, what is really going on is an ingenious way of creating problems for children, the crucial first step in learning. In higher grade levels the creation of need may be accomplished through involving students in planning for their own educational experiences, operating their own student governments, or designing procedures to place the student on his own resources with ever increasing opportunities for self-direction.

The importance of the relevance principle for communication can also be observed in the other helping professions. Giving persons psychological tests which they have not asked for, for example, is often a frustrating experience for the beginning counselor. He is quite likely to find that his client has little or no interest in the valuable information the counselor would like to give him. Social workers know that giving a client information he sees no need for is unlikely to be either accepted or acted upon. Worse still, the social worker who insists upon providing unnecessary information is likely to be regarded by his clients as ignorant or as an annoying busybody. Dieticians are often frustrated because, despite the vast quantities of information they have about the "right" things to eat and ways to prepare it, the persons they want to help frequently ignore the information and go right on eating what they like and cooking the way their mothers did. It is a common complaint of clergymen everywhere that the people who need sermons most are the ones who never come to church.

Donald Snygg once pointed out that "there is nothing in this world so useless as answers we do not have problems for!" It is the attempt to provide such answers which frequently results in failures of communication in all aspects of the helping professions. Helpers who truly want to communicate with their clients will need to be sensitive to the needs of their clients and skillful in relating what they have to convey to those needs.

INFORMATION AND CENSORSHIP

The principle of relevance is also operative with respect to information or experience clients need but cannot acquire. People need information in order to deal with life. If they cannot get it when they need it, they may be plunged even deeper into the problems they face. Without access to accurate information, adjustments to life must be made on the basis of distorted or inaccurate data. There can be no place for censorship in effective helping processes. Rather, the process requires helping clients to obtain whatever information is needed with the greatest possible dispatch.

Sometimes information may be withheld by well-meaning persons "for fear of hurting" those they work with, or for fear their clients may not be adequate to deal with the problems the information creates for them. Nurses and doctors, for example, have been known to lie to patients with terminal cancer who asked them if they would get well. Such well-meaning attempts to shield the patient often result in robbing him of the opportunity to do something he might like before it is too late. Proper planning can only occur in the light of accurate information.

This question also arises with teachers and counselors who may have to decide what information to provide a student or client. Should a child be told his intelligence test scores, for example? Applying the principle that there is no information about himself that a person ought not have, the answer would seem to be unequivocably, "yes." However, the problem of communication involves more than simply providing information. It is a question of meaning. To provide a person with a set of scores he doesn't understand may actually have the effect of providing him with false information. The helper who supplies information, therefore, has an additional responsibility to be sure it is understood. This may be such a difficult, time-consuming task that a helper may prefer to eschew the giving of information in the first place. The principle that a person ought to know the facts of how he stands with relationship to other people, providing he wants to know this, is still a good one. But the time required to assure his adequate understanding (granting the competence of the helper to do so) may be so large a factor as to warrant withholding information—not on the grounds of whether it is good for the student, but whether the helper has the time and energy available for the necessary clarification or the wish to engage in the discussion.

The methods helpers have used to relate information to need are extraordinarily varied. Many counselors, for example, have learned to wait for their clients to express a need to know. They do this because they have learned it is more efficient that way. They know that information given prior to need is often fruitless and may even be destructive to the helping relationship. As a consequence they have come to rely upon the client's own drives for health, recognizing that if they are successful in helping the client to search for meaning then, sooner or later, he must come to realize he lacks important information. At this point the counselor can help him to get it in whatever way is most appropriate at the time. For example, the mother who has come at last to the conclusion that her child needs special help can then be helped to find the appropriate agency for the purpose. If the same information had been given to her when she first came for aid, it might have given her the impression that the helper was not interested in the case and was trying to pass the problem on to another helper. Or, she might have felt very guilty and frustrated at being unable to care for the child herself. It is not an easy matter to admit that one has failed with his own child. Information about where and how to send one's child to an agency or institution of some sort must be preceded by the prior question of whether to send him at all. Even that can only be dealt with when one has come to terms with his own inadequacies. It is, after all, the client whom counselors hope to help change. Waiting for his need to set the pace is no loss of efficiency. There is little point for the counselor, social worker, or pastor to tell his client what he cannot use. This may only convey to him how little he is understood by the very people who are trying to help him.

Teachers, too, have discovered by experience that self-direction is an effective way of helping students relate information to need. What students need to know, they search out with ingenuity and vigor. What is more, knowledge acquired through such research is far more likely to be permanent and pertinent to their future needs. Accordingly, modern educators devote much time and attention to getting students involved in the learning process and creating needs they never knew they had. They do this because it makes learning more efficient and the presentation of information more likely to result in learning, which is what teaching is all about.

Social workers have learned in practice the value of "confrontation with reality"—that is, the importance of permitting a client to come face to face with his problems, to take the consequences of his own behavior or misbehavior. A potent source of information for everyone is the feedback he perceives following his own behavior. From such feedback, important data is obtained of a very personal sort. Protecting a person from such information may constitute a kind of censorship wherein the individual is robbed of experience that could be truly significant in his return to health. Overprotection from consequences may also destroy the opportunity to learn the things required to make a more adequate adjustment. The delinquent, continuously excused for his misbehavior, may be led by this experience to *expect* to escape responsibility for his actions and so cause him to perceive no necessity for better kinds of adjustment.

The attempt to relate information to need is also an important goal of the public speaker or writer. He does this through various devices aimed at helping his audience to identify with the information being provided. The authors of this book, for example, have attempted to relate information to the reader's own personal experience and needs for understanding. Sometimes this has been done by telling the reader a story with which he could identify. Attempts have also been made to seek his involvement through homely examples, by contrasting points of view or pointing out similarities with his own experience. The writers have even tried on occasion to do this by creating problems for readers.

INFORMATION MUST BE RELEVANT TO IMMEDIATE NEED

It is not enough that information should seem important to the receiver; it must also be related to his current problems or interests if it is to be truly effective. People perceive what they need to perceive, but immediate needs are always far more pressing and pertinent than those at a distance. Psychological distance, it should be noted, is not the same as physical distance. It has to do with *perceived* distance of an event to the self, rather than real distance in time and space. The snake behind the glass in the zoo, though only a few inches from us, is much farther away psychologically than the snake in the grass we meet face to face at a distance of several feet. To tell a woman who has just broken up with her lover, "Never mind, there will be many others," is seldom likely to be helpful if it is even comprehended at all. It is rarely helpful to give people information they will not need for years to come. Failure to understand this fact produces much of the disenchantment of the teenager when adults, with the best of intentions, attempt to provide young people with good advice.

It is the immediate problem that calls for solution. A little boy asked his mother where babies came from. "Oh, dear!" thought the mother, "the time has come!" So she sat him down and explained the matter in detail. When she was through, the little boy wailed, "But I didn't want to know all that!" A great many of the failures of communication between adults and children are largely wasted effort because information provided has little relationship to immediate need.

Another application of this principle is to be found in the lack of relationship usually found between an individual's stated self-ideal and behavior. Many have assumed that a person's stated goals of "what he would like to be" were important motivators of behavior. Logically, it would seem to be true that the way to help someone change would be to have him examine what he would like to be and what he now is, then make himself behave in the new ways. Unfortunately, this rarely turns out to be helpful. For most of us, the self-ideal (if we have thought about it at all) is something we dig up to tell people when they ask us what we would like to become. Even if this is a fairly true aspiration, it seldom affects our behavior because it is too remote from present matters to be of much concern. It is an academic exercise with little or no dynamic effect on moment to moment behavior. Immediate goals are the ones that affect behavior.

Long-term goals initiate and direct behavior, but they do not sustain it. If one's behavior is to be maintained along a path toward the attainment of a major goal, the process of becoming must be enhancing and reinforcing, or else a person will not continue. A person goes to college to get a degree, but that goal will not keep him there. The nature of the day to day experiences will determine whether or not he will continue to seek a degree. If the process of becoming "educated" proves to be a satisfying one the individual will remain until he takes his degree and perhaps continue to do further work toward a higher degree. If the process is not satisfying, he will drop out and pursue some other course of action. Long-term goals are significant only as they can be translated into more immediate steps for action. Almost anyone can observe in the people about him how far-off goals, no matter how explicitly stated, are frequently belied by short-term actions. The student who loudly protests that he wants to be a doctor more than anything in the world, and who nevertheless fails his required courses for entrance into medical school is a common example. As a matter of fact, it is a major problem of the helping professions to assist people in bringing their short-term aspirations into closer touch with long ones.

INFORMATION MUST BE RELATED
TO EXISTING MEANINGS

The Importance of Fit

Whether information can be truly communicated will be dependent on the readiness of the receiver to absorb it. We have already seen that the meaning of events is a question of the relationship of an experience to the existing organization of the perceptual field. It is only as the person discovers the relationship of new experience to that which is already in existence that it can be comprehended, which is another way of saying that it can be given meaning. We have also observed that meanings often exist in a kind of hierarchy in which complex ones are dependent upon the prior existence of simpler concepts. This is why age and experience are important variables in learning—not for their own sake, but because they provide opportunities for the development of earlier meanings on which later ones can be built.

A great many of the frustrations in communication come about because communicators have not been successful in helping communicatees perceive the place of new information in their existing fields of awareness. This failure to relate the new to the old results in what Festinger has called cognitive dissonance. He points out how difficult it is to absorb new ideas when they cannot be brought into harmony with those already present. Piaget also made much of this fact in his descriptions of growth in children's reasoning. He called it the "problem of the match." Prescott Lecky talked of the need of the individual for self-consistency and pointed out that the acquisition of meaning was a consequence of a person's attempts to achieve order in his experience.

Perhaps the clearest examples of the effects of the importance of fit are to be observed in trying to communicate with someone who speaks a different language. A common language is a tremendous assistance in the development of common meanings. Even without the language barrier, however, we can see the importance of this principle in operation when we find ourselves in a social situation where our usual expectancies do not fit, as, for example, when we go to an unfamiliar church with a friend and find ourselves confused at how to behave in this new setting. Information can only be comprehended if it can somehow be fitted to what is already there. What does not fit is likely to be rejected if it is apprehended at all.

SPEED AND PACING

Communication takes time. While information can be transmitted from one person to another with great speed, its comprehension is another matter. The meaning of information has to do with the individual's discovery of the relationship of new information to what is already there in his perceptual field. This requires a searching of the field, matching and adjustment of new understandings into the total gestalt. All of this takes time. One of the most common destroyers of communication is the impatience of the communicator. Effective lecturers know that it is a rare audience, indeed, which can be expected to carry away more than one or two new ideas. The speed of communication must be determined by the rate of comprehension, not the capacity of the communicator to deliver his message.

Time spent in making certain meanings are conveyed is not time wasted. There is no point in speaking if receivers can't hear. People in the helping professions often destroy their own effectiveness for failure to recognize the time required for communication. They become so preoccupied with "covering the subject," "getting on with the discussion," "presenting the facts," or "coming to a decision" that their clients or students are lost in the race. People do not put up with this for long. They have too many more important things to do so they "turn the speaker off," "drop out," fall asleep, or amuse themselves in the best ways they can. One needs but remember his own behavior listening to a speaker deliver his message without apparently caring whether his audience hears it or not to find similar examples for himself. It is lucky for many speakers that people are mostly well-mannered. On the other hand, it might improve the quality of speaking if audiences were less so and speakers had to take the full consequences of their behavior.

Effective communication calls for pacing material to the comprehension of the hearers. The principle of pacing is well known to educators, and many efforts of curriculum planners are devoted to finding ways to adjust subject matter to the readiness of children to deal with it. This is a question of both speed of presentation and relationship of the new to what already is comprehended. Good teachers do this as they try to meet the individual needs of children in their classes. Unfortunately, the principle is also often violated because of built-in inflexibilities in some schools which do not really permit the kind of adaptation to readiness that is necessary for effective communication. Among the worst offenders is the grade-level concept, which requires all children to deal with a specific curriculum at a particular time, ready or not. The importance of pacing is equally evident in other helping professions, and equally glaring examples of violations of the principle may be observed in the practice of counseling, social work, pastoral care, nursing, or whatever the relationship of helper and helpee.

While communication may often fail because the receiver is not yet ready to comprehend it, it can also be rendered ineffective or useless when receivers are long past the readiness point. Who has not passed a very dull hour listening to a speaker tell him interminably what he already knew? Many a helper has made himself unproductive by providing information his student, client, or patient has already had or has long since passed beyond. One of the interesting developments in recent educational research has been the discovery that many children are ready to learn very difficult concepts at much earlier ages than we had formerly supposed. Even complex economic concepts, we now know, can be taught in the very early grades if it is necessary or desirable to do so. The question is not whether the children are ready, but whether the teachers are.

The Value of Simplicity

Other things being equal, the simpler material is the more likely it is to be comprehended. Simplicity really refers to fit in the experience of the receiver. What is simple is a highly individual matter. What is easy for the student of calculus will seem quite different when the same material is presented to the person struggling with basic combinations of multiplication. The importance of simplicity seems very obvious, but, alas, it is frequently violated in practice. There are even some people in the helping professions who honestly believe it is good for persons to be confronted with terribly difficult and complex tasks. They operate on the principle: "the harder the better." To be sure, people need to confront problems, but information complex beyond the subject's readiness to grasp it can only result in discouragement and despair.

Other communicators make themselves ineffective because they are really more interested in the impressions they are making than in communicating. So, graduate students and learned scholars often turn out to be dreadful writers. They really don't care what they communicate so long as they create an impression of their own erudition. They write to impress their colleagues or their bosses. Whether anyone else comprehends is a matter of minor concern. It is the cleverness or the "scholarliness" of their style which intrigues them. Indeed, if others don't understand them, they may even take this as further proof of their own superiority. "If he doesn't comprehend it when I've said it so beautifully, that just proves how difficult it is. How wonderful I am and how stupid he is!"

People who really want to communicate do not regard simplicity as unscholarly. They recognize simplicity as one of the rules which affects communication and use it to make communication more successful. The goal of science itself is to make things comprehensible by reducing events to the simplest possible terms. This is known as the "Law of Parsimony."

Principles and Details in Communication

A variation of the need for simplicity in communication can be observed in the general or specific character of information. Communication is a function of the overlap of perceptual fields. The field of meanings existing for different people will vary a great deal more with respect to details than with respect to general principles. There is almost no end to the number of details one can find in a given body of information. Principles, however, are fewer and more comprehensive so that by emphasizing general principles the helper is much more likely to facilitate change in meaning than if he concentrates upon details. This fact has led Bruner and others to emphasize the importance of the "structure" of knowledge rather than the facts of knowledge. They point out that general principles are much more likely to find translation into the existing field of information than details, and advocate that education orient teaching to emphasize principles rather than details. Unfortunately, much provision of information for other people emphasizes exactly the opposite. It focuses attention upon details rather than structure. Professors, for example, frequently fill their lectures with details, test their students on details in objective examinations, and concentrate so exclusively on the students' handling of details that students soon "get the message"; it is the details that are important. These they then try to memorize. Unfortunately, unrelated facts are difficult to fit into already existing information without the unifying principles which give them meaning and so they are quickly lost. Emphasis upon the structure of knowledge is much more likely to find consistency or match within the learner's experience.

The application of any of the principles of effective communication is dependent upon the sensitivity of the communicator to what is going on in the listener. Good communicators are continuously searching the feedback they get from their audiences and adjusting their own behavior accordingly to assure maximum impact. Many of the principles discussed in the pages above can be observed in operation in the behavior of effective public speakers. Whether by accident or design, good speakers have learned to apply these principles in their presentations and adjust from moment to moment to the current condition of their audiences. An interesting example of this is the famous speech made years ago by Russell Conwell who traveled the Chautauqua circuit giving a speech entitled, "Acres of Diamonds." This single speech was so immensely successful that Mr. Conwell amassed a fortune which he later used to found Temple University. The structure of this speech is a very simple one. Throughout, a basic thought is stated in the simplest possible terms, then illustrated in ways that make it possible for the hearer to fit the principle to his own need and daily experience. This pattern is repeated over and over throughout the address.

OPENNESS AND COMMUNICATION

A major factor in determining the success of communication will be the condition of the receiver. In Chapter 6 we saw how the experience of threat interferes with the individual's perceptions by creating tunnel vision and forcing the defense of self. Both of these phenomena interfere with communication. Every human being has the insatiable task of enhancing himself. To do this he must also defend himself against humiliation and degradation. Psychological barriers are therefore needed to maintain existence. No organism can deal with everything simultaneously. Selection is necessary. People take in what they need and defend themselves against what is disruptive or destructive. Highly self-actualized persons, as we have seen, are maximally open to the world. Deeply threatened ones are surrounded by walls which isolate them from human intercourse. They have such impermeable defense systems that they are almost impossible to penetrate.

Barriers established in response to the experience of threat are even more important for communication because of the cyclic effects of the threat counter-threat spiral which has the potential to destroy the very dialogue of communication and, even, in its extremes to result in destruction of the communicators themselves. Once begun, the experience of threat may bounce back and forth from one communicator to the other, spiraling upward to increased intensity and interfering more and more with communication. It is brought about in part by attempts at self-defense and in part by retaliatory attacks (also a kind of defense) of one against the other. Imagine, for example, a pleasant conversation going on between Robert and Clifford represented by (A) in Fig. 5. In this conversation Robert and Clifford are fairly open to each other and their conversation moves back and forth quite easily, with little resistance and a maximum of comprehension. In the course of this conversation (B) Clifford says something to Robert which, intentionally or not, seems to Robert quite uncomplimentary. Robert is hurt by this comment and feels threatened. Accordingly, his defenses rise to protect himself from Clifford and that, of course, begins to interfere with his abilities to grasp what Clifford is saying. As a further defense he lets loose a mildly cutting remark at Clifford. Now Clifford (C), feeling himself under attack, raises his own defenses and retaliates in kind. This just proves what Robert thought in the first place—that Clifford was trying to insult him.

Fig. 5 Threat and Counter-Threat in Communication

For Persons		For Nations
	Robert (Russia?) Clifford (China?)	
open dialogue	A	freedom of commerce and communication
cutting remarks, insults	B	harassment; breaking walls and trade barriers
angry retorts, insults, and slander	C	"police action"; tanks and aircraft
leave the scene or punish the adversary		atomic bombs

Therefore, he raises his defenses still higher and looses a tougher retort, which only forces Clifford to do the same. So the spiral is well on its way. The greater the threat the less the ability to hear, and the greater the necessity to respond with greater threat. If something doesn't happen to stop this interaction, the pressure may eventually build up such a head of steam that it can only be resolved by some kind of drastic action (D).

This spiraling effect of threat and counter threat, of course, is not limited to individuals only. It also happens to nations, as illustrated on the right-hand side of Fig. 5. Between nations the spiral can escalate to such heights that threat eventually becomes intolerable and war breaks out to eliminate the threat posed by the "enemy." This can be done by physically wiping him out or by reducing his capacity to threaten to a point where it can be successfully coped with. Once embarked on a threat counter-threat spiral, it is difficult to stop, and communication is likely to get worse unless the experience of threat can somehow be reduced and the channels of communication reopened.

Breaking the deadly threat counter-threat cycle will call for some combination of the following.

1/ Attention to the feelings involved in the process of dialogue. Preoccupation of the participants with action (who did what to whom and what is to be done in retaliation) inflames the threat counter-threat cycle. It obscures the causes of difficulty and turns the attention of the dialogue from the sources of cure. To resolve a threat, one or both parties must become concerned with the feeling aspect. In the helping professions this is a major task of helpers, and finds expression in almost everything they do.

2/ Absorbing or draining off feelings of threat. If one or both parties can find a way to respond with less threat than they receive, the vicious circle can be interrupted and temperatures can be given opportunity to decrease. The helper does this in many ways: He may absorb the threat, as the teacher does when he lets a child work off his anger in some harmless fashion or as the counselor does in maintaining his "cool" and remaining unshockable at what his client has to tell him.

3/ Contributing to the personal feelings of security in participants. Positive feelings about self make possible greater toleration of threat and less need for self-defense. Helpers accomplish this goal through helping clients to achieve greater feelings of self-actualization either through their own interactions with their helpees or through the manipulation of external events to this end.

4/ Adjusting the interchange to the tolerance levels of the reactors. Matters are consciously arranged to assure that communications have as little inflammability as possible. The helper cannot do this for his client. He can, however, control his own responses or set an example by his own behavior. To do this requires a great deal of sensitivity on the part of the helper and a high degree of self-discipline.

5/ Recognition of difference. The appreciation of the fact of difference and its value in human affairs will, of itself, help to lower the temperature of interactions. It contributes to the feeling that "it is all right to be me" and acceptance of a similar right in others. For this reason much of the work of helpers revolves around the recognition and acceptance of difference expressed in innumerable ways in the various branches of these professions.

Because of the experiences we have had in a lifetime of growing up, almost anyone is touchy about something and has built up defenses to protect himself against hurt. These defenses are likely to seem essential to the people who have them, and they do not willingly or quickly give them up. They cannot be ignored if communication is to be effective. Communication is not a matter of bargaining or slick operations, but rather a matter of discovering mutual meanings. An atmosphere of force and coercion can only disrupt this process or, worse still, involve us in a disastrous cycle of threat and counter-threat.

A further difficulty with threat in communication is the fact that symbols of hostility and the reasons for people's anger, etc., generally outlast the conditions which created them. Therefore, the effects of threat carry on far beyond the original confrontation, and failures of communication may continue for long periods even after the reasons for hostility may have disappeared. Notable examples of this can be seen in feuds which sometimes occur in the mountains of Appalachia or in family quarrels between husband and wife who go about not speaking to one another long after they have forgotten the original source of their anger.

Just as threat interferes with communication, challenge tends to improve it. People hear and respond more effectively to matters they feel able to cope with. In order to gain the maximum facilitating effects of challenge, while at the same time avoiding the inhibiting effects of threat, many workers in the helping professions have learned to let their clients, students, parishioners, or patients set the pace.

Each human being is a neatly balanced system continuously in the process of seeking fulfillment. This drive does not let him rest. It continually pushes him forward, but each individual also has within him his own checks and balances—his accelerators, brakes, and safety valves. How far and how fast he will go depends upon how he sees himself and the situations in which he is involved. Because his drive is insatiable, he must move if the way seems open to him and within his capacities. But the drive for fulfillment will also not permit him to behave in ways which seem likely to destroy his self-realization.

When things are too threatening for people physically, they may faint. When things are too much for them in counseling, they avoid the topic. When things are too much for students in school, they go away from there by sleeping (more politely, daydreaming) or perhaps dropping out. Persons in the helping professions must either learn to wait or find ways of helping their charges to see events in new and challenging ways.

Effective helpers learn to work *with* these checks and balances rather than *against* them. They learn to follow the lead of their students, counselors, and parishioners. They know their clients will confront what they need to when they can, and so helpers devote their attention to creating the conditions which will make this possible.

AUTHORITY AND COMMUNICATION

An interesting illustration of the effects of challenge and threat on communication may be observed in people's responses to unearned authority. "Unearned authority" is that prestige and status which a helper or leader has when he first confronts the people he seeks to help. The group leader, for example, comes to the meeting with built-in status and authority because he is the "leader," perhaps also because he has a doctor's degree, wrote a book, has a reputation in the community, or whatever. This authority is called "unearned" because it was not given to him by the people he now seeks to communicate with. He may have earned it elsewhere, but not with these people. Over a period of time he may earn authority with them as group members discover, each for himself, what the leader has to offer. Each invests the leader with more or less authority, dependent upon his experience of him as a person, as a knower, speaker, demonstrator, or sensitive or insensitive human being. In the beginning, of course, there is only unearned authority and it is only with experience that this gives way to positive or negative earned authority. Unearned authority, for most people, is likely to be threatening. Accordingly, all of the effects of threat discussed in this book are likely to accompany the interaction and get in the way of effective communication. It is a common observation that students and clients simply do not hear teachers and group leaders in the very first sessions. Instructions given, advice proffered, information outlined—all have a very low incidence of comprehension and must almost always be repeated in more or less detail on later occasions. With increased experience on the part of clients, students, parishioners, or group members the leader is given more or less positive or negative authority. If the earned authority is positive, the leader's words are likely to be received as challenging and enhancing. If the earned authority is negative, the case may be quite the opposite. These effects may be so pervasive as to cancel out such ordinary drawbacks as lack of experience and the like. Herman Wessels wrote of a young first-year teacher he had known:

> When he left last June for further study there was an astounding outpouring of affection on the part of his students, and this surprised him. For he had come to us shy and not too sure of himself, and he had found his steadfast purpose through these bright, seeking youngsters whom he taught. He emerged as a person who carried the authority not of age and life experience, but the authority of commitment and true caring.

Communication is immensely increased by positive earned authority, so much so that some of the usual crutches to aid communication may no longer be necessary. When unearned authority is high, for example, college students take notes. As earned authority increases, less notes are likely to be taken. In the case of negative earned authority, this happens because the student has discovered that what the teacher has to say is not important. Where there is a high degree of positive earned authority, however, there may also be a slackening off of note-taking for a different reason, because people are less likely to forget what important people say!

LISTENING SIDE OF COMMUNICATION

To this point, we have been talking about communication as a function of the helper as sender. But communication is a problem of interaction —a matter of overlap of perceptual fields. Most helpers are deeply dependent upon the give and take of language or some other form of transferring human meaning. For most it is necessary to be not only effective senders, but to also be attentive receivers. People must know how to listen.

Much of the data needed by helping persons to carry out their tasks is obtained in communication with their clients, students, or patients. To make effective use of this data, helpers must learn to listen with great care to what the helpee is seeking to express. We have already seen how communication can break down between people talking with each other even with the best of intentions. The difficulties of communication are much greater when persons are ignorant, feel threatened, or are unhappy or intentionally seeking to deceive. To penetrate through such barriers and to really understand the persons he is working with calls for disciplined control of his own needs on the part of the helper and skillful tuning-in to the messages his client is conveying.

Effective listening is also important for another reason. The act of listening itself conveys messages to those attended to. In ordinary social discourse the careful listener is paying the speaker the highest form of compliment. He is saying in effect, "You are a truly significant person to me and what you are saying is important." So, also, the teacher is teaching the student important things about himself by listening to him. He may be conveying, for example, "I really care about you and what you think and believe." Such a message is no small matter. It is an active, living demonstration which may speak far more loudly and clearly to the student than what the teacher is speaking about. The importance of the message conveyed by careful listening is even more important in the case of unhappy or maladjusted persons with deep feelings of deprivation and alienation. For such persons, being really listened to is much more than mere communication; it is a therapeutic experience in itself! For counselors, psychiatrists, social workers, and pastoral counselors engaging in face-to-face communication with disturbed and troubled subjects, careful listening is an essential for successful practice.

Skill in careful listening is not acquired by accident. Most effective helpers actively work at it. At least in the beginning, its acquisition requires conscious effort. Most conversations in daily life are hardly attended to. We do not expect hearers to remember much of what we have to say in the usual give and take of casual talk. Much conversation is not even intended to convey very much. It is engaged in to amuse and enhance ourselves. So, two people who appear to be talking with one another are not so much holding a conversation; they are taking turns at self-enhancement! Each is waiting more or less patiently for the other to finish so that he can go on with his own story. That kind of communication would never do for serious attempts at helping others where much deeper and more meaningful understanding is required. Helpers have to work at listening. It is a basic skill of the trade. It is often a difficult and exhausting one, besides, as any good counselor or social worker has long since discovered.

The kind of listening required for effective helping, of course, is much more than mere attention to words. It is the active search for meaning already discussed in Chapter 10. "Listening with the third ear" involves attending to all that the client, student, or patient is expressing, not just verbally but nonverbally as well, in his gestures, movements, inflections, even by what he specifically does not say. Carl Rogers has called the disciplined listening of helpers "non-evaluative listening." By this he means a reading of the whole person, an attempt to understand the nature of what is there, of who and what and how the helper is, clearly and accurately, without the distortion of the helper's own judgments, preconceptions, or values. It is to achieve this kind of discipline over one's self that psychotherapy or counseling is often advocated as part of the training of persons entering the helping professions for work with disturbed or deprived persons.

SELECTED READINGS

Starred entries indicate appearance in whole or in part in Donald L. Avila, Arthur W. Combs, and William W. Purkey, *The Helping Relationship Sourcebook* (Boston: Allyn & Bacon, 1971).

Brill, N. Communication with low income families. *Journal of Home Economics,* 1966, **58,** 631–635.

Gibb, J. R. Defensive communication. *The Journal of Communication,* 1961, **11,** 141–148.

Hayakawa, S. I. *Language in thought and action.* New York: Harcourt, Brace & World, 1964.

Kelley, E. C. Communication and the open self. *ETC, A Review of General Semantics,* 1954, **10,** 96.

MacDonald, J. B. Gamesmanship in the classroom. *National Association of Secondary School Principals Bulletin,* 1966, **50,** 31–68.

Mehrabian, A. et al. Immediacy: An indicator of attitudes in linguistic communication. *Journal of Personality,* 1966, **34,** 26–34.

Riek, T. *Listening with the third ear.* New York: Grove Press, 1948.

* Roethlisberger, F. J. Barriers to communication between man. In S. I. Hayakawa (Ed.), *The use and misuse of language.* Greenwich, Conn.: Fawcett, 1962, 41–46.

Shapiro, J., Foster, C. P. & Powell, T. Facial and bodily cues of genuineness, empathy, and warmth. *Journal of Clinical Psychology,* 1968, **24,** 233–236.

* White R. K. Misperception and the Vietnam War. *Journal of Social Issues,* 1966, **22,** 1–154.

Winick, C. & Holt, H. Seating position as nonverbal communication in group analysis. *Psychiatry,* 1961, **24,** 171–182.

14

Varied Roles of Helpers

There is nothing magical about the helping professions. Techniques of helping are not confined to professionals. Everyone at some time in his life engages in counseling, teaching, administering, advising, or any of the other practices upon which the helping processes depend. The things a helper does are no different from those employed by people in many walks of life. What makes his function unique is the disciplined way in which he employs himself and his techniques. Helping relationships are not identical with life but special conditions designed to strengthen the helpee's capacity to deal with life. This often requires protecting people and temporarily sheltering them from the ordinary pressures of the world they live in while they work out new and more satisfying ways of coping. To this end, counselors create warm and friendly relationships for threatened and hostile clients, and teachers speak of education as "preparation for life." It is precisely because they are different from ordinary life that helping relationships have value.

The professional helper is not "just another person." He must be a significant other, informed, disciplined, experienced, and skillful in carrying out his special role. His manifest objective is increased adequacy of client, student, or patient. Whatever he does in helping will be dependent upon his skill in mobilizing events to this end. This is no haphazard process. It must be predictable and controllable. It is not enough for helpers to operate on faith nor to do what "might help" without some reason to believe that outcomes will be positive rather than negative. This is not to suggest that helpers must at all times and in all places be clearly able to predict the full consequences of whatever they do. At this stage of our knowledge no man can be expected to meet that requirement. Responsible professional service, however, is not fortuitous. It must be predicated upon reasonable presumptions of positive effect. To be "significant," an "other" must have direction.

Procedures must be congruent with principles and purposes. Techniques employed without such understanding are mere tinkering. Applied to the manipulation of things, the price of such fortuitous approaches to problems may sometimes be justified; applied to human beings it is surely unacceptable, especially for persons claiming to be professional helpers. Teachers, counselors, and social workers need to acquire effective techniques and ways of working with people; but these must be used as products of understanding and expressions of dynamics rather than important ends in their own right.

HELPING REQUIRES CHOOSING

From the thousands of possibilities open to him, a helper has to make choices. The ways in which effective helpers work are almost as varied as the human personalities who carry them out. What a given counselor, teacher, nurse, pastor, or supervisor selects for appropriate ways of operating will be determined, in the first place, by events inside his self— especially his personal needs and the nature of his beliefs about himself; the people he must work with; the purposes of the peculiar task he is engaged in; and the personal solutions he has found to questions about the nature of man, human capacities, and the dynamics of change in human personality. The choices he makes will also be affected by peculiar conditions outside himself, including the need of his clients, the time available to do whatever he must in order to be helpful, the degree of control he has over the conditions of helping, and the special demands imposed upon him by the job description under which he is operating. A helper will also have to choose which aspect to focus his attentions on—the client, the environment, the helper's self and relationships, or some combination of these.

Sometimes helpers may choose to work straightforwardly in controlling and directing the behavior of those they seek to help. For example, the behavior modification therapist seeks to do this by trying to "shape" the behavior of clients through techniques of reinforcement. Helpers may also seek to remove annoying habits by hypnosis. A child may be taught the skills he needs to engage in social activities with his peers. The reward and punishment technique for teaching has long been practiced in our public schools. Manipulations may also be directed at the environment as when a social worker seeks to improve the conditions of slum housing or when a school principal acts to provide better learning conditions for the children in his school.

Methods of helping through control and direction of students, clients, and patients are impatiently rejected by some workers in the helping professions, and the word "manipulation" has sometimes been regarded as though it were synonymous with "evil." As we have seen, there is no such thing as a good or a right method of helping. The principle applies to manipulation. Of itself, it is neither good nor bad. It has acquired its bad name because it seems to some helpers undemocratic, a kind of violation of the dignity and integrity of the individual; or perhaps because it is not appropriate or effective with the kinds of problems some helpers must deal with. However, there is nothing inherently wrong with manipulation per se. All helpers manipulate something—the environment, the client, or themselves—to create a helping relationship. Like any other method it may be used appropriately or inappropriately, positively or negatively, depending upon the skill and understanding of the helper.

Persons in the helping professions generally tend to specialize in one of four ways of working:

1. Through changing the environment.
2. Through face-to-face, one-to-one relationships.
3. Through relationships in groups.
4. Through other people.

While all these ways of working are dependent upon the same basic principles of human behavior, each requires its own special knowledge, skills, and relationships; each has also developed its appropriate programs of training. Each way of working has its peculiar advantages and drawbacks, depending upon the personal perspective of the helper. The way in which he chooses to operate will be dependent upon questions such as: "Do I want to influence few or many?" "Do I find greater satisfactions in working at deeply personal levels or more remote impersonal ones?" "Am I more interested in rehabilitation of persons in need of help, or do I want to make my contribution through forestalling the *need* for rehabilitation by programs of prevention?" Or, "Should I direct my energies toward encouraging self-actualization?" These are not matters of right or wrong, better or worse. They are matters of choice about ways of using self—not only in the service of others, but, just as importantly, for achieving personal fulfillment of the helper himself. The helper who is not receiving some personal satisfactions from helping is not only cheating himself, but is also probably cheating his clients.

1. CHANGING THE ENVIRONMENT

All helpers at one time or another will be called upon to exert some influence upon the environment of those they seek to help. Sometimes this will be quite direct and at other times it may be only occasional or fortuitous. For some helpers it will represent the primary way in which they seek to work with other people; for others it will be a device utilized only on occasion. In the broadest sense, it could be said that all forms of helping are accomplished through effecting some kind of change in the helpee's environment. Changing a parent's attitudes through teaching changes the environment for his child. Even the changes produced in psychotherapy by the most nondirective counselor are brought about by the relationship created by the therapist's presence and behavior, a form of modifying the client's environment.

The physical world is the place where we live and provides us with the physical needs for growth and survival. Whatever can be done to make it more productive, healthful, and beautiful must be a primary goal of everyone interested in the welfare of man. It is also a major social problem of our times and, no matter what a helper does in his professional role, exerting his influence as a private citizen to create a better environment for mankind must certainly remain a major responsibility. The human questions posed for the professional helper's assistance, however, are seldom likely to be answered by changing the physical aspects of environment since man is a social animal and his growth and development as a human being are essentially dependent on people. The environment in which the professional helper must usually work includes the people surrounding his client or student. Changing the people environment, however, is not easily brought about. As we have seen in Chapter 2, the older a person gets the larger is the world to which he is responding and the less and less likely it becomes that the helper will be in a position to change it. If the environment surrounding his client is to be changed at all, more often than not, it will have to be done by the client or student himself; and, it will be necessary for the helper to exert his efforts primarily through the person who has come for help.

2. ONE–TO–ONE RELATIONSHIP

The goal of the helping professions, no matter by whom it is practiced, is to produce some change in individuals. Even change in society can only be brought about in the final analysis through changes in individual people. Some helpers, like counselors or nurses, work almost exclusively with individuals. But all helpers must, at one time or another, whether superficially or in depth, carry out some part of their functions in a face-to-face relationship with one other person. The first thought of most people confronted with the necessity for helping someone else in this way is to give them advice by telling them what the facts are or what they ought to do. Over thousands of years people have developed a great number of techniques for doing this. Among some of the more common are convincing people, marshaling the evidence, exhorting people to be good, ordering or forbidding, explaining, persuading, advising, threatening, seducing, suggesting, guiding, rewarding, punishing, making people feel guilty, or using religious influence. Of course, people *can* be helped in these ways. Indeed, given the right circumstances, people can be helped by almost anything. Every few years we are treated to some startling new technique for helping people. It becomes a fad for a time and then quietly dies away. Even the most ridiculous of these techniques in their heyday may produce important changes in people. If people *believe* a thing is helpful, that is often enough to make it work.

Helping people in one-to-one relationships might be thought of as a continuum of purpose—from interviews (*getting* information *from* the client) through advising (*giving* information or guidance) to counseling and psychotherapy (facilitating personal discovery of meaning at deeper and deeper levels).

Many of the needs people have for help can be provided by the simple expedient of providing information. It is helpful, indeed, to be told what time it is, how to get to a strange part of the city, how to figure out one's income tax, or how to solve an intellectual problem. The helping relationships required for providing such information are comparatively simple and straightforward. The more human or personal problems in which people need assistance, however, are rarely the consequence of a lack of information. When people misbehave it is rarely because they do not know what they ought to do. The serious problems with which people need help are likely to be moral ones, matters of decision, desire, hope, frustration, or deprivation. As a consequence, when they come for help their need is not so much for information, despite the fact that this may be the tenor of their original request. Most persons who come to counselors for assistance already have most of the information they need. Certainly it is true that people need information in order to deal effectively with life. Withholding information which could help a person to get better quicker is cruel and inhuman. On the other hand, giving people information which they do not need or cannot use only sidetracks the helping process. Generally speaking, people in trouble want, not so much to be told as, to be understood. Modern practices of counseling and psychotherapy, therefore, are much less concerned with giving people information and are much more concerned with discovering how to develop effective relationships with persons in need of help.

IMPORTANCE OF THE RELATIONSHIP

Early in the history of counseling, it was assumed that the advice given by counselors made the difference. Later on, helping was thought to be a function of the *methods* which counselors used; practitioners argued at great length about whether directive or nondirective methods were most efficacious. More recently, the *relationship* of counseling has been regarded as the most significant aspect. At first, this came about because counselors focused on the facilitating effect of the relationship on the exploration of meaning. Now, we are beginning to understand that it does much more than simply facilitate: It teaches as well. If one looks at the kinds of behaviors advocated for the practice of good counseling in most modern schools of thought, he might ask himself in each instance, "What would the client be likely to learn about self from experiencing this behavior?" He will find that the answers lead to the characteristics of self-actualization, positive views of self, openness to experience and feelings of identification toward others. Reversing the process and asking, "What kinds of behavior would be required to teach a person a positive self, openness to experience or deep feelings of identification?" leads directly to descriptions of relationships almost universally advocated for effective counseling. In the one-to-one encounter it is the relationship which counts in facilitating exploration of self and the world and in providing new experiences of self in the form of positive feedback from a significant member of the outside world.

To establish an effective face-to-face relationship the helper must learn to use himself optimally. If he uses himself too little, no relationship is established at all. On the other hand, by using himself too much he may run the risk of so dominating the relationship as to destroy or delay the client's own growth and fulfillment. The intimate one-to-one relationship of counseling requires highly developed skills in listening, empathy, self-discipline, and patience. Much of these helpers' training is devoted to practicing and refining these qualities to ever greater perfection.

The preoccupation of nonprofessional counselors with what they are saying often gets in the way of the careful listening practiced by professionals. Casual counselors talk too much. Professional counselors know that it is the activity of the client which brings about change and that it is his talking and exploring which need to be encouraged. To this end they spend much time and effort in the course of their training learning to be empathic and disciplining themselves to listen with great care in order to understand how things seem in the private worlds of their clients. Effective counseling requires patience. Professional counselors have learned from much experience that counseling takes time. Inexperienced counselors often impede their own success for failure to understand the important fact that the deeper, more important, and fundamental the change in a human personality, the longer will be the process of change. A proper appreciation of this fact can save the beginner a great deal of heartache and his client a good deal of frustration. It will keep him from pushing the helpee too hard and save himself from discouragement and disillusionment through a proper perspective of what he can and cannot accomplish.

Of all the helping professions, counselors and psychotherapists have responsibility for working most intimately with the sick, the frightened, the deprived, and the deeply maladjusted. As a consequence the training of these kinds of workers is deeply concerned with developing relationships that are carefully designed to produce maximum rapport and freedom of communication. Much attention is paid to the messages conveyed to clients by the relationships created. Counselors seek to make their relationships nonthreatening, caring, secure, and encouraging for clients. Noncounselors, on the other hand, often bypass these important considerations in their preoccupation with what they are trying to say to the student or parent with whom they are in dialogue. In the process they hinder possibilities of effective results, for clients typically learn far more from the established relationship than from the specifics of what is said.

Academic training for the one-to-one way of working usually requires that counselors and therapists emphasize the study of clinical, individual, or humanistic psychologies rather than more orthodox, objective approaches to human behavior. Most training programs also call for some kind of personal participation in counseling whereby the beginning counselor can experience the process as consumer. In this way he has opportunity to improve understanding by seeing the process from the client's perspective. At the same time it affords an opportunity to become better acquainted with himself and his own hangups, an awareness necessary for the kind of self-discipline required in effective practice of counseling.

3. HELPING THROUGH GROUPS

One of the most effective ways in which people help one another is through the formation of groups. The one-to-one relationship of counseling is in itself a kind of group; but helping people in a one-to-one, face-to-face relationship is likely to be a pretty slow business. Often it will be much more efficient to work with people in larger numbers. Helpers such as group workers, group therapists, teachers, etc., carry out their helping functions primarily through working with groups. All helpers, regardless of their specialty, need to be capable of operating in these ways with some measure of competence.

Throughout man's history, leaders have assembled men in groups from time to time to provide them with information or to band together for some common cause. For the oldest of the helping professions—priests and teachers—the group approach has always been a primary technique for helping. More recently, we have come to understand the value of the group experience itself as a vehicle for the exploration and discovery of new meanings about self and the world. As a consequence, people in the helping professions everywhere are experimenting in a variety of ways with the use of groups for advancing human growth and fulfillment. Major questions in education, for example, are how to group children for most effective learning and how to use group discussion as a tool of teaching. Social workers are experimenting extensively with groups for family therapy and community action programs. Counselors and psychologists are much concerned with basic encounter groups, group play therapy, and the utilization of groups for the advancement of mental health. Occupational and recreational therapy have become most important branches of the healing arts, and human relations experts are concerned with the problems of group conflict and its resolution.

Through the use of groups the number of persons who can be helped by the professions is enormously increased. A group, however, is not an entity in itself. To change a group it is still necessary to change the hearts and minds of the individual people of whom the group is composed. Therefore, whatever is done to help people in groups must still be directed toward the individual members of the group and must produce some change in their personal modes of perception. The kinds of group experiences constructed by the helper to achieve these ends may vary widely from groups that are little more than pleasant pasttimes to intensely therapeutic groups, from completely spontaneous to rigidly controlled groups, from purely objective discussions to deeply personal explorations of meaning. They can generally be classified in four major categories: conversation, instruction, decision, or discovery groups.

CONVERSATION GROUPS

These are the least controlled of group techniques and differ very little from the social dialogue engaged in by everyone of us in interacting with others on a more or less casual basis. The prototype may be found in the college student's "bull session," a pleasant pasttime in which one seeks to regale others by descriptions or stories of things he knows or events which have happened to him. A bull session is pure entertainment, a device for self-enhancement. Ordinarily it proceeds at considerable speed as one person after another tells a story, an anecdote, or makes a comment. Verbal participation is likely to be high in such casual conversation, and the group tends to maintain a size so that everyone can get a chance to speak. If waiting gets too long, the session is likely to break up into smaller groups where more people have a chance to comment. Most of the talk is descriptive—"I saw . . . ," "Did you read where . . . ?" "Once I . . . ," "My uncle has . . . ," and so on. Conversation moves like a game of "one-upmanship" in which one person tells a story and someone else tells another to top it. Learning in such a group is likely to be at a low ebb. The bull session is used by most professional helpers, if at all, only occasionally as a means of establishing rapport.

INSTRUCTION GROUPS

These kinds of groups are brought together, almost exclusively, to show or tell participants something—usually through some form of lecture or demonstration. They may range in size from a very few to the millions reached by the wonders of our electronic age. Most of the activity in such groups is performed by the leader. Learners are primarily passive. Their task is to listen, watch, and absorb. The center of everyone's attention is on the content or subject matter being presented. Everything depends upon the skill of the helper in making his presentation, and he is ordinarily not very concerned with the problems of the atmosphere for learning or of aiding processes of discovery in the learner. Whatever interaction occurs is likely to be confined to that between teacher and student. Interactions of students with students are limited, if they exist at all. In earlier chapters we have seen that learning always consists of two aspects: acquiring new information or experience and discovering its meaning. Instruction groups can often be effective ways of accomplishing the former, but leave much to be desired as ways of achieving the latter.

Historically, instruction groups have been the major paths through which teachers attempted to carry out their helping roles. Much teaching, especially at the college level, is even now carried on in this time-honored lecture-demonstration tradition. Modern concepts of teaching and learning, however, no longer accept so narrow a view of the task. "Telling" is no longer regarded as the primary function of teachers. Indeed, we have now developed marvelous mechanical devices that are more effective than teachers in providing people with information—radio, television, motion pictures, programmed instruction, audio-visual techniques, and computers. Accordingly, the information phase of learning is increasingly being turned over to such gadgets while the teacher devotes himself to the more important problems of helping students discover the meaning of information provided, a major objective they share with the other professions.

DECISION GROUPS

Some groups are formed with a primary purpose to arrive at a consensus or decision on some matter. Almost everyone is familiar with such groups and has participated in them at one time or another. A group of people come together to study a question and arrive at some solution or program of action, perhaps to nominate a slate of officers, decide where to go on a picnic, formulate a set of rules for a school system, negotiate a contract, or settle a dispute among members. The group proceeds by sharing information on the problem, listening to proposals and counter-proposals for solution, and sooner or later taking a vote to record its decision, and then moves on to other business. Such groups can often prove highly useful in bringing about agreement on some plan of action. In this respect they have limited applicability for the helping process, which seeks more fundamental change in personal meanings. Most helpers are much less concerned with the decisions made by their clients than with facilitating the processes of exploration and discovery which underlie a helpee's choice of actions. For the professional helper, the quality and direction of the discussion preceding decisions may be much more important than the final vote.

The prior experience of persons in decision groups, in fact, raises problems for helpers, for decision groups have the unhappy effect of coercing their members to arrive at the approved solutions once the group has reached a point of decision. Even the "democratic" procedure of taking a vote can have this effect, for a vote is often no more than a way of stopping a discussion. When the vote is taken, discussion halts and the minority is coerced into whatever decision the majority has arrived at. Experience of this sort can seriously interfere with the freedom of the individual to explore and move in directions unique to his own needs. It is a common observation that "a man convinced against his will, is of the same opinion still." So, the behavior of a minority member of a decision group is often quite unaffected by his participation. Worse still, if he has often experienced its coercive effects, he may learn to approach group encounters on later occasions with suspicion and fear. This creates problems for helpers, because people who have experienced such groups develop an expectancy that this is the way in which a group "ought" to operate. As a consequence they often delay or destroy the effectiveness of helping groups set up for other purposes until group leaders have been able to help them perceive that the new situation is quite different from what they have experienced before.

Discovery Groups

In the past twenty or thirty years, special types of groups have been developed by various branches of the helping professions to aid students, clients, and patients explore and discover new and more adequate understandings of themselves and their relationships to the world. Leaders of such groups generally concentrate much more upon the group process than upon specific outcomes to be obtained from the process. Emphasis is on the experience of participating in the group and what the individual can make of it. Because of the highly personal character of helping group participation, a supportive atmosphere is also much more necessary for success. A great deal also depends upon the skill of the leader in creating an atmosphere which makes self-disclosure possible. Helping groups are now in wide use in many aspects of the helping professions and are generally used for three kinds of purposes:

1/ Sensitivity training. Group experiences are used to aid participants in developing increased sensitivity to themselves and to other people. Some forms of these groups have also been called encounter groups or confrontation sessions. Sensitivity groups have been particularly popular in the training of workers in the helping professions, the training of executives in industry, and in public relations work. They are being increasingly employed as regular parts of training programs for persons entering the various helping professions.

2/ Group therapy. Groups are used in this instance for their therapeutic value, especially in assisting patients or clients with personality problems. Such techniques have been widely used, for example, with prison inmates, potential juvenile delinquents, marital problems, parent education, and the like.

3/ Learning groups. In this instance, group techniques are used to assist students in the exploration and discovery of the meaning of ideas in many content fields. Contrary to the general belief of many that teaching is primarily a matter of "telling," modern approaches to education increasingly rely upon various types of group experiences to assist students in the exploration and discovery of new meanings about themselves and the world they live in.

Keeping Perspective

Whenever people hit upon a new technique or idea for dealing with human problems, there is likely to follow a period of testing in which the idea is tried in an infinite variety of ways. In this process the idea may be pushed to the limit and applied as a "pure case," or it may be interpreted in the most bizarre fashion. Such a period in the exploration of new ideas is also likely to be characterized by persons who develop great loyalty and enthusiasm for their particular innovations. Since there are no "right" answers for dealing with human beings, even the wildest techniques may work for some people—especially if they believe they will. This evidence of success may serve to corroborate the particular prejudices of the innovator, resulting for a time in numbers of people staunchly advocating with great fervor the merits of a particular approach. This seems to be a necessary part of the evolution of almost any new idea and, of course, has its values in providing a wide variety of test situations. In time, as the froth beaten up by all this activity settles down, the true dimensions of the new concept begin to emerge and are fitted into the fabric of our understanding with a clearer understanding of their limitations and possibilities. With all the ferment and excitement going on in the field of human relations in our time, this process happens very frequently. Persons working in the helping professions must be keenly aware of such forces at work and evaluate them properly, for the sake of students, clients, or parishioners and for the growth of the helper himself.

One of the areas where this kind of experimentation is currently going on most extensively is in the field of group activities, known as basic encounter. The variations being tried by proponents of these groups cover a vast range. There are groups which emphasize loving and caring and groups which insist upon confronting each other in brutal fashion. Groups have single leaders, multiple leaders, and no leaders at all. There are large groups, small ones, groups that meet only once, and groups that meet for long periods. Some "Marathon" groups, meet for forty-eight hours, and permit group members to leave the room only to use the lavatory. Some groups even meet in the nude. Out of all this, we will in time no doubt discover more precisely what groups can and cannot do and how to operate them with maximum efficiency. In the meantime, it is important to be aware that such terms as counseling, basic encounter, group therapy, and the like, cannot be understood as entities. One cannot simply be for them or against them, because the terms which designate them tell us nothing about what goes on within them. One cannot know, for example, what to think about basic encounter without knowing who is involved; the purpose of the group members; and especially the philosophy, goals, and beliefs of the group leader.

Since people only do what they would rather, a helping group cannot long maintain itself unless its members feel it is an experience of value. It is possible to demand the presence of young children in a group. Students can be required to go to school, but, generally speaking, as people become adults they do not remain in groups that do not provide them with some kinds of satisfaction. Accordingly, to help people in groups it is necessary very early in the experience to provide participants with experiences that encourage them to drop their defenses, to perceive accurately the nature of the group in which they are engaged, and to discover some inkling of what the experience may have to offer them.

The degree of personal commitment achieved in a group can often be clearly observed by listening to the level of conversation. With little or no commitment, people talk to one another at fingertip lengths. Their talk is mostly descriptive and usually pertaining to events outside themselves: "There was this man and . . . ," "Did you read where . . . ?" "My cousin once. . . ." As commitment begins to occur, one is likely to hear expressions with beginning references to self: "I read that . . . ," "Can you tell me if. . . ?" "I went to see. . . ." Such comments are still likely to be highly descriptive. With still greater commitment, tentative involvements of self begin to show themselves: "I don't know about that . . . ," "Do you suppose that . . . ?" "I doubt if. . . ." Even closer to self, one next hears comments such as: "I wonder about . . . ," "I am not sure about this, but . . . ," "It seems to me. . . ." Much closer to self are comments like, "Well, I thought . . . ," "I don't really care for . . . ," "I enjoy. . . ." At the deepest levels of commitment one may even hear, what some psychologists call "gut" talk: "I hate . . . ," "That makes me so mad!" "I love."

HELPING PEOPLE THROUGH OTHERS

Throughout this volume we have been dealing with the problems of the helping professions primarily conceived as dialogue or encounter between a helper and one or more helpees. Helpers in any of the branches of these professions, however, from time to time will need to work in settings where it will be necessary to work with and through other people to accomplish the goals of helping.

So, teachers seek to help children through working with parents; school psychologists attempt to exert influence on a child's welfare by conferring with his teachers; social workers may meet with judges or city councils to bring about changes helpful to the persons they serve in their home communities. It is notorious that people who are good at their jobs get promoted to administrative or supervisory roles. Thus, an expert counselor or teacher may find himself in a position where he no longer works with clients or children, but must exert his influence through his impact upon counselors and teachers. Under these circumstances, helping effects must be produced at second or third hand. For some, such as administrators, supervisors, and consultants in the helping professions, operating remotely may even be the kind of practice most feasible for them.

The techniques required for operating at second hand will frequently differ from those employed when working more directly with clients. The basic dynamics of behavior do not change, however, when applied at first or second hand. The fundamental principles guiding the supervisor or consultant are the same as those which guide the teacher, social worker, or counselor—even though the practices engaged in may vary greatly from those which might be used in face-to-face encounters. Helpers working with and through other people will still have to find their own best ways of using themselves, their knowledge, and their skills to advance the helping cause.

Among the special problems of helping indirectly is the frustration of having to rely on others to get things done. Desirable goals seem so clear to those who hold them, and things which *ought* to be done seem so obvious and necessary. This is especially true if they have been formulated at some distance from the scene of action. When one is away from the pressures and protected from the harassment of immediate events, proper paths for action can often be seen with great clarity. For helpers at the front line who are immersed in the problems of students and clients, matters may be perceived very differently when immediate pressures and responsibilities immensely compound the issues faced. To avoid compounding frustration, the patience and understanding demanded of persons operating on the face-to-face level is even more essential when it is necessary to work with and through other persons. This is true with the capacity for acceptance also. Helpers, too, must be accepted where they are, and encouraged and supported in the processes of moving forward. The farther away the helper must work from the scene of direct involvement, the more difficult to keep the lines of communication open both ways. Effective helping from more remote levels of operation depends upon open communication, and many an otherwise good program has disintegrated for failure to recognize and deal with the importance of this question.

WHO IS THE CLIENT?

Many a helper forced to work in secondary roles makes himself ineffective because of his confusion about who is his client. The client is the person who comes to the helper, the person with whom he is most intimately in touch. Let us use the example of a school psychologist. A teacher asks him for help in working with a difficult child. If the school psychologist sees his role exclusively as one of working in a face-to-face relationship with the child, at the time of her complaint the psychologist is likely to reply: "Very well, Miss Atwood. Send him down to my office and I'll see what I can do with him." In making this response he has lost a valuable opportunity to be of assistance and has made himself less effective as a consultant. The proper client for a consultant is *whoever he is confronting*. The school psychologist who sees himself in this broader role does not make the mistake of sending his primary client away. Instead he tells Miss Atwood, "I can see how difficult it must be for you to work with him. Sit down and let's talk about it." He begins his work by trying to help Miss Atwood. He recognizes that helping the child involves helping his teacher to be able to deal with the child more effectively. Indeed, since the teacher is going to have to live with the child, and vice versa, for the remainder of the school year, success will most likely be reached with and through the teacher. As he helps Miss Atwood deal with her frustrations and talk about her problem, he is contributing directly to her strength and capacity to carry out her job and be better able to deal with the child who is her current problem. When school psychologists work this way, they frequently do not have to work with the child at all. Sometimes the therapy provided the teacher by an opportunity to discuss her problem is enough to give her new courage to try again and insight to try new approaches. Even if this does not occur, at the end of the session with Miss Atwood the psychologist can still arrange to see the child and talk some more with the teacher on another occasion. The helping relationship is applied by the consultant to everyone he consults.

An additional complication for helpers working in consultant, administrative, or supervisory roles is created by the authority attached to such positions. Often this is likely to hinder creativity, create resistance, and destroy communication between first- and second-level helpers. In earlier chapters we have spoken of the importance of "visibility" in fostering helping relationships. This is particularly important for helpers working at more remote levels of the helping process. Generally speaking, the greater the authority of the administrator or supervisor, the greater is the anxiety and fear of encounter with him. It is probably no accident that one of the most frequent complaints of administrators is that their jobs are so lonely! It is probable that failures to make themselves visible to their employees and too great an emphasis upon the authority of their positions are the reasons for such a sad state of affairs. To carry out their work effectively, helpers working at the supervisory or consultant level will have to deal with these problems. How they deal with them and how they choose to work with those who seek their help must, of necessity, be a matter of personal choice.

SELECTED READINGS

Berzon, B., Pious, C. & Farson, R. The therapeutic event in group psychotherapy: A study of subjective reports by group members. *Journal of Individual Psychology,* 1963, **19,** 204–212.

Bradford, L., Benne, K. & Gibb, J. R. *T-group theory and laboratory method.* New York: Wiley, 1964.

Bugental, J. F. T. *The search for authenticity: An existential-analytic approach to psychotherapy.* New York: Holt, Rinehart & Winston, 1965.

Caplan, G. *Concepts of mental health and consultation: The application in public health social work.* Children's Bureau, U.S. Department of Health, Education and Welfare, Washington, D.C., 1959.

Ginott, H. G. *Group psychotherapy with children,* New York: McGraw Hill, 1961.

Marrow, A. J., Bowers, D. G. & Seashore, S. E. *Management by participation.* New York: Harper & Row, 1967.

Miel, A. *Creativity in teaching.* Belmont, Calif.: Wadsworth, 1961.

O'Banion, T. & O'Connell, A. *The shared journey: An introduction to encounter.* Englewood Cliffs, N.J.: Prentice-Hall, 1970.

Rogers, C. R. A note on "the nature of man." *Journal of Counseling Psychology,* 1957, **4,** 199–203(b).

Stoller, F. H., The long weekend. *Psychology Today.* 1967, **1,** 28–33.

Truax, C. B. & Wargo, D. G. Psychotherapeutic encounters that change behavior: For better or for worse. *American Journal of Psychotherapy,* 1966, **22,** 499–520.

15

The Helper as Person and Citizen

A helper is much more than an automaton which knows something. He is a warm-blooded, living, human being with his own needs, capacities, hopes, fears, loves, and aspirations. In addition to these characteristics which they share in common with all other human beings, helpers have assumed, or have had thrust upon them, the responsibility for creating relationships helpful for other people. How effectively the helper carries out this task will be dependent upon how well he has learned to make use of his particular talents and personality for the realization of his own and society's purposes. This we have earlier called the "self as instrument" concept. The success of a helper will depend not only on what he knows, but even more on the kind of person he is and how effectively he has learned to behave in his important task. The fact of his personness is the most important determinant in his relationships with others. The helper's self is the primary tool he has to work with and, like the tools of any good craftsman, needs care and attention to assure maximum usefulness. While no one can ever escape from his own personality, a helper can learn to use himself in ways that are more fulfilling to himself and the world in which he lives.

THE HELPER AS A PERSON

ROLES AND METHODS IN HELPING

A good deal of discussion goes on among persons in the helping professions concerning the proper role of the counselor, teacher, administrator, social worker, or nurse. The term "role" ordinarily refers to some form of acting, so we speak of "playing a role." Examining the functions of the professional helper in that light, however, is not likely to be very helpful. It focuses attention on the wrong question. It is possible, of course, for teachers, counselors, or social workers to act a part in the relationships they have with their clients and students. But such relationships can seldom be maintained for very long, for people behave according to their perceptions—and the moment a person's guard is down, his fundamental beliefs become apparent to those he interacts with in spite of himself.

Basic feelings have a way of penetrating through facades. From early childhood, people develop a high degree of sensitivity to the genuineness of those with whom they must interact. As a consequence, the professional helper who attempts to "play" a role, professes what he does not believe in, or tries to be what he is not, may only serve to make his students or clients uneasy or afraid and is very likely to produce a feeling that he is a phony. This can be observed in the "control panic" unhappily experienced by some beginning teachers. When assigned to an unusually lively or difficult class, first efforts at capturing attention meet with little success. To meet this problem the teacher searches for "methods to handle them." If these methods fit him, things may quiet down. If they do not, the class senses this and begins a process of exploration aimed at finding out what the limits are. This launches a spiral of trying and testing, which rises higher and higher as the teacher desperately "tries more things" in which he really has no confidence; the students, made more and more uncertain by lack of consistent structure, search ever more wildly to discover the limits. If long continued, this dervish may end with the students in control and the teacher reduced to a state of utter helplessness. Many a beginning teacher has suffered through this nightmare, brought on by a "gimmick approach," and some have been so demoralized as to leave the profession forever. Others, having found out the hard way, learn to distrust other people's methods or devices which do not fit them and so, on later occasions, manage their classes more effectively.

The kind of communication required for most helping relationships calls for openness in the helper, a willingness to level with his students or clients. Carl Rogers includes the quality of genuineness in the counselor as one of the basic requirements for successful counseling practice along with congruence, empathy, and unconditional positive regard. Aspy, Carkhuff, Truax and others have tested these hypotheses with counselors and teachers and they find that these are, indeed, qualities of effective helpers. Genuine relationships have also been discussed by Sidney Jourard as "self-disclosure." His researches demonstrate the importance of self-disclosure for helping relationships in several professional groups. Further confirmation of the importance of genuineness is found in the Florida studies in the helping professions reported in Chapter 1.

One needs to know what he can expect of other persons in order to guide his own behavior safely and satisfyingly in a relationship. This calls for feedback from others which has the feel of solidity. Psychologists sometimes call this "making one's self visible." Without this quality, effective relationships become almost impossible and encounters become confused and frustrating. Take, for example, the dilemma of a child with a teacher unwilling to be who she is. After six months of living with a teacher, most children have a pretty clear idea as to what she is really like. If, however, the teacher refuses to accept such an evaluation and insists she is something else, the child who must live with her is in a difficult predicament. If he treats his teacher the way he knows she is, she rejects him. On the other hand, he cannot treat her the way she says she is except by trying to act out what he does not really believe. This he can only do so long as he can keep his mind on it. The moment he forgets, he behaves in terms of his beliefs about what she really is like and is back in the soup again!

Effective encounters are dependent upon the ability of the persons involved to predict probable reactions with accuracy. Participants must know what to expect from each other. This is especially true with people in authority. If they do not make themselves visible so that we know who they are, what they are thinking, and where they stand, it becomes impossible to predict their behavior. Thus, relationships with them become increasingly dangerous. Generally speaking, there is only one thing to do with this kind of relationship, and that is to stay as far away from it as possible.

IMPORTANCE OF AUTHENTICITY

Authenticity is a prime quality of effective helpers. With authenticity, many things become easy; without it, helpers create unnecessary barriers for themselves and those they seek to help. Helpers willing to be openly and honestly who they are have a tremendous advantage. They can forget themselves and so give themselves much more freely to the task at hand. Their interactions tend to be straightforward, uncomplicated, and hence, more likely to be appropriate. Like being in high gear, the relationship between concept and action is direct. Helpers who find it necessary to concentrate attention on "playing a role" or "using right methods" introduce deviations in the route from idea to behavior. The methods helpers use must fit them so that they come into use smoothly and naturally. Preoccupation with techniques is certain to make them seem contrived. When learning to dance, one watches his feet and falls all over them. When he learns to relax and "go with the music," dancing improves and both dancer and partner get far more pleasure out of the performance. So it is with methods. Authenticity frees the helper to devote his full attention to the problems at hand. His behavior can be smoothly congruent and *en rapport* with students, clients, and the world.

Effective helpers seem to be characterized by a capacity to trust their own organisms. Their behavior seems almost intuitive rather than rational. In his excellent book *Life in Classrooms,* Philip W. Jackson writes of the teachers he studied:

> When called on to justify their professional decisions, for example, my informants often declared that their classroom behavior was based more on impulse and feeling than on reflection and thought. In other words, they were more likely to defend themselves by pointing out that a particular course of action *felt* like the right thing to do, rather than by claiming that they *knew* it to be right. As the structure of a teaching session or of a class day unfolds, the teacher frequently behaves like a musician without a score. He ad-libs. (Jackson, P. W., p. 145, 1968)

No doubt, this kind of straightforward trust in self will appear to some persons extremely hazardous. It is so, of course, if the helper's thinking and belief systems are poorly or inaccurately formed. The fact that everyone behaves in terms of his beliefs is unlikely to be rescinded very soon. Whether we like it or not, all of us are at the mercy of the belief systems of those we trust ourselves to. Mixed-up thinking is very likely to produce mixed-up behavior. But the helper whose thinking is clear and consistent, whose motives are positive and humane, and whose experience has provided effective ways of working with others need not frighten anyone. All human interaction is built upon beliefs. A set of beliefs well thought out and thoroughly tested in experience *deserves* to be trusted.

A person with a position is always likely to reveal a stronger posture than a person without. Even a negative conviction, if it is clear and unambiguous, may be easier for a student or client to relate to than a vacillating stance. This is one of the reasons for the rejection of eclecticism as a workable philosophy for helpers. Choosing methods or techniques from widely divergent sources may be highly effective, providing they are tied together by an internally consistent theoretical or philosophical position. An eclectic approach in which a helper is trying things "because they might work" is likely to be a disaster. Clients and patients deserve better of the helping relationship than such a "smorgasbord approach." Helping people is far too important for playing games because too much is at stake. The helper with a consistent system of beliefs can disclose himself and maintain his client's confidence; the helper without such a system dares not disclose himself lest his client discover the disordered state of his thinking. The authentic helper is more visible and the impression he conveys is likely to be one of confidence, assurance, and strength. On the other hand, the helper without authenticity is likely to create an impression of doubt, hesitation, dishonesty, and a sneaking suspicion in the minds of his clients that he really is a fraud.

THE HELPER'S OWN SELF-ACTUALIZATION

Helping relationships require that helpers either postpone their own immediate needs for fulfillment or find important satisfactions in being of service to their students. To do this, helpers need to be well-disciplined. Self-discipline, however, is not an easy thing to maintain unless the helper himself is achieving a significant degree of self-actualization in his own life. Deeply deprived persons are likely to find it difficult or impossible to be too concerned about fulfilling the needs of others. Their own needs are far too pressing.

What people perceive is a function of need, and even in fairly well-adjusted persons this selective effect upon perception is likely to produce a degree of distortion in what they attend to. Freud once pointed out that misbehaviors we recognize in others are apt to be those we have wrestled within ourselves. Even in the psychological clinic it is not uncommon to find that beginning clinicians tend to see their own hangups in the cases they diagnose.

Helpers need to have themselves well in hand. Otherwise, the question of who is helping whom is likely to become confused. A complete reversal of roles for helper and helpee is not uncommon in teaching and counseling. This can easily happen with a resistant student or client who has learned how to keep outsiders from approaching his private feelings by asking them questions about their lives and experiences. The unwary helper can be seduced by this gambit. He replies to the questions he is asked, assuming that the client really wants to know and because it eases the conversation and seems to contribute to rapport. Unless he is aware of what is going on, he may soon discover that he is doing all the talking and using the experience to ventilate his own feelings!

Self-discipline can sometimes cover up the effects of mild deprivation, but even with the most rigorous personal discipline it is probably not possible for highly inadequate persons to overcome that handicap to becoming an effective helper. All helping relationships require personal discipline. But self-discipline, no matter how strenuously applied, can rarely substitute sufficiently for positive feelings about self. Positive feelings about self make strenuous efforts at self-discipline less necessary. Accordingly, counselor-training programs often recommend and even require that counselors in training go through the experience themselves.

The capacity for self-acceptance characteristic of self-actualizing persons also contributes greatly to the establishment of effective helping relationships. It makes those people much more compassionate. This, of course, is a facilitating characteristic of great importance for the relationship. Research also demonstrates that acceptance of self is closely related to acceptance of others—that is to say, persons willing and able to confront who they are with clarity and honesty are much more likely to be able to do this with those they interact with. Such acceptance is an important property for helping.

Helpers do not have to be perfect. If they were there would be very few in the profession. What *is* necessary is an accurate, realistic view of themselves, their assets, and their limitations. Persons engaged in the helping professions must do so responsibly. In accepting a request for help, the helper assumes the responsibility not to exceed his competence. To hold out a hope to someone else which cannot be delivered is cruel and inhuman. Worse still, since clients can only judge the value of a helping relationship by their experience of it, a bad experience may have the additional effect of preventing the client from ever getting the help he needs because of his loss of faith in the process. Good helpers do not exceed their competence. The greater the self-actualization of the helper, the greater will be the degrees of freedom within which he can operate effectively. Whatever the level of personal fulfillment, however, persons engaged in the helping professions must have clear understandings of themselves, their talents, and their limitations.

THE PERSONAL SELF AND PROFESSIONAL SELF

Beginners in the helping professions sometimes cause themselves and others much unhappiness over a confusion of their roles as persons and professional workers. A person's self and role are not the same. The self has to do with whom a person is. It consists of his personal belief systems, his peculiar ways of seeing himself, and his relationship to the world. The professional role, on the other hand, has to do with a specialized relationship to other people. It defines a set of proper responsibilities and appropriate ways of behaving for the particular encounter in question. Of course, it is true that these two concepts are related, but they are by no means identical. Effective helpers need to be authentic people, and the self they display in the helping relationship should, indeed, be genuine. While the self must be expressed authentically in the professional role, however, it does not follow that the professional role should pervade the private life of the helper. One can live the philosophy of helping and apply it to his own life. Attempting to live the *practice* of the various forms of the helping professions, however, may only serve to complicate effective relationships in one's private life.

The self is what one is and so must be the same in all of life's situations. The expression of self in behavior may vary widely depending upon the nature of interactions encountered. The relationships one has with his wife, his friends, or his co-workers do not call for the person's professional role but his role as husband, friend, or colleague. The helper who seeks to be teacher or counselor to his wife, friends, or colleagues may find that he has only succeeded in frustrating and antagonizing them. What they are likely to experience is a hidden agenda—a feeling of being tolerated, used, or manipulated. Beginning counselors, for example, often make themselves obnoxious going about "treating" everyone they come in contact with. Treating a person who hasn't asked for it, or teaching a person who doesn't want such a relationship, can be a form of blatant lack of acceptance. It imposes a relationship and so robs others of their right to choose for themselves.

Helpers are not immune to the effects of the self-concept on perception and may even be blinded by their professional roles. Pediatricians, concerned about a child's health, have been known to strap a child's arm to a board so that he could not bend his elbow and put his thumb in his mouth, not thinking what this frustration does to the *mental* health of the child. Public health nurses and social workers often complain about people who live in shacks but nevertheless own television sets. They forget that if they lived in such squalid conditions they, too, might wish to have what little joy and beauty a television set could bring them. Psychologists deeply concerned about a client's behavior have been known to overlook the evidence of brain damage in clients. Clergymen, too, may be so deeply concerned with the problem of a parishioner's sins that instead of helping they "cast the first stone." Roles must be appropriate for the relationship in which they are used. It is important for helpers to keep perspectives clear.

The intense concentration of effort involved in many of the helping professions is a most exhausting experience. In addition, the rigorous self-discipline required to carry out some of these relationships effectively requires a kind of setting of one's self aside in the interests of other people. Even the healthiest self must still seek fulfillment, and this is a search which cannot long be denied. This is not to suggest that successful performance in the helping professions may not, in itself, be a form of fulfillment. It is, indeed, a source of great satisfaction for effective helpers. But the self is more than "professional." It is also personal, man or woman, husband or wife, citizen, friend, or any of a thousand other possibilities. These, too, require care and feeding. It is important, therefore, that persons engaged in the helping professions avail themselves of opportunities to engage in activities which are less demanding and more directly fulfilling of personal needs. The old adage that "all work and no play makes Jack a dull boy" has relevance for the helping professions. The most effective teachers, counselors, nurses, and psychologists known to the authors of this book are people who do not work at their professional roles full time.

THE HELPER'S SELF

SELF-ACCEPTANCE

If the self of the helper plays so important a part in the helping relationship, we may ask the question, "What can a potential helper do to make his self more effective?" In a sense, this entire book is an attempt to define what a helper is like and to point to ways for achieving excellence as a practitioner. It is probable, however, that no book can do much more than that. The development of an effective helper is a highly personal matter having to do with the growth of a particular self and its own discovery of how it needs to operate. The achievement of such goals cannot be accomplished by a book. It must be reached by a person who is actively working with people and searching for personal solutions. A book can do no more than provide some general guidelines for the search.

To become an effective teacher, counselor, social worker, or nurse is just that—a process of becoming. It is a matter of growth and occurs in gradual fashion over an extended period of time. This is a discovery that is often disappointing to beginners in the helping professions. With much enthusiasm and goodwill, they enter upon their training experience and expect that becoming an expert counselor or teacher is only a matter of learning the necessary tricks of the trade. Usually they are quickly disillusioned, but some never get over their early belief that it is only a matter of being a clever manipulator of the right things at the right time. People *grow* to be effective helpers and growth takes time.

The growth of expert helpers does not come about overnight. *Techniques* of helping, like changes of costume, can sometimes quickly be put on. The development of an effective "self as instrument," however, is not achieved by the skillful employment of gadgets or gimmicks. It is the product of increasingly differentiated perceptions, of maturing beliefs, values, and understandings. These, we have seen, are matters of personal growth. It is true that some persons enter the helping professions with high levels of sensitivity and systems of belief about themselves and others far advanced over other beginners. Some even enter their professional education at levels superior to those achieved by some of their fellows on graduation. There is room to grow, however, for every helper so long as he remains in the profession and approaches his tasks with openness and intent to learn. In some activities of life, experience can be superseded by mechanical shortcuts or clever manipulations; but there are few substitutes for experience in the helping professions. Skill in helping is dependent upon the person of the helper, and changing persons can only be accomplished through changing experience. Recognition of this fact can save the beginning professional worker a good deal of heartache and grief. Many an otherwise likely candidate has destroyed his own effectiveness by reason of his impatience. Sudden changes rarely happen in students, clients, or patients. Nor do they occur in persons studying the helping professions.

Professional workers in training are much more likely to make progress toward their goals if they can begin with an honest acceptance of themselves where they are. We have already seen that an attitude of acceptance is a major characteristic of adequate personalities. It is also a basic requirement for the helping relationship. An effective helper is one who has learned how to use himself effectively and efficiently to carry out his own and society's purposes. The problem of becoming an effective professional worker, then, is not a question of trading one's old self in for a new one. Rather, it is a matter of learning how to use the self one has and how to improve it slowly over a period of time. A very good place for the professional worker, then, to start his professional growth is by applying the principle of acceptance to himself, to begin his growth with the declaration, "It's all right to be me!"

PERCEPTIONS—KEYS TO CHANGE

An earlier chapter (Chapter 6) discussed at some length the difficulties involved in trying to change a person's behavior by concentrating on behavior itself. The principle also applies to the efforts of counselors, teachers, and social workers to bring about changes in themselves. If it were true that people changed simply by knowledge about what ought to be done, then education professors would be by far the best teachers; psychologists and psychiatrists, the best adjusted; nurses and doctors, the healthiest; and ministers the most serene. But everyone knows that that is not true! The attempt to change themselves by a direct attack on behavior is especially likely to be disappointing for trainees in the helping professions—not only because it puts prime attention in the wrong places, but also because it interferes with the very relationship the profession depends upon to accomplish its ends.

Concentration of attention on behavior is probably responsible for the dismaying research finding that beginning counselors are less like expert counselors in their beliefs about helping relationships than a random group of people taken off the streets! Similarly, beginning teachers overly preoccupied with using the "right" methods are likely to be poorer teachers. As they begin intensive study of how they "ought to be," for a time, they become less authentic than before they started. Like learning to drive an automobile, the beginner may know as much about the mechanics of a car as the experienced driver but when he learns to drive he must concentrate attention on precisely what he is doing; consequently, he over-drives. This, of course, requires correction and recorrection, producing erratic operation and demanding attention to very near goals like avoiding the curb, slowing down before the corner, seeing what is coming from behind, and a thousand other details. The experienced driver's field of attention expands to broader questions of where he is going, how to get there, and to events at some distance from his current location. The sooner the beginner can give up his preoccupation with details (by developing some mastery of them, of course) the sooner he will be free to devote his attention to larger issues and longer-range objectives.

Preoccupation with his own behavior is likely to make the helper less effective for another reason: It takes his attention off his students or clients. The essence of helping relationships is communication. Communication, however, requires listening, and it is impossible to listen to others while preoccupied with one's self.

For maximum growth the helper must explore not his own behavior, but his system of beliefs or perceptions. In Chapter 1 we observed that effective helpers could be clearly distinguished from poor ones by the nature of their beliefs about themselves, about the people they work with, about their purposes and values, and about the nature of the helping process. It is in these areas, then, that exploration is needed to advance helper growth most effectively. The process of learning to be an effective professional worker is a matter of continuous exploration of beliefs and meanings. It begins with an attitude that it is good to look and fun to try. It is stimulated by new and challenging experience, by study and innovation. It is immensely facilitated by interaction with people. The inspiration of dialogue and confrontation with others is especially important because people are the subject of helping efforts, the vehicles in which the outcomes occur, and the primary laboratory in which understandings about the helping process are born. The growth of persons in the helping professions begins with the *study of* people but finds its greatest advances in active *interactions with* them. It is in these directions that the beginner must search for personal growth.

Growth Potential of Helping Itself

One of the most potent stimulators of growth for the helper, of course, is his own participation in the practice of helping. Counselors, for example, cannot walk hand in hand with clients through the intimate phases of their lives without having the experience add something important to their own understanding. Similarly, successful experiences in teaching, nursing, supervision, administration, and social work must leave their inevitable mark upon the professional helper and enrich his own field of experience, for human encounters are two-way streets.

Successful participation in helping relationships is, in itself, an experience in fulfillment. In earlier chapters we have observed that whatever is experienced is experienced forever. We have also seen how the self may expand to include other persons. As a consequence, the helper's encounters with the clients, students, and patients with whom he is identified greatly extend his own experience and the impact of his person. A friend once pointed out to the authors three sources of immortality available to everyone. One kind, he said, is the immortality we achieve through our blood lines. This is a tenuous foothold, however, for our hereditary links may be easily broken by the failure of our children or their descendants to reproduce. A second kind of immortality, he pointed out, is that which is promised us in the tenets of religion. That may be a comforting thought. It could also conceivably be wrong. The only kind of immortality we can all be sure of, he maintained, is that which we achieve as a consequence of the impact we have upon the people in the world we live in. So the helper affects his client and the client affects the helper and each goes away from the interaction changed in more or less degree as a consequence of the experience. He will never be the same again. All his future contacts will be affected because of this significant experience. "This," said our friend, "is a kind of immortality we can all be sure of. If in time we achieve the others also, that's like icing on the cake."

THE HELPER AS CITIZEN

The professional role of helpers demands a special responsibility for assisting individuals to the achievement of greater fulfillment. This, in itself, is an important contribution to society. But the responsibility of helpers does not stop there. People in the helping professions live and work in society. They were citizens before they were teachers, counselors, social workers, or nurses, and the responsibilities of citizenship cannot lightly be set aside by anyone. Persons in the helping professions, like everyone else, must come to some kind of terms with the world they live in. Hopefully, they will do so constructively. The helper's responsibility as a citizen requires more than repairing the casualties of the system as a counselor might, or preventing future failures as a teacher may. His responsibility as a citizen is to contribute as best he can to the construction of a truly fulfilling society. He has to do this for his own sake as a person living in a society. He has to do it also for the sake of those who are dear to him and, because the persons he is trying to help are products of society, his professional role as helper demands he do what he can to make the world a better place to live in.

Persons in the helping professions have several advantages in this process, for the very professions they are engaged in were established by society in the first place to further meet human needs. Because societies are made up of individuals, the successful carrying out of their professional responsibilities leads directly to the enhancement of individuals and hence to the improvement of society. Participation in the helping professions does more. By the very nature of these professions, practitioners operate at the core of human problems. Their daily work keeps them closely in touch with human beings in more or less intimate ways. Carl Rogers once suggested that what we learn about human beings in the processes of counseling, for example, is similar to the contributions which the X ray made to our understanding of human physiology. Participation in the helping professions keeps one closely in touch with the raw stuff of which human personality is composed. The insight and understanding of people and their behavior obtained by effective helpers can be of immense value for understanding the dynamics of society and contributing to its improvement.

Much has been written about the effects of society upon human beings. Anthropologists, sociologists, historians, and observers of the social scene in general provide us with daily evidence of these effects through all our communicative media. The volume of these productions is sometimes overwhelming. Most of this information is descriptive in nature; it tells us what the current scene is or speculates on how it got this way. Unhappily, it usually gives us very few clues as to what may be done about matters. Knowing that the problems of youth arise from our "affluent society," or the breakdown of the American family because so many mothers are going to work is likely to be of very little help in doing something about these problems. No one in his right mind would suggest we give up our affluence, and anyone who thinks he can convince this generation of mothers to give up their jobs is out of touch with reality. Analyses of the social scene are tremendously valuable in explaining events. They are also useful in providing the data for broad social planning. In the final analysis, fundamental changes in society only come about as individual people change.

Certainly, it is true that persons are affected by their societies. It is also true that societies are made up of individuals. Indeed, the reason people come together to form groups in the first place is to improve their chances of achieving greater fulfillment. Societies are what people make them. A society which does not provide fulfillment is soon abandoned or changed so that it will. Because societies are made up of people, a change in people inevitably has its effects upon society as well. Because of their special knowledge and experience, good helpers can make important contributions to social change by sharing what they know and by committing themselves to action wherever their special talents can be made useful. How they do this, of course, must be a very individual matter depending upon the helper's self, his situation, and the degree of involvement he chooses. Like learning to help in his professional role, what he does in aiding society must hinge upon learning to use himself effectively as an instrument for human welfare. How he does this will be an individual matter; whether he does it at all will depend upon the strength of his concern and his willingness to get in the act in the first place.

Human institutions tend to be conservative, and over a period of time they develop a kind of hardening of the arteries. This inertia is often maddening and leaves many people discouraged in their attempts to produce change in the world about them. People do not *have* to be futile, however. What is needed is a proper perspective of what can be done and how. Human interaction *can* be meaningful and human beings *can* change their behavior. Persons rarely change as rapidly as we would like, however, and groups of people are likely to change even more slowly. The belief that human effort is of no avail, however, is simply not valid. Such an attitude can only make failure a foregone conclusion. It defeats itself. What is needed is a clear understanding of the dynamics of behavior change and the interactions of persons with the societies they live in. With this perspective, helpers can escape the immobilizing effects of discouragement and disillusion and free themselves to operate in closer touch with reality and, hence, also, with greater likelihood of success.

RESPONSIBILITY FOR CHANGE

Perhaps the most frequently heard excuse for personal inaction is the one that begins, "They won't let me. . . ." "They" may be bosses, parents, teachers, principals, supervisors, politicians, almost anybody. The implication is that one could do so much if only these nefarious influences were not preventing him. The vast majority of reasons given by teachers, for example, for the failure of students to learn lie almost anywhere except with the teacher himself—the children weren't motivated, were improperly prepared last year, were lazy, came from bad home situations, etc. The tendency to place the blame for failure on others is by no means confined to teachers. It is a common excuse for inaction employed by helpers in all of the professions whether counselors, supervisors, social workers, nurses, psychiatrists, or clergymen.

Sometimes it is true that supervisors, administrators, or other persons impose restrictions upon freedom. Equally as often obstructions turn out to exist only in the minds of the complainants. When the accuracy of the "they won't let me" explanation for inaction is investigated, "they" are often amazed to hear of the roadblocks "they" are presumed to have placed in the way of progress. Obstructions to change do not have to be real, however. If someone thinks they exist, that is enough. Rosenthal and others have called this the "self-fulfilling prophecy" and demonstrated that when people believe a thing is so, they are very likely to behave in ways that make it so. Counselors who believe their clients are resisting are likely to create resistance, and social workers convinced that nothing can be done are not likely to try very hard to bring about changes and so increase the likelihood that nothing will be done.

Even in circumstances where the attitudes of others really do interfere with innovations, a good deal can still be accomplished. Obstructions to human efforts can seldom be kept in force full time. Much can, therefore, be done in the times between. Teachers often complain, for example, that they cannot do the things they would like to because their principal will not let them. Most principals, however, are busy people and few have time to observe what is going on in a teacher's classroom very often. When the classroom door is closed, nobody but the teacher and the students know what goes on in there, and often the students aren't quite sure either!

Large changes often frighten people, especially if they are widely advertised in advance. This creates its own resistance. The very same changes can often be brought about without opposition if they are instituted as "normal" procedures minus trumpets and fanfare. In every life situation there is always some room to maneuver, a degree of slack which permits a certain amount of movement. The helper who systematically takes up this slack as far as he can soon finds that he has still more room to maneuver. People get used to his operating there. They assume it is normal, relax attention, and so provide a little more room to wriggle. Operating over a period of time by a process of continuous "taking up the slack," considerable change may be brought about. Later, because the matter never became an issue, no one is quite sure how it happened. Meanwhile, it has gotten well-established and, if successful, has built a case for continuance.

THE HELPER AS AGENT OF CHANGE

To be effective as an agent of change in the world he lives in, the helper must begin with a feeling that it is truly important to exert himself. Few people can sustain much interest in unimportant events. Unfortunately, in the complicated society we live in, it is easy to overlook many serious questions. People are so busy dealing with the personally important matters they confront every day, that what is crucial for other people or with respect to broader issues seems much less pressing. It is easy for helpers to become preoccupied with their tasks. The success of counselors is likely to be judged by the satisfaction of clients; the success of teachers is likely to be measured by student performance in the subject the teacher teaches. These are the urgent questions for the helper. They are also the sources of his rewards and the criteria for his professional advancement. Such matters have built-in importance and can easily preempt the helper's total time and energy. This is a pity for two reasons: It shirks the helper's broader responsibility to the society he lives in and robs society of help from persons whose unique talents and experience are specially relevant for dealing with human problems.·

Just as the helper is only likely to deal with that which seems important to him, society does the same. Whatever change a helper seeks in a group must, therefore, somehow come to seem desirable in the perceptions of the persons he hopes to influence. There must be some kind of confrontation with the problem in such fashion that it appears both personal and pressing. With some issues, this may be comparatively easy; with others it may be very difficult. Many social problems are regarded by almost everyone as needing solution. Others, even when they seem important, appear neither personal nor pressing and so their resolution may be long postponed. This has happened with persons not directly affected with respect to such problems as civil rights, poverty in our cities, care of the mentally ill, rehabilitation of criminals, to name but a few. Under such circumstances the confrontation of people with problems may have to be made sufficiently dramatic in order to bring them into the forefront of attention. This is a major function of demonstrations, protests, strikes, and riots.

It is not enough for helpers hoping to be change agents to think good thoughts. Ideas must somehow be translated into behavior if they are to have any impact whatsoever. People do not respond to unexpressed thoughts. The data from which they draw their conclusions is the behavior of people who seem important to them. To be effective, helpers must act. This does not mean that everything a person thinks must necessarily be expressed. As a matter of fact, in the interests of maximum impact, behavior may sometimes have to be expressed less drastically than belief. At first glance such a statement may sound like a denial of the principle of authenticity we have spoken of earlier. Not at all. People may *believe* whatever they wish. Behavior though, because it directly interacts with others, must be relevant and responsible. So, a man who believes he must be honest may speak out forcefully against racism knowing full well it will be threatening to his hearers because he *intends* to force a distasteful confrontation. The same honest man may "pull his punches" when his sister inquires how he likes her hat because he is also kind and loves his sister—values that are more important at that moment than being impeccably honest.

Since people behave in terms of their perceptions, persons hoping to change behavior must be concerned with the *meaning* of what they do in the experience of those they hope to influence. To be unconcerned with the consequences of one's behavior is to be little more than self-indulgent. If the helper's behavior imposes unnecessary barriers to move-ment or destroys the causes he seeks to advance, everyone loses. No one is required to say all he believes. Authenticity has to do with personal integrity and its expression in overall behavior. It does not demand that the behaver satisfy the demands of observers making their judgments from limited samples of his behavior. To be who he is will often require a person to behave in ways that are neither acceptable nor understood by outside observers.

The production of change has to do with maintaining a proper balance between challenge and threat, which we have had occasion to refer to many times in this volume. Maximum change is likely to be produced when we are successful in finding ways of challenging people without threatening them. One reason for the ineffectiveness of many who take a radical position for social change is their insistence upon behaving in the full measure of belief without regard for its effects upon others. The radical demands full expression of himself and full acceptance by others. This is a strain on both. In the process he often makes himself so threat-ening to those he would like to change that he leaves them no alternative but to reject him and his message altogether. As a consequence, he may end up creating opposition and resistance to the very ends he sought. The dynamics affecting human interrelationships cannot be made inop-erative by ignoring them. To do so may only result in frustration and failure.

By contrast, the liberal is often a most important agent of social change because the position he takes is far enough away from where people are as to force them to think about the matter. Yet, he is not so far from the status quo as to constitute threat and thus force rejection of a new idea or defense of the old positions. Without compromising his beliefs or abandoning eventual goals, he adjusts his demands to a real-istic appraisal of what is currently possible. This is not to suggest that there may not be times and places when radical or revolutionary con-cepts may be in order. Radicals can and have had stunning effects upon human affairs in the course of history. Persons who choose this way of forcing confrontation do so at the risk of destroying themselves in the process—but on occasion even that may be deemed a price well worth paying. There are social causes so important that personal considerations need to be sacrificed for larger goals.

As members of the social order, persons in the helping professions need to have a proper perspective of what can honestly be expected from their society. People in the helping professions sometimes get the feeling that they are not properly appreciated by the institutions they are involved in or the people they work with. Society often seems ungrateful for the contributions which helpers make. So, social workers bewail the fact that they are often misunderstood by the communities they are seeking to help, teachers complain that the public seems woefully disinterested in the problems of the schools, counselors are shocked at the ingratitude of clients, and nurses are hurt that their patients so quickly forget them. Actually, this is a common fate of all workers in our society. A democratic society *expects* each person to do his job. An interdependent society can only exist that way. This is especially true for the helping professions established expressly to serve other people. Society takes for granted they will do their jobs. It also reserves the right to kick like fury if it doesn't believe the job is being done. This is the democratic way, and persons in the helping professions who feel they are not appreciated by the society need only to ask themselves, "When was the last time I dropped in at the police station to tell them what a good job they are doing?" "When did I last call up the sewage disposal works to express my appreciation for what they are doing?" For that matter, "When was the last time I wrote my congressman or senator with something other than a complaint?"

CONFLICTING DEMANDS ON THE HELPER

The professional role of the helper makes him responsible for aiding individuals to reach their maximum fulfillment. The personal role of the helper requires him to behave as a citizen in ways that protect and enhance his society. Fortunately, these goals are generally congruent, but at times they may come temporarily into conflict with one another. For example, a child caught in a disapproved act may beg his teacher not to inform his parents. A client tells his counselor that he has been shoplifting, or his social worker that he plans to commit suicide. The problems created by such confrontations must be met by helpers. What will the helper do about them? The answers are not simple. They are further complicated by the fact that the helper probably would not have the information in the first place had he not been successful in creating an atmosphere in which the helper felt safe in talking about such unacceptable matters. Similar conflicts come about when some agency of society attempts to impose upon the helper a requirement which he feels is contrary to his conception of his professional role. This situation might arise when a teacher is told that he may not teach evolution or is required by a principal to lead children in daily prayers—an act which has been declared unconstitutional. It might occur, too, when a counselor or nurse is requested by an authority to divulge what a client or patient said.

Matters like these raise difficult problems of the proper relationship between professional roles and citizenship roles of the helper. When they occur there will always be people about with simple answers. Solutions, however, are not simple except for those people who haven't really thought about the question, or for those who have thought about them a great deal and arrived at solutions which now seem self-evident. The resolution of these kinds of problems for helpers confronted with them for the first time is likely to involve a good deal of anguish and distress. Pat answers will seldom suffice. Each helper must think matters through for himself and arrive at his own decisions. After that, he must also be willing to take the consequences, whatever they may be. The process of making such decisions is painful. The pain is by no means lost, however; it is precisely by wrestling with such knotty problems that vision becomes clear, understandings are sharpened, philosophies are made more congruent, and the growth of the helper is achieved.

THE HELPER'S OWN ECONOMY

Persons in the helping professions are likely to have many demands made upon them, especially if they are good at their jobs. The numbers of people in the world needing help are very great, and the number of professional helpers is still very few. As a consequence, the demands for aid to which people in the helping professions are likely to be subjected will often be well nigh overwhelming. This raises difficult problems for the helper in his role as both helper and citizen. He probably entered the profession in the first place because he sincerely wanted to be of help to other people. When he finds that the number of requests which come to him so far outrun his capacities to deliver, there is real danger that he may become discouraged, disillusioned, or embittered by his experience.

People in need of help can be terribly exacting of those who seem to be in positions to assist them. As a consequence, persons in the helping professions are likely to be subjected to great demands from their constitutents. This is especially true for those professions dealing with problems of maladjustment. Desperate people have little time to think of the problems of others. They are likely to be extraordinarily sensitive to slights and demanding of attention from helpers. To deal with such persons requires the "patience of Job," a capacity to absorb hostility, and a depth of concern sufficient to carry the helper through long periods of little or no apparent progress. Fundamental changes in people take place slowly, and often the helper may never see the effects of what he has done because they do not become manifest until long after the helpee has left him. The significance of what has been said or done to a person may not become obvious to him until days, months, or even years later.

The effectiveness of professional helpers will be dependent upon how they choose to use themselves as instruments. Some of these decisions will be predetermined by the titles they bear or the accepted practices defined by their place of employment. But even in the most rigidly pre-scribed settings, there will still be many decisions remaining to be made about whom to work with, how to spend time, and how to go about the helping task. How well a helper can cope with the varied demands made upon him will be dependent upon his understanding of his clients, the nature of the helping task, the extent of his compassion, and the depth of personal resources he has to call upon. Often it will be necessary to operate for long periods on the strength of these concepts and resources without immediate knowledge of results.

In making decisions about how to use themselves, helpers will cer-tainly make mistakes. This is inevitable. Mistakes must be expected. They must also be forgiven. The compassion helpers advocate for others must equally well be applied to themselves. The helper consumed with guilt or asking too much of himself may only end up making himself ineffective.

Helpers are persons, too, and must be permitted the privileges of be-ing human. There may even be times when helpers will have to say "no" to requests which are made of them. This may be an anguished decision for helpers, accompanied by feelings that they have somehow betrayed their trust. But, like everyone else, helpers have limitations and, because of those limitations or because of limits imposed by outside events, it will sometimes be necessary to reject requests for help. Indeed, not to do so might result in compounding problems for students or clients. Coun-selors, for example, who take on too many clients, may end up teaching their clients that the process has little to offer. Teachers who cannot bear to hurt a child by saying "no" when they should, may only lead their pupils on to greater disillusionment and a sense of betrayal at a later date.

Because of their limitations or because of the circumstances in which they have to work, there may even be times when helpers decide to do less than their best. This is a decision which any human being has a right to make; but, having made it, it ought to be clearly perceived for what it is—a human decision and not an inevitable fact. A guidance counselor in high school may decide to spend his time seeing every member of the senior class for fifteen minutes instead of working more intensively with a few. That decision is his prerogative. It should not, however, be rationalized as making himself more effective.

A human being is a dynamic economy. Each has its assets and liabilities, its strengths and its weaknesses. This economy cannot long be violated. Instead, it must be accepted and worked with. Helpers need to be able accurately and realistically to assess their limitations and accept them for what they are. They are not required to be all things to all people. Indeed, if they try, they are almost certainly doomed to failure. Being human, they, too, need times of respite to regain perspective and composure.

Working in the helping professions is a thrilling, fulfilling experience when it is done well. It is also demanding and exhausting. What is required of the helper is that:

1. He see himself, his professional role, and society in proper perspective.
2. He demand of each of these the maximum of its potential.
3. He make honest decisions about what is really worth fighting for.
4. He be willing to take the consequences of those decisions.

After that, having done the best he can with what he's got and where he is, who can ask any more of him?

There are few right answers in the helping professions. How a helper carries out his task must be a matter of choosing how to use himself most effectively and efficiently in carrying out his own and society's purposes. The choices he makes and the resulting consequences cannot be escaped. What can be assured is that his choices are based upon the broadest, richest understandings a helper can acquire. That is a lifelong project for which this book can suggest but a bare beginning.

SELECTED READINGS

Starred entry indicates appearance in Donald L. Avila, Arthur W. Combs, and William W. Purkey, *The Helping Relationship Sourcebook* (Boston: Allyn & Bacon, 1971).

Block, J. & Thomas, H. Is satisfaction with self a measure of adjustment? *Journal of Abnormal and Social Psychology,* 1955, **51,** 254–259.

Gordon, C. & Gergen, K. J. *The self in social interaction: Volume 1: Classic and contemporary perspectives.* New York: Wiley, 1968.

Lantz, D. L. Changes in student teachers' concepts of self and others. *Journal of Teacher Education,* 1964, **15,** 200–203.

* Lawton, G. Neurotic interaction between counselor and counselee. *Journal of Counseling Psychology,* 1958, **5,** 28–33.

Meyer B. Self-acceptance of nurses and acceptance of patients: An exploratory investigation. *Nursing Research,* 1965, **14,** 346–350.

Rosenthal, R. & Jacobson L. *Pygmalion in the classroom.* New York: Holt, Rinehart & Winston, 1968(a).

Ziferstein, I. Psychological habituation to war: A sociological case study. American Journal of Orthopsychiatry, 1967, **37,** 457–468.

Bibliography

Abramson, P. (Ed.) Discipline: Not the worst problem . . . but bad. *Grade Teacher,* 1968, **86,** 151–163.

Adams, H. B. Mental illness; Or interpersonal behavior patterns? *American Psychologist,* 1964, **19,** 191–197.

Adams, J. S. Reduction of cognitive dissonance by seeking consonant information. *Journal of Abnormal and Social Psychology,* 1961, **62,** 74–78.

Adorno, T. W. *The authoritarian personality.* New York: Harper, 1950.

Allport, F. H. *Theories of perception and the concept of structure.* New York: Wiley, 1965.

Allport, G. W. The use of personal documents in psychological science. *Social Science Research Council Bulletin,* 1942.

Allport, G. W. The ego in contemporary psychology. *Psychological Review,* 1943, **50,** 451–468.

Allport, G. W. *Becoming.* New Haven: Yale University Press, 1955.

Allport, G. W. *Pattern and growth in personality.* New York: Holt, Rinehart & Winston, 1961.

Amatora, S. A. Similiarity in teacher and pupil personality. *Journal of Psychology,* 1954, **37,** 45–51.

Ames, A. Visual perception and the rotating trapezoidal window. *Psychological Monographs,* 1951, **65,** 7.

Ames A. *An interpretative manual: The nature of our perceptions, prehensions and behavior.* Princeton, N.J.: Princeton University Press, 1955.

Ames, L. B. The sense of self on nursery school children as manifested by their verbal behavior. *Journal of Genetic Psychology,* 1952, **81,** 193–232.

Amos, W. E. & Orem, R. C. *Managing student behavior.* St. Louis: Green Publishing Co., 1967.

Anderson, H. H. *Creativity and its cultivation.* New York: Harper & Row, 1959.

Appelbaum, S. A. The problem solving aspect of suicide. *Journal of Projective Techniques and Personality Assessment,* 1963, **27,** 259–268.

Arbuckle, D. S. Self ratings and test scores on two standardized personality inventories. *Personnel Guidance Journal,* 1958, **37,** 292–293.

Arbuckle, D. S. & Boy, A. V. Client-centered therapy in counseling students with behavior problems. *Journal of Counseling Psychology,* 1961, **8,** 136–139.

Arkoff, A. Some workers in improvement. *Adjustment and mental health.* New York: McGraw Hill, 1968, pp. 284–307.

Aronson E., Carlsmith, J. M. & Darley, J. M. The effects of expectancy on volunteering for an unpleasant experience. *Journal of Abnormal and Social Psychology,* 1963, **66,** 220–224.

Asch, M. J. Nondirective teaching in psychology: An experimental study. *Psychological Monographs,* 1951, **65,** iii–24.

Aspy, D. N. Maslow and teachers in training. *Journal of Teacher Education,* 1969, **20,** 303–309.

Aspy, D. N. How did he get there? *Peabody Journal of Education,* 1969, **47,** 152–153.

Aspy, D. N. The effect of teacher-offered conditions of empathy, positive regard and congruence upon student achievement. *Florida Journal of Educational Research,* 1969, **11,** 39–49.

Ausubel, D. P. The prestige motivation of gifted children. *Genetic Psychology Monograph,* 1951, **42,** 53–117.

Ausubel, D. P. A new look at classroom discipline. *Phi Delta Kappan,* 1961, **43,** 25–30.

Ausubel, D. P. A teaching strategy for culturally deprived pupils: Cognitive and motivational considerations. *School Review,* 1963, **71,** 454–463.

Avila, D. L. & Purkey, W. W. Intrinsic and extrinsic motivation: A regrettable distinction. *Psychology in the Schools,* 1966, **3,** 206–208.

Avila, D. L., Combs, A. W., & Purkey, W. W. *The helping relationship sourcebook.* Boston: Allyn & Bacon, 1971.

Axline, V. M. *Play therapy.* Boston: Houghton Mifflin, 1947.

Axline, V. M. *Dibs: In search of self.* Boston: Houghton Mifflin, 1964.

Bach, G. R. The marathon group: 1. Intensive practice of intimate interaction. *Psychological Reports,* 1966, **18,** 995–1002.

Bagby, J. A cross cultural study of perceptual predominance in binocular rivalry. *Journal of Abnormal and Social Psychology,* 1957, **54,** 331–334.

Ball, G. Speaking without words. *American Journal of Nursing,* 1960, **60,** 692–693.

Barlow, J. A. *Stimulus and response.* New York: Harper & Row, 1968.

Barrett, H. O. An intensive study of 32 gifted children. *Personnel and Guidance Journal,* 1957, **36,** 192–194.

Bartlett, F. C. *Remembering.* (Rev. ed.) Cambridge, England: Cambridge University Press, 1932.

Bartley, S. H. *Principles of perception.* New York: Harpers, 1958.

Battle, E. S. & Rotter, J. B. Children's feelings of personal control as related to social class and ethnic group. *Journal of Personality,* 1960, **31,** 482–490.

Beard, R. M. *An outline of Piaget's developmental psychology for students and teachers.* New York: Basic Books, 1969.

Beatty, W. H. & Clark, R. A self-concept theory of learning: A learning theory for teachers. In H. C. Lindgren (Ed.), *Readings in educational psychology.* New York: Wiley, 1968.

Becker, A. H. *The function of relationship in pastoral counseling.* (Doctoral dissertation, Boston University) Boston, Mass.: University Microfilms, 1958. No. 58-3087.

Beker, J. The influence of school camping on the self-concepts and social relationships of sixth grade children. *Journal of Educational Psychology,* 1960, **51,** 352–356.

Beloff, H. & Beloff, J. Unconscious self evaluation using a stereoscope. *Journal of Abnormal and Social Psychology,* 1959, **59,** 275–278.

Benton, J. A., Jr. Perceptual characteristics of Episcopal pastors. Unpublished doctoral dissertation, University of Florida, 1964.

Beres, D. Perception, imagination and reality. *International Journal of Psychoanalysis,* 1960, **41,** 327–334.

Berger, E. M. The relation between expressed acceptance of self and expressed acceptance of others. *Journal of Abnormal and Social Psychology,* 1952, **47,** 778–782.

Bergin, A. E. Some implications of psychotherapy research for therapeutic practice. *Journal of Abnormal Psychology,* 1966, **71,** 235–246. See also, *International Journal of Psychiatry,* 1967, **3,** 136–150.

Berkowitz, L. et al. The interest, value and relevance of fear arousing communication. *Journal of Abnormal and Social Psychology,* 1960, **60,** 37–43.

Bertocci, P. A. The psychological self, the ego and personality. *Psychological Review,* 1945, **52,** 91–99.

Berzon, B., Pious, C. & Farson, R. E. The therapeutic event in group psychotherapy: A study of subjective reports by group members. *Journal of Individual Psychology,* 1963, **19,** 204–212.

Bettelheim, B. *Truants from life.* Glencoe, Ill.: Free Press, 1955.

Bettleheim, B. *Love is not enough.* New York: Collier Books, 1965.

Bettelheim, B. *The empty fortress: Infantile autism and the birth of the self.* New York: Free Press, 1967.

Bettelheim, B. Where self begins. *Child and Family,* 1968, **7,** 5–12.

Bieri, J. Changes in interpersonal perceptions following social interaction. *Journal of Abnormal and Social Psychology,* 1953, **48,** 61–66.

Bieri, J. & Trieschman, A. Learning as a function of perceived similarity to self. *Journal of Personality,* 1956, **25,** 213–223.

Bigge, M. L. *Learning theories for teachers.* New York: Harper & Row, 1964.

Bills, R. E. About people and teaching. *Bulletin of the Bureau of School Service,* College of Education, University of Kentucky, 1955.

Bills, R. E. Personality changes during student centered teaching. *Journal of Educational Research,* 1956, **50,** 121–126.

Binet, A. Les idees modernes sur les enfants. Paris: Ernest Flamarion, 1909 (Cited from Hunt, 1961).

Birney, R. C., Burdick, H. & Teevan, R. C. *Fear of failure,* New York: Van Nostrand, 1969.

Bischof, L. *Interpreting personality theories.* New York: Harper & Row, 1964.

Block, J. & Thomas, H. Is satisfaction with self a measure of adjustment? *Journal of Abnormal and Social Psychology,* 1955, **51,** 254–259.

Blommers, P. & Coffield, W. Effects of non-promotion on educational achievement in the elementary school. *Journal of Educational Psychology,* 1956, **46,** 237–249.

Bonner, H. *On being mindful of man.* Boston: Houghton Mifflin, 1965.

Borislow, B. Self-evaluation and academic achievement. *Journal of Counseling Psychology*, 1962, **9**, 246–254.

Bousfield, W. A. & Cohen, B. H. The occurence of clustering in the recall of randomly arranged associates. *Journal of Psychology*, 1955, **36**, 67–81.

Bowers, N. D. & Soar, R. S. *Evaluation of laboratory human relations training for classroom teachers. Studies of human relations in the teaching-learning process: V. Final report.* U.S. Office of Education Contract. No. 8143. Columbia, S.C.: University of South Carolina, 1961.

Bowers, W. J. *Student dishonesty and its control in college.* New York: Bureau of Applied Social Research, Columbia University, 1964.

Bradford, L., Benne, K. & Gibb, J. R. *T-group theory and laboratory method.* New York: Wiley, 1964.

Bradway, K. P. & Robinson, N. M. Significant I. Q. changes in twenty-five years. *Journal of Educational Psychology*, 1961, **52**, 74–79.

Brammer, L. M. & Shostrom, E. L. *Therapeutic psychology; Fundamentals of counseling and psychotherapy.* Englewood Cliffs, N.J.: Prentice-Hall, 1960.

Brandt, R. M. The accuracy of self estimate: A measure of self concept reality. *Genetic Psychology Monographs*, 1958, **58**, 55–99.

Brill, N. Communication with low income families. *Journal of Home Economics*, 1966, **58**, 631–635.

Brim, O. G., Jr. College grades and self estimates of intelligence. *Journal of Educational Psychology*, 1954, **45**, 477–484.

Brock, T. C. & Grant, L. D. Dissonance, awareness, and motivation. *Journal of Abnormal and Social Psychology*, 1963, **67**, 53–60.

Brookes, R. M. & Goldstein, A. G. Recognition by children of inverted photographs of faces. *Child Development*, 1963, **34**, 1033–1040.

Brookover, W. B. *The relationships of self-images to achievement of junior high school subjects.* United States Office of Education. Project No. 845, East Lansing, Mich., 1960.

Brookover, W. B., Paterson, A. & Thomas, S. Self-concept of ability and school achievement. *Sociology of Education*, 1964, **37**, 271 and 278.

Brown, B. B. *An investigation of observer-judge ratings of teacher competence.* Final Rept. No. D-182, Contract No. OF-6-10-288, Bureau of Research, U.S. Department of Health, Education, and Welfare, Office of Education, 1969.

Brownfain, J. J. Stability of the self concept as a dimension of personality. *Journal of Abnormal and Social Psychology*, 1952, **47**, 597–606.

Bruner, J. S. The art of discovery. *Harvard Educational Review*, 1961, **31**, 21–32.

Bruner, J. S. On perceptual readiness. In E. P. Hollander & R. G. Hunt (Eds.), *Current perspectives in social psychology: Readings with commentary.* New York: Oxford, 1963, 42–47.

Bruner, J. S. *Toward a theory of instruction.* New York: W. W. Norton, 1966.

Brunkan, R. J. & Sheni, F. Personality characteristics of ineffective, effective, and efficient readers. *Personnel and Guidance Journal*, 1966, **44**, 837–844.

Bugental, J. F. T. *The search for authenticity: An existential-analytic approach to psychotherapy.* New York: Holt, Rinehart & Winston, 1965.

Bugental, J. F. T. (Ed.) *Challenges of humanistic psychology.* New York: McGraw-Hill, 1967.

Buhler, C. B. Human life goals in the humanistic perspective. *Journal of Humanistic Psychology,* 1967, **7**, 36–52.

Butler, J. M. The interaction of client and therapist. *Journal of Abnormal and Social Psychology,* 1952, **47**, 366–378 (supplement).

Caliguri, J. Self concept of the poverty child. *Journal of Negro Education,* 1966, **35**, 280–282.

Calvin, A. D. & Holtzman, W. H. Adjustment and discrepancy between self concept and inferred self. *Journal of Consulting Psychology,* 1953, **17**, 39–44.

Cantor, N. *The teaching learning process.* New York: Holt, Rinehart & Winston, 1953.

Cantril, H. *The why of man's experience.* New York: Macmillan, 1950.

Cantril, H. *Human nature and political systems.* New Brunswick, N.J.: Rutgers University Press, 1961.

Cantril, H. The human design. *Journal of Individual Psychology,* 1964, **20**, 129–136.

Cantril, H. Sentio, Ergo Sum: "Motivation" reconsidered. *The Journal of Psychology,* 1967, **65**, 91–107.

Caplan, G. *Concepts of mental health and consultation: The application in public health social work.* Washington, D.C., Children's Bureau, U.S. Dept. of Health, Education and Welfare, 1959.

Caplin, M. D. Self concept, level of aspiration, and academic achievement. *The Journal of Negro Education,* 1968, **37**, 435–439.

Carkhuff, R. R. & Berenson, B. G. *Beyond counseling and therapy.* New York: Holt, Rinehart & Winston, 1967.

Carkhuff, R. R. & Truax, C. B. *Toward counseling and psychotherapy: Training and practice.* Chicago, Ill.: Aldine, 1967.

Carkhuff, R. R. & Truax, C. B. Toward explaining success and failure in interpersonal learning experiences. *Personnel and Guidance Journal,* 1966, **44**, 723–728.

Carlson, R. Stability and change in the adolescent's self-image. *Child Development,* 1965, **36**, 659–666.

Carlton, L. & Moore, R. H. Culturally disadvantaged children can be helped. *NEA Journal,* 1966, **9**, 13–14.

Carlton, L. & Moore, R. H. *Reading, self-directive dramatization and self concept.* Columbus, Ohio: Charles E. Merrill, 1968.

Carter, T. P. The negative self concept of Mexican-American students. *School and Society,* 1968, **96**, 217–219.

Cartwright, R. D. Self-conception patterns of college students, and adjustment to college life. *Journal of Counseling Psychology,* 1963, **10**, 47–52.

Chansky, N. M. & Taylor, M. Perceptual training with young mental retardates. *American Journal of Mental Deficiency,* 1964, **68**, 460–468.

Chickering, A. W. Self concept, ideal self concept, and achievement. *Dissertation Abstracts,* 1958, **29**, 164.

Chodorkoff, B. Self-perception, perceptual defense, and adjustment. *Journal of Abnormal and Social Psychology,* 1954, **49,** 508–512.

Chodorkoff, B. Alcoholism and ego function. *Quarterly Journal Studies on Alcohol,* 1964, **25,** 292–299.

Chowdhry, K. & Newcomb, T. M. The relative abilities of leaders and non-leaders to estimate opinions of their own groups. *Journal of Abnormal and Social Psychology,* 1952, **47,** 51–57.

Cohen, A. Cognitive tuning as a factor affecting impression formation. *Journal of Personality,* 1961, **29,** 235–245.

Cohen, J. Psychological time. *Scientific American,* 1964, **211,** 116–124.

Cohen, L. D. Level of aspiration behavior and feelings of adequacy and self-acceptance. *Journal of Abnormal and Social Psychology,* 1954, **49,** 84–86.

Combs, A. W. Phenomenological concepts in non-directive therapy. *Journal of Consulting Psychology,* 1948, **12,** 197–208.

Combs, A. W. A phenomenological approach to adjustment theory. *Journal of Abnormal and Social Psychology,* 1949, **44,** 29–35.

Combs, A. W. Intelligence from a perceptual point of view. *Journal of Abnormal and Social Psychology,* 1952, **47,** 662–673. (b)

Combs, A. W. Counseling as a learning process. *Journal of Counseling Psychology,* 1954, **1,** 31–36.

Combs, A. W. The myth of competition. *Childhood Education,* 1957, **33,** 264–269. (a)

Combs, A. W. New horizons in field research: The self concept. *Educational Leadership,* 1958, **15,** 315–319.

Combs, A. W. & Snygg, D. *Individual behavior: A perceptual approach to behavior.* New York: Harper & Brothers, 1959.

Combs, A. W. What can man become? *California Journal for Instructional Improvement,* 1961, **4,** 15–23.

Combs, A. W. The personal approach to good teaching. *Educational Leadership,* 1964, **21,** 369–378.

Combs, A. W. Some basic concepts in perceptual psychology. Speech given at APGA Convention, 14 April 1965, Session #239, Minneapolis, Minn.

Combs, A. W. *The professional education of teachers: A perceptual view of teacher preparation.* Boston: Allyn & Bacon, 1965.

Combs, A. W. Fostering self direction. *Educational Leadership,* 1966, **23,** 373–387.

Combs, A. W. et al. *Florida studies in the helping professions.* (University of Florida Social Science Monograph No. 37) University of Florida Press, Gainesville, Fla., 1969.

Combs, A. W., Courson, C. C. & Soper, D. W. The measurement of self concept and self report. *Educational and Psychological Measurement,* 1963, **23,** 439–500. (b)

Combs, A. W. & Soper, D. W. The self, its derivative terms and research. *Journal of Individual Psychology,* 1957, **12,** 134–145.

Combs, A. W. & Soper, D. W. *The relationship of child perceptions to achievement and behavior in the early school years.* Cooperative Research Project No. 814, University of Florida, Gainesville, Fla., 1963.

Combs, A. W. & Soper, D. W. Perceptual organization of effective counselors. *Journal of Counseling Psychology,* 1963, **10,** 222–226. (c)

Combs, A. W. & Soper, D. W. The helping relationship as described by "good" and "poor" teachers. *Journal of Teacher Education,* 1963, **14,** 64–67. (a)

Combs, A. W. & Taylor, C. The effect of perception of mild degrees of threat on performance. *Journal of Abnormal and Social Psychology,* 1952, **47,** 420–424. (a)

Combs, C. F. Perception of self and scholastic underachievement in the academically capable. *Personnel and Guidance Journal,* 1964, **43,** 47–51.

Combs, C. F. A study of the relationship between certain perceptions of self and scholastic underachievement in academically capable high school boys. *Dissertation Abstracts,* 1964, **24,** 620. (b)

Connelly, C. J. Threatening the sense of self worth. *Childhood Education,* 1964, **4,** 20.

Conwell, R. H. *Acres of diamonds.* New York: Harper & Row, 1943.

Cook, W. E. The motivation of delinquent adolescent girls for achievement in school. Unpublished masters thesis, Ohio State University, 1964.

Coopersmith, S. Relationship between self-esteem and sensory (perceptual) constancy. *Journal of Abnormal and Social Psychology,* 1964, **68,** 217–222.

Coopersmith, S. *The antecedents of self esteem.* San Francisco: Freeman Press, 1967.

Coudert, J. *Advice from a failure.* New York: Dell, 1965.

Courson, C. The relationship of certain perceptual factors to adequacy. Unpublished doctoral dissertation, University of Florida, 1963.

Courson, C. The use of inference as a research tool. *Educational and Psychological Measurement,* 1965, **25,** 1029–1038.

Courson, C. Personal adequacy and self-perception in high school students: A study of behavior and internal perceptual factors. *Journal of Humanistic Psychology,* 1968, **8,** 29–38.

Craddick, R. A. Height of Christmas tree drawings as a function of time. *Perceptual and Motor Skills,* 1963, **17,** 335–339.

Crandall, V. J. & Sinkeldam, C. Children's dependent and achievement behaviors in social situations and their perceptual field dependence. *Journal of Personality,* 1964, **32,** 1–22.

Cronbach, L. J. *Essentials of psychological testing.* New York: Harper, 1960.

Crovetto, L. L., Fischer, A. M. & Boudreaus, J. L. *The pre-school child and his self-image.* Division of Instruction and Division of Pupil Personnel, New Orleans Public Schools, 1967.

Crowne, D. P. & Stephens, M. W. Self-acceptance and self-evaluative behavior: A critique of methodology. *Psychological Bulletin,* 1961, **58,** 104–121.

Crutchfield, R. S. Conformity and character. *American Psychologist,* 1955, **10,** 91–98.

Culler, I. B. Stability of self concept in schizophrenia. *Journal of Abnormal Psychology,* 1966, **71,** 275–279.

Davids, A. & Lawton, M. H. Self concept, mother aversions and food aversions in emotionally disturbed children. *Journal of Abnormal and Social Psychology,* 1961, **62,** 309–314.

Davidson, H. & Lang, G. Children's perceptions of their teacher's feelings toward them related to self-perception, school achievement and behavior. *Journal of Experimental Education*, 1960, **29**, 107–118.

Davis, J. M. Personality, perceptual defense and stereoscopic perception. *Journal of Abnormal and Social Psychology*, 1959, **58**, 398–402.

Davitz, J. R. Fear, anxiety and the perception of others. *Journal of General Psychology*, 1959, **61**, 169–173.

Davitz, J. R. & Davitz, L. J. The communication of feelings by content-free speech. *Journal of Communication*, 1959, **9**, 6–13. (a)

Davitz, J. R. & Davitz, L. J. Nonverbal vocal communication of feeling. *Journal of Communication*, 1961, **2**, 81–86.

Dearborn, D. C. & Simon, H. A. Selective perception: A note on the departmental identifications of executives. *Sociometry*, 1958, **21**, 140–144.

Dee, F. S., Arndt, C. & Meyer B. Self-acceptance of nurses and acceptance of patients: An exploratory investigation. *Nursing Research*, 1965, **14**, 346–350.

De Haan, R. F. *Accelerated learning programs.* Washington, D.C.: Center for Applied Research in Education, 1963.

Delaney, D. J. & Heiman, R. A. Effectiveness of sensitivity training on the perception of non-verbal communication. *Journal of Counseling Psychology*, 1966, **13**, 436–440.

Deutsch, M. Minority group and class status as related to social and personality factors in scholastic achievement. (Society for Applied Anthropology, Cornell University, Ithaca, N.Y. Monograph No. 2.) 32 pages, 1960.

Dexter, L. A. *The tyranny of schooling.* New York: Basic Books, 1964.

Dickman J. F. The perceptual organization of person-oriented versus task-oriented student nurses. Unpublished doctoral dissertation, University of Florida, 1967.

Diggory, J. *Self evaluation.* New York: Wiley, 1966.

Diller, L. Conscious and unconscious self-attitudes after success and failure. *Journal of Personality*, 1954, **23**, 1–12.

Dinitz, S., Scarpitti, F. R. & Reckless W. C. Delinquency vulnerability: A cross group and longitudinal analysis. *The American Sociological Review*, 1962, **27**, 515–517.

Dixon, W. R. & Morse, W. C. The prediction of teaching performance: Empathic potential. *Journal of Teacher Education*, 1960, **11**, 351–364.

Dombrow, R. A study of the relationship between therapist's empathy for patients and changes in patient's self-concepts during therapy. *Dissertation Abstracts*, 1966, **27B**, 301–302.

Draguns, J. G. & Multari, G. Recognition of perceptually ambiguous stimuli in grade school children. *Child Development*, 1961, **32**, 541–550.

Durr, W. K. & Schmatz, R. R. Personality differences between high-achieving and low-achieving gifted children. *Reading Teacher*, 1964 **17**, 251–254.

Eisen, N. H. Some effects of early sensory deprivation on later behavior: The quandam hard of hearing child. *Journal of Abnormal and Social Psychology*, 1962, **65**, 338–342.

Eisner, W. W. *Think with me about creativity.* Dansville, N.Y.: Owen Publishing Co., 1964.

Ellena, W. J., Stevenson, M. & Webb, H. V. *Who's a good teacher?* Washington, D.C., American Association of School Administrators, National Education Association, 1961.

Engel, E. The role of content in binocular resolution. *American Journal of Psychology,* 1956, **69,** 87–91.

Engel, E. Binocular methods in psychological research. In E. P. Kilpatrick (Ed.), *Explorations in transactional psychology.* New York: New York University Press, 1961, 290–305.

Engel, M. The stability of the self-concept in adolescence. *Journal of Abnormal and Social Psychology,* 1959, **58,** 211–215.

English, H. B. Education of the emotions. *Journal of Humanistic Psychology,* Spring, 1961, 101–109.

English, H. B. *Dynamics of child development.* New York: Holt, Rinehart & Winston, 1961.

Epstein, S. Unconscious self evaluation in a normal and schizophrenic group. *Journal of Abnormal and Social Psychology,* 1955, **50,** 65–70.

Erikson, E. M. The concept of identity in race relations. *Daedalus,* 1966, **95,** 141–171.

Evaluation as feedback and guide. 1967 Yearbook. Washington, D.C., Association for Supervision and Curriculum Development. National Education Association.

Fair, J. A comprehensive high school studies learning. *Educational Leadership,* 1959, **16,** 351–354.

Farquhar, W. W. *A comprehensive study of the motivational factors underlying achievement of eleventh grade high school students.* United States Office of Education Cooperative Research Report No. 846, January 1968, Michigan State University, United States Office of Education Office of Research and Publications.

Fausti, R. P. & Luker, A. H. Phenomenological approach to discussion. *Speech Teacher,* 1965, **14,** 19–23.

Festinger, L., Peicken, H. W. & Schacter, S. *When prophecy fails.* Minneapolis: University of Minnesota Press, 1956.

Festinger, L. *A theory of cognitive dissonance.* Stanford, Calif.: Stanford University Press, 1957.

Festinger, L. Cognitive dissonance. *Scientific American,* 1964, **207,** 93–107.

Fey, W. F. Acceptance of self and others and its relation to therapy readiness. *Journal of Clinical Psychology,* 1954, **10,** 269–271.

Fiedler, F. E. The concept of an ideal therapeutic relationship. *Journal of Consulting Psychology,* 1950, **14,** 239–245. (b)

Fiedler, F. E. A comparison of therapeutic relationships in psychoanalytic, non-directive and Adlerian therapy. *Journal of Consulting Psychology,* 1950, **14,** 436–445. (a)

Field, J. *A life of one's own.* Great Britain: Hunt, Barnard, 1955.

Fink, M. B. Self concept as it relates to academic underachievement. *California Journal of Educational Research,* 1962, **13,** 57–62.

Fisher, W. Better self-images. *The Instructor,* 1968, **78,** 95.

Flanders, N. A. *Teacher influence, pupil attitudes and achievement: Studies in interaction analysis.* Final Report, Project No. 397, 1960, Cooperative Research Program, United States Office of Education, Washington, D.C.

Frank, J. D. *Persuasion and healing.* Baltimore: Johns Hopkins Press, 1961.

Frank, L. *Nature and human nature.* New Brunswick, N.J.: Rutgers University Press, 1951.

Frankel, E. Effects of a program of advanced summer study on the self-perceptions of academically talented high school students. *Exceptional Children,* 1964, **30,** 245–249.

Frankl, V. E. *Man's search for meaning: An introduction to logotherapy.* Boston: Beacon, 1963.

Freer, J. J. The effects of scholastic success and failure on the relationship among self-concept, ideal self, and level of aspiration. *Dissertation Abstracts,* 1961, **22,** 347.

French, J. P. R. Overcoming resistance to change. *Human Relations,* 1948, **1,** 512–532.

Freud, A. *The ego and the mechanisms of defense.* New York: International Universities Press, 1946.

Freud, S. *A general introduction to psychoanalysis.* Garden City, N.Y.: Garden City Publishing Co., 1920.

Freud, S. *The problem of anxiety.* New York: Norton, 1936.

Freud, S. *An outline of psychoanalysis.* New York: Norton, 1949.

Friedman, I. Phenomenal, ideal and projected conceptions of self. *Journal of Abnormal and Social Psychology,* 1955, **51,** 611–615.

Fromm, E. *Escape from freedom.* New York: Holt, Rinehart & Winston, 1941.

Fromm, E. *Man for himself.* New York: Holt, Rinehart & Winston, 1957.

Fromm, E. *The sane society.* New York: Holt, Rinehart & Winston, 1955.

Fromm, E. *Art of loving: An inquiry into the nature of love.* New York: Harper & Row, 1956.

Frostig, M. Visual perception in brain-injured children. *American Journal of Orthopsychiatry,* 1963, **33,** 665–671.

Frymier, J. R. *The relationship of certain behavioral characteristics to perception.* Unpublished doctoral dissertation, University of Florida, 1957.

Frymier, J. R. Professionalism in context. *Ohio State Law Journal,* 1965, **26,** 53–65. (a)

Frymier, J. R. *The nature of educational method.* Columbus, Ohio: Charles Merrill, 1965. (b)

Frymier, J. R. Measuring creativity and delinquency proneness with a picture preference scale. Mimeographed. The Ohio State University, February, 1966.

Frymier, J. R. & Thompson, J. H. Motivation: The learner's mainspring. *Educational Leadership,* 1965, **22,** 567–570.

Gage, N. L. Explorations in the understanding of others. *Educational and Psychological Measurement,* 1953, **13,** 14–26.

Gage, N. L. Exploration of teacher's perceptions of pupils. *Journal of Teacher Education,* 1958, **9,** 97–101.

Gage, N. L. (Ed.) *Handbook of research on teaching.* A project of the American Educational Research Association. Chicago: Rand McNally, 1963.

Gebel, A. S. Self perception and leaderless group discussion status. *Journal of Social Psychology,* 1950, **40,** 309–318.

Gergen, K. J. & Wishnov, B. Others' self-evaluations and interaction anticipation as determinants of self-presentation. *Journal of Personality and Social Psychology*, 1965, **2**, 348–358.

Getzels, J. W. & Jackson, P. W. *Creativity and intelligence: Explorations with gifted students*. New York: Wiley, 1962.

Getzels, J. W. & Jackson, P. W. The teacher's personality and characteristics. In N. L. Gage (Ed.), *Handbook of research on teaching*. Chicago: Rand McNally, 1963, 506–582.

Gibb, J. R. A climate for learning. *Adult Education*, 1958, **9**, 19–21.

Gibb, J. R. Defensive communication. *The Journal of Communication*, 1961, **11**, 141–148.

Gibb, J. R. et al. *Dynamics of participative groups*. New York: Jolin Swift, 1961.

Gibb, J. R. & Gibb, L. M. *Applied group dynamics*. Washington, D.C.: National Training Laboratories, 1955.

Gibby, R. G., Sr. & Gibby, R. G., Jr. The effects of stress resulting from academic failure. *Journal of Clinical Psychology*, 1967, **23**, 35–37.

Gibson, E. J. Perceptual learning. *Annual Review of Psychology*, 1963, **14**, 29–56.

Gillham, H. L. *Helping children accept themselves and others*. New York: Bureau of Publications, Teachers College, Columbia University, 1959.

Ginott, H. G. *Group psychotherapy with children*. New York: McGraw-Hill, 1961.

Ginott, H. G. *Between parent and child: New solutions to old problems*. New York: Macmillan, 1965.

Ginott, H. G. *Between parent and teenager*. New York: Macmillan, 1968.

Gladstone, R. *A set of principles of teaching derived from experimental psychology*. (2nd ed.) Stillwater, Oklahoma: Oklahoma State University Press, 1967.

Goins, J. T. Visual perceptual abilities and early reading progress. (University of Chicago Press Supplementary Educational Monograph No. 87) February 1958.

Gollob, H. F. & Dittes, J. E. Effects of manipulated self-esteem on persuasibility depending on threat and complexity of communication. *Journal of Personality and Social Psychology*, 1965, **2**, 195–201.

Gooding, C. T. An observational analysis of the perceptual organization of effective teachers. Unpublished doctoral dissertation, University of Florida, 1964.

Goodman, H. Self-insight, empathy and perceptual distortion: A study of the relationships between measures of self-insight, empathy, and perceptual distortion as obtained from ratings made by individuals on themselves and others in their group. *Dissertation Abstracts*, 1953, **13**, 120.

Goodman, M. Expressed self-acceptance and interspousal needs: A basis for mate selection. *Journal of Counseling Psychology*, 1965, **11**, 129–135.

Gordon, C. & Gergen, K. J. *The self in social interaction. Vol. I: Classic and contemporary perspectives*. New York: Wiley, 1968.

Gordon, I. J. Observing from a perceptual viewpoint. *Journal of Teacher Education*, 1959, **10**, 280–284.

Gordon, I. J. & Wood, P. C. Relationship between pupil self evaluation, teacher evaluation of the pupil and scholastic achievement. *Journal of Educational Research,* 1963, **56,** 440–443.

Gordon, I. J. *Studying the child in school.* New York: Wiley, 1966.

Gordon, I. J. New conceptions of children's learning and development. Washington, D.C., Association for supervision and curriculum development, National Education Association, 1966, 49–73.

Gordon, I. J. A parent education approach to provision of early stimulation for the culturally disadvantaged. A final report on the Ford Foundation, Gainesville, Fla.: Institute for Development of Human Resources, 1967.

Gordon, I. J. *Human development from birth through adolescence.* (2nd ed.) New York: Harper & Row, 1969.

Gordon, I. J. & Combs, A. W. Perception and the learner. *Review of Educational Research,* 1958, **28,** 433–444.

Gordon, T. *Group-centered leadership: A way of releasing the creative power of groups.* Boston: Houghton Mifflin, 1955.

Goslin, D. A. *The search for ability.* New York: Russell Sage Foundation, 1963.

Gowan, J. C. Factors of achievement in high school and college. *Journal of Counseling Psychology,* 1960, **7,** 91–95.

Greene, G. *Sex and the college girl.* New York: Dial Press, 1964.

Grimes, J. W. & Allensmith, W. Compulsivity, anxiety, and school achievement. *Merrill-Palmer Quarterly of Behavior and Development,* 1961, **7,** 247–271.

Grossack, M. Cues, expectations and first impressions. *Journal of Psychology,* 1953, **35,** 245–252.

Grossack, M. M. Some effects of cooperation and competition upon small group behavior. *Journal of Abnormal and Social Psychology,* 1954, **49,** 341–348.

Grossack, M. M. Perceived Negro group belongingness and social rejection. *The Journal of Psychology,* 1954, **38,** 127–130. (a)

Grossack, M. M. Some personality characteristics of Southern Negro students. *The Journal of Social Psychology,* 1957, **46,** 125–131.

Guilford, J. P. Three faces of intellect. In R. E. Ripple (Ed.), *Readings in learning and human abilities.* New York: Harpers, 1964, 46–64.

Guller, I. B. Stability of self concept in schizophrenia. *Journal of Abnormal Psychology,* 1966, **71,** 275–279.

Haarer, D. L. A comparative study of self concept of ability between institutionalized delinquent boys and non-delinquent boys enrolled in public schools. Unpublished doctoral dissertation, Michigan State University, 1964. See also *Dissertation Abstracts,* **XXV,** 6410.

Haas, H. I. & Maehr, M. L. Two experiments on the concept of self and the reaction of others. *Journal of Personality and Social Psychology,* 1965, **1,** 100–105.

Haberman, M. & Raths, J. High, average, low—and what makes teachers think so. *Elementary School Journal,* 1968, **68,** 241–245.

Haefner, D. Some effects of situational threat on group behavior. *Journal of Abnormal and Social Psychology,* 1954, **49,** 445–453.

Haimowitz, M. L. Criminals are made, not born. In M. L. Haimowitz & N. R. Haimowitz (Eds.), *Human development: Selected readings.* New York: Thomas Y. Crowell, 1960, 359–375.

Hall, C. S. & Lindzey, G. *Theories of personality.* New York: Wiley, 1957.

Hall, E. T. *The silent language.* Greenwich, Conn.: Fawcett, 1959.

Hamachek, D. E. A study of the relationships between certain measures of growth and the self-images of elementary school children. *Dissertation Abstracts,* 1961, **21,** 2193.

Hamachek, D. E. Dynamics of the self. *Wisconsin Journal of Education,* 1969, **101,** 7–9.

Hamachek, D. E. & Mori, I. Need structure, personal adjustment and academic self concept of beginning education students. *Journal of Educational Research,* 1964, **58,** 158–162.

Harlow, H. The nature of love. *The American Psychologist,* 1958, **13,** 673–685.

Harlow, H. & Harlow, M. K. Social deprivation in infant monkeys. *Scientific American,* 1962, **207,** 136–146.

Harlow, H. F. Love in infant monkeys. *Scientific American,* 1959, **200,** 68–74.

Harrington, M. *The other America.* Baltimore, Md.: Penguin Books, 1963.

Harvey, O. J. et al. *Conceptual systems and personality organization.* New York: Wiley, 1961.

Hastings, P. K. A relationship between visual perception and level of personal security. *Journal of Abnormal and Social Psychology,* 1952, **47,** 552–560.

Hastorf, A. H. & Myro, G. The effect of meaning on binocular rivalry. *American Journal of Psychology,* 1959, **72,** 393–400.

Havighurst, R. The development of the ideal self in childhood and adolescence. *Journal of Educational Research,* 1946, **40,** 241–257.

Hayakawa, S. I. Suicide as a communicative act. *ETC: A review of general semantics,* 1957, **15,** 46–51.

Hayakawa, S. I. *Language in thought and action.* New York: Harcourt, Brace & World, 1964.

Heider, F. *The psychology of interpersonal relations.* New York: Wiley, 1958.

Heine, R. W. A comparison of patients' reports on psycho-therapeutic experience with psychoanalytic, non-directive and Adlerian therapists. *Journal of Psychotherapy,* 1953, **7,** 16–23.

Herman, Sister Mary. Self concept of the Negro child. *Catholic School Journal,* 1966, **66,** 62–63.

Heron, W. The pathology of boredom. *Scientific American,* 1957, **196,** 52–56.

Hess, E. H. Imprinting in animals. *Scientific American,* 1958, **198,** 81–90.

Hilgard, E. R. Human motives and the concept of self. *American Psychologist,* 1949, **4,** 374–382.

Hilgard, E. & Bowers, G. *Theories of learning.* New York: Appleton-Century-Crofts, 1966.

Hill, T. T. Attitudes toward self: An experimental study. *Journal of Educational Sociology,* 1957, **30,** 395–397.

Hitt, W. D. Two models of man. *American Psychologist,* 1969, **24,** 651–658.

Honzik, M. P., Macfarlane, J. W. & Allen, J. The stability of mental test performance between two and eighteen years. In W. Dennis (Ed.), *Readings in child psychology.* Englewood Cliffs, N.J.: Prentice Hall, 1963, 223–232.

Horowitz, R. E. Racial aspects of self-identification in nursery school children. *Journal of Psychology,* 1939, **7,** 91–99.

House, R. J. T-group education and leadership effectiveness: A review of the empiric literature and a critical evaluation. *Personnel Psychology,* 1967, **20,** 1–31.

Hummel, R. & Sprinthall, N. Underachievement related to interests attitudes, and values. *The Personnel and Guidance Journal,* 1965, **44,** 388–395.

Hunt, J. M. *Intelligence and experience.* New York: Ronald Press, 1961.

Hunt, J. M. The implications of changing ideas on how children develop intellectually. *Children,* 1964, **11,** 83–91.

Hunt, J. M. Traditional personality theory in the light of recent evidence. In R. G. Brown, R. A. Newell & H. G. Vonk (Eds.), *Behavioral implications for curriculum and teaching: Interdisciplinary readings.* Dubuque, Iowa: William C. Brown, 1969.

Huntingfield, G. & Spegil, I. M. Achievement motivation and field independence. *Journal of Consulting Psychology,* 1960, **24,** 550–551.

Ittelson, W. H. The involuntary bet. *Vogue,* March 15, 1952, 76–77 and 127,

Ittelson, W. H. *The Ames demonstrations in perception.* Princeton, N.J.: Princeton University Press, 1952.

Ittelson, W. H. & Cantril, H. *Perception: A transactional approach.* New York: Doubleday, 1954.

Ittelson, W. H. & Slack, C. The perception of persons as visual objects. In R. Taguiri & L. Petrullo (Eds.), *Person perception and interpersonal behavior.* Stanford, Calif.: Stanford University Press, 1958, 210–228.

Ittelson, W. H. *Visual space perception.* New York: Springer, 1960.

Jackson, P. W. *Life in classrooms.* New York: Holt, Rinehart & Winston, 1968.

Janis, I. L. & Feshback, S. Effects of fear-arousing communication. *Journal of Abnormal and Social Psychology,* 1953, **48,** 78–92.

Janis, I. L. Personality correlates of susceptibility to persuasion. *Journal of Personality,* 1954, **23,** 504–518.

Jersild, A. *In search of self.* New York: Bureau of Publications, Teachers College, Columbia University, 1952.

Jersild, A. T. Voice of the self. *NEA Journal,* 1965, **54,** 23–25.

Johnson, T. J., Feigenbaum, R. & Weiby M. Some determinants and consequences of the teacher's perception of causation. *Journal of Educational Psychology,* 1964, **55,** 237–246.

Jones, A., Braden, I. & Wilkinson, H. J. Information deprivation as a motivational variable. *Journal of Experimental Psychology,* 1961, **62,** 126–137.

Jones, W. S., Jr. Some correlates of the authoritarian personality in a quasi-therapeutic situation. Unpublished doctoral dissertation, University of North Carolina, 1961.

Jourard, S. M. The study of self-disclosure. *Scientific American,* 1958, **198,** 77–82. (b)

Jourard, S. M. & Lasakow, P. Some factors in self-disclosure. *Journal of Abnormal and Social Psychology*, 1958, **56,** 91–98. (a)

Jourard, S. Self-disclosure and other cathexis. *Journal of Abnormal and Social Psychology*, 1959, **59,** 428–431.

Jourard, S. *Personal adjustment.* New York: Macmillan, 1963.

Jourard, S. *The transparent self.* New York: Von Nostrand, 1964.

Jourard, S. *Disclosing man to himself.* New York: Van Nostrand, 1968.

Jourard, S. Healthy personality and self-disclosure. In H. G. Brown, R. A. Newell & H. G. Vonk (Eds.), *Behavioral implications for curriculum and teaching: Interdisciplinary readings.* Dubuque, Iowa: William C. Brown, 1969.

Kapp, K. W. *Toward a science of man in society.* The Hague: Martinus Nijhoff, 1961.

Katona, G. *Psychological analysis of economic behavior.* New York: McGraw-Hill, 1951.

Katz, D. et al. *Productivity, supervision and morale in an office situation, Part I.* Institute for Social Research, University of Michigan, Ann Arbor, Mich., 1950.

Kelley, E. C. *Education for what is real.* New York: Harper, 1947.

Kelley, E. C. Communication and the open self. *ETC: A Review of General Semantics,* 1954, **10,** 96.

Kelley, E. C. *In defense of youth.* Englewood Cliffs, N.J.: Prentice-Hall, 1962.

Kelley, E. C. *Another look at individualism.* Detroit, Mich.: Wayne State University, College of Education, 1962.

Kelley, E. C. The meaning of wholeness. In S. I. Hayakawa (Ed.), *ETC: A Review of General Semantics.* 1969, 26, 7–15.

Kelly, F. J. & Veldman, D. J. Delinquency and school dropout behavior as a function of impulsivity and non-dominant values. *Journal of Abnormal and Social Psychology,* 1964, **69,** 190–194.

Kimble, G. A. & Garmezy, N. *Principles of general psychology* (2nd ed.) New York: Ronald Press, 1956.

Kirk, S. A. *Early education of the mentally retarded: An experimental study.* Urbana, Ill.: University of Illinois Press, 1958.

Klein, G. S. The personal world through perception. In R. R. Blake, & G. V. Ramsey (Eds.), *Perception.* New York: Ronald Press, 1951, 328–355.

Klein, G. S., Holdt, R. R. & Spence, D. P. Cognition without awareness: Subliminal influences upon conscious thought. *Journal of Abnormal and Social Psychology,* 1958, **57,** 255–266.

Kohler, W. *Gestalt psychology.* New York: Liveright, 1947.

Kolers, P. A. It loses something in the translation. *Psychology Today,* 1969, **2,** 32–35.

Korchin, S. J. & Basowitz, H. Perceptual adequacy in a life stress. *Journal of Psychology,* 1954, **38,** 495–502.

Kounin, J. S. & Gump, P. V. Ripple effect in discipline. *Elementary School Journal,* 1958, **59,** 158–162.

Kounin, J. S. Managing emotionally disturbed children in regular classrooms: A replication and extension. *Journal of Special Education,* 1968, **2,** 129–135.

Kowitz, G. T. Test anxiety and self-concept. *Childhood Education,* 1967, **44,** 162–165.

Kuenzli, A. E. *The phenomenological problem.* New York: Harper & Brothers, 1959.

Kvareceus, W. C. et. al. *Negro self-concept: Implications for school and citizenship.* New York: McGraw-Hill, 1965.

Kvaraceus, W. C. Poverty, education and race relations. In W. C. Kvaraceus, J. S. Gibson & T. J. Curtin (Eds.), *Poverty, education and race relations: Studies and proposals.* Boston: Allyn & Bacon, 1967, 3–10.

Lafferty, J. C. Values that defeat learning. *National Association of Secondary School Principals Bulletin,* 1968, **52,** 201–212.

Lakin, M. Some ethical issues in sensitivity training. *American Psychologist,* 1969, **24,** 923–928.

Lamy, M. E. Relationship of self-perceptions of early primary children to achievement in reading. In I. J. Gordon (Ed.), *Human development: Readings in research.* Chicago: Scott, Foresman & Co., 1965, 251.

Landsman, T. Factors influencing individual mental health. *Review of Educational Research,* 1962, **32,** 464–475.

Lane, H. A. *On educating human beings.* Chicago: Follett, 1964.

Lantz, D. L. Changes in student teachers' concepts of self and others. *Journal of Teacher Education,* 1964, **15,** 200–203.

Lantz, D. L. Relationship between classroom emotional climate and concepts of self, others and ideal among elementary student teachers. *Journal of Educational Research,* 1965, **59,** 80–83.

Lanzetta, J. T., Axelrod, H., Haefner, D. & Langham, P. Some effects of situational threat on group behavior. *Journal of Abnormal and Social Psychology,* 1954, **49,** 445–453.

Laury, G. V. & Murloo, A. M. Subtle types of mental cruelty to children. *Child and Family,* 1967, **6,** 28–34.

Lawton, G. Neurotic interaction between counselor and counselee. *Journal of Counseling Psychology,* 1958, **5,** 28–33.

Lay, F. Language facilitation among delinquent boys. *Journal of Communication,* 1965, **15,** 216–225.

Lazarus, R. S. & Longo, N. The consistency of psychological defenses against threat. *Journal of Abnormal and Social Psychology,* 1953, **48,** 495–499.

Learning and mental health in the school. 1966 Yearbook. Washington, D.C., Association for Supervision and Curriculum Development. National Education Association.

Lecky, P. *Self-consistency: A theory of personality.* New York: Island Press, 1945.

Lee, L. C., Kagan J. & Rabson, A. Influence of preference for analytic category upon concept acquisition. *Child Development,* 1963, **34,** 433–442.

Lefcourt, H. M. Risk taking in Negro and white adults. *Journal of Personality and Social Psychology,* 1965, **2,** 765–770.

Leichty, M. M. Family attitudes and self-concept in Vietnamese and U.S. children. *American Journal of Orthopsychiatry,* 1963, **33,** 38–50.

Levanway, R. W. The effect of stress on expressed attitude toward self and others. *Journal of Abnormal and Social Psychology,* 1955, **50,** 225–226.

Levinson, B. M. Culture and mental retardation. *Psychological Record,* 1958, **8,** 27–38.

Lewin, K., Dembs, T., Festinger, L. & Sears, P. S. Level of aspiration. In J. McV. Hunt (Ed.), *Personality and the behavior disorders. Vol. 1.* New York: Ronald Press, 1944, 333–378.

Liddle, G. P. Psychological factors involved in dropping out of school. *High School Journal,* 1962, **45,** 276–280.

Liddle, G. P. The secondary school as an instrument for preventing juvenile delinquency. *High School Journal,* 1964, **47,** 146.

Lifton, W. M. *Working with groups.* New York: Wiley, 1966.

Lilly, J. & Shurley, J. T. Experiments in solitude, in maximum achievable physical isolation with water suspension, of intact healthy persons. In B. E. Flaherty (Ed.), *Psychophysiological aspects of space flight.* New York: Columbia University Press, 1961, 238–247.

Lippitt, R. *Feedback process in the community context.* Washington, D.C., National Training Laboratory, National Education Association, 1965.

Lippitt, R. & White, R. K. An experimental study of leadership and group life. In G. E. Swanson, T. M. Newcomb & E. L. Hartley (Eds.), *Readings in social psychology.* (Rev. ed.) New York: Henry Holt, 1952.

Livingston, R. B. How man looks at his own brain: An adventure shared by psychology and neuro-physiology. In S. Koch (Ed.), *Psychology: A study of a science.* New York: McGraw-Hill, 1962, 51–99.

Lloyd, J. The self-image of a small black child. *Elementary School Journal,* 1967, **67,** 406–411.

Logan, F. A. & Wagner, A. R. *Reward and punishment.* Boston: Allyn & Bacon, 1965.

Luchins, A. S. The problem of truth in the study of perception. *Psychological Record,* 1963, **13,** 213–220.

Luckey, E. B. Implications for marriage counseling of self perceptions and spouse perceptions. *Journal of Counseling Psychology,* 1960, **7,** 3–9.

Ludwig, D. L. & Maehr, M. L. Changes in self-concept and stated behavior preferences. *Child Development,* 1967, **38,** 453–467.

Luft, J. On nonverbal interaction. *Journal of Psychology,* 1966, **63,** 261–268.

MacDonald, J. B. Gamesmanship in the classroom. *National Association of Secondary School Principals Bulletin,* 1966, **50,** 51–68.

MacKinnon, D. W. The nature and nurture of creative talent. *American Psychologist,* 1962, **17,** 484–495.

MacLeod, J. Sensitivity training, What's that? Is it for a local church? *International Journal of Religious Education,* 1966, **43,** 8–9.

Maehr, M. L., Menking, J. & Nafeger, S. Concept of self and the reaction of others. *Sociometry,* 1962, **25,** 353–357.

Maehr, M. L. Some limitations of the application of reinforcement theory to education. *School and Society,* 1968, **96,** 108–110.

Mahler, C. A. & Caldwell, E. *Group counseling in secondary schools.* Chicago: Science Research Associates, 1961.

Makarenko, A. S. *The collective family: A handbook for Russian parents.* Garden City, N.Y.: Doubleday, 1967.

Malcolm X. *The autobiography of Malcolm X.* New York: Grove Press, 1964.

Malpass, L. F. Some relationships between students' perceptions of school and their achievement. *Journal of Educational Psychology,* 1953, **44,** 475–482.

Marrow, A. J. *Behind the executive mask.* New York: American Management Association, 1964.

Marrow, A. J. Risks and uncertainty in action research. *Journal of Social Issues,* 1964, **20,** 5–20.

Marrow, A. J. Gomberg's "Fantasy." *Trans-action.* Sept./Oct. 1966.

Marrow, A. J., Bowers, D. G. & Seashore, S. E. *Management by participation.* New York: Harper & Row, 1967.

Marshall, H. H. The effect of punishment of children: A review of the literature and a suggested hypothesis. *Journal of Genetic Psychology,* 1965, **106,** 23–33.

Marshall, J. The evidence. *Psychology Today,* 1969, **2,** 48–52.

Maslow, A. H. *Motivation and personality.* New York: Harper, 1954.

Maslow, A. H. Creativity in self-actualizing people. In H. H. Anderson (Ed.), *Creativity and its cultivation.* New York: Harper & Brothers, 1959, 83–95.

Maslow, A. H. *New knowledge in human values.* New York: Harper, 1959.

Maslow, A. H. *Toward a psychology of being.* New York: Van Nostrand, 1962.

Maslow, A. H. The creative attitude. *The Structuralist,* 1963, **3,** 4–10.

Matarayya, J. D. Psychotherapeutic processes. *Annual Review of Psychology,* 1965, **16,** 181–224.

Matson, F. W. (Ed.) *Being, becoming, and behavior.* New York: George Braziller, 1967.

May, R. *Man's search for himself.* New York: W. W. Norton, 1953.

May, R. (Ed.) *Existence.* New York: Basic Books, 1958.

May, R. (Ed.) *Existential psychology.* New York: Random House, 1961.

Mayer, C. L. The relationship of early special class placement and the self-concepts of mentally handicapped children. *Exceptional Children,* 1966, **33,** 77–81.

McCallon, E. L. Teacher characteristics and their relationship to change in the congruency of children's perception of self and ideal-self. *Journal of Experimental Education,* 1966, **34,** 84–88.

McCandless, B. R. & Castaneda, A. Anxiety in children, school achievement, and intelligence. *Child Development,* 1956, **27,** 379–382.

McClintok, C. G. & Davis, J. Changes in the attribute of "Nationality" in the self-percept of the "stranger." *Journal of Social Psychology,* 1958, **48,** 183–193.

McGinnies, E. Emotionality and perceptual defense. *Psychological Review,* 1949, **56,** 244–251.

McGinnies, E. & Adornetto, J. Perceptual defense in normal and schizophrenic observers. *Journal of abnormal and social psychology,* 1952, **47,** 833–837.

McGrath, J. E. & McGrath, M. Effects of partisanship on perceptions of political figures. *Public Opinion Quarterly,* Spring 1962.

McIntyre, C. J. Acceptance by others and its relation to acceptance of self and others. *Journal of Abnormal and Social Psychology,* 1952, **47,** 624–625.

McNeil, E. B. *The quiet furies: Man and disorder.* Englewood Cliffs, N.J.: Prentice-Hall, 1967.

Mead, G. H. *Mind and society.* Chicago: University of Chicago Press, 1934.

Mead, M. The young adult. In E. Ginzburg (Ed.), *Values and ideals of American youth.* New York: Columbia University Press, 1961, 37–51.

Mehrabian, A. et al. Immediacy: An indicator of attitudes in linguistic communication. *Journal of Personality,* 1966, **34,** 26–34.

Meinhart, N. T. Love is the essence of nursing. *RN,* August 1968, 69–70.

Melzack, R. The perception of pain. *Scientific American,* 1961, **204,** 41–49.

Menninger, K. A. *Man against himself.* New York: Harcourt, Brace & World, 1938, 1968.

Meyer, B. et al. Self-acceptance of nurses and acceptance of patients: An exploratory investigation. *Nursing Research,* 1965, **14,** 346–350.

Miel, A. *Creativity in teaching.* Belmont, Calif.: Wadsworth, 1961.

Mitchell, C. D., Harlow, H. F., Raymond, C. J. & Ruppenthal, G. C. Long term effects of total social isolation upon behavior of Rhesus monkeys. *Psychological Reports,* 1966, **18,** 567–580.

Montague, Ashley. *Man in process.* New York: Mentor Books, 1961.

Morgan, E. M. *A comparative study of self-perceptions of aggressive and withdrawn children.* Unpublished doctoral dissertation, University of Florida, 1961.

Morrison, K. *Management counseling of small business in the United States.* The University of Mississippi: Mississippi Industrial and Technological Research Commission, July, 1963.

Morse, W. C. Self-concept in the school setting. *Childhood Education,* 1964, **41,** 195–198.

Mouly, G. J. *Psychology for effective teaching.* (2nd ed.) New York: Holt, Rinehart & Winston, 1968.

Moustakas, C. *The self: Exploration in personal growth.* New York: Harper, 1956. (a)

Moustakas, C. *The teacher and the child.* New York: McGraw-Hill, 1956. (b)

Moustakas, C. E. *Loneliness.* Englewood Cliffs, N.J.: Prentice-Hall, 1961.

Moustakas, C. E. *The authentic teacher: Sensitivity and awareness in the classroom.* Cambridge, Mass.: Howard A. Doyle Publishing Co., 1966.

Mudra, D. A new look at leadership. *Journal of Health, Physical Education and Recreation,* 1964, **35,** 30 and 86.

Murphy, G. *Personality: A biosocial approach to origins and structure.* New York: Harper, 1947.

Murphy, G. & Spohn, H. E. *Encounter with reality.* Boston: Houghton Mifflin, 1968.

Murray, E. J. Learning theory and psychotherapy: "Biotropic versus sociotropic approaches." *Journal of Counseling Psychology,* 1963, **10,** 250–255.

Murray, H. A. *Thematic apperception test*. Cambridge, Mass.: Harvard University Press, 1943.

Mussen, P. H. *The psychological development of the child*. Englewood Cliffs: N.J.: Prentice-Hall, 1963.

Neill, A. S. *Summerhill*. New York: Hart Publishing, 1960.

Newcomb, T. M. Persistence and regression of changed attitudes: Long-range studies. *Journal of Social Issues*, 1963, **19**, 3–14.

O'Banion, T. & O'Connell, A. *The shared journey: An introduction to encounter*. Englewood Cliffs, N.J.: Prentice-Hall, 1970.

Omwake, K. T. The relation between acceptance of self and acceptance of others shown by three personality inventories. *Journal of Consulting Psychology*, 1954, **18**, 443–446.

Orr, J. F. *An analysis of some projective data and correlated behavioral data of the Kellogg leadership study*. Unpublished master's thesis, University of Florida, 1959.

Otto, H. A. The Minerva experience: Initial report. In J. F. Bugental (Ed.), *Challenges of humanistic psychology*. New York: McGraw-Hill, 1967, 119–124.

Page, E. Teacher comments and student performance: A seventy-four classroom experiment in school motivation. *Journal of Educational Psychology*, 1958, **49**, 173–181.

Paris, N. M. T-grouping: A helping movement. *Phi Delta Kappan*, 1968, **49**, 460–463.

Parker, J. The relationship of self-report to inferred self-concept. *Educational and Psychological Measurement*, 1966, **26**, 691–700.

Paschal, B. J. A concerned teacher makes the difference. *The Arithmetic Teacher*, 1966, **13**, 203–205.

Patterson, C. H. *Counseling and psychotherapy: Theory and practice*. New York: Harper, 1959.

Patterson, C. H. The self in recent Rogerian theory. *Journal of Individual Psychology*, 1961, **17**, 5–11.

Payne, D. A. The concurrent and predictive validity of an objective measure of academic self-concept. *Educational and Psychological Measurement*, 1962, **22**, 773–780. (a)

Payne, D. A. & Farquhar, W. W. The dimensions of an objective measure of academic self concept. *Journal of Educational Psychology*, 1962, **53**, 187–192.

Pearl, D. Ethnocentrism and the self concept. *Journal of Social Psychology*, 1954, **40**, 137–147.

Perceiving, behaving, becoming: A new focus for education. 1962 Yearbook. Washington, D.C., Association for Supervision and Curriculum Development. National Education Association.

Perkins, H. V. Factors influencing change in children's self-concepts. *Child Development*, 1958, **29**, 221–230.

Perry, D. C. Self acceptance in relation to adjustment. *Dissertation Abstracts*, 1961, **22**, 317–318.

Pettigrew, T., Allport, G. & Barnett, E. Binocular resolution and percept of race in South Africa. *British Journal of Psychology*, 1958, **49**, 265–278.

Phillips, B. N., Hindsman, E. & Jennings, E. Influence of intelligence on anxiety and perception of self and others. *Child Development*, 1960, **31**, 41–45.

Piaget, J. & Elkind, D. (Ed.), *Six psychological studies*. New York: Random House, 1967.

Pilisuk, M. Cognitive balance and self-relevant attitudes. *Journal of Abnormal and Social Psychology*, 1962, **65**, 95–103.

Pilisuk, M. Anxiety, self-acceptance, and open-mindedness. *Journal of Clinical Psychology*, 1963, **19**, 387–391.

Pinneau, S. R. & Milton, A. The ecological veracity of the self-report. *Journal of Genetic Psychology*, 1958, **93**, 249–276.

Postman, L. & Bruner, J. S. Perception under stress. *Psychological Review*, 1948, **55**, 314–323.

Premack, D. Toward empirical behavior laws: I, positive reinforcement. *Psychological Review*, 1959, **66**, 219.

Prentice, W. C. H. Some cognitive aspects of motivation. In R. J. C. Harper et al. (Eds.), *The cognitive processes*. Englewood Cliffs, N.J.: Prentice-Hall, 1961, 400–411.

Privette, G. Transcendent functioning. *Teachers College Record*, 1965, **66**, 733–739.

Proshanky, H. The effects of reward and punishment on perception. *Journal of Psychology*, 1942, **13**, 295–305.

Purkey, W. W. The self and academic achievement. Gainesville, Fla.: University of Florida. *Florida Educational Research and Development Council Research Bulletin*, 1967, Vol. 3, No. 1.

Purkey, W. W. The search for self: Evaluating student self-concepts. Gainesville, Fla.: University of Florida. *Florida Educational Research and Development Council Research Bulletin*, 1968, Vol. 4, No. 2.

Purkey, W. W. *Self concept and school achievement*. Englewood Cliffs, N.J.: Prentice-Hall, 1970.

Putman, L. J. A communication on communication. *Improving college and university teaching*, 1966, **14**, 148–150.

Rabinowitz, M. The relationship of self-regard to the effectiveness of life experiences. *Journal of Counseling Psychology*, 1966, **13**, 139–143.

Rabkin, L. Y. The disturbed child's perception of parental attributes. *Dissertation Abstracts*, 1963, **24**, 2566.

Raimy, V. C. Self-reference in counseling interviews. *Journal of Consulting Psychology*, 1948, **12**, 143–163.

Reckless, W. C., Dinitz, S. & Murray, E. Self concept as an insulator against delinquency. *American Sociological Review*, 1956, **21**, 744–746.

Reckless, W. C., Dinitz, S. & Kay, B. Self component in potential delinquency. *American Sociological Review*, 1957, **22**, 566–570.

Reckless, W. C. & Dinitz, S. Pioneering with self-concept as a vulnerability factor in delinquency. *The Journal of Criminal Law, Criminology and Police Science*, 1967, **58**, 515–523.

Redl, F. & Wineman, D. *Children who hate*. Glencoe, Ill.: Free Press, 1951.

Redl, F. & Wineman, D. *Controls from within*. Glencoe, Ill.: Free Press, 1952.

Reed, C. F. & Cuadra, C. A. The role-taking hypothesis in delinquency. *Journal of Consulting Psychology,* 1957, **21,** 386–390.

Reed, H. B. The learning and retention of concepts. I. The influence of set. *Journal of Experimental Psychology,* 1946, **36,** 71–87.

Reed, H. B. Implications for science education of a teacher competence research. *Science Education,* 1962, **46,** 473–486.

Renzaglia, G. A., Henry, D. R. & Rybolt, G. A. Estimation and measurement of personality characteristics and correlates of their congruence. *Journal of Counseling Psychology,* 1962, **9,** 71–78.

Rezler, A. G. Influence of needs upon the student's perception of his instructor. *Journal of Educational Research,* 1965, **58,** 282–286.

Riek, T. *Listening with the third ear.* New York: Grove Press, 1948.

Riessman, F. *The culturally deprived child.* New York: Harper, 1962.

Risley, T. R. Learning and lollipops. *Psychology Today,* 1968, **7,** 28–31.

Rivlin, L. G. Creativity and the self-attitudes and sociability of high school students. *Journal of Educational Psychology,* 1959, **50,** 147–152.

Roberts, W. Believing is seeing. *Saturday Review,* Oct. 19, 1968, 62.

Robinson, M. P. *The burning of the rotunda.* Richmond, Va.: F. J. Mitchell Printing Co., 1921.

Roe, A. A psychologist examines 64 eminent scientists In W. B. Barbe (Ed.), *Psychology and education of the gifted.* New York: Appleton-Century-Crofts, 1965, 234–242.

Roethlisberger, F. J. & Dickson, W. J. *Management and the worker.* Cambridge, Mass.: Harvard University Press, 1950.

Roethlisberger, F. J. Barriers to communication between men. In S. I. Hayakawa (Ed.),*The use and misuse of language.* Greenwich, Conn.: Fawcett Publications, 1962, 41–46.

Rogers, C. R. *Counseling and psychotherapy: Newer concepts in practice.* Boston: Houghton Mifflin, 1942.

Rogers, C. R. Some observations on the organization of personality. *American Psychologist,* 1947, **2,** 358–368.

Rogers, C. R. *Client-centered therapy.* Boston: Houghton Mifflin, 1951.

Rogers, C. R. A note on "the nature of man." *Journal of Counseling Psychology,* 1957, **4,** 199–203. (b)

Rogers, C. R. A process conception of psychotherapy. Report given to the annual conference of the American Psychological Association, New York City, September 2, 1957.

Rogers, C. R. The characteristics of a helping relationship. *Personnel and Guidance Journal,* 1958, **37,** 6–16.

Rogers, C. R. A theory of therapy, personality, and interpersonal relationships, as developed in the client-centered framework. In S. Koch (Ed.), *Psychology: A study of a science.* New York: McGraw-Hill, 1959, 184–256. (a)

Rogers, C. R. Toward a theory of creativity. In H. H. Anderson (Ed.), *Creativity and its cultivation.* New York: Harper, 1959, 69–82.

Rogers, C. R. *On becoming a person.* Boston: Houghton Mifflin, 1961.

Rogers, C. R. Freedom and commitment. *ETC: A Review of General Semantics,* 1965, **22,** 133–152.

Rogers, C. R. The therapeutic relationship: Recent theory and research. *Australian Journal of Psychology,* 1965, **17,** 95–108. (b)

Rogers, C. R. The interpersonal relationship in the facilitation of learning. In R. R. Leeper (Ed.), *Humanizing education: The person in the process.* Washington, D.C., Association for Supervision and Curriculum Development, National Education Association, 1967, 1–18.

Rogers, C. R. A plan for self-directed change in an educational system. *Educational Leadership,* 1967, **24,** 717–731.

Rogers, C. R. The therapeutic relationship: Recent theory and research. In B. Babladelis & S. Adams, (Eds.), *The shaping of personality.* Englewood Cliffs, N.J.: Prentice-Hall, 1967, 466–477. (a)

Rogers, C. R. *Coming into existence.* Cleveland: World Publishing Co., 1967.

Rogers, C. R. *Freedom to learn.* Columbus, Ohio: Merrill Publishing Co., 1969.

Rogers, C. R. & Skinner, B. F. Some issues concerning the control of behavior. *Science,* 1956, **124,** 1057–1066.

Rogers, C. R. & Dymond, R. F. *Psychotherapy and personality change.* Chicago: University of Chicago Press, 1954.

Rosenfeld, H. & Zander, A. The influence of teachers on aspirations of students. *Journal of Educational Psychology,* 1961, **52,** 1–11.

Rosenthal, R. & Jacobson, L. Teacher expectations for the disadvantaged. *Scientific American,* 1968, **218,** 19–23. (b)

Rosenthal, R. & Jacobson, L. *Pygmalion in the classroom.* New York: Holt, Rinehart & Winston, 1968.

Roth, R. M. The role of self-concept in achievement. *Journal of Experimental Education,* 1959, **27,** 265–281.

Rotman, C. B. & Golburgh, S. J. Group counseling of mentally retarded adolescents. *Mental Retardation,* 1967, **5,** 13–16.

Ruesch, J. & Kees, W. *Nonverbal communication.* Berkeley, Calif.: University of California Press, 1956.

Ruff, G. E. Isolation and sensory deprivation. In S. Arieti (Ed.), *American handbook of psychiatry.* New York: Basic Books, 1966, 385–405.

Ryans, D. G. Some relationships between pupil behavior and certain teacher characteristics. *Journal of Educational Psychology,* 1961, **52,** 82–90.

Sampson, E. E. Achievement in conflict. *Journal of Personality,* 1963, **31,** 510–516.

Sarason, I. G. *Personality: An objective approach.* New York: Wiley, 1966.

Sarason, I. G. Verbal learning, modeling and juvenile delinquency. *American Psychologist,* 1968, **23,** 254–266.

Sargent, S. S. Humanistic methodology in personality and social psychology. In J. F. T. Bugental (Ed.), *Challenges of humanistic psychology.* New York: McGraw-Hill, 1967, 127–132.

Scarpitti, F. R., Murray, E., Dinitz, S. & Reckless, W. C. The "good" boy in a high delinquency area: Four years later. *American Sociological Review,* 1960, **25,** 555–558.

Scheerer, M. Problem solving. *Scientific American,* 1963, **208,** 118–128.

Scheidell, T. M. et al. Feedback in small group communication. *Quarterly Journal of Speech*, 1966, **2**, 273–278.

Schultz, D. P. *Sensory restrictions: Effects on behavior.* New York: Academic Press, 1965.

Schultz, J. L. A cross-sectional study of the development, dimensionality, and correlates of the self concept in school-age boys. *Dissertation Abstracts*, 1966, **26**, 5883.

Schutz, W. C. *Joy: Expanding human awareness.* New York: Grove Press, 1967.

Sears, P. S. & Sherman, V. S. *In pursuit of self esteem: Case studies of eight elementary school children.* Belmont, Calif.: Wadsworth, 1964.

Seeman, M. Alienation and learning in a hospital setting. *American Sociological Review*, 1962, **27**, 772–782.

Selye, H. The two-edged sword of stress. In R. G. Brown, R. A. Newell & H. G. Vonk (Eds.), *Behavioral implications for curriculum and teaching: Interdisciplinary readings.* Dubuque, Iowa: Wm. Brown Book Co., 1969.

Senesh, L. The economic world of the child. *Instructor*, 1963, **72**, 77–79.

Severin, F. T. *Humanistic viewpoints in psychology.* New York: McGraw-Hill, 1965.

Sewell, W. H., Harris, C. W. & Mussen, P. H. Relationship among child training practices. *American Sociological Review*, 1955, **20**, 137–148.

Shainberg, D. Personality restriction in adolescents. *Psychiatric Quarterly*, 1966, **40**, 258–270.

Shapiro, J. G. Agreement between channels of communication in interviews. *Journal of Consulting Psychology*, 1966, **30**, 535–538.

Shapiro, J. G., Foster, C. P. & Powell, T. Facial and bodily cues of genuineness, empathy, and warmth. *Journal of Clinical Psychology*, 1968, **24**, 233–236.

Shaw, M. C. & Alves, G. J. The self concept of bright academic underachievers. *Personnel and Guidance Journal*, 1963, **42**, 401–403.

Shaw, M. C. & Black, M. D. The reaction to frustration of bright high school underachievers. *California Journal of Educational Research*, 1960, **11**, 120–124. (b)

Shaw, M. C., Edson, K. & Bell, H. The self concept of bright underachieving high school students as revealed by an adjective check list. *Personnel and Guidance Journal*, 1960, **39**, 193–196.

Shaw, M. C. & McCuen, J. T. The onset of academic underachievement in bright children. *Journal of Educational Psychology*, 1960, **51**, 103–108.

Sheere, E. T. An analysis of the relationship between acceptance of and respect for self and acceptance of and respect for others in ten counseling cases. *Journal of Consulting Psychology*, 1949, **13**, 169–175.

Sherman, M. & Dey, C. B. The intelligence of isolated mountain children. *Child Development*, 1932, **3**, 279–290.

Shurley, J. T. The hydro-hypodynamic environment. *Proceedings of the Third World Congress of Psychiatry.* Toronto, Canada: University of Toronto Press, 1963, 232–237.

Silverman, I. Self esteem and differential responsiveness to success and failure. *Journal of Abnormal and Social Psychology*, 1964, **69**, 115–119.

Skeels, H. M., Updergraff, R., Wellman, B. L. & Williams, H. M. A study of environmental stimulation: An orphanage preschool project. *University of Iowa Study of Child Welfare*, 1938, **15**, 191.

Skeels, H. M. A study of the effects of differential stimulation on mentally retarded children: A follow-up report. *American Journal of Mental Deficiencies*, 1941, **42**, 340–350.

Skeels, H. M. & Dye, H. B. A study of the effects of differential stimulation on mentally retarded children. *Proceedings of the American Association of Mental Defects*, 1939, **44**, 114–136.

Skinner, B. F. *Science and human behavior*. New York: Free Press, 1953.

Skinner, B. F. A case history in the scientific method. *American Psychologist*, 1956, **11**, 221–223.

Skinner, B. F. Why we need teaching machines. *Harvard Educational Review*, 1961, **32**, 377–398.

Skinner, B. F. *The technology of teaching*. New York: Appleton-Century-Crofts, 1968.

Smith, H. C. *Sensitivity to people*. New York: McGraw-Hill, 1966.

Smith, W. M. Past experience and the perception of visual size. *American Journal of Psychology*, 1952, **65**, 389–403.

Snyder, W. U. *Casebook of non-directive psychotherapy*. Boston: Houghton Mifflin, 1947.

Snygg, D. The psychological basis of human values. In D. Ward (Ed.), *Goals of economic life*. New York: Harper & Brothers, 1953, 335–364.

Syngg, D. A cognitive field theory of learning. In W. B. Waetjen & R. R. Leeper (Eds.), *Learning and mental health in the school*. Washington, D.C., Association for Supervision and Curriculum Development, National Education Association, 1966.

Snygg, D. & Combs, A. W. The phenomenological approach and the problems of "unconscious" behavior. *Journal of Abnormal and Social Psychology*, 1950, **45**, 523–528.

Solley, C. M. & Murphy, G. *Development of the perceptual world*. New York: Basic Books, 1960.

Sontag, L. W., Baker, C. T. & Nelson, V. L. Mental growth and personality development: A longitudinal study. In W. R. Goller (Ed.), *Readings in the psychology of human growth and development*. New York: Holt, Rinehart & Winston, 1962, 418–429.

Soper, D. W. & Combs, A. W. The helping relationship as seen by teachers and therapists. *Journal of Consulting Psychology*, 1962, **26**, 288.

Spielberger, C. D. The effects of manifest anxiety on the academic achievement of college students. *Mental Hygiene*, 1962, **46**, 420–426.

Spielberger, C. D. & Weitz, H. Group counseling and the academic performance of anxious college freshmen. *Journal of Counseling Psychology*, 1962, **9**, 195–204. (b)

Staines, J. W. The self-picture as a factor in the classroom. *British Journal of Education Psychology*, 1958, **28**, 97–111.

Stinnett, T. M. & Huggett, A. J. The profession of teaching. In *Professional problems of teachers*, New York: Macmillan, 1966.

Stock, D. An investigation into the interrelations between the self-concept and feelings directed toward other persons and groups. *Journal of Consulting Psychology*, 1949, **13**, 176–180.

Stoller, H. The long weekend. *Psychology Today*, 1967, **1**, 28–33.

Stotland, E. Effects of public and private failure on self evaluation. *Journal of Abnormal and Social Psychology*, 1958, **56**, 223–229.

Stotland, E. Self-esteem group interaction, and group influence on performance. *Journal of Personality*, 1961, **29**, 273–284.

Strang, R. M. *The adolescent views himself: A psychology of adolescence.* New York: McGraw-Hill, 1957.

Strong, D. J. & Feder, D. Measurement of the self-concept: A critique of the literature. *Journal of Counseling Psychology*, 1961, **8**, 170–180.

Strunk, O., Jr. Note on self-reports and religiosity. *Psychological Report*, 1958, **4**, 29.

Strunk, O. *Religion, A psychological interpretation.* New York: Abingdon Press, 1962.

Suinn, R. M., Osborne, D. & Winfree, P. The self-concept and accuracy of recall of inconsistent self-related information. *Journal of Clinical Psychology*, 1963, **18**, 473–474.

Sullivan, H. S. *Conceptions of Modern Psychiatry.* (2nd ed.) New York: W. W. Horton, 1955.

Sweetland, A. & Childs, O. The effect of emotionality on concept formation. *Journal of Genetic Psychology*, 1958, **59**, 211–218.

Swinn, R. M. & Hill, M. Influence of anxiety on the relationship between self acceptance and acceptance of others. *Journal of Consulting Psychology*, 1964, **28**, 116–119.

Taba, H. *School culture: Studies of participation and leadership.* Washington, D.C.: American Council on Leadership, 1955, 86–118.

Tagiuri, R. & Petrulo, L. *Person, perception, and interpersonal behavior.* Stanford, Calif.: Stanford University Press, 1958.

Taylor, C. & Combs, A. W. Self-acceptance and adjustment. *Journal of Consulting Psychology*, 1952, **16**, 89–91.

Taylor, D. M. *Consistency of the self-concept.* Unpublished doctoral dissertation, Vanderbilt University, 1953.

Thomas, S. An experiment to enhance self-concept of ability and raise school achievement among low-achievement ninth grade students. *Dissertation Abstracts*, **XXVI**, 1966, 4870.

Thompson, L. Perception patterns in three Indian tribes. *Psychiatry*, 1951, **14**, 255–263.

Tillich, P. *The courage to be.* New Haven: Yale University Press, 1959.

Torrance, E. P. Creative and critical evaluative attitudes of teachers. *Rewarding creative behavior*, Englewood Cliffs, N.J.: Prentice-Hall, 1965, 75–84.

Torrance, E. P. Rationalizations about test performance as function of self-concepts. *Journal of Social Psychology*, 1954, **39**, 211–217.

Tournier, P. *The meaning of persons.* New York: Harper, 1957.

Trent, R. D. The relationship between expressed self acceptance and expressed attitudes toward Negro and white in Negro children. *Journal of Genetic Psychology*, 1957, **91**, 25–31.

Truax, C. B. An approach toward training for the aide-therapist: Research and implications. Symposium presented at the American Psychological Association Convention, Chicago, September 1965. (a)

Truax, C. B. et al. Changes in self-concepts during group psychotherapy as a function of alternate sessions and vicarious therapy pre-training in institutionalized mental patients and juvenile delinquents. *Journal of Consulting Psychology*, 1966, **30**, 309–314. (a)

Truax, C. B. et al. Empathy, warmth, genuineness. *Rehabilitation Record*, 1966, **7**, 10–11.

Truax, C. B. et al. Therapist empathy, genuineness, and warmth and patient therapeutic outcome. *Journal of Consulting Psychology*, 1966, **3**, 395–401. (d)

Truax, C. B., Carkhuff, R. R. & Kodman, F. Relationships between therapist-offered conditions and patient change in group psychotherapy. *Journal of Clinical Psychology*, 1965, **21**, 327–329. (b)

Truax, C. B. & Wargo, D. G. Psychotherapeutic encounters that change behavior: For better or for worse. *American Journal of Psychotherapy*, 1966, **22**, 499–520.

Usher, R. H. *The relationship of perceptions of self, others and the helping task to certain measures of college faculty effectiveness.* Unpublished doctoral dissertation, University of Florida, 1966.

Van Buskirk, C. Performance on complex reasoning tasks as a function of anxiety. *Journal of Abnormal and Social Psychology*, 1961, **62**, 201–249.

Van Kaam, A. *Existential foundations of psychology.* Pittsburgh: Duquesne University Press, 1966.

Verba, S. *Small groups and political behavior: A study of leadership.* Princeton, N.J.: Princeton University Press, 1961.

Walsh, A. M. *Self-concepts of bright boys with learning difficulties.* New York: Bureau of Publications, Teachers College, Columbia University, 1956.

Wann, T. W. (Ed.) *Behaviorism and phenomenology: Contrasting bases for modern psychology.* Chicago: University of Chicago Press, 1964.

Wapner, S. et al. *The body percept.* New York: Random House, 1965.

Ward, P. & Bailey, J. A. Community participation and attitudinal changes among teacher education students. *The Personnel and Guidance Journal*, 1966, **44**, 628–630.

Watson, J. B. *Behaviorism.* (Rev. ed.) Chicago: University of Chicago Press, 1930.

Wattenberg, W. W. & Clifford, C. Relation of self concepts to beginning achievement in reading. *Child Development*, 1964, **35**, 461–467.

Weaver, T. T. Effects of positive and negative personality evaluations on the self concepts of high school seniors. *Dissertation Abstracts*, 1965, **26**, 1785–1786.

Webster, S. W. & Kroger, M. N. A comparative study of selected perceptions and feelings of Negro adolescents with and without white friends in integrated urban high schools. *Journal of Negro Education*, 1966, **35**, 55–60.

Webster, S. W. *Discipline in the classroom.* San Francisco: Chandler, 1968.

Wessels, H. M. Four teachers I have known. *Saturday Review of Literature*, June 7, 1961.

White, R. K. Misperception and the Vietnam war. *Journal of Social Issues,* 1966, **22,** 1–154.

White, W. & Porter, T. Self concept reports among hospitalized alcoholics during early periods of sobriety. *Journal of Counseling Psychology,* 1966, **13,** 352–355.

Wilhelms, F. T. & Siemans, R. E. A curriculum for personal and professional development. In *Changes in teaching education: An appraisal.* Washington, D.C., National Commission on Teacher Education and Professional Standards, National Education Association, 1963.

Williams, C. D. The elimination of tantrum behavior by extinction procedures. *Journal of Abnormal and Social Psychology,* 1959, **59,** 269.

Williams, T. R. The personal-cultural equation in social work and anthropology. *Social Casework,* 1959, **40,** 74–80.

Williams, W. C. The use of force. From *The farmer's daughter and other stories.* Philadelphia: New Directions, 1961.

Winick, C. & Holt, H. Seating position as nonverbal communication in group analysis. *Psychiatry,* 1961, **24,** 171–182.

Wittreich, W. J. The honiphenomenon. *Journal of Abnormal and Social Psychology,* 1952, **47,** 705–712.

Wohlwill, J. F. Perceptual learning. *American Review of Psychology,* 1966, **17,** 201–232.

Wolman, B. B. *The unconscious mind: The meaning of Freudian psychology.* Englewood Cliffs, N.J.: Prentice-Hall, 1968.

Wrightsman, L. S., Jr. Effects of anxiety, achievement, motivation, and task importance upon performance on an intelligence test. *Journal of Educational Psychology,* 1962, **53,** 150–156.

Wylie, R. C. *The self-concept: A critical survey of pertinent research literature.* Lincoln, Neb.: University of Nebraska Press, 1961.

Ziferstein, I. Psychological habituation to war: A sociological case study. *American Journal of Orthopsychiatry,* 1967, **37,** 457–468.

Zimmerman, I. L. & Allebrand, G. N. Personality characteristics and attitudes toward achievement of good and poor readers. *The Journal of Educational Research,* 1965, **59,** 28–30.

Zoolalion, C. Factors related to differential achievement among boys in ninth grade algebra. *Journal of Education Research,* 1965, **58,** 205–207.

Reference Index

The contributions of many authors have influenced the writing of this book. Their numbers are so great, in fact, that reference to each of them in the text itself would seriously detract from readability. To provide for ease of reading and, at the same time, to acknowledge their deep appreciation for the fine work of other writers, the present authors have therefore included this Reference Index. By means of this simple guide, interested readers may locate references appropriate to the discussion of various points throughout the text. Page and line references indicate the approximate point at which the work of other authors is especially relevant. Complete standard citations of the particular work referred to may be found in the Bibliography (pages 312–339).

CHAPTER 1/ WHAT IS A PROFESSIONAL HELPER?

CHAPTER 2/   TWO WAYS OF LOOKING AT BEHAVIOR

CHAPTER 3/   SELF–CONCEPT: PRODUCT AND PRODUCER OF EXPERIENCE

CHAPTER 4/   A HUMANISTIC VIEW OF MOTIVE

CHAPTER 5/ THE CRUCIAL CHARACTER OF MEANING

CHAPTER 6/ LEARNING AS MEANING CHANGE

CHAPTER 7/ THE LIMITS OF MAN'S BECOMING

CHAPTER 8/   FREEDOM AND SELF–ACTUALIZATION

CHAPTER 9/ GOALS AND PURPOSES OF HELPING

CHAPTER 10/ DEVELOPING UNDERSTANDING

CHAPTER 11/   ESTABLISHING HELPING RELATIONSHIPS

CHAPTER 12/   AIDING THE SEARCH FOR NEW MEANING

CHAPTER 13/ COMMUNICATION

CHAPTER 14/ VARIED ROLES OF HELPERS

CHAPTER 15/   THE HELPER AS PERSON AND CITIZEN

Index

Page references for authors listed in this index indicate points in the text at which their work is especially relevant, whether specific reference appears on that page or not. See Reference Index for further information.